Modern Studies in

ON NOAM CHOMSKY

MODERN STUDIES IN PHILOSOPHY is a series of anthologies presenting contemporary interpretations and evaluations of the works of major philosophers. The editors have selected articles designed to show the systematic structure of the thought of these philosophers, and to reveal the relevance of their views to the problems of current interest. These volumes are intended to be contributions to contemporary debates as well as to the history of philosophy; they not only trace the origins of many problems important to modern philosophy, but also introduce major philosophers as interlocutors in current discussions.

MODERN STUDIES IN PHILOSOPHY is prepared under the general editorship of Amelie Oksenberg Rorty, Livingston College, Rutgers University.

GILBERT HARMAN is Professor of Philosophy at Princeton University.

Modern Studies in Philosophy

Amelie Oksenberg Rorty
General Editor

ON NOAM CHOMSKY
Critical Essays

EDITED BY GILBERT HARMAN

Anchor Books
Anchor Press/Doubleday
Garden City, New York

This anthology has been especially prepared for Anchor Books and has never before appeared in book form.

Anchor Books edition: 1974

Library of Congress Cataloging in Publication Data

Harman, Gilbert, comp.
  On Noam Chomsky.

  (Modern studies in philosophy)
  Contents: Harman, G. Introduction.—Hollander, J. Coiled Alizarine.—Searle, J. Chomsky's revolution in linguistics. [etc.]
  Includes bibliographies.
  1. Chomsky, Noam—Addresses, essays, lectures. 2. Linguistic research—United States—Addresses, essays, lectures. I. Title.
P85.C47H3   410′.92′4
ISBN 0-385-03765-1
Library of Congress Catalog Card Number 74-3558

Contents

Introduction

It is appropriate that a volume of the Modern Studies in Philosophy Series should be devoted to Noam Chomsky since nothing has had a greater impact on contemporary philosophy than Chomsky's theory of language. For the same reason, it would also be appropriate for such a volume to appear in a Modern Studies in Linguistics Series, a Modern Studies in Psychology Series, or a Modern Studies in Anthropology Series, because Chomsky's theory has had a major impact on these subjects too. More precisely Chomsky has let us see that there is a single subject of language and mind which crosses departmental boundaries. Although this book appears in the Modern Studies in Philosophy Series, it contains essays by not only philosophers, but by linguists, psychologists, and an anthropologist—not that the authors are easily classified in this way; furthermore it is intended not only for students of philosophy but for anyone interested in Chomsky's theory of mind and language.

The first essay, by John Searle, gives an admirably clear presentation of Chomsky's theory and contains a useful introductory bibliography. The final essay is a review of John Lyons' *Noam Chomsky* by Dell Hymes which discusses the historical background of Chomsky's theory and possible connections between his theory of language and his politics. The remaining papers can be roughly grouped into three sections. First come those mainly concerned with methodological questions and with the relation between Chomsky's linguistics and psychology: Lees's review of *Syntactic Structures;* Putman's early paper and Quine's later discussion of methodological issues; Bever, Lackner, and Kirk on the "psychological reality" of deep structure; and an essay that Bever has written especially for this volume. Second come papers concerned with Chomsky's claim that his theory represents a modern defense of rationalism and the theory of innate ideas: the excerpts from Ross's dissertation (published here for the first time); my review of *Language and Mind;* and Nagel's article on linguistics and epistemology. The remaining papers, by Katz, Davidson, Stampe, Lewis, and Partee, discuss questions of grammar, meaning, and logical analysis.

In his review of *Syntactic Structures,* Lees argues that the transition from structural linguistics to Chomsky's theory of transformational grammar is like the transition from alchemy to chemistry. He says that a low-level science of classification, experiment, and precise measurement has given way to an advanced science characterized by the construction and testing of theories. Now, it is clear enough that Chomsky has provided a framework for the construction of theories of language and of grammars of particular languages; but there has been a certain amount of controversy over the ways in which such theories and grammars are to be tested. This controversy represents one of the methodological issues that comes up again and again in the first group of papers (and recurs in many of the other papers too).

Lees argues that one test of a grammar is whether it accounts for speakers' intuitions. A particular generative grammar of the sort that Chomsky describes will, among other things, predict that certain utterances are grammatical and that others are ungrammatical. Lees says that such predictions can be tested directly against speakers' intuitions of grammaticality. But others (including Chomsky) are dubious about this sort of direct test. Speakers can to some extent distinguish "deviant" from "nondeviant" utterances, to use Putnam's terminology (following Ziff); in other words, they can make what Bever calls "judgments of acceptability." But it is not clear that speakers can intuitively distinguish between ungrammaticality and other kinds of deviance. Is Chomsky's example *colorless green ideas sleep furiously* grammatically deviant or semantically or logically deviant? People have disagreed about this, and, as Partee notes, Chomsky has changed his mind twice about this example.

As Chomsky's theory has developed, it has become increasingly clear that grammaticality has to be interpreted as a highly theoretical notion, not easily tested by appeals to intuition. Partee mentions Chomsky's willingness at one point to count as grammatical obviously deviant utterances like *I saw himself* and *will I please help you tomorrow?* In other words, Chomsky foresees that the unacceptability of such utterances may have to be accounted for by semantic principles of interpretation rather than by principles of grammar alone. Bever describes some other examples in which still different principles might be needed to explain intuitive judgments of acceptability.

This leads to a more complicated picture than Lees's. If intuitive judgments of speakers provide the test of grammar, the test is not a test of grammar alone but of grammar, semantics, theory of perceptual strategy (as Bever calls it), and so forth. But suppose that two different packages of grammar, semantics, theory of perceptual strategy, etc. predicted the same intuitive judgments of acceptability.

Would there be any reason to choose one rather than another? Would it even make sense to suppose that one package was right, the other wrong? This is one of the issues that Putnam discusses. His suggestion is that grammatical notions may have to be regarded as relative to one's choice of grammar. Similarly, Quine is worried about possible evidence in a case like this in which two packages might predict the same judgments of acceptability. Quine is particularly skeptical about further appeals to speakers' intuitions in support of one analysis of the structure of a sentence as against other analyses.

A different type of evidence about structure comes from the "click" experiments of Bever and others. A report on one of these experiments is included here. In Bever's paper, he says more about these experiments and what he takes them to show. Whether such evidence might help settle Quine's worries is an open question.

This is only one way to look at the methodological issues—as if Chomsky's theories and grammars were somehow suspect on the grounds that it is not clear how they are to be tested. There is also a complementary way to see things. We might just as easily decide that Chomsky's theories and grammars represent science at its best, so that the methodological issue is how to extract a moral about the proper relation between psychological theory and evidence. From this perspective, the moral might be that the evidential relation is more indirect than has been supposed by most psychologists and philosophers. Bever's paper could then be seen as a paradigm of method in psychology. Behavior is not to be explained directly but as the result of the complex interaction of a number of different mental systems.

Let me turn now to a more specific methodological issue. When Chomsky introduced his theory of transformational grammar, he provided a powerful framework in which grammars of natural languages could be written. Now Putnam observes that the framework is, in a sense, too powerful: it puts hardly any restrictions on grammar. Therefore, to say that a transformational grammar exists for any natural language is to say something relatively trivial if no further constraints are placed on what counts as a transformational grammar.

One obvious constraint, mentioned by Lees, is that grammar must be learnable. A natural language is a language that children can learn as their first language. Any grammar that could not be learned in this way can be ruled out as the grammar of a possible natural language. What is wanted, though, is a more formal statement of the constraint. What distinguishes grammars that can be learned from grammars that cannot?

The idea suggests itself that learning theory might indicate formal constraints on learnable grammars. But Chomsky discovered that existing psychological theories of learning are no help at all. If they are specific enough to put any constraints on grammar, they appear to put such strong constraints that it would be impossible for a child to learn any existing natural language. Chomsky concluded that there is something wrong with existing psychological theories of learning.

A different approach to learning would be to get an account of language learning which one would then try to generalize into a better general psychological theory of learning. However, as a result of his attempts to see what constraints are to be placed on learnable grammars, Chomsky has come to believe that language learning may involve a specific faculty or ability that is not involved in other learning.

This reasoning depends on the particular nature of the sorts of constraints there seem to be on rules in transformational grammars, so I have included here excerpts from Ross's dissertation on this subject. Chomsky's argument that the child has an "innate schematism" for grammar is sympathetically discussed by Searle, and by me in my review of *Language and Mind*.

Chomsky has also said that his conclusions about language learning vindicate the old rationalist theory of innate ideas, as defended by Descartes and Leibniz. His claim raises a number of philosophical and historical issues that are difficult to separate. One is whether there is any interesting sense in which a child has what Chomsky calls "tacit knowledge" of principles of universal grammar. Searle and Nagel express doubts about this, which they take to be crucial for the claim that Chomsky has resuscitated rationalism.

Turning now to a different issue, let me recall that philosophers have long been interested in the logical analysis of sentences of ordinary language, an enterprise which they have distinguished from grammatical analysis on the grounds that logical form is often quite different from grammatical form. But Chomsky's distinction between surface grammatical structure and deep structure changes this picture. For example, Katz argues that logical form can be defined in terms of grammatical structure if that structure includes deep as well as surface structure. On the other hand, Quine warns that the logician has purposes that are different from those of the grammarian. Where the grammarian is concerned to analyze natural language, the logician may wish to find a better notation, better in the way that algebra is more useful than ordinary English for certain purposes.

Nonetheless, one can be concerned with the logic of natural language and, in that case, Katz's point seems well taken. Furthermore, if our "package" consisting of grammar, semantics, theory of perceptual strategy, and so forth, permits a logical analysis of sentences of the language in question, then there is an additional test of the package over and above speakers' intuitions of acceptability: we can also see whether the package accounts for intuitions about logical properties and relations.

Similarly, Chomsky's grammatical analysis may make possible a theory of truth in a language of the sort that Davidson describes. Adding this to the "package" yields further tests. Davidson points out, for example, that we can bring out the structural differences between *I persuaded John to leave* and *I expected John to leave* by appeal to truth conditions, without needing the appeal Chomsky makes in this connection to the intuitive differences in the ways in which we understand these sentences.

Nevertheless, a number of complaints have been directed at Katz's proposal, partly because he assumes that he can give a firm foundation for a distinction between analytic and synthetic judgments. As Quine and Bever indicate, the issue is more complex than Katz allows. Another complaint concerns Katz's identification of the meaning of an utterance with its "semantic representation" in the "package" that Katz envisions. Davidson and Lewis think that meaning is instead a matter of truth conditions; Searle (following Grice) thinks that meaning involves speakers' intentions. This is largely a verbal issue. Semantic representations, truth conditions, and speakers' intentions can all be found somewhere in Lewis' account of linguistic conventions. (One aspect of this verbal issue is pursued by Stampe in his investigation of the meaning of meaning. His essay is itself an example of the sort of combined logical and grammatical analysis that Chomsky's theory makes possible.)

As Searle remarks, within the framework that Chomsky has created there is a dispute concerning the relation between grammar and meaning, syntax and semantics. Chomsky assumes that syntax and semantics can be distinguished and, in particular, that there is a level of deep syntactic structure that is distinct from a level of logical and semantical representation. Other linguists have argued that these distinctions cannot be made and that syntax and semantics are inextricably intertwined. The issue is a complex and obscure one and it is controversial how the issue should be stated. It is even in dispute whether there is a real nonverbal issue at all. For one perspective on the controversy, see Partee's admirably clear essay.

G. H.

Coiled Alizarine*

for Noam Chomsky

Curiously deep, the slumber of crimson thoughts:
While breathless, in stodgy viridian,
Colorless green ideas sleep furiously.

Chomsky's Revolution in Linguistics*

JOHN SEARLE

I

Throughout the history of the study of man there has been a fundamental opposition between those who believe that progress is to be made by a rigorous observation of man's actual behavior and those who believe that such observations are interesting only in so far as they reveal to us hidden and possibly fairly mysterious underlying laws that only partially and in distorted form reveal themselves to us in behavior. Freud, for example, is in the latter class, most of American social science in the former.

Noam Chomsky is unashamedly with the searchers after hidden laws. Actual speech behavior, speech *performance,* for him is only the top of a large iceberg of linguistic *competence* distorted in its shape by many factors irrelevant to linguistics. Indeed he once remarked that the very expression "behavioral sciences" suggests a fundamental confusion between evidence and subject matter. Psychology, for example, he claims is the science of mind; to call psychology a behavioral science is like calling physics a science of meter readings. One uses human behavior as evidence for the laws of the operation of the mind, but to suppose that the laws must be laws of behavior is to suppose that the evidence must be the subject matter.

In this opposition between the methodology of confining research to observable facts and that of using the observable facts as clues to hidden and underlying laws, Chomsky's revolution is doubly interesting: first, within the field of linguistics, it has precipitated a conflict which is an example of the wider conflict; and secondly, Chomsky has used his results about language to try to develop general anti-behaviorist and anti-empiricist conclusions about the nature of the human mind that go beyond the scope of linguistics.

His revolution followed fairly closely the general pattern described in Thomas Kuhn's *The Structure of Scientific Revolutions:* the ac-

* Reprinted with permission from The New York Review of Books © 1972 New York Review, Inc.

cepted model or "paradigm" of linguistics was confronted, largely by Chomsky's work, with increasing numbers of nagging counterexamples and recalcitrant data which the paradigm could not deal with. Eventually the counterexamples led Chomsky to break the old model altogether and to create a completely new one. Prior to the publication of his *Syntactic Structures* in 1957, many, probably most, American linguists regarded the aim of their discipline as being the classification of the elements of human languages. Linguistics was to be a sort of verbal botany. As Hockett wrote in 1942, "Linguistics is a classificatory science."[1]

Suppose, for example, that such a linguist is giving a description of a language, whether an exotic language like Cherokee or a familiar one like English. He proceeds by first collecting his "data," he gathers a large number of utterances of the language, which he records on his tape recorder or in a phonetic script. This "corpus" of the language constitutes his subject matter. He then classifies the elements of the corpus at their different linguistic levels: first he classifies the smallest significant functioning units of sound, the *phonemes,* then at the next level the phonemes unite into the minimally significant bearers of meaning, the *morphemes* (in English, for example, the word "cat" is a single morpheme made up of three phonemes; the word "uninteresting" is made up of three morphemes: "un," "interest," and "ing"), at the next higher level the morphemes join together to form *words* and *word classes* such as noun phrases and verb phrases, and at the highest level of all come sequences of word classes, the possible *sentences* and *sentence types.*

The aim of linguistic theory was to provide the linguist with a set of rigorous methods, a set of discovery procedures which he would use to extract from the "corpus" the phonemes, the morphemes, and so on. The study of the meanings of sentences or of the uses to which speakers of the language put the sentences had little place in this enterprise. Meanings, scientifically construed, were thought to be patterns of behavior determined by stimulus and response; they were properly speaking the subject matter of psychologists. Alternatively they might be some mysterious mental entities altogether outside the scope of a sober science or, worse yet, they might involve the speaker's whole knowledge of the world around him and thus fall beyond the scope of a study restricted only to linguistic facts.

---

[1] Quoted in R. H. Robins, *A Short History of Linguistics* (Indiana University Press, 1967), p. 239.

Structural linguistics, with its insistence on objective methods of verification and precisely specified techniques of discovery, with its refusal to allow any talk of meanings or mental entities or unobservable features, derives from the "behavioral sciences" approach to the study of man, and is also largely a consequence of the philosophical assumptions of logical positivism. Chomsky was brought up in this tradition at the University of Pennsylvania as a student of both Zellig Harris, the linguist, and Nelson Goodman, the philosopher.

Chomsky's work is interesting in large part because, while it is a major attack on the conception of man implicit in the behavioral sciences, the attack is made from within the very tradition of scientific rigor and precision that the behavioral sciences have been aspiring to. His attack on the view that human psychology can be described by correlating stimulus and response is not an a priori conceptual argument, much less is it the cry of an anguished humanist resentful at being treated as a machine or an animal. Rather it is a claim that a really rigorous analysis of language will show that such methods when applied to language produce nothing but falsehoods or trivialities, that their practitioners have simply imitated "the surface features of science" without having its "significant intellectual content."

As a graduate student at Pennsylvania, Chomsky attempted to apply the conventional methods of structural linguistics to the study of syntax, but found that the methods that had apparently worked so well with phonemes and morphemes did not work very well with sentences. Each language has a finite number of phonemes and a finite though quite large number of morphemes. It is possible to get a *list* of each; but the number of *sentences* in any natural language like French or English is, strictly speaking, infinite. There is no limit to the number of new sentences that can be produced; and for each sentence, no matter how long, it is always possible to produce a longer one. Within structuralist assumptions it is not easy to account for the fact that languages have an infinite number of sentences.

Furthermore the structuralist methods of classification do not seem able to account for all of the internal relations within sentences, or the relations that different sentences have to each other. For example, to take a famous case, the two sentences "John is easy to please" and "John is eager to please" look as if they had exactly the same grammatical structure. Each is a sequence of *noun-copula-adjective-infinitive verb*. But in spite of this surface similarity the grammar of the two is quite different. In the first sentence, though it is not apparent from the surface word order, "John" functions as the direct object of the verb to please; the sentence means: it is easy for someone to please John. Whereas in the second "John" functions as the subject of the verb to please; the sentence means: John is eager that he please someone. That this is a difference in the *syntax* of the sentences comes out clearly in the fact that English allows us to form the noun phrase "John's eagerness to please" out of the second, but not "John's easiness to please" out of the first. There is no easy or natural way to account for these facts within structuralist assumptions.

Another set of syntactical facts that structuralist assumptions are inadequate to handle is the existence of certain types of ambiguous sentences where the ambiguity derives not from the words in the sentence but from the syntactical structure. Consider the sentence "The shooting of the hunters is terrible." This can mean that it is terrible that the hunters are being shot or that the hunters are terrible at shooting or that the hunters are being shot in a terrible fashion. Another example is "I like her cooking." In spite of the fact that it contains no ambiguous words (or morphemes) and has a very simple superficial grammatical structure of noun-verb-possessive pronoun-noun, this sentence is in fact remarkably ambiguous. It can mean, among other things, I like what she cooks, I like the way she cooks, I like the fact that she cooks, even, I like the fact that she is being cooked.

Such "syntactically ambiguous" sentences form a crucial test case for any theory of syntax. The examples are ordinary pedestrian English sentences, there is nothing fancy about them. But it is not easy to see how to account for them. The meaning of any sentence is determined by the meanings of the component words (or morphemes) and their syntactical arrangement. How then can we account for these cases where one sentence containing unambiguous words (and morphemes) has several different meanings? Structuralist linguists had little or nothing to say about these cases; they simply ignored them. Chomsky was eventually led to claim that these sentences have several different syntactical structures, that the uniform *surface* structure of, e.g., "I like her cooking" conceals several different *underlying* structures which he called "deep" structures. The introduction of the notion of the deep structure of sentences, not always visible in the surface structure, is a crucial element of the Chomsky revolution, and I shall explain it in more detail later.

One of the merits of Chomsky's work has been that he has persistently tried to call attention to the puzzling character of facts that are so familiar that we all tend to take them for granted as not requiring explanation. Just as physics begins in wonder at such obvious facts as that apples fall to the ground or genetics in wonder that plants and animals reproduce themselves, so the study of the structure of language begins in wondering at such humdrum facts as that "I like her cooking" has different meanings, "John is eager to please" isn't quite the same in structure as "John is easy to please," and the equally obvious but often overlooked facts that we continually find ourselves saying and hearing things we have never said or heard before and that the number of possible new sentences is infinite.

The inability of structuralist methods to account for such syntactical facts eventually led Chomsky to challenge not only the methods but the goals and indeed the definition of the subject matter of linguistics given by the structuralist linguists. Instead of a taxonomic goal of classifying elements by performing sets of operations on a corpus of utterances, Chomsky argued that the goal of linguistic description should be to construct a theory that would account for the infinite number of sentences of a natural language. Such a theory would show which strings of words were sentences and which were not, and would provide a description of the grammatical structure of each sentence.

Such descriptions would have to be able to account for such facts as the internal grammatical relations and the ambiguities described above. The description of a natural language would be a formal deductive theory which would contain a set of grammatical rules that could generate the infinite set of sentences of the language, would not generate anything that was not a sentence, and would provide a description of the grammatical structure of each sentence. Such a theory came to be called a "generative grammar" because of its aim of constructing a device that would generate all and only the sentences of a language.

This conception of the goal of linguistics then altered the conception of the methods and the subject matter. Chomsky argued that since any language contains an infinite number of sentences, any "corpus," even if it contained as many sentences as there are in all the books of the Library of Congress, would still be trivially small. Instead of the appropriate subject matter of linguistics being a randomly or arbitrarily selected set of sentences, the proper object of study was the speaker's underlying knowledge of the language, his "linguistic competence" that enables him to produce and understand sentences he has never heard before.

Once the conception of the "corpus" as the subject matter is rejected, then the notion of mechanical procedures for discovering linguistic truths goes as well. Chomsky argues that no science has a mechanical procedure for discovering the truth anyway. Rather, what happens is that the scientist formulates hypotheses and tests them against evidence. Linguistics is no different: the linguist makes conjectures about linguistic facts and tests them against the evidence provided by native speakers of the language. He has in short a procedure for *evaluating* rival hypotheses, but no procedure for *discovering* true theories by mechanically processing evidence.

The Chomsky revolution can be summarized in the following chart:

	Structuralism	*Generative Grammar*
Subject Matter	corpus of utterances	speaker's knowledge of how to produce and understand sentences, his linguistic competence
Goal	classification of the elements of the corpus	specification of the grammatical rules underlying the construction of sentences
Methods	discovery procedures	evaluation procedures

Most of this revolution was already presented in Chomsky's book *Syntactic Structures*. As one linguist remarked, "The extraordinary and traumatic impact of the publication of *Syntactic Structures* by Noam Chomsky in 1957 can hardly be appreciated by one who did not live through this upheaval."[2] In the years after 1957 the spread of the revolution was made more rapid and more traumatic by certain

2 Howard Maclay, "Overview," in D. Steinberg and L. Jakobovits, eds., *Semantics* (Cambridge University Press, 1971), p. 163.

special features of the organization of linguistics as a discipline in the United States. Only a few universities had separate departments of linguistics. The discipline was (by contrast to, say, philosophy or psychology), and still is, a rather cozy one. Practitioners were few; they all tended to know one another; they read the same very limited number of journals; they had, and indeed still have, an annual get-together at the Summer Linguistics Institute of the Linguistic Society of America, where issues are thrashed out and family squabbles are aired in public meetings.

All of this facilitated a rapid dissemination of new ideas and a dramatic and visible clash of conflicting views. Chomsky did not convince the established leaders of the field but he did something more important, he convinced their graduate students. And he attracted some fiery disciples, notably Robert Lees and Paul Postal.

The spread of Chomsky's revolution, like the spread of analytic philosophy during the same period, was a striking example of the Young Turk phenomenon in American academic life. The graduate students became generative grammarians even in departments that had traditionalist faculties. All of this also engendered a good deal of passion and animosity, much of which still survives. Many of the older generation still cling resentfully to the great traditions, regarding Chomsky and his "epigones" as philistines and vulgarians. Meanwhile Chomsky's views have become the conventional wisdom, and as Chomsky and his disciples of the Sixties very quickly become Old Turks a new generation of Young Turks (many of them among Chomsky's best students) arise and challenge Chomsky's views with a new theory of "generative semantics."

II

The aim of the linguistic theory expounded by Chomsky in *Syntactic Structures* (1957) was essentially to describe syntax, that is, to specify the grammatical rules underlying the construction of sentences. In Chomsky's mature theory, as expounded in *Aspects of the Theory of Syntax* (1965), the aims become more ambitious: to explain all of the linguistic relationships between the sound system and the meaning system of the language. To achieve this, the complete "grammar" of a language, in Chomsky's technical sense of the word, must have three parts, a *syntactical* component that generates and describes the internal structure of the infinite number of sentences of the language, a *phonological* component that describes the sound structure of the sentences generated by the syntactical component, and a *semantic* component that describes the meaning structure of the sentences. The heart of the grammar is the syntax; the phonology and the semantics are purely "interpretative," in the sense that they describe the sound and the meaning of the sentences produced by the syntax but do not generate any sentences themselves.

The first task of Chomsky's syntax is to account for the speaker's understanding of the internal structure of sentences. Sentences are not unordered strings of words, rather the words and morphemes are grouped into functional constituents such as the subject of the sentence, the predicate, the direct object, and so on. Chomsky and other grammarians can represent much, though not all, of the speaker's knowledge of the internal structure of sentences with rules called "phrase structure" rules.

The rules themselves are simple enough to understand. For example, the fact that a sentence (S) can consist of a noun phrase (NP) followed by a verb phrase (VP) we can represent in a rule of the form: S → NP + VP. And for purposes of constructing a grammatical theory which will generate and describe the structure of sentences, we can read the arrow as an instruction to rewrite the left-hand symbol as the string of symbols on the right-hand side. The rewrite rules tell us that the initial symbol S can be replaced by NP + VP. Other rules will similarly unpack NP and VP into their constituents. Thus, in a very simple grammar, a noun phrase might consist of an article (Art) followed by a noun (N); and a verb phrase might consist of an auxiliary verb (Aux), a main verb (V), and a noun phrase (NP). A very simple grammar of a fragment of English, then, might look like this:

1. S → NP + VP
2. NP → Art + N
3. VP → Aux + V + NP
4. Aux → (can, may, will, must, etc.)
5. V → (read, hit, eat, etc.)
6. Art → (a, the)
7. N → (boy, man, book, etc.)

If we introduce the initial symbol S into this system, then construing each arrow as the instruction to rewrite the left-hand symbol with the elements on the right (and where the elements are bracketed, to rewrite it as one of the elements), we can construct *derivations* of English sentences. If we keep applying the rules to generate strings until we have no elements in our strings that occur on the left-hand side of a rewrite rule, we have arrived at a "terminal string." For example, starting with S and rewriting according to the rules mentioned above, we might construct the following simple derivation of the terminal string underlying the sentence "The boy will read the book":

S

NP + VP (by rule 1)

Art + N + VP (by rule 2)

Art + N + Aux + V + NP (by rule 3)

Art + N + Aux + V + Art + N (by rule 2)

the + boy + will + read + the + book (by rules 4, 5, 6, and 7)

The information contained in this derivation can be represented graphically in a tree diagram of the following form:

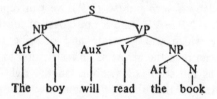

This "phrase marker" is Chomsky's representation of the syntax of the sentence "The boy will read the book." It provides a description of the syntactical structure of the sentence. Phrase structure rules of the sort I have used to construct the derivation were implicit in at least some of the structuralist grammars; but Chomsky was the first to render them explicit and to show their role in the derivations of sentences. He is not, of course, claiming that a speaker actually goes consciously or unconsciously through any such process of applying rules of the form "rewrite X as Y" to construct sentences. To construe the grammarian's description this way would be to confuse an account of competence with a theory of performance.

But Chomsky does claim that in some form or other the speaker has "internalized" rules of sentence construction, that he has "tacit" or "unconscious" knowledge of grammatical rules, and that the phrase structure rules constructed by the grammarian "represent" his competence. One of the chief difficulties of Chomsky's theory is that no clear and precise answer has ever been given to the question of exactly how the grammarian's account of the construction of sentences is supposed to represent the speaker's ability to speak and understand sentences, and in precisely what sense of "know" the speaker is supposed to know the rules of the grammar.

Phrase structure rules were, as I have said, already implicit in at least some of the structuralist grammars Chomsky was attacking in *Syntactic Structures*. One of his earliest claims was that such rules, even in a rigorous and formalized deductive model such as we have just sketched, were not adequate to account for all the syntactical facts of natural languages. The entering wedge of his attack on structuralism was the claim that phrase structure rules alone could not account for the various sorts of cases such as "I like her cooking" and "John is eager to please."

First, within such a grammar there is no natural way to describe the ambiguities in a sentence such as "I like her cooking." Phrase structure rules alone would provide only one derivation for this sentence; but as the sentence is syntactically ambiguous, the grammar should reflect that fact by providing several different syntactical derivations and hence several different syntactical descriptions.

Secondly, phrase structure grammars have no way to picture the differences between "John is easy to please" and "John is eager to please." Though the sentences are syntactically different, phrase structure rules alone would give them similar phrase markers.

Thirdly, just as in the above examples surface similarities conceal underlying differences that cannot be revealed by phrase structure grammar, so surface differences also conceal underlying similarities. For example, in spite of the different word order and the addition of certain elements, the sentence "The book will be read by the boy" and the sentence "The boy will read the book" have much in common: they both mean the same thing—the only difference is that one is in the passive mood and the other in the active mood. Phrase structure grammars alone give us no way to picture this similarity. They would give us two unrelated descriptions of these two sentences.

To account for such facts, Chomsky claims that in addition to phrase structure rules the grammar requires a second kind of rule, "transformational" rules, which transform phrase markers into other phrase markers by moving elements around, by adding elements, and by deleting elements. For example, by using Chomsky's transformational rules, we can show the similarity of the passive to the active mood by showing how a phrase marker for the active mood can be converted into a phrase marker for the passive mood. Thus, instead of generating two unrelated phrase markers by phrase structure rules, we can construct a simpler grammar by showing how both the active and the passive can be derived from the same underlying phrase marker.

To account for sentences like "I like her cooking" we show that what we have is not just one phrase marker but several different underlying sentences each with a different meaning, and the phrase markers for these different sentences can all be transformed into one phrase marker for "I like her cooking." Thus, underlying the one sentence "I like her cooking" are phrase markers for "I like what she cooks," "I like the way she cooks," "I like the fact that she cooks," etc. For example, underlying the two meanings, "I like what she cooks" and "I like it that she is being cooked," are the two phrase markers:[3]

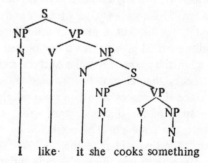

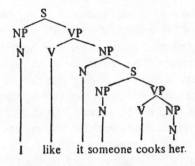

Different transformational rules convert each of these into the same derived phrase marker for the sentence "I like her cooking." Thus, the ambiguity in the sentence is represented in the grammar by phrase markers of several quite different sentences. Different phrase markers produced by the phrase structure rules are transformed into the same phrase marker by the application of the transformational rules.

Because of the introduction of transformational rules, grammars of Chomsky's kind are often called "transformational generative grammars" or simply "transformational grammars." Unlike phrase structure rules which apply to a single left-hand element in virtue of its shape, transformational rules apply to an element only in virtue of its position in a phrase marker: instead of rewriting one element as a string of elements, a transformational rule maps one phrase marker into another. Transformational rules therefore apply after the phrase structure rules have been applied; they operate on the output of the phrase structure rules of the grammar.

Corresponding to the phrase structure rules and the transformational rules respectively are two components to the syntax of the language, a *base component* and a *transformational component*. The base component of Chomsky's grammar contains the phrase structure rules, and these (together with certain rules restricting which combinations of words are permissible so that we do not get nonsense sequences like "The book will read the boy") determine the *deep structure* of each sentence. The transformational component converts the deep structure of the sentence into its *surface structure*. In the example we just considered, "The book will be read by the boy" and the sentence "The boy will read the book," two surface structures are derived from one deep structure. In the case of "I like her cooking," one surface structure is derived from several different deep structures.

At the time of the publication of *Aspects of the Theory of Syntax* it seemed that all of the semantically relevant parts of the sentence, all the things that determine its meaning, were contained in the deep structure of the sentence. The examples we mentioned above fit in nicely with this view. "I like her cooking" has different meanings because it has different deep structures though only one surface structure; "The boy will read the book" and "The book will be read by the boy" have different surface structures, but one and the same deep structure, hence they have the same meaning.

This produced a rather elegant theory of the relation of syntax to semantics and phonology: the two components of the syntax, the base component and the transformational component, generate deep structures and surface structures respectively. Deep structures are the input to the semantic component, which describes their meaning. Surface structures are the input to the phonological component, which describes their sound. In short, deep structure determines meaning, surface structure determines sound. Graphically the theory of a language was supposed to look like this:

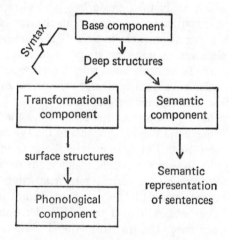

Phonological representation of sentences

The task of the grammarian is to state the rules that are in each of the little boxes. These rules are supposed to represent the speaker's competence. In knowing how to produce and understand sentences, the speaker, in some sense, is supposed to know or to have "internalized" or have an "internal representation of" these rules.

The elegance of this picture has been marred in recent years, partly by Chomsky himself, who now concedes that surface structures determine at least part of meaning, and more radically by the younger Turks, the generative semanticists, who insist that there is no boundary between syntax and semantics and hence no such entities as syntactic deep structures.

III

Seen as an attack on the methods and assumptions of structural linguistics, Chomsky's revolution appears to many of his students to be not quite revolutionary enough. Chomsky inherits and maintains from his structuralist upbringing the conviction that syntax can and should be studied independently of semantics; that form is to be characterized independently of meaning. As early as *Syntactic Structures* he was arguing that "investigation of such [semantic] proposals invariably leads to the conclusion that only a purely formal basis can provide a firm and productive foundation for the construction of grammatical theory."[4]

The structuralists feared the intrusion of semantics into syntax because meaning seemed too vaporous and unscientific a notion for use in a rigorous science of language. Some of this attitude appears to survive in Chomsky's persistent preference for syntactical over semantic explanations of linguistic phenomena. But, I believe, the desire to keep syntax autonomous springs from a more profound philosophical commitment: man, for Chomsky, is essentially a syntactical animal. The structure of his brain determines the structure of his syntax, and for this reason the study of syntax is one of the keys, perhaps the most important key, to the study of the human mind.

It is of course true, Chomsky would say, that men use their syntactical objects for semantic purposes (that is, they talk with their sentences), but the semantic purposes do not determine the *form* of the syntax or even influence it in any significant way. It is because form is only incidentally related to function that the study of language as a formal system is such a marvelous way of studying the human mind.

[4] Noam Chomsky, *Syntactic Structures* (Mouton & Co., 1957), p. 100.

It is important to emphasize how peculiar and eccentric Chomsky's over-all approach to language is. Most sympathetic commentators have been so dazzled by the results in syntax that they have not noted how much of the theory runs counter to quite ordinary, plausible, and common-sense assumptions about language. The common-sense picture of human language runs something like this. The purpose of language is communication in much the same sense that the purpose of the heart is to pump blood. In both cases it is possible to study the structure independently of function but pointless and perverse to do so, since structure and function so obviously interact. We communicate primarily with other people, but also with ourselves, as when we talk or think in words to ourselves. Human languages are among several systems of human communication (some others are gestures, symbol systems, and representational art) but language has immeasurably greater communicative power than the others.

We don't know how language evolved in human prehistory, but it is quite reasonable to suppose that the needs of communication influenced the structure. For example, transformational rules facilitate economy and so have survival value: we don't have to say, "I like it that she cooks in a certain way," we can say, simply, "I like her cooking." We pay a small price for such economies in having ambiguities, but it does not hamper *communication* much to have ambiguous sentences because when people actually talk the context usually sorts out the ambiguities. Transformations also facilitate communication by enabling us to emphasize certain things at the expense of others: we can say not only "Bill loves Sally" but also "It is Bill that loves Sally" and "It is Sally that Bill loves." In general an understanding of syntactical facts requires an understanding of their function in communication since communication is what language is all about.

Chomsky's picture, on the other hand, seems to be something like this: except for having such general purposes as the expression of human thoughts, language doesn't have any essential purpose, or if it does there is no interesting connection between its purpose and its structure. The syntactical structures of human languages are the products of innate features of the human mind, and they have no significant connection with communication, though, of course, people do use them for, among other purposes, communication. The essential thing about languages, their defining trait, is their structure. The so-called "bee language," for example, is not a language at all because it doesn't have the right structure, and the fact that bees apparently use it to communicate is irrelevant. If human beings evolved to the point where they used syntactical forms to communicate that are quite unlike the forms we have now and would be beyond our present comprehension, then human beings would no longer have language, but something else.

For Chomsky language is defined by syntactical structure (not by the use of the structure in communication) and syntactical structure is determined by innate properties of the human mind (not by the needs of communication). On this picture of language it is not surprising that Chomsky's main contribution has been to syntax. The semantic results that he and his colleagues have achieved have so far been trivial.

Many of Chomsky's best students find this picture of language implausible and the linguistic theory that emerges from it unnecessarily cumbersome. They argue that one of the crucial factors shaping syntactic structure is semantics. Even such notions as "a grammatically correct sentence" or a "well-formed" sentence, they claim, require the introduction of semantic concepts. For example, the sentence "John called Mary a Republican and then SHE insulted HIM"[5] is a well-formed sentence only on the assumption that the participants regard it as insulting to be called a Republican.

Much as Chomsky once argued that structuralists could not comfortably accommodate the syntactical facts of language, so the generative semanticists now argue that his system cannot comfortably account for the facts of the interpenetration of semantics and syntax. There is no unanimity among Chomsky's critics—Ross, Postal, Lakoff, McCawley, Fillmore (some of these are among his best students)— but they generally agree that syntax and semantics cannot be sharply separated, and hence there is no need to postulate the existence of purely syntactical deep structures.

Those who call themselves generative semanticists believe that the generative component of a linguistic theory is not the syntax, as in the above diagrams, but the semantics, that the grammar starts with a description of the meaning of a sentence and then generates the syntactical structures through the introduction of syntactical rules and

[5] As distinct from "John called Mary beautiful and then she INSULTED him."

lexical rules. The syntax then becomes just a collection of rules for expressing meaning.

It is too early to assess the conflict between Chomsky's generative syntax and the new theory of generative semantics, partly because at present the arguments are so confused. Chomsky himself thinks that there is no substance to the issues because his critics have only rephrased his theory in a new terminology.[6]

But it is clear that a great deal of Chomsky's over-all vision of language hangs on the issue of whether there is such a thing as syntactical deep structure. Chomsky argues that if there were no deep structure, linguistics as a study would be much less interesting because one could not then argue from syntax to the structure of the human mind, which for Chomsky is the chief interest of linguistics. I believe on the contrary that if the generative semanticists are right (and it is by no means clear that they are) that there is no boundary between syntax and semantics and hence no syntactical deep structures, linguistics if anything would be even more interesting because we could then begin the systematic investigation of the way form and function interact, how use and structure influence each other, instead of arbitrarily assuming that they do not, as Chomsky has so often tended to assume.

It is one of the ironies of the Chomsky revolution that the author of the revolution now occupies a minority position in the movement he created. Most of the active people in generative grammar regard Chomsky's position as having been rendered obsolete by the various arguments concerning the interaction between syntax and semantics. The old time structuralists whom Chomsky originally attacked look on with delight at this revolution within the revolution, rubbing their hands in glee at the sight of their adversaries fighting each other. "Those TG [transformational grammar] people are in deep trouble," one warhorse of the old school told me. But the traditionalists are mistaken to regard the fight as support for their position. The conflict is being carried on entirely within a conceptual system that Chomsky created. Whoever wins, the old structuralism will be the loser.

[6] Cf., e.g., Noam Chomsky, "Deep Structure, Surface Structure, and Semantic Interpretation," in D. Steinberg and L. Jakobovits, eds., *Semantics* (Cambridge University Press, 1971).

IV

The most spectacular conclusion about the nature of the human mind that Chomsky derives from his work in linguistics is that his results vindicate the claims of the seventeenth-century rationalist philosophers, Descartes, Leibniz, and others, that there are innate ideas in the mind. The rationalists claim that human beings have knowledge that is not derived from experience but is prior to all experience and determines the form of the knowledge that can be gained from experience. The empiricist tradition by contrast, from Locke down to contemporary behaviorist learning theorists, has tended to treat the mind as a *tabula rasa,* containing no knowledge prior to experience and placing no constraints on the forms of possible knowledge, except that they must be derived from experience by such mechanisms as the association of ideas or the habitual connection of stimulus and response. For empiricists all knowledge comes from experience, for rationalists some knowledge is implanted innately and prior to experience. In his bluntest moods, Chomsky claims to have refuted the empiricists and vindicated the rationalists.

His argument centers around the way in which children learn language. Suppose we assume that the account of the structure of natural languages we gave in Section II is correct. Then the grammar of a natural language will consist of a set of phrase structure rules that generate underlying phrase markers, a set of transformational rules that map deep structures onto surface structures, a set of phonological rules that assign phonetic interpretations to surface structures, and so on. Now, asks Chomsky, if all of this is part of the child's linguistic competence, how does he ever acquire it? That is, in learning how to talk, how does the child acquire that part of knowing how to talk which is described by the grammar and which constitutes his linguistic competence?

Notice, Chomsky says, several features of the learning situation: The information that the child is presented with—when other people address him or when he hears them talk to each other—is limited in amount, fragmentary, and imperfect. There seems to be no way the child could learn the language just by generalizing from his inadequate experiences, from the utterances he hears. Furthermore, the child acquires the language at a very early age, before his general intellectual faculties are developed.

Indeed, the ability to learn a language is only marginally dependent on intelligence and motivation—stupid children and intelligent children, motivated and unmotivated children, all learn to speak their native tongue. If a child does not acquire his first language by puberty, it is difficult, and perhaps impossible, for him to learn one after that time. Formal teaching of the first language is unnecessary: the child may have to go to school to learn to read and write but he does not have to go to school to learn how to talk.

Now, in spite of all these facts the child who learns his first language, claims Chomsky, performs a remarkable intellectual feat: in "internalizing" the grammar he does something akin to constructing a theory of the language. The only explanation for all these facts, says Chomsky, is that the mind is not a *tabula rasa,* but rather, the child has the form of the language already built into his mind before he ever learns to talk. The child has a universal grammar, so to speak, programmed into his brain as part of his genetic inheritance. In the most ambitious versions of this theory, Chomsky speaks of the child as being born "with a perfect knowledge of universal grammar, that is, with a fixed schematism that he uses, . . . in acquiring language."[7] A child can learn any human language on the basis of very imperfect information. That being the case, he must have the forms that are common to all human languages as part of his innate mental equipment.

As further evidence in support of a specifically human *"faculté de langage"* Chomsky points out that animal communication systems are radically unlike human languages. Animal systems have only a finite number of communicative devices, and they are usually controlled by certain stimuli. Human languages, by contrast, all have an infinite generative capacity and the utterances of sentences are not predictable on the basis of external stimuli. This "creative aspect of language use" is peculiarly human.

One traditional argument against the existence of an innate language learning faculty is that human languages are so diverse. The differences between Chinese, Nootka, Hungarian, and English, for ex-

[7] Noam Chomsky, "Linguistics and Philosophy," in S. Hook, ed., *Language and Philosophy* (NYU Press, 1969), p. 88.

ample, are so great as to destroy the possibility of any universal grammar, and hence languages could only be learned by a general intelligence, not by any innate language learning device. Chomsky has attempted to turn this argument on its head: In spite of surface differences, all human languages have very similar underlying structures; they all have phrase structure rules and transformational rules. They all contain sentences, and these sentences are composed of subject noun phrases and predicate verb phrases, etc.

Chomsky is really making two claims here. First, a historical claim that his views on language were prefigured by the seventeenth-century rationalists, especially Descartes. Second, a theoretical claim that empiricist learning theory cannot account for the acquisition of language. Both claims are more tenuous than he suggests. Descartes did indeed claim that we have innate ideas, such as the idea of a triangle or the idea of perfection or the idea of God. But I know of no passage in Descartes to suggest that he thought the syntax of natural languages was innate. Quite the contrary, Descartes appears to have thought that language was arbitrary; he thought that we arbitrarily attach words to our ideas. Concepts for Descartes are innate, whereas language is arbitrary and acquired. Furthermore Descartes does not allow for the possibility of *unconscious* knowledge, a notion that is crucial to Chomsky's system. Chomsky cites correctly Descartes's claim that the creative use of language distinguishes man from the lower animals. But that by itself does not support the thesis that Descartes is a precursor of Chomsky's theory of innate ideas.

The positions are in fact crucially different. Descartes thought of man as essentially a language-using animal who arbitrarily assigns verbal labels to an innate system of concepts. Chomsky, as remarked earlier, thinks man as essentially a syntactical animal producing and understanding sentences by virtue of possessing an innate system of grammar, triggered in various possible forms by the different human languages to which he has been exposed. A better historical analogy than with Descartes is with Leibniz, who claimed that innate ideas are in us in the way that the statue is already prefigured in a block of marble. In a passage of Leibniz Chomsky frequently quotes, Leibniz makes

> . . . the comparison of a block of marble which has veins, rather than a block of marble wholly even, or of blank tablets, i.e., of what

is called among philosophers, a tabula rasa. For if the soul resembles these blank tablets, truth would be in us as the figure of Hercules is in the marble, when the marble is wholly indifferent to the reception of this figure or some other. But if there were veins in the block which would indicate the figure of Hercules rather than other figures, this block would be more determined thereto, and Hercules would be in it as in some sense innate, although it would be needful to labor to discover these veins, to clear them by polishing, and by cutting away what prevents them from appearing. Thus, it is that ideas and truths are for us innate, as inclinations, dispositions, habits, or natural potentialities, and not as actions, although these potentialities are always accompanied by some actions, often insensible, which correspond to them.[8]

But if the correct model for the notion of innate ideas is the block of marble that contains the figure of Hercules as "disposition," "inclination," or "natural potentiality," then at least some of the dispute between Chomsky and the empiricist learning theorists will dissolve like so much mist on a hot morning. Many of the fiercest partisans of empiricist and behaviorist learning theories are willing to concede that the child has innate learning capacities in the sense that he has innate dispositions, inclinations, and natural potentialities. Just as the block of marble has the innate capacity of being turned into a statue, so the child has the innate capacity of learning. W. V. Quine, for example, in his response to Chomsky's innateness hypothesis argues, "The behaviorist is knowingly and cheerfully up to his neck in innate mechanisms of learning readiness." Indeed, claims Quine, "Innate biases and dispositions are the cornerstone of behaviorism."[9]

If innateness is the cornerstone of behaviorism what then is left of the dispute? Even after all these ecumenical disclaimers by behaviorists to the effect that of course behaviorism and empiricism require innate mechanisms to make the stimulus-response patterns work, there still remains a hard core of genuine disagreement. Chomsky is arguing not simply that the child must have "learning readiness," "biases," and "dispositions," but that he must have a *specific* set of linguistic mechanisms at work. Claims by behaviorists that general learning strategies are based on mechanisms of feedback, information processing, analogy, and so on are not going to be enough.

---

[8] G. Leibniz, *New Essays Concerning Human Understanding* (Open Court, 1949), pp. 45–46.

[9] W. V. O. Quine, "Linguistics and Philosophy," in S. Hook, ed., *Language and Philosophy* (NYU Press, 1969), pp. 95–96.

One has to postulate an innate faculty of language in order to account for the fact that the child comes up with the right grammar on the basis of his exposure to the language.

The heart of Chomsky's argument is that the syntactical core of any language is so complicated and so specific in its form, so unlike other kinds of knowledge, that no child could learn it unless he already had the form of the grammar programmed into his brain, unless, that is, he had "perfect knowledge of a universal grammar." Since there is at the present state of neurophysiology no way to test such a hypothesis by inspection of the brain, the evidence for the conclusion rests entirely on the facts of the grammar. In order to meet the argument, the anti-Chomskyan would have to propose a simpler grammar that would account for the child's ability to learn a language and for linguistic competence in general. No defender of traditional learning theory has so far done this (though the generative grammarians do claim that their account of competence is much simpler than the diagram we drew in Section II above).

The behaviorist and empiricist learning theorist who concedes the complexity of grammar is faced with a dilemma: either he relies solely on stimulus-response mechanisms, in which case he cannot account for the acquisition of the grammar, or he concedes, à la Quine, that there are innate mechanisms which enable the child to learn the language. But as soon as the mechanisms are rich enough to account for the complexity and specificity of the grammar, then the stimulus-response part of the theory, which was supposed to be its core, becomes uninteresting; for such interest as it still has now derives entirely from its ability to trigger the innate mechanisms that are now the crucial element of the learning theory. Either way, the behaviorist has no effective reply to Chomsky's arguments.

V

The weakest element of Chomsky's grammar is the semantic component, as he himself repeatedly admits.[10] But while he believes that

---

[10] I am a little reluctant to attribute the semantic component to Chomsky, since most of its features were worked out not by him but by his colleagues at MIT; nonetheless since he incorporates it entirely as part of his grammar I shall assess it as such.

the semantic component suffers from various minor technical limitations, I think that it is radically inadequate; that the theory of meaning it contains is too impoverished to enable the grammar to achieve its objective of explaining all the linguistic relationships between sound and meaning.

Most, though not all, of the diverse theories of meaning advanced in the past several centuries from Locke to Chomsky and Quine are guilty of exactly the same fallacy. The fallacy can be put in the form of a dilemma for the theory: either the analysis of meaning itself contains certain of the crucial elements of the notion to be analyzed, in which case the analysis fails because of circularity; or the analysis reduces the thing to be analyzed into simpler elements which lack its crucial features, in which case the analysis fails because of inadequacy.

Before we apply this dilemma to Chomsky let us see how it works for a simple theory of meaning such as is found in the classical empirical philosophers, Locke, Berkeley, and Hume. These great British empiricists all thought that words got their meaning by standing for ideas in the mind. A sentence like "The flower is red" gets its meaning from the fact that anyone who understands the sentence will conjoin in his mind an idea of a flower with an idea of redness. Historically there were various arguments about the details of the theory (e.g., were the ideas for which general words stood themselves general ideas or were they particular ideas that were made "general in their representation"?). But the broad outlines of the theory were accepted by all. To understand a sentence is to associate ideas in the mind with the descriptive terms in the sentence.

But immediately the theory is faced with a difficulty. What makes the ideas in the mind into a *judgment?* What makes the sequence of images into a representation of the *speech act of stating* that the flower is red? According to the theory, first I have an idea of a flower, then I have an idea of redness. So far the sequence is just a sequence of unconnected images and does not amount to the judgment that the flower *is* red, which is what is expressed in the sentence. I can assume that the ideas come to someone who understands the sentence in the form of a judgment, that they just are somehow connected as representing the speech act of stating that the flower is red—in which case we have the first horn of our dilemma and the theory is circular, since it employs some of the crucial elements of the notion of meaning in the effort to explain meaning. Or on the other hand if I do not assume the ideas come in the form of a judgment then I have only a sequence of images in my mind and not the crucial feature of the original sentence, namely, the fact that the sentence *says* that the flower is red—in which case we have the second horn of our dilemma and the analysis fails because it is inadequate to account for the meaning of the sentence.

The semantic theory of Chomsky's generative grammar commits exactly the same fallacy. To show this I will first give a sketch of what the theory is supposed to do. Just as the syntactical component of the grammar is supposed to describe the speaker's syntactical competence (his knowledge of the structure of sentences) and the phonological component is supposed to describe his phonological competence (his knowledge of how the sentences of his language sound), so the semantic component is supposed to describe the speaker's semantic competence (his knowledge of what the sentences mean and how they mean what they mean).

The semantic component of a grammar of a language embodies the semantic theory of that language. It consists of the set of rules that determine the meanings of the sentences of the language. It operates on the assumption, surely a correct one, that the meaning of any sentence is determined by the meaning of all the meaningful elements of the sentence and by their syntactical combination. Since these elements and their arrangement are represented in the deep structure of the sentence, the "input" to the semantic component of the grammar will consist of deep structures of sentences as generated by the syntactic component, in the way we described in Section II.

The "output" is a set of "readings" for each sentence, where the readings are supposed to be a "semantic representation" of the sentence; that is, they are supposed to be descriptions of the meanings of the sentence. If for example a sentence has three different meanings the semantic component will duplicate the speaker's competence by producing three different readings. If the sentence is nonsense the semantic component will produce no readings. If two sentences mean the same thing, it will produce the same reading for both sentences. If a sentence is "analytic," that is, if it is true by definition because the meaning of the predicate is contained in the meaning of the subject (for example, "All bachelors are unmarried" is analytic because the meaning of the subject "bachelor" contains the meaning of the predicate "unmarried"), the semantic component will produce a reading for the sentence in which the reading of the predicate is contained in the reading of the subject.

Chomsky's grammarian in constructing a semantic component tries to construct a set of rules that will provide a model of the speaker's semantic competence. The model must duplicate the speaker's understanding of ambiguity, synonymy, nonsense, analyticity, self-contradiction, and so on. Thus, for example, consider the ambiguous sentence "I went to the bank." As part of his competence the speaker of English knows that the sentence is ambiguous because the word "bank" has at least two different meanings. The sentence can mean either I went to the finance house or I went to the side of the river. The aim of the grammarian is to describe this kind of competence; he describes it by constructing a model, a set of rules, that will duplicate it. His semantic theory must produce two readings for this sentence.

If, on the other hand, the sentence is "I went to the bank and deposited some money in my account" the semantic component will produce only one reading because the portion of the sentence about depositing money determines that the other meaning of bank—namely, side of the river—is excluded as a possible meaning in this sentence. The semantic component then will have to contain a set of rules describing which kinds of combinations of words make which kind of sense, and this is supposed to account for the speaker's knowledge of which kinds of combinations of words in his language make which kind of sense.

All of this can be, and indeed has been, worked up into a very elaborate formal theory by Chomsky and his followers; but when we have constructed a description of what the semantic component is supposed to look like, a nagging question remains: What exactly are these "readings"? What is the string of symbols that comes out of the semantic component supposed to *represent* or *express* in such a way as to constitute a description of the meaning of a sentence?

The same dilemma with which we confronted Locke applies here: either the readings are just paraphrases, in which case the analysis is circular, or the readings consist only of lists of elements, in which case the analysis fails because of inadequacy; it cannot account for the fact that the sentence expresses a *statement*. Consider each horn of the dilemma. In the example above when giving two different readings for "I went to the bank" I gave two English paraphrases, but that possibility is not open to a semantic theory which seeks to explain competence in English, since the ability to understand paraphrases presupposes the very competence the semantic theory is seeking to explain. I cannot explain general competence in English by translating English sentences into other English sentences. In the literature of the Chomskyan semantic theorists, the examples given of "readings" are usually rather bad paraphrases of English sentences together with some jargon about "semantic markers" and "distinguishers" and so on.[11] We are assured that the paraphrases are only for illustrative purposes, that they are not the real readings.

But what can the real readings be? The purely formal constraints placed on the semantic theory are not much help in telling us what the readings are. They tell us only that a sentence that is ambiguous in three ways must have three readings, a nonsense sentence no readings, two synonymous sentences must have the same readings, and so on. But so far as these requirements go, the readings need not be composed of words but could be composed of any formally specifiable set of objects. They could be numerals, piles of stones, old cars, strings of symbols, anything whatever. Suppose we decide to interpret the readings as piles of stones. Then for a three-ways ambiguous sentence the theory will give us three piles of stones, for a nonsense sentence, no piles of stones, for an analytic sentence the arrangement of stones in the predicate pile will be duplicated in the subject pile, and so on. There is nothing in the formal properties of the semantic component to prevent us from interpreting it in this way. But clearly this will not do because now instead of explaining the relationships between sound and meaning the theory has produced an unexplained relationship between sounds and stones.

When confronted with this objection the semantic theorists always make the same reply. Though we cannot produce adequate readings

[11] For example, one of the readings given for the sentence "The man hits the colorful ball" contains the elements: [Some contextually definite] (Physical object) (Human) (Adult) (Male) (Action) (Instancy) (Intensity) [Collides with an impact] [Some contextually definite] (Physical Object) (Color) [[Abounding in contrast or variety of bright colors] [Having a globular shape]]. J. Katz and J. Fodor, "The Structure of a Semantic Theory," in *The Structure of Language,* J. Katz and J. Fodor, eds., (Prentice-Hall, 1964), p. 513.

at present, ultimately the readings will be expressed in a yet to be discovered universal semantic alphabet. The elements in the alphabet will stand for the meaning units in all languages in much the way that the universal phonetic alphabet now represents the sound units in all languages. But would a universal semantic alphabet escape the dilemma? I think not.

Either the alphabet is a kind of a new artificial language, a new Esperanto, and the readings are once again paraphrases, only this time in the Esperanto and not in the original language; or we have the second horn of the dilemma and the readings in the semantic alphabet are just a list of features of language, and the analysis is inadequate because it substitutes a list of elements for a speech act.

The semantic theory of Chomsky's grammar does indeed give us a useful and interesting adjunct to the theory of semantic competence, since it gives us a model that duplicates the speaker's competence in recognizing ambiguity, synonymy, nonsense, etc. But as soon as we ask *what* exactly the speaker is recognizing when he recognizes one of these semantic properties, or as soon as we try to take the semantic theory as a *general* account of semantic competence, it cannot cope with the dilemma. Either it gives us a sterile formalism, an uninterpreted list of elements, or it gives us paraphrases, which explain nothing.

Various philosophers working on an account of meaning in the past generation[12] have provided us with a way out of this dilemma. But to accept the solution would involve enriching the semantic theory in ways not so far contemplated by Chomsky or the other Cambridge grammarians. Chomsky characterizes the speaker's linguistic competence as his ability to "produce and understand" sentences. But this is at best very misleading: a person's knowledge of the meaning of sentences consists in large part in his knowledge of how to use sentences to make statements, ask questions, give orders, make requests, make promises, warnings, etc., and to understand other people when they use sentences for such purposes. Semantic

---

[12] In, e.g., L. Wittgenstein, *Philosophical Investigations* (Macmillan, 1953); J. L. Austin, *How to Do Things with Words* (Harvard, 1962); P. Grice, "Meaning," in *Philosophical Review* 1957; J. R. Searle, *Speech Acts, An Essay in the Philosophy of Language* (Cambridge University Press, 1969); and P. F. Strawson, *Logico-Linguistic Papers* (Methuen, 1971).

competence is in large part the ability to perform and understand what philosophers and linguists call *speech acts.*

Now if we approach the study of semantic competence from the point of view of the ability to use sentences to perform speech acts, we discover that speech acts have two properties, the combination of which will get us out of the dilemma: they are governed by rules and they are intentional. The speaker who utters a sentence and means it literally utters it in accordance with certain semantic rules and with the intention of invoking those rules to render his utterance the performance of a certain speech act.

This is not the place to recapitulate the whole theory of meaning and speech acts,[13] but the basic idea is this. Saying something and meaning it is essentially a matter of saying it with the intention to produce certain effects on the hearer. And these effects are determined by the rules that attach to the sentence that is uttered. Thus, for example, the speaker who knows the meaning of the sentence "The flower is red" knows that its utterance constitutes the making of a statement. But making a statement to the effect that the flower is red consists in performing an action with the intention of *producing in the hearer the belief* that the speaker is committed to the existence of a certain state of affairs, as determined by the semantic rules attaching to the sentence.

Semantic competence is largely a matter of knowing the relationships between semantic intentions, rules, and conditions specified by the rules. Such an analysis of competence may in the end prove incorrect, but it is not open to the obvious dilemmas I have posed to classical empiricist and Chomskyan semantic theorists. It is not reduced to providing us with paraphrase or a list of elements. The glue that holds the elements together into a speech act is the semantic intentions of the speaker.

The defect of the Chomskyan theory arises from the same weakness we noted earlier, the failure to see the essential connection between language and communication, between meaning and speech acts. The picture that underlies the semantic theory and indeed Chomsky's whole theory of language is that sentences are abstract objects that are produced and understood independently of their role in communication. Indeed, Chomsky sometimes writes as if sentences

[13] For an attempt to work out some of the details, see J. R. Searle, *Speech Acts,* Chapters 1–3.

were only incidentally used to talk with.[14] I am claiming that any attempt to account for the meaning of sentences within such assumptions is either circular or inadequate.

The dilemma is not just an argumentative trick, it reveals a more profound inadequacy. Any attempt to account for the meaning of sentences must take into account their role in communication, in the performance of speech acts, because an essential part of the meaning of any sentence is its potential for being used to perform a speech act. There are two radically different conceptions of language in conflict here: one, Chomsky's, sees language as a self-contained formal system used more or less incidentally for communication. The other sees language as essentially a system for communication.

The limitations of Chomsky's assumptions become clear only when we attempt to account for the meaning of sentences within his system, because there is no way to account for the meaning of a sentence without considering its role in communication, since the two are essentially connected. So long as we confine our research to syntax, where in fact most of Chomsky's work has been done, it is possible to conceal the limitations of the approach, because syntax can be studied as a formal system independently of its use, just as we could study the currency and credit system of an economy as an abstract formal system independently of the fact that people use money to buy things with or we could study the rules of baseball as a formal system independently of the fact that baseball is a game people play. But as soon as we attempt to account for meaning, for semantic competence, such a purely formalistic approach breaks down, because it cannot account for the fact that semantic competence is mostly a matter of knowing how to talk, i.e., how to perform speech acts.

The Chomsky revolution is largely a revolution in the study of syntax. The obvious next step in the development of the study of language is to graft the study of syntax onto the study of speech acts. And this is indeed happening, though Chomsky continues to fight a rearguard action against it, or at least against the version of it that the generative semanticists who are building on his own work now present.

[14] E.g., meaning, he writes, "need not involve communication or even the attempt to communicate," *Problems of Knowledge and Freedom* (Pantheon Books, 1971), p. 19.

There are, I believe, several reasons why Chomsky is reluctant to incorporate a theory of speech acts into his grammar: First, he has a mistaken conception of the distinction between performance and competence. He seems to think that a theory of speech acts must be a theory of performance rather than of competence, because he fails to see that competence is ultimately the competence to perform, and that for this reason a study of the linguistic aspects of the ability to perform speech acts is a study of linguistic competence. Secondly, Chomsky seems to have a residual suspicion that any theory that treats the speech act, a piece of speech behavior, as the basic unit of meaning must involve some kind of a retreat to behaviorism. Nothing could be further from the truth. It is one of the ironies of the history of behaviorism that behaviorists should have failed to see that the notion of a human action must be a "mentalistic" and "introspective" notion since it essentially involves the notion of human *intentions*.

The study of speech acts is indeed the study of a certain kind of human behavior, but for that reason it is in conflict with any form of behaviorism, which is conceptually incapable of studying human behavior. But the third, and most important reason, I believe, is Chomsky's only partly articulated belief that language does not have any essential connection with communication, but is an abstract formal system produced by the innate properties of the human mind.

Chomsky's work is one of the most remarkable intellectual achievements of the present era, comparable in scope and coherence to the work of Keynes or Freud. It has done more than simply produce a revolution in linguistics; it has created a new discipline of generative grammar and is having a revolutionary effect on two other subjects, philosophy and psychology. Not the least of its merits is that it provides an extremely powerful tool even for those who disagree with many features of Chomsky's approach to language. In the long run, I believe his greatest contribution will be that he has taken a major step toward restoring the traditional conception of the dignity and uniqueness of man.

BIBLIOGRAPHY

A brief bibliography of works relevant to the issues discussed in this article:
1. Noam Chomsky, *Syntactic Structures* (Humanities Press, 1957).

Chomsky's first book, now out of date, but still required reading as the classic statement of the attack on structuralism.

2. Noam Chomsky, *Language and Mind* (Harcourt, Brace and World, 1968, 1972). A series of three lectures Chomsky gave in Berkeley in 1967. This is the clearest statement by Chomsky of the relations between his theory of language and his theory of human nature. Start reading Chomsky's work with this book. It is now available in an enlarged edition containing three extra articles.

3. Noam Chomsky, *Cartesian Linguistics* (Harper & Row, 1966). An attempt to trace the ancestry of Chomsky's theory of language from the rationalist philosophers of the seventeenth century.

4. Noam Chomsky, *Topics in the Theory of Generative Grammar* (Humanities Press, 1966). I believe this to be the simplest and easiest to understand statement by Chomsky of his fundamental linguistic notions, though developments since it was published make some parts of it out of date.

5. Noam Chomsky, *Aspects of the Theory of Syntax* (MIT Press, 1965). The classic statement of Chomsky's mature theory as described in Section II of this article. Most current controversies, over e.g., generative semantics, take this book as their starting point. It is hard to follow, unless you have read, say, numbers 2, 4, and 6 of this bibliography first.

6. John Lyons, *Noam Chomsky* (Viking Press, Modern Masters, 1970). The simplest and clearest introduction to Chomsky's work and to the basic notions of generative grammar. It is rather uncritical, especially about the alleged connection between Chomsky's linguistics and his politics, but it is the best book with which to begin the study of generative grammar. Read it first, then read Chomsky.

7. D. Steinberg and L. Jakobovits, *Semantics, An Interdisciplinary Reader in Philosophy, Linguistics and Psychology* (Cambridge University Press, 1971). An absurdly expensive ($16.50) but useful collection of essays. Several attack the adequacy of the account of language given in *Aspects of the Theory of Syntax*. [Paperback edition, 1974.–Ed.]

8. J. R. Searle, ed., *The Philosophy of Language* (Oxford University Press, 1971). A paperback collection of essays covering both the speech act analysis of language and generative grammar.

9. J. L. Austin, *How to Do Things with Words* (Harvard University Press, 1962). Austin's William James Lectures given at Harvard in 1955. It contains the classic exposition of the theory of speech acts.

10. J. R. Searle, *Speech Acts, An Essay in the Philosophy of Language* (Cambridge University Press, 1969). Contains the theory of speech acts that underlies the remarks in Section V of this article.

11. D. A. Reibel and S. A. Schane, eds., *Modern Studies in English, Readings in Transformational Grammar* (Prentice-Hall, 1969). Genera-

tive grammar has spawned a sizable anthology industry. Of the collections devoted exclusively to syntax, this and the next seem to me the most useful, though both contain some fairly technical articles.

12. R. A. Jacobs and P. S. Rosenbaum, eds., *Readings in English Transformational Grammar* (Ginn & Company, 1970). All the articles in this volume are concerned with the notion of deep structure. The book is built around the theme of assessing, criticizing, and eventually revising the conception of syntax in *Aspects of the Theory of Syntax.*

Review of *Syntactic Structures**

ROBERT B. LEES

Syntactic structures. By NOAM CHOMSKY. Pp. 116. 's-Gravenhage: Mouton & Co., N.V., 1957.

During the past twenty-five years of development in the field of linguistics it has become customary, especially among anthropologists, to regard linguistics as a very advanced, systematic, precise, powerful —in short, 'scientific' discipline. Social scientists, seeking greater precision in the formulation of their special theories, look with envy upon the very exact grammatical statements and the impressive laboratory-phonetic descriptions which are to be found in the pages of linguistic journals, and the linguist himself has come to believe in some instances that he alone among social scientists points the way to a new scientific revolution in our understanding of human behavior.

Before considering in detail the contents of Chomsky's monograph it is useful to re-examine our notions of science and linguistics, for this little book on syntactic structure has much to say about the status of linguistics as a science.[1] Admitting that that typically western insti-

* Reprinted by permission of the author and the Linguistic Society of America from *Language* 33 (1957), pp. 375–407.

[1] The monograph reviewed here is a version of some parts abstracted from a much larger work now in preparation, together with summaries of other materials previously published and unpublished. The reviewer was privileged to read a first version of the larger work—*The Logical Structure of Linguistic Theory*, pp. 752 + li (Cambridge, Mass., 1956)—and now finds it difficult to refrain from referring to topics and results which appear there but not in the book under review. This discussion may therefore serve in part as a preview of the author's detailed statement of his theory of language.

The reader will profit also from three other publications of Chomsky's: Systems of syntactic analysis, *Journal of symbolic logic* 18.242–56 (1953); Semantic considerations in grammar, *Report of the sixth annual Round Table Meeting on Linguistics and Language Teaching* (= *Monograph series on languages and linguistics*, No. 8) 141–50 (1955); Three models for the description of language, *IRE transactions on information theory*, Vol. IT-2, No. 3 (1956). See also his doctoral dissertation, *Transformational analysis* (MS; University of Pennsylvania, 1955).

The reviewer is a member of the Research Laboratory of Electronics, Massachusetts Institute of Technology, where his work is supported in part by the U. S. Army (Signal Corps), the U. S. Air Force (Office of Scientific Research,

tution which we call science is marked by a number of different kinds of activity, such as the use of precise measurement, complicated technical devices, laboratory experiments, or statistical analysis of masses of data, such activities as these are not nearly so characteristic of scientific method as is theory construction and validation. This may be seen most clearly when we compare in the overall history of one of the physical sciences the various stages of achievement through which the science has passed.

Consider as an example the development of chemistry as we know it today. While some chemical knowledge is very old indeed, all that the ancient world knew of chemistry can be considered a kind of accumulated tradition of folk lore, the rules of thumb passed on from one generation of embalmers, tanners, and cosmeticians to the next, a kind of practical engineering for the householder and artisan. With medieval alchemical study, though it was under the influence of gold-seeking and magic, began the first systematic recording of chemical properties, and, along with the careful observations, the first clumsy theories of chemical behavior, culminating in the rather fanciful but seriously intended phlogiston theory of combustion. With the proposal of this erroneous theory and its subsequent demise in favor of Lavoisier's more satisfactory oxygen theory of burning, alchemical lore graduated from magical engineering to scientific discipline. It is not so much the correctness of Lavoisier's explanation which ushered in the scientific era for chemistry, as the change in attitude which accompanied the whole controversy over combustion theories. From that controversy on, chemistry has been concerned less with observation and classification of curious reactions and more and more with the proposal and validation of theories to account for chemical behavior.

Once it has developed beyond the prescientific stage of collection and classification of interesting facts, a scientific discipline is characterized essentially by the introduction of abstract constructs in theories and the validation of those theories by testing their predictive power. Scientific theories are marked not only by freedom from internal contradiction, but also by maximal cohesion with other branches of knowledge, maximal validity in coverage of known data, and maximal elegance of statement. Freedom from internal contradiction is required for making predictions, for from contradictory state-

Air Research and Development Command), and the U. S. Navy (Office of Naval Research), and in part by the National Science Foundation.

ments any assertion may be deduced. Cohesion with other theories is required so that contradictions will not appear in the areas of overlap of data. Maximal coverage is desirable because it is the very purpose of scientific theories to explain by means of generalizations our understanding of particular events and our intuitive perception of their interrelations. Elegance or simplicity of statement compensates for the inevitable limitations on validation which are entailed by finite size of the corpus of data available to us at any time; it may be thought of as a measure of the degree of generality achieved. When scientific prediction diverges from our prescientific, intuitive perception of empirical relations, either the theory is at fault or our perception in error; but when they coincide, the proposed theory is thereby greatly strengthened.

The term 'intuition' may also be used in a different sense in connection with linguistic theories. The empirical data which a linguistic theory must explain consists not only of the noises which talking people produce, but also of various kinds of judgments they can make and feelings they may have about linguistic data. For example, a speaker knows which sounds or words rime, and he can say when a sentence is grammatically permitted or excluded, whether or not he has ever before heard the particular rime or sentence in question. These judgments are sometimes referred to as linguistic intuitions. They are part of the linguistic data to be accounted for, and they must be distinguished from the intuitive or prescientific perceptions which the linguist, qua scientist, has about the data, and which he renders explicit or formalizes, and thus eliminates, by means of his linguistic theory.

While some areas of systematic knowledge are still characterized largely by minute observations and cataloging, but as yet by little useful generalization, for example in the areas of psychology, economics, medicine, and sociology, some fields of knowledge have reached such an advanced stage of development that their basic problems can be stated very succinctly, and their structure is so well understood that we can now begin to construct axiomatic theories to render explicitly and rigorously just what their content is and means. Thus, we might formulate the fundamental problem of physical chemistry as follows: given the detailed nuclear and electronic structure of an atom, what will be the predicted chemical properties of that substance?

Linguistics and science. How does linguistic science measure up against this conception of scientific theory? Is it possible to state exactly the fundamental problem of linguistics? Confining our attention to that branch of language studies dealing with grammar—grammar in the broad sense: the study of linguistic structures as a whole—at what stage of development are our ideas on grammar? Do we deal with grammatical theories, and if so, are those theories characterized by consistency, cohesion with other branches of behavioral science, elegance of statement, i.e. powerful generality, and compatibility with linguistic intuition? These are serious questions which we must all face honestly.

It would seem that our conception of what the grammar of a language is like is all too often of the purely taxonomic, data-cataloging sort. When we compare a modern descriptive grammar with an old-fashioned prescriptive grammar of a century ago, we are accustomed to dismiss the latter as unscientific, especially to the extent that it slavishly reproduces Latin and Greek grammatical categories in an effort to order the data of a non-classical language. But what more is our descriptive grammar than another reordering of the data—now, to be sure, according to a less traditional scheme of categories, but nonetheless according to an arbitrary set of descriptive labels which has become fossilized within linguistic tradition? Thus, without giving any internal linguistic justification, no reasons derived from a theory of language structure and behavior, the empirical data are organized in our descriptive grammar into chapters on Phonemes, Morphophonemics, Word-formation, The Noun, The Verb, Particles, and possibly Syntax, the whole intended from the very beginning to be just a classification of utterance fractions so that they may be successively mentioned from the first to the last page of the grammar in some manner other than randomly.[2]

This long digression into the position of grammar among the sciences seemed appropriate here because, in the reviewer's opinion, Chomsky's book on syntactic structures is one of the first serious at-

[2] It is interesting to note that Hayward Keniston, who describes himself as a humanist, criticizes linguistics as not speculative enough and too bound to a description of physical entities; see *Monograph series on languages and linguistics* 7.146–52 (1954). While criticisms of this sort on the part of humanists may often be interpreted to mean something like 'Linguistics is too scientific, not vague enough', it would be far healthier for us to take it quite literally to mean, 'Linguistics is not scientific enough, too atomistic and taxonomic.'

tempts on the part of a linguist to construct within the tradition of scientific theory-construction a comprehensive theory of language which may be understood in the same sense that a chemical, biological theory is ordinarily understood by experts in those fields. It is not a mere reorganization of the data into a new kind of library catalog, nor another speculative philosophy about the nature of Man and Language, but rather a rigorous explication of our intuitions about our language in terms of an overt axiom system, the theorems derivable from it, explicit results which may be compared with new data and other intuitions, all based plainly on an overt theory of the internal structure of languages; and it may well provide an opportunity for the application of explicit measures of simplicity to decide preference of one form over another form of grammar.

Discovery, decision, or evaluation? Before going on to examine particularities it is necessary to clarify one essential issue which may well prove to be an obstacle to understanding for many a linguist reader. Although Chomsky discusses this point at some length (§ 6.1), it is so important that it can easily bear repetition here.

Nearly all American scholarly work in the field of descriptive and structural linguistics is strongly and unmistakably oriented toward the problem of providing linguistics with a mechanical procedure for discovering the correct grammar of any given language, or better, of some given corpus.[3]

Let us consider first this latter, subsidiary notion which some have entertained, namely, that the linguist has discharged his task once he has specified exactly the constituency of some previously selected, presumably representative text. This criticism is intended to apply equally well to the study of extinct languages, for while the corpus of materials available at any one time for a contemporary language may be vastly larger than the few extant inscriptions for the extinct

---

[3] Pursuit of this goal is seen in perhaps its best and most resolute form in the works of Zellig S. Harris: Discontinuous morphemes, *Language* 21.121–27 (1945); Morpheme to utterance, *Language* 22.161–83 (1946); *Methods in structural linguistics* (Chicago, 1951); Discourse analysis, *Language* 28.1–30 (1952); Distributional structure, *Word* 10.146–62 (1954); Phoneme to morpheme, *Language* 31.190–222 (1955); Co-occurrence and transformation in linguistic structure, *Language* 33 (1957). Following Harris, Rulon Wells attempted to provide a firm basis for discovery of grammatical structure: Immediate constituents, *Language* 23.81–117 (1947); but he denied there (93) that it would be an entirely mechanical procedure.

one, it is nevertheless still finite. Now, for any finite set of objects, say phonemes or words, there are innumerable ways to specify exactly the content and arrangement of those elements, and if this were all that a grammar had to do, there would indeed be a completely mechanical and trivial way to discover grammar. But when we require of the grammar, as does any scientist, that the statements in it be maximally general, it is because we suppose that in this way these statements may be used to predict correctly a maximum number of new elements and sequences which do NOT occur in the finite corpus of data with which we start. Thus we may reasonably expect of a grammar that it account not merely for the sentences of the text in hand, but also for many other sentences which have never been uttered before, but which could be uttered naturally by a speaker of the language in question. There is no obvious mechanical way to generate such a maximally general set of statements.

Time and time again a grammatical proposal is criticised in our literature with the questions: how do you know where to draw that boundary in the stream of speech? what airtight method have you given us by means of which we may transform our transcriptions or tape-recordings into strings of phonemes or grammatical formulas? how did you find these syntactic categories before having analyzed the morphology, or these stresses before those junctures? It is asked, in other words, that the linguist specify just how the elements which make up the grammar of a language have been elicited from Nature, how they have been educed from the physical data; this is very much as if it had been demanded of Kekulé that for the success of his theory of carbon compounds he specify exactly how he fixed upon the notion of the six-membered benzene ring. We must take full note here of just what is being required of linguistic theory when we desire that it provide us with a mechanical means for constructing the grammar of a given language, that it provide us, in other words, with a 'discovery procedure'.

It is necessary in this connection to distinguish clearly between this question of grammatical criteria, motivation, and aims on the one hand, and on the other, the independent and trivial question of the physical arrangement or presentation of the grammatical description, once it has been constructed.[4]

Not even the most advanced of the physical sciences, not to men-

---

[4] Wells, Immediate constituents § 46.

tion the whole remaining less exact body of scientific knowledge, is so powerful as to provide a discovery procedure for its area of interest. There is no known mechanical procedure in all of advanced theoretical physics which will permit an expert physicist to find the laws of nature which connect the readings on the meters of his laboratory one with another or each with the phenomena outside of the laboratory. It is a common misconception on the part of many a scientist, strange to say, that correct scientific theories are discovered by making many observations of nature, that somehow the right answers just leap up out of the laboratory notebook if only we have measured enough things accurately.

This is not to say that the scientist can neglect his proficiency in the use of well established and effective laboratory techniques or that the linguist can afford to omit learning how to deal with the informant and collect useful data. Every scientist uses as a source for inspiration in the construction of new models for nature all that he has learned about older successful models and all that he can learn about model construction from older experienced scientists.

American linguistic canons are particularly characterized by this confusion of field and laboratory techniques for data collection and classification on the one hand and model construction or grammar writing on the other. The confusion is further compounded by the often-heard suggestion that statistical methods, that is, elaborate counting techniques, will not only reveal the correct analysis but even explicate linguistic behavior.[5] Statistical methods ARE in a sense mechanical, nearly everyone knows how to count, they are amenable to machine manipulation in electronic computers, and every statistical formula, even if misapplied, will yield a concrete number, a statistic; but, though much material may be thereby easily summarized, it is not thereby explained. Recent suggestions that phonemic and morphemic segmentation be mechanized by a statistical technique are best regarded as devices for generating hypotheses about linguistic boundaries which must then be validated grammatically. There does not seem to be any demonstrable connection between the grammatical

[5] Charles F. Hockett, in a review of Shannon and Weaver's *The mathematical theory of communication, Language* 29.69–93, esp. 87–88 (1953), proposed that morphemic segmentation might be mechanized by a statistical technique. Similar suggestions are attempted by Harris, Phoneme to morpheme, and by Seymour B. Chatman, Immediate constituents and expansion analysis, *Word* 11.377–85 (1955).

significance of a form and its relative frequency of occurrence, as some statistical theories assume; in fact, it is not even clear that the latter frequency exists as a definable quantity.

The linguistic units postulated by a grammar are constructed much like the concepts of proton, covalent bond, or gene: they are postulated because of the great predictive power which they lend to the theory, but they are not brought to light in the data by a process of induction. And the theories by means of which we order our experiences, on the street or in the laboratory, are generated only by those flashes of insight, those perceptions of pattern, which mark off the brilliant scientist from the dull cataloger of data.[6]

If then we cannot require of linguistic meta-theory that it provide a discovery procedure for linguistics, a procedure for generating grammars mechanically, perhaps one might ask for the next best thing, a mechanical procedure for recognizing a correct grammar (from among all the possible alternatives: i.e. we do the generating, the machine rejects all the wrong ones). Again this would be a rather extravagant request, for even such a well-grounded discipline as classical mathematics cannot boast a 'decision procedure' which would determine mechanically whether any given statement is a theorem or not (except in the most trivial logical calculi). Therefore it does not seem at all over-modest to seek important results on the basis of still weaker demands.

Thus, we might relax our requirements for a linguistic meta-theory to the weaker position of what Chomsky has termed an 'evaluation procedure', a mechanical way to evaluate two proposed grammars on the basis of explicit criteria of excellence and reject one as inferior to the other. It would then no longer be the responsibility of the grammarian to state rigorously HOW he managed to find the particular grammar proposed. Any manipulatory or heuristic principles or devices which he may have found useful or stimulating play no role within the theory itself, once it is constructed.

It may seem strange to some linguists that a grammar can be considered to be a theory of a particular language, and not just a reordering or abbreviation of a text (§ 6.1). But when we consider the generality which must be required of a grammar, in order that it permit the prediction of an unbounded number of new sentences, just as

[6] Cf. Carl G. Hempel, *Fundamentals of concept formation* 36–37 (International encyclopedia of unified science 2.7; Chicago, 1952).

any speaker himself can generate them, we see that it is analogous not to a herbarium, anatomical map, or library catalog, but rather to a scientific theory embodying proposed laws of nature.

Now, although no natural science can claim even a true evaluation procedure, Chomsky guesses that linguistics might very well permit this degree of theoretical power, and that we shall be in a much better position to determine this if we would only give up our ambitious attempts to provide a discovery or decision procedure for our grammars. To reject the worse alternative of a pair of proposed theories, the best that the natural scientist can do is to propose a so-called 'crucial experiment'; but linguistics may be able to go one step further and formulate rigorous criteria of excellence of grammars. Chomsky, in the course of axiomatizing grammatical structure, has proposed some ways in which this might be done in the future. For example, with a satisfactory and comprehensive linguistic meta-theory, the notation for structural statements might be standardized, and then the number of symbols used in a grammar would be a measure of its generality.

The belief that linguistics is a discovery procedure for grammars has led quite naturally to the uncritical acceptance of another troublesome assumption, that of phonemic bi-uniqueness. By this is meant that for a transcription to be phonemic, it is necessary that it be unique in two directions: not only must each string of phonemic symbols be pronounceable in one and only one way, but also every utterance must be transcribable in one and only one way in terms of the phonemes. This latter condition of unique transcribability not only is superfluous for linguistics, it does not even render properly the desired condition of natural, automatic transcribability (for every sound type in every environment there should be some one natural transcription), since bi-uniqueness may be achieved in any number of trivial ways. One need only set up a scheme to reject all but some one possible transcription for any utterance, say the first one in any ordered list of all possible ones.[7]

---

[7] See below for a case in which superfluous rules can be eliminated by rejecting this principle of bi-uniqueness. Cf. Bernard Bloch, Phonemic overlapping, *American speech* 16.278–84 (1941); Hockett, review of Martinet's *Phonology as functional phonetics, Language* 27.340 (1951). Chomsky, Halle, and Lukoff have chosen to reject the principle of bi-uniqueness entirely in their article On accent and juncture in English, *For Roman Jakobson* 65–80 (The Hague, 1956).

Levels. There is an important and immediate result from our agreement to surrender the requirement for a discovery procedure, namely that much of the motivation for a strict isolation of grammatical levels is thereby lost,[8] i.e. there is no longer any strong reason to insist that phonemic description (say) be entirely independent of and antecedent to syntactic description. Now there can be no charge of circularity in the use of syntactic criteria to isolate phonemic entities which must in turn be used later on to determine those very syntactic units used.[9] If one does not demand a mechanical procedure for deriving a grammar from the data, there can be no question of a compulsory order in which various units must be specified. Nor is there any notion of circularity of definition involved in the specification of empirical elements, since the latter must be sharply distinguished from definitions in the strict sense, which are agreements on how technical terms are to be introduced into a theory. Furthermore, even if one did establish an order of discovery, and phonemic analysis were prior to syntactic analysis, any dependence of the latter upon the former would, ipso facto, imply a corresponding relation in the opposite direction, and it is hard to see just how an injunction against 'mixture of levels' could be formulated rigorously, unless this injunction is taken to mean complete irrelevance of phonemics to syntax.

Conditions on grammars. If, then, a grammar, once constructed, is validated by the application of some explicit criteria of simplicity (say, minimal number of symbols used), is this sufficient to guarantee that it will add something to our knowledge of language or languages? Shall we still have to regard similarities in speech behavior among

[8] At the same time the whole concept of linguistic level can be reformulated much more rigorously.

[9] Cf. William G. Moulton, Juncture in modern standard German, *Language* 23.225 fn. 14 (1947); H. A. Gleason, Jr., *An introduction to descriptive linguistics* 66, 175 (New York, 1955); On quite different grounds, grammatical criteria for phonemic analysis have been advocated by Kenneth L. Pike, Grammatical prerequisites to phonemic analysis, *Word* 3.155 (1947), More on grammatical prerequisites, *Word* 8.106–21 (1952). In a review of Harris's *Methods*, *Language* 28.507 fn. 8, Murray Fowler erroneously construes Harris's references to the use of meaning criteria in that work as the major cause of his failure to provide a discovery procedure (though Harris's methods in fact make no use of semantic criteria), and uses this charge of circularity as his strongest criticism of distributional analysis. Cf. also Eugene A. Nida, The analysis of grammatical constituents, *Language* 24.173 (1948); Hockett, review of Martinet 341.

various languages to be some fortuitous convergence of otherwise unrelated linguistic evolutions? Speakers of every language employ
phonemes, morphemes, sentences, immediate constituents, vowels,
consonants, and more or less rigid ordering of these in utterances.
Speakers of all languages acquire the ability during childhood to extend indefinitely the use of the grammatical patterns of their language
to produce an endless stream of new sentences, no one of which may
ever have been uttered before in all linguistic history, but each of
which is nevertheless immediately recognizable by any of those speakers to be fully grammatical. If a grammar is to be of any more general
interest than a handbook for learning the language of which it purports to be the description, then clearly it must satisfy more conditions than maximum simplicity.

To ensure the significance of a grammar, Chomsky would impose
two further types of conditions upon it: a set of so-called 'internally
linguistic' conditions, and a set of 'external conditions' (§ 6.1). If
a grammar is to explicate the kinds of linguistic behavior mentioned
above, it must meet not only the internal requirement of simplicity,
but must be so constructed that all the linguistic units and concepts
used can be shown to be special cases of more general definitions
embodied in a linguistic meta-theory, a theory of language; otherwise there would be no reason to expect that our knowledge of how
speakers of any one language used it to communicate had any relation
at all to what the grammar of other languages could elucidate about
communication among their speakers.

Furthermore, if it is to be useful in explicating the behavior of
speakers, a grammar must be able to satisfy certain external, empirical requirements. It must permit us to generate automatically all
and only the grammatical sentences of the language, else it could not
be called a description at all. Moreover, these sentences cannot be
restricted to some finite corpus, say a text, or the set of all sentences
which had been uttered up to the time of the construction of the
grammar, else it could not account for the fact that speakers are able
to extend the corpus indefinitely.

Clearly, some kind of recursive rules will be required in order that
a finite grammar generate an infinite set of sentences. Although the
morpheme inventory of a language is finite in size at any one time,
and sentences must be constructed of morpheme sequences, the number of sentences is unlimited because there is no meaningful upper

bound which may be placed on the length of sentences, even though any given sentence must be finite in length.

Furthermore, speakers exhibit a fairly consistent ability to grade sequences of morphemes by degree of acceptability as utterances, even when they are meaningless (as in nonsense verse, like Lewis Carroll's Jabberwocky); therefore a grammar must permit the construction of a scale of grammaticalness (Chap. 2, fn. 2; Chap. 5, fn. 2). This scale extends from indisputably bona fide sentences such as *Birds sing,* through various degrees of grammaticalness as in *Their black, round, squares of milk don't fit today, She would have been being silly then,* or *Whom are you seeming?,* all the way to clearly ungrammatical sequences such as *Mine dispose out umpire the.*[10]

Still another external condition which one could impose on a useful grammar, one which Chomsky has found particularly expedient in lending support to a given analysis (Chap. 8), is that it explicate our intuitive understanding of ambiguous sentences by providing two or more different automatic derivations for them. It should also yield different derivations for sentences which, though very similar in apparent outward form, are understood differently. Thus, *He bought stock for me* can be understood in two ways: either it means *He bought stock; the stock was for me,* or it means *He bought stock; he did it for me,* and an adequate grammar of English would, we hope, automatically provide two different analyses for that sentence. This is not simply a question of two different meanings for the preposition *for,* but rather of two different phrase-structures; this becomes apparent when we nominalize the sentence with an *ing*-transformation into two different transforms: *His buying stock for me (was . . .)* and *His buying stock (was for me).*

Similarly, the two sentences *It was proved by Fermi* and *It was proved by induction,* though they appear to be of the same outward form, i.e. have the same constituent structure, are understood differently, and this must be accounted for by an adequate grammar. Again, this is not merely a difference in meaning between *Fermi* and *induction;* the first sentence must be related to *Fermi proved it* (by a passive transformation), while the second is related to *X proved it by induction.*

The information source model. Given these various conditions which might be placed upon a grammar, especially the indispensable

[10] Cf. David L. Olmsted, review of *Psycholinguistics, Language* 31.50 (1955).

requirement that it at least permit the generation of all the grammatical sentences of the language, what is the weakest sort of model for language which we could entertain?

It is fashionable for information theoreticians, communications engineers, and some linguists to seek an explication of linguistic phenomena in some statistical model of language.[11] While it would be silly to deny the usefulness of such models for an understanding of certain problems in science, such as the behavior of ideal gases, there does seem to be good reason to believe that language, and more particularly grammar, is essentially a nonstatistical structure, and is rather to be understood with the help of combinatory or algebraic models.

One recent suggestion is that speech be considered the output of a kind of finite automaton which generates sentences from left to right as it changes from state to state with its conditional probabilities, a kind of Markov chain of predispositions to emit the next symbol with a likelihood dependent only upon which state the machine is in at the moment. When these states are identified with the immediately preceding n symbols in a string of linguistic symbols, such a model yields its special case, the nth-order approximation to bona fide text, where grammaticalness might be interpreted as 'high-order approximation'.[12] There is at least this one strong objection to all such conceptions of language: there is no reason whatever to believe that the relative frequency of occurrence (or limit thereof, i.e. the probability) of a sentence or any other sequence, even if this could be rigorously determined, has anything at all to do with its grammaticalness. Thus, there are countless sentences so short as to be of undisputed grammaticalness, whose relative frequency of occurrence must be very much smaller than such longer and more involved, but more common, sentences as *Any resemblance to persons living or dead is entirely coincidental.* If linguistic description is merely a matter of replacing all very low probabilities with zero, then many an impec-

[11] See Hockett, *A manual of phonology* 3–14 (Baltimore, 1955). Cf. also Claude E. Shannon and Warren Weaver, *The mathematical theory of communication* (Urbana, Ill., 1949); Hockett, review of Shannon and Weaver 86–87; Benoit Mandelbrot, Structure formelle des textes et communication, *Word* 10.1–27 (1954); id., Simple games of strategy occurring in communication through natural languages, *Trans. IRE*, PGIT-3. 124–37 (1954).

[12] Shannon and Weaver 13–15; George A. Miller, *Language and communication* 83–86 (New York, 1951); Kellogg Wilson, *Psycholinguistics: A survey of theory and research problems* 46 (Baltimore, 1954).

cable sentence such as *Birds eat* would have to be rejected because it is hardly ever said.

Furthermore, the fact that among successive orders of approximation there appear randomly various grammatical sequences as well as various ungrammatical ones at EVERY level of approximation shows that the order is not relevant to grammaticalness.

A somewhat more powerful model of a finite-state machine, the first in order which could be at all seriously considered as a model of language, would permit the generation of infinitely many sentences using a finite apparatus, a so-called finite-state Markov process, as information source. Chomsky has shown[13] this model to be inadequate to account for natural language with its recursive nesting of constructions within one another. Chapter 3 is a nontechnical review of his arguments.

Involved in all such considerations is the notion that a grammar may be described as though it were a kind of machine, of whatever sort. This is not intended as another banal example of scientism on the part of the modern grammarian, for there is a clear relation between the essential properties of a mechanical device and the structure of a scientific theory. In order that a theory, and therefore also a grammar, be perfectly public and reproducible, but at the same time effective, it is necessary that the predictions afforded by the theory be an automatic consequence of its premises and arguments. If then the appropriate notations be set up, the derivation of its predictions from its premises may be translated into machine terms, and, depending upon how complicated an algebra was employed in the theory, the derivations may be mechanized inside an actual physical machine, such as an electronic computer. There is a body of mathematical literature dealing in detail with the properties of such machines.[14] An ordinary electronic computer would suffice to generate the sentences permitted by a finite-state model, mentioned above. To yield derivations for the sentences of a natural language, a machine would require more power than this, say at least as much as an automaton with infinite memory (or, as it is usually called, a Turing machine).[15] But there is as yet no indication that any of the the-

---

[13] Three models (cf. fn. 1).

[14] E.g., S. C. Kleene, *Introduction to metamathematics,* esp. Chap. 13 (Princeton, 1952).

[15] Ibid.; see also J. G. Kemeny, Man viewed as a machine, *Scientific American,* April 1955, 58–67, for a particularly graphic description of the Turing

orems from the mathematics of Turing machines is at all revealing linguistically. In other words, it is of no interest that a Turing machine would suffice in power to account for grammar; the important question is: exactly WHICH particular Turing machines out of the infinite possible kinds best explicate the linguistic behavior of speakers. Specification of the internal structure which such a machine would have to have is just the study of grammar, and the algebra which it would have to obey is not likely to be an interpretation of any system known or studied independently in classical mathematics.

Phrase-structure grammar. The most immediately interesting feature of Chomsky's researches into English syntax and grammatical theory is his rigorous attempt to construct a grammar on the basis of a carefully axiomatized and consistently detailed level of 'phrase-structure', that is, roughly, 'bracketing' or, as it is usually termed in linguistics, immediate-constituent analysis (Chap. 4).[16] He has brought out clearly the resulting difficulties which inevitably beset any such serious attempt.

While the communication engineer assumes language to be an interpretation of some weak version of Turing machine, the linguist, more sophisticated in matters of natural language, has assumed that the sentences of a language may each be analyzed into a linearly concatenated sequence of immediate constituents, and that this bracketing or parsing operation may be performed at various levels of generality to yield a hierarchical branching-diagram, such that any unit at any level is just a certain continuous string within some sentence or else a class of such strings drawn from different but grammatically equivalent sentences.

The difficulties which arise in such a simple-minded model, e.g. with discontinuous components and portmanteau morphemes, have been the topic of much recent methodological discussion.[17] But,

---

machine. Even if such a machine were *powerful* enough to reproduce all of human behavior, as Kemeny suggests, it does not seem to this reviewer any more fruitful as an approach to an understanding of this behavior than computer theory is revealing in the explication of grammatical facts.

[16] The independence of phrase-structure from forms, order and construction has also been pointed out by Hockett, Two models of grammatical description, *Word* 10.218–20 (1954). Wells also notes the independence of sequence from 'construction' (= phrase structure) in IC analysis.

[17] Cf. Floyd G. Lounsbury, A semantic analysis of the Pawnee kinship usage, *Language* 32.159–62 (1956); Sol Saporta, Morph, morpheme, archimorpheme, *Word* 12.9–14 (1956).

previous to Chomsky's attempt, no one has really taken seriously any set of criteria of adequacy and simplicity in the construction of a grammar of any one language, has ever really followed out to its last implication any consistent method of representing the sentences of any one language in a revealing, intuitively satisfying way. Chomsky is, then, one of the first to emphasize clearly the ever compounding difficulties attendant upon any such grammatical description based exclusively on such a phrase-structure model, and he is the first to offer a constructive suggestion for circumventing these difficulties.

Before going on to this suggestion, let us first note some of these inadequacies of a phrase-structure grammar (Chap. 5). First, there are many instances of sentences understood quite differently, but for which there seem to be no grounds within phrase-structure for assigning different representations without introducing either intolerably complex or arbitrarily unmotivated or unintuitive machinery. For example, there is no way in such a grammar to say that *What are you looking for?* and *What are you running for?* have different structures. As is shown by a simple paraphrase, the first sentence contains a prepositional phrase *for what,* while the second contains an interrogative *what for* 'why', but there is no mechanism for associating a sentence with its paraphrase, and the two sentences appear therefore to have identical constituent structures.

Similarly, there are many cases of ambiguous sentences for which only a single analysis seems justified.[18] Thus, the sentence *This teacher's marks are very low* is understood in two ways: 'This teacher gives low marks' or 'This teacher gets low marks'. There is no reason, however, for assigning two different immediate-constituent analyses, nor is there any word in the sentence which may be said to have two different lexical meanings (homophony).

Then there are also cases where two or more analyses would result for a single unambiguous construction, if we agree to apply the most obvious criteria of simplicity to our grammar. For example, within English phrase-structure there would be grounds for assigning to the sentence *The dog is barking* both the analysis Noun phrase (*the dog*) + Auxil. verb phrase (*is –ing*) + Verb phrase (*bark*), and also the analysis Noun phrase (*the dog*) + Copula (*is*) + Adjective (*barking*). The latter analysis is clearly a counterintuitive result, but considerations of simplicity in the analysis of certain other sentences

---

[18] The inadequacy of IC analysis of ambiguous sentences is also recognized by Hockett, Two models 218.

require such a treatment: *The dog is a friendly animal* (NP + *is* + NP) and *Barking is a sign of excitement* (NP + *is* + NP), therefore: NP = V-*ing*.

Another type of difficulty is encountered when we try to formulate such rules as that of conjunction. To specify which sequences may appear on the two sides of the conjunction *and,* it would be necessary to designate more than the internal immediate-constituent construction of each component, for they must be constituents of the same kind and derivation to yield fully grammatical conjunctions. Furthermore, even if conjunctions could be described simply as constituents of the same internal and external structure, connected by means of a conjunction morpheme, sentences of the following sort could not be described as 'imperative plus declarative': *Hurry up or you'll be late, Come here and I'll tell you a story* unless the notion of imperative and declarative sentence types is relinquished.

This whole notion of sentence type is, as a matter of fact, quite unmotivated in a phrase-structure grammar. Thus, there is no way to show that *John hit Bill* and *Bill was hit by John* are related, though of different constituent structure, in a way that *John hit Bill* and *Bill hit John* are not, though of similar structure.

Another notion which it would seem an adequate grammar should explicate is the fairly consistent choice of one type of construction to be more basic or central than another more marginal or derived type. Thus, active sentences are thought to underlie passives (as in the previous paragraph), statements are more basic than questions, main clauses are more central structures than dependent clauses. But there is no compelling reason on the basis of constituent structure to order constructions in this natural way.

Perhaps the most severe defect of a grammar expressed exclusively in terms of a phrase-structure hierarchy, or branching-diagrams, is the extreme complexity required even for the simplest type of sentences, and the great difficulty of stating this phrase-structure in terms of units which may contain one another as constituents. While a branching-diagram can be constructed individually for any one given sentence (i.e. every sentence has at least one specifiable phrase-structure), there is no set of expansion or parsing rules which will yield properly the phrase-structure of ALL the sentences, unless extensive portions of the grammar are restated several times. If these uneconomical repetitions are permitted, then the grammar fails to state the near identity in structure between those parts which must be repeated. For example, all of the mechanism which provides the proper combinations of adjective and noun in such sentences as NP + *is* + A (*Roses are red, Men are numerous,* but not *This man is numerous*) will have to be repeated for such sentences as (*The* +) A + NP + VP (*Red roses smell good, Numerous men go there,* but not *This numerous man is coming*).

Transformations. One of the two most far-reaching results of Chomsky's study is then his discovery of a new level of linguistic structure which at once sweeps away most of the difficulties encountered in any attempt to extend phrase structure beyond a description of the most central declarative sentences of the language. (Chap. 7.) For a given rule to apply within this level of grammatical description the derivational history of an expression must be taken into account for each rule serves to convert, or transform, one constituent structure into another.

The basic idea behind this new level of structure was obviously derived from those manipulations characteristic of Harris's discourse analysis: a sentence whose phrase structure differs from those already set up in the grammar may nevertheless exhibit a whole set of internal correlations or selections identical with those found in simpler, already described sentences.[19] In other words, a more marginal sentence or construction may be described as a transform of some underlying, more central structure. Harris, in order to find some core of essential, basic propositions of which all the various sentences of a discourse might be said to be merely various versions, has permitted different sentences to be collapsed into prototypes if they differ in statable grammatical ways from one another; e.g. a passive sentence

---

[19] But it is also interesting to note that, in a sense, transformational analysis is essentially a formalization of a long-accepted, traditional approach to grammatical relations. To cite only a single example of classical grammatical thought which is basically a kind of transformation theory: 'It is different when we come to such a combination as *an early riser,* which it is quite impossible to turn into *a riser who is early.* Here the adjunct is a shifted subjunct of the verb contained in the substantive *riser: he rises* (vb) *early* (adv) = *he is an early* (adj) *riser* (sb)'—Otto Jespersen, *A modern English grammar* 2.283 § 12.12. Here Jespersen correctly perceives that the difference in the way that we understand, on the one hand, *he is an early riser,* and, on the other, *he is an early bird* can be accounted for by regarding the former as a transform of *he rises early,* the latter as a transform of the pair *he is an X* and *early bird* (which in turn is a transform of *the bird is early*).

may be transformed into its active form if this will facilitate the collapse.[20]

Chomsky, on the basis of somewhat different motives, has been led to set up a whole level of grammatical transformations to deal with all the difficulties encountered in trying to state explicitly a complete and simple immediate-constituent grammar. Here the phrase-structure rules need be used to generate only a central core of simplest sentences, the KERNEL, in which only a very limited number of sentence types appears (roughly, the shortest active indicative assertions). All other grammatical sentences of the language can be generated by means of these transformations and may be said to have a derived constituent structure. Now, for example, *What are you looking for?* can be described as a what-question transform of *You are looking for it,* and *What are you running for?* as a why-question transform from *You are running.* Or we may say that passives are less central than actives since the transformation which generates passives from actives is not reversible, as there is no way of identifying the prepositional phrase with *by* which contains the subject of the active. Thus, *The blow hurt John → John was hurt by the blow,* but not *John was hurt by the bridge → *The bridge hurt John,* or *John was elected by the following week → *The following week elected John.*

The anatomy of grammar. Grammar is now seen as a structure of three main interrelated levels of rules, each developed as a different kind of concatenation algebra. The lowest level contains morpho-phonemic and phonemic rules in which there is a relation, for the most part order-preserving, between the parts of each representation of an utterance and the temporally arranged parts of the real utterance, and in which, for each sublevel, all the constituents may be developed in a derivation simultaneously. There is a 'highest' level, the level of phrase-structure, which yields branching diagrams, in which any given rule can develop only one constituent at a time in order that each rule be required to take into consideration only the results of the immediately preceding rule[21] and in which there are

---

[20] Harris, *Language* 28.18–25; Co-occurrence and transformation.

[21] For example, suppose that the representation of a sentence, NP + VP (i.e. noun-phrase plus verb-phrase) is to be developed next, and is rewritten directly as *Dogs + can + swim,* then there is no specification of the phrase-structure in the result, since there is no way to tell which of the developed elements originated as NP and which as VP. But if the development proceeds

no clearly definable sublevels, but rather only whole sets of representations for any given derived utterance. In the 'intermediate' transformation level each rule must take into consideration the phrase-structure and transformational history of the representations of utterances to which it applies, the rules of transformation may each apply to more than one string, and may furthermore be reapplied to yield the necessary recursiveness for infinite extension.

In such a grammar there would seem to be no particular place of honor accorded to just those considerations which figure most prominently in a traditional grammatical description, viz. so-called 'morphemics'. Descriptive grammatical sketches are, in large part at least, simply more or less elaborate morpheme-order charts. It is seldom found necessary to justify either the particular classes of morphemes selected for detailed treatment (say, bases which precede final -*s* plural, but not bases which precede final -*y* as in *muddy, icy, tiny*), even when they are quite small (as in adjectives in -*er*), or the particular diagnostic stigma chosen to distinguish the members from all other morphemes. But now, viewing a grammar as a theory which will generate all and only grammatical sentences by means of naturally chosen, maximally simple, unrepeated rules, all bases and all those affixal morphemes which are required for stating phrase-structures (because they are correlated with other morphemes external to their own base or construction) will appear somewhere among the constituent-structure rules. And after the application of all transformations and phrase-structure expansions, before the application of morphophonemic and lower-level rewritings, each sentence will be represented morphemically; the concatenated units at this level are MORPHEMES, for the most part inflectional morphemes and morphological heads, i.e. bases.

Before morphemes can be spelled out phonemically, it will of course usually be necessary to pass through one or more sublevels of mappings which will select the appropriate morphophonemic shapes of heterogeneous morphemes when these selections can be stated simply in terms of the surrounding morphemic environment. (Here e.g. the various shapes for the past-tense verbal morpheme

in two steps—S = NP + VP, NP = *dogs*, VP = *can* + *swim*, expanding each phrase separately—the phrase-structure is preserved at each step: S = NP + VP = *dogs* + VP = *dogs* + *can* + *swim*, and we can say that *dogs* is a NP and *can* + *swim* is a VP.

will be selected according as the base is weak, strong, irregular, etc.)

Halle has pointed out[22] the following very interesting consequence of basing the grammar upon rule-simplicity rather than upon arbitrary and unmotivated principles, such as bi-uniqueness of phonemic transcription. In American descriptive grammars, allomorphic selections conditioned by both the choice of the surrounding morphemes and by the more immediate phonemic environment are all lumped together (sometimes in two subdivisions) into a morphophonemics, and then rules for the allophonic selections are stated as part of the phonology, with the usual insistence that the phonemic transcription preserve bi-uniqueness and phonetic reality, i.e. a unique transcription for every different perceived segment. The lack of certain phonemic contrasts in positions of neutralization is either ignored or said to devolve upon the defective distribution of the (neutralized) phonemes. In many cases, however, this division entails needless duplication of statement and results therefore in loss of generality in the grammar.

Consider the common case, as in the following Turkish example, of final devoicing, or neutralization of voiced-voiceless contrasts in final positions: final morphophonemic b, d, ǰ, g, ɢ, r, and l are devoiced to [p, t, č, k, q] and [r̥, l̥]. Since the traditional treatment recognizes [r̥, l̥] (devoiced r and l) as allophones of /r, l/, but [p, t, č, k, q] as separate phonemes, the rule of devoicing must be stated twice (if we would avoid setting up two new r and l phonemes just for this case), once as a morphophonemic rule for /b, d, ǰ, g, ɢ/ and again as an allophonic rule for /r, l/. In Chomsky's (and Halle's) conception of grammar, one need consider, after morphophonemic rewritings of the first kind (morphemically conditioned), only one last linguistic level before stating the phonic values of its units in a series of unrepeated phonetic rules, among which appears this rule of devoicing for all stops and liquids. Although it is not bi-unique, this last linguistically significant level may be called phonemic, especially since it is the first level at which the units are all directly describable in terms of the phonetic system used, say a distinctive-feature system, boundary-markers, and phonetic rules.

As the following successive representations of a sample Turkish sentence show, any transcription lower than the last would contain

[22] Personal communication. Halle will adopt this view in his forthcoming work *The sounds of Russian.*

obviously subphonemic writings, such as the devoiced allophones of the otherwise homogeneous phoneme /r/:

{Ahmed + Sg + General + Book + Sg + Def Obj + Mehmed + Sg + Dative + Give + Aorist + 3rd Sg #} (string of morphemes which results from application of all syntactic rules in phrase-structure and transformation levels)

⟨ahmed + O + O + | kitab + O + I + | mehmed + O + E + | ver + ɪr + O #⟩ (string of morphophonemes which results from application of all morphophonemic spelling rules for morphemes)

/ahmed + kitabi + mehmede + verir #/ (string of phonemes, each characterizable as some maximally nonredundant set of features, which results from application of phonemic rules)

[ahmed | kitabɪ | mehmede | verir #] (a phonetic representation which results from application of phonetic rules specifying vowel harmony)

[ahmet | kitabɪ | mehmede | verir̦ #] (a further phonetic representation after application of phonetic rule of final voicing: [b d j g ɢ r l] = [p t č k q r̦ l̦])

[aạmɛt̠'k'it̠'abɪmɛɛmɛd̠ɛvɛr̆ir̦] (a still further phonetic representation after application of other phonetic rules. Continues until all phonemes have been described in terms of ALL available features, at which point the linguistic description is ended, since any further specification of sounds would introduce only new free variations or subliminal distinctions.)

It is not yet completely clear just what structure is required for the level in which phonemic representations (in the sense intended here) are converted into representations in terms of the minimally contrastive phonetic features which the analyst chooses. Something like the following may suffice: the phonemic representation is first rewritten as a series of feature bundles in which the number of features used to specify each phoneme is minimized by the elimination of all redundant features. Then by means of a series of phonetic rules the redundant features are added to each phoneme in some simplest manner until they have all become specified to such an exact degree that any further distinctions would serve to introduce only phonetic differences which are always in free variation. At this point the linguistic description is at an end, and further specification of noises is a question of physics or physiology. This whole level is then characterized by the unique use of the features mentioned as its alphabet.

The successive representations in a derivation will gradually approach bi-uniqueness, but it is never necessary to require this condition.

Chomsky avoids those philosophical problems entailed by the use of class notation in the grammar, such as were of concern to early phonemicists: is a phoneme an actual noise-occurrence (a phone-token), a class of similar noise-occurrences (a phone-type), a class of similar phone-types (allophone), a class of allophones, or merely (sic) an abstraction corresponding to one of these, or, say, a certain pair of these, as in the Prague concept of the phoneme as a phonological opposition? Once a grammar has been acknowledged to be the THEORY of some language, all grammatical units which appear in it may be accorded the same status as the notions in any physical or chemical theory. For instance, the volume which appears, symbolized by the letter V, in the gas law $pV = nRT$ is not an actual gas volume, nor even a class of gas volumes, it represents volumes in a theory of ideal gas behavior. So too we shall say that a concept such as phoneme, noun-phrase, or auxiliary verb, which occurs in the algebra of a language, in its grammar, REPRESENTS a certain string of noises, or a certain type of string of noises. (Within the phrase-structure part of the grammar, then, any string might have many different representations: e.g. $NP = T + A + N = T + black + N = T + A + shoe = the + A + shoe = the + black + shoe =$ etc.) And it is just one of the tasks of linguistic meta-theory to specify exactly the nature of this relation of naming or representing which holds between concepts in the grammar and real pieces of speech, or between one representation of a string and another.

Needless to say, the structure of such algebras of grammatical levels, representation relations, etc. has nothing to do with the particular graphic devices used to mention or manipulate them on paper. A valid grammatical statement is just as valid whether it is affirmed in an abstruse algebraic notation or in plain words. Finally, it is not the use of mathematical symbols and formulaic statement which renders a given treatment 'formal'. Mathematical formality in an interpreted system means rigorous statement of how each symbol is related to the empirical datum which it represents.

Theory of grammar. The other most important result of Chomsky's theory of language is his very strict axiomatization of linguistic theory. He has chosen to take seriously the requirement that a grammar be not merely an arbitrary reorganization of some corpus, but (in a specifiable sense) a simplest machine which will generate all and only the grammatical sentences of a language. But in order to devise an adequate measure of simplicity, it is incontrovertibly necessary first to specify in exact and minute detail just what the internal structure of a grammar and a grammatical level is, and just exactly how the levels are related to one another. Then the grammar of any one language can be required to meet a set of relatively weak external requirements of conformity to the meta-theory of grammar.

It may be that, in our great enthusiasm to introduce linguistic relativity as an antidote to prescriptive classicism, we have also thrown out all grammatical theory, like the proverbial baby with the bath water. The theory of universal grammatical categories, like Ptolemaic astronomy, while quite wrong, was more in need of revision than of repudiation. This is not to say that the descriptive linguist has no theory of language at all. He believes, it is true, that all languages have phonemes and morphemes, that all sentences have immediate constituents, etc. But at the same time, he inhibits the development of a comprehensive theory of language by favoring an exaggerated relativity of arbitrarily chosen form classes.

Replacing erroneous semantic notions with strictly specified 'formal' categories was, to be sure, an advance, especially where those categories correspond well to intuitive notions of structural equivalence. The so-called formal analysis has the one advantage of permitting the analysis of any given sentence in the presence of a correct grammar, by reference only to the rules and to the sentence itself, while the older semantic classifications would require additional knowledge of the meanings.[23] But merely specifying the membership of a class by means of more explicit notation, such as a diagnostic environment or an exact list, does not provide any deeper understanding of the category involved.

The correctness of a grammatical statement is assured not by the arbitrarily chosen differentia, semantic or formal, but by the analyst's correct perception of the underlying phrase-structure or transformational history. For example, to separate nouns from verbs in English is certainly necessary, but to do so by defining them as classes of morphemes which may occur before certain final affixes (rather than certain others) is just as arbitrary and ad hoc as is a separation on the basis of 'means person, place, or thing, etc.' versus 'means action,

[23] Gleason, *Introduction* 92–95.

etc.' In the 'formal' analysis there is no motivated reason for choosing the particular affixes used rather than some others, or for using any other differentiae which happen to specify the members of the desired class. Nor is there ever any serious attempt to catalog ALL POSSIBLE classes on the basis of the following affix, as would be necessary if this were the true analytic criterion, for the analyst knows full well that to do so would yield a very detailed but completely vacuous morpheme-order chart, and not the desired categories of noun and verb. Given a set of meaningful categories or morpheme classes, it is always possible to find or devise some explicit 'formal' property which will serve to specify just which elements belong to the list of members of the various categories. This is just as arbitrary as any semantic classification which accomplishes the same task; and as for explicitness, nothing could be more explicit than a simple listing of the members.

Furthermore, the 'formal' analysis is no more generalizing than the semantic. To include *sheep, oxen, alumni,* etc. among nouns requires special rules, just as special rules are required to accommodate meanings within the semantic specification other than 'person, place, or thing'. Such ad-hoc rules, whether semantic or formal, require special invention for each individual case, and thus add little to our understanding of grammatical categories. Only when an individual category in some language can be shown to be a special case of a more general notion of 'grammatical category' applying within a linguistic metatheory to all languages, are we justified in seeing this as a real step toward elucidating the behavior of speakers of that language.

Meaning in linguistics. So far we have said nothing at all about the vexed question of semantic criteria in linguistics (Chap. 9). There is a very simple explanation for this neglect: if the term 'meaning' is taken in its ordinary, everyday sense, this notion turns out to be simply irrelevant to grammatical theory and analysis. It is however not at all irrelevant to language study, and it may even be that part of linguistic studies which is of the greatest interest to the majority of our profession. But the study of meaning and its relation to grammar has been woefully confused by the widespread confounding of reference, meaning, synonymy, 'differential meaning', informant response, amount of 'information', significance, grammatical equivalence, truth-preserving equivalence, and mutual substitutability. No single concept involved in linguistic tradition has caused such widespread misunderstanding and entailed such a plethora of polemic as has that of meaning, with the possible exception of the 'phonetic law' of the Junggrammatiker. The linguist not only is beset, as is any other behavioral scientist, with all the classical philosophical problems inherent in the notion of meaning, but also must now deal with the added difficulty of identification with one or another of the several schools of linguistic philosophy at odds with one another over the question of whether and (if so) how meaning enters into linguistic analysis.

There are two other scholarly disciplines in which serious attempts have been made to clarify problems involved in this area: philosophy and psychology. Now, while philosophy seems to have succeeded fairly well in elucidating the notions involved in the relation of denotation, that is, all that is meant by reference or naming, there seems to have been little progress so far in explicating the concept of meaning. Although many formal systems have been constructed to deal with semantics, even the best of them assume as basic, primitive notions the relation of synonymy and/or the property of significance, and it is just these very concepts which are so unclear. It is advisable in any case to avoid entirely any use of the term 'meaning' (as a noun) and to speak instead exclusively of a relation 'means', or to be even more careful, using just 'is significant' (= 'has a meaning') and 'is synonymous with' (= 'has the same meaning as').

As for the second discipline mentioned above, it does not seem at all unlikely that if a full explication of significance and synonymy (and therefore also of 'meaning') is forthcoming, it will be found in some psychological or psycholinguistic theory. But, at least for the present, any such theory is far beyond current achievements in complexity and power.

Although it seems quite clear, at least to Chomsky and the present reviewer, that semantic criteria of analysis are neither useful in nor indeed pertinent to grammar, nevertheless we might expect that insight into grammatical structure, and the ways in which sentences are understood, would yield directly a better understanding of significance and synonymy. This is especially true if we seek to formulate grammatical statements in such a way as best to explain ambiguities in and centrality of structure, and when we employ for this a kind of transformation for which lexicosemantic content may very well be an invariant. Thus it would be a great step forward if it could be shown that all or most of what is 'meant' by a sentence is contained in the kernel sentences from which it is derived. And much of the obscurity beclouding the idea of meaning may very well have resulted in large measure from a restrictive overconcern with lexical items and dictionary entries to the exclusion of the sentence, for while the former are seen in many but by no means all cases to participate in a relation of denotation or naming, it may be that it is only the latter unit, the sentence, which is truly significant, i.e. has a 'meaning'.

It might be of value to bring together here several clarifying notions on some of the things that meaning CANNOT be and some of the reasons why meaning in its ordinary usage cannot be pertinent to grammatical analysis.[24]

MEANING AND REFERENCE. The first confusion which we must dispose of, one in which the reviewer himself has indulged,[25] is the suggestion that meaning is nothing more nor less than REFERENCE, the simple, fairly well understood notion of denotation between an expression and a material object which it denotes. However, there are many expressions which refer to the same object but are not synonymous, for example *the largest city in the world* and *London;* both expressions denote the city of London, but the meaning of the former, as well as that of the latter (if indeed it may be said to have any meaning at all) will remain unaffected after New York has surpassed London in size, though they will then have begun to denote two different objects. Synonyms, if they have any denotation at all, are always co-referent; thus synonymy is a narrower, more complex, and obscurer notion than co-reference, and the latter is a necessary but not a sufficient condition for the former, for all meaningful, referential expressions.[26]

MEANING AND DISTRIBUTION. It has been suggested, especially of-

[24] For similar discussions, see Yehoshua Bar-Hillel, Logical syntax and semantic, *Language* 30.230–37 (1954), and an answer by Chomsky, Logical syntax and semantics: Their linguistic relevance, *Language* 31.36–45 (1955).

[25] Meaning in three linguistic theories, read before the Linguistic Forum, University of Michigan, in 1953, and again before the Washington Linguistic Club in 1954.

[26] Note that some expressions do not seem to have any meaning, in its ordinary sense, e.g. *to* in *he likes to sing.* Other expressions have no reference, e.g. *the average American* and *mermaid,* unless we are willing to people the universe with countless imaginary objects. Cf. also C. E. Bazell, The choice of criteria in structural linguistics, *Word* 10.132 (1954); Miller. *Language and communication* 160.

ten by linguists, whose attention has been focused on linguistic form, that meaning is just a certain kind of distribution in linguistic frames.[27] This would presumably mean that the two expressions having the same meaning, again in the ordinary sense of meaning, must share a common distribution, i.e. they must be mutually substitutable, holding some parameter constant, and this distributional fact must serve then to explicate synonymy.

Some logicians have proposed that meaning be explicated with the notion of truth-preserving substitutability. This view is untenable, for in the true sentence *I'm certain that everyone knows quicksilver is quicksilver,* replacement of the last word by its synonym, *mercury,* will render the sentence false.

Mutual substitutability in all linguistic frames with the preservation of grammaticalness is usually taken as the basic distributional criterion of grammatical analysis.[28] This notion will not serve as an explication of meaning, however, for it is not a sufficient condition for synonymy, as may be seen from such expressions as *cerise* and *ecru,* which, though they are quite different in meaning, may be freely substituted in all relevant frames used for grammatical analysis with no change in grammaticalness. Nor is this notion a necessary condition for synonymy, for such expressions as *highball* and *a drink of diluted spirits served with ice in a tall glass,* though they are synonymous, will not occur grammatically in the same linguistically diagnostic frames e.g. the latter does not occur before the plural morpheme or before the noun *glass* as in *highball glass).*

A somewhat weaker proposal—that 'degree of synonymy', if such could indeed be defined, is given by 'degree of similarity of distribution'—is also likely to fail, for there is at least some reason to expect that a word may occur more frequently in the frames of its antonym

---

[27] See Nida, A system for the description of semantic elements, *Word* 7.1–14 (1951); id., The identification of morphemes, *Language* 24.430 (1948); Norman A. McQuown, review of Harris's *Methods, Language* 28.501 (1952); and possibly Harris, *Methods* 7 fn. 4, 365 fn. 6, and Distributional structure 155–58. But per contra cf. Bar-Hillel's article 233 and Chomsky's reply 44, as well as Miller, *Language and communication* 112.

[28] It is interesting to note, however, that no author has yet taken such a distributional criterion really seriously and examined *all* possible frames for substitutability, whether to establish synonymy *or* grammatical equivalence, i.e. form-class membership. What is really used is substitution in 'diagnostic' frames; and these are chosen quite arbitrarily—which is sufficient to show the futility of a discovery procedure for grammatical analysis by substitution techniques.

than in those of its synonyms; thus, if we could specify all the environments in which *dry* occurs, we would probably also find *wet* there more often than (say) *destitute of moisture*.

MEANING AND INFORMANT RESPONSE. Among the empirical bases of grammatical analysis one of the most important is the informant's indication of which utterance fractions are the same and which are different—that is to say, the data which distinguish free variation from contrast.[29] While it is almost universally recognized that repetitions of 'sames' must be isolated from contrasting segments or utterances, it has also been almost universally assumed that this information must be semantic. Thus, it is supposed that 'phonemic difference' cannot be recognized before the phonemes have been isolated by the analyst for fear that the contrary would involve circularity. The bland assumption that an assertion of sameness or difference is a semantic criterion has introduced endless confusion into the question of meaning in linguistics and the basis of grammatical analysis (§ 9.2.6).[30]

THE EMPIRICAL BASIS OF LINGUISTIC ANALYSIS. That the informant response test is not a semantic criterion has been clearly demonstrated by Chomsky,[31] especially for the case of phonemic analysis. He

[29] Cf. Gleason, *Introduction* 182.

[30] Bloch has attempted to eliminate the need for the informant's response entirely by basing an apparently mechanical analysis scheme upon distributional criteria; see A set of postulates for phonemic analysis, *Language* 24.3–46 (1948); Studies in colloquial Japanese IV. Phonemics, *Language* 26.89–90 (1950). That his postulate system does not provide a true discovery procedure can be seen at least from its use of nonmechanizable notions such as 'general definition', see Contrast, *Language* 29.59–60 (1953). Lounsbury, while defending complete independence of semantics and linguistics, still assumes that informant response is a semantic criterion; see A semantic analysis of the Pawnee kinship usage, *Language* 32.190–91 (1956).

See also Einar Haugen, Directions in modern linguistics, *Language* 27.219 (1951); Eli Fischer-Jørgensen, The phonetic basis for identification of phonemic elements, *JASA* 24.611, 615 (1952); Lounsbury, *Oneida verb morphology* 16 fn. 8 (New Haven, 1953); Paul L. Garvin, review of Jakobson, Fant, and Halle's *Preliminaries to speech analysis, Language* 29.476 (1953). Harris avoids this confusion in phonemic analysis by advocating the use of pair tests (*Methods* 31–32), and alludes to a distinction between informant response and semantic criteria in the phrase 'meaning-like distinction between utterances which are not repetitions of each other' (7 fn. 4); see also 29 fn. 1, but 173, 363 (appendix to § 12.41), and 365 fn. 6. The confusion is also avoided by Halle, The strategy of phonemics, *Word* 10.200 (1954), and by Hockett, *Manual* 144–45.

[31] Semantic considerations (cf. fn. 1).

points out with compelling cogency that 'difference of meaning' is completely irrelevant to 'phonemic distinctness', since homonyms prove it to be an insufficient condition, while synonyms prove it to be an unnecessary one.

This point is of such general interest that a brief summary may not be out of place here. The usually stated canon is that if a phonic difference in some environment entails a meaning difference, then the phonic difference is an instance of a phonemic contrast. In other words, difference of meaning is a criterion to distinguish free variation from contrast. Consider the following crucial types, in which the transcriptions followed by an asterisk[32] are in question:

(1) [mi:t* mi: æt ðʌ mi:t* maɟkɪt]   *Meet me at the meat market.*
(2) [ðɪs ɟu:t* ɪz ʌ skuɛɟ ɟut*]   *This root is a square-root.*
(3) [ðɪs li:f* ɪz ɪn oʊk ɫi:f*]   *This leaf is an oak-leaf.*

In case 1 (homophony) the informant will indicate that the two identically transcribed phone-token sequences are different in meaning, yet we know them to be identical phonemically. Therefore, difference in meaning is not a sufficient condition for phonemic contrast.

In case 2 (synonymy) the informant indicates no meaning difference, yet the forms are phonemically distinct. Therefore meaning difference cannot be a necessary condition for contrast. We conclude that semantic contrast is irrelevant to phonemic contrast.

In case 3 (free variation) the lack of meaning difference will lead the analyst to identify [l] and [ɫ] correctly in the given environment.

If it be supposed that meaning difference can nevertheless serve to distinguish case 2 from case 3 for a whole set of phone-token pairs, each illustrating the same proposed phonemic contrast, by the fact that a meaning difference must be found in at least one such pair if the given phonic difference is phonemic, this can only be because the analyst has been able previously to identify corresponding members of the pairs as phonemically identical. For example, in some other illustration of case 2:

[ðɛɟz sʊt* an mae su:t*]   *There's soot on my suit.*

The informant may indicate that [ʊ] and [u:] are in contrast because of the meaning difference. This can be used to verify the phonemic

---

[32] The starred examples are taken from Eli Fischer-Jørgensen's discussion of this question in her article The commutation test and its application to phonemic analysis, *For Roman Jakobson* 140–51 (The Hague, 1956).

contrast of /ʊ/ and /u/ only if the [ʊ] of [sʊt] has been identified with that of [ɜʊt] and the [u:] of [su:t] with that of [ɜu:t]. But this cannot be done on the basis of the meaning-difference criterion, since now the environments are no longer identical.

The use of such meaning criteria to distinguish free variation from contrast appears even more hopeless when we note the many cases in which two phone-types are in contrast in one environment but in free variation in another. This is the case with many pairs of English vocalic nuclei in contrast under strong stress but freely interchangeable under weak stress, such as /ow/, /o/, and possibly /ʌ/; or, for many dialects, /iy/ and /i/ before /g/ or /ŋ/, and /t/ and /č/ before /r/.

The method actually employed by the analyst in all such crucial cases is some version of the 'pair-test'[33] (§ 9.2.4), with or without collecting the superfluous information on meaning. It is important to keep in mind that such tests are designed not only to determine whether two segments sound alike or different to the native speaker for one presentation, but also to determine whether the identification or distinction is made consistently. For this reason, the tested pair is presented to the informant in massive, randomized replication. Furthermore, by tape recording techniques such comparisons as that of the [u:] of [su:t] with the [u:] of [ɜu:t] may be made.

It has been objected that an informant might easily learn to distinguish free variants, as in case 3 above, and thus invalidate the results. This is just the reason for including a consistency test, for if an informant does in fact distinguish [l] from [ł] consistently in all examples tested, then the distinction is not a case of free variation at all, but one of synonymy, and the analyst might expect eventually to uncover nonsynonymous examples.

The same arguments for the independence of grammatical intuition from the meanings of the forms may be given for other levels of analysis.[34] Difference of meaning cannot be used as evidence for

[33] For a clear statement of the pair-test technique in phonemic analysis, see Harris, *Methods* 31–32; id., Distributional structure, *Word* 10.158–59 (1954); Halle, Strategy, *Word* 10.200 (1954); Chomsky, Semantic considerations.

[34] It hardly seems necessary to document the use of a semantic criterion in the identification of morphemes, since this principle is almost universal in contemporary linguistic works. See for instance Bloch, English verb inflection, *Language* 23.399–418 (1947); Hockett, Problems of morphemic analysis, *Language* 23.341 (1947); Moulton, Juncture, *Language* 23.218 (1947); Nida, System, *Word* 7.2 (1951); Lounsbury, *Oneida verb morphology* 11; C. F. Voegelin,

morphemic distinctness without introducing a vast number of otiose morphemic splits. For example, the morpheme *yellow* has several unrelated meanings, such as 'color between orange and green', 'cowardly', 'venal', but there would be no grammatical advantage in morphemically separating any two semantically distinct instances in identical environments. Similarly, meaning contrast is not a sufficient criterion for difference in constituent structure; in the following sentence, for either of its two meanings, the constituent structure is identical morpheme by morpheme: *It was prohibited by a new law,* which means either 'A new law prohibited it' or else '. . . prohibited it by means of a new law.'

Meaning difference is also not a necessary criterion either for morphemic distinctness or for constructional contrast. *Nearsighted* and *myopic,* though identical in meaning, are different morphemically. *He took off his coat* is constructionally different from *He took his coat off,* but they are synonymous. If it be objected that, after all, no two tokens are ever really quite synonymous,[35] this is tantamount to surrendering semantic distinction as an analytic criterion.

Often the canon is modified somewhat to read: any two phonemically identical tokens which share some common ELEMENT of meaning are morphemically identical.[36] This hypothetical common element, if indeed meanings have elements, is the same kind of ad-hoc designator of morpheme membership as the arbitrary differentia mentioned above, a designator of form-class membership. It is just as easy (or difficult) to discover something common to the meanings of *yellow* (color) and *yellow* (cowardly) as to the meanings of the morphemically distinct *bat* (baseball) and *bat* (animal), if the notion of meaning is extended sufficiently. (We consider the two cases of *bat* to be morphemically different because they are derived from the two different grammatical categories animate noun and inanimate noun, as required by our sentence-generating grammar of English. The two instances of *yellow,* on the other hand, are, to the best of our knowledge, categorically identical adjectives.)

Distinctive features and meaning equivalence, *Language* 24.133 (1948); John Lotz, Speech and language, *JASA* 22.713–14 (1950); Bar-Hillel, Logical syntax, *Language* 30.230 (1954); Gleason, *Introduction* 54–55, 77, 79, 109.

[35] See for instance Nida, System 6, Identification 431–32.

[36] See Nida, System 9; Ward H. Goodenough, Componential analysis and the study of meaning, *Language* 32.207–8 (1956); but Harris, Distributional structure 152.

Recognizing that, if meaning were explained in terms of a person's total social and psychological response to expressions, there would probably be no true synonyms, some have suggested that grammatical analysis must be based upon some notion of DEGREE of semantic similarity.[37] No one, however, has yet shown how meanings might be quantified or how in practice a degree of synonymy could be used to isolate grammatical units.

Many writers have treated meaning in linguistics as though it could be partitioned into various 'kinds of meaning'. In particular they have attempted to isolate among the parts of total meaning that portion determined solely by the linguistic environment, the so-called 'structural' or 'grammatical' meaning, as distinguished from the lexical or connotative meaning.[38] This would seem to be nothing more than a strange and unorthodox use of the word 'meaning' to denote linguistic distribution.

Others, seeking to allay feelings of guilt at the use of apparently semantic criteria when testing for distinctness of units, have emphasized a strict separation of 'meaning' from 'differential meaning'.[39] This use of a very misleading term, differential meaning, for the major empirical datum of linguistic analysis merely compounds the confusion, for the term is clearly a misnomer either for 'difference in meaning' (not a certain KIND of meaning), which is a useless semantic criterion, or for mere 'difference', a criterion whose kind depends upon how the informant's response has been elicited.

If, then, because of the arguments offered above, semantic criteria, such as 'difference in meaning', have been withdrawn as useful evidence for grammatical structure, there would seem to be nothing in the linguistic data to indicate to the analyst which utterances or utterance fractions must be compared and contrasted to test which tentative structural units. First, this is not a valid argument in favor of semantic criteria any more than it is in favor of any other possible criteria, say chemical, political, or theological. Second, as we see from the practice of linguists, though unfortunately not from their own de-

[37] Nida, Identification 437 fn. 40; also Harris, Distributional structure 157.
[38] See Bloch, English verb inflection 399–400 § 1.2; Lounsbury, *Oneida verb morphology* 18, Pawnee kinship usage 189; Martin Joos, Description of language design, *JASA* 22.708 (1950); Gleason, *Introduction* 55.
[39] Especially Henry Lee Smith, Jr., and George L. Trager. See for example Smith, review of Carroll's *The study of language, Language* 31.61 (1955); *Linguistic science and the teaching of English* 11–12 (Cambridge, Mass., 1956).

scriptions of linguistic methodology, the criterion actually used in all crucial cases is either the informant's response in carefully designed pair-tests or other elicitation techniques, so constructed as to be completely indifferent to meanings, or else the linguist's own Sprachgefühl[40] is called upon to provide the correct analysis, after which any ad-hoc rule may be devised to designate the results. But any serious and consistent attempt to use synonymy simply yields the wrong answers.

INFORMATION AND MEANING. It might be well to take note of just one last invalid suggestion for the explication of meaning, which has been offered perhaps in the hope that some powerful mathematical treatment could be borrowed from the communications engineer to clarify an obscure semantic notion.[41]

Given a code with which messages may be formulated and transmitted and some process of generating messages such that to each code symbol a probability may be attached, then to every message may be associated a quantity, called 'amount of information', which varies appropriately with the uncertainty of the receiver in his identification of the message transmitted.[42] The amount of information may then be used to devise various other measures, as for the efficiency of a code or the capacity of a transmission channel.

Perhaps because of the somewhat unfortunate choice of the technical term 'information', which is colloquially very close to the term 'meaning', it has been supposed that the two concepts may be related. But since any number of different meanings may be attached to a

[40] It is precisely this *Sprachgefühl*, this intuitive notion about linguistic structure, which, together with the sentences of a language, forms the empirical basis of grammatical analysis; and it is precisely the purpose of linguistic science to render explicit and rigorous whatever is vague about these intuitive feelings. This is apparently what Hockett means in his discussion of 'empathy' in phonemic analysis, *Manual* 146–47.

[41] See for instance Joos, review of Locke and Booth's *Machine translation of languages, Language* 32.294 (1956); but per contra cf. Wilson, *Psycholinguistics* 46.

[42] There have been many popular treatments of information theory since Shannon's original papers in the *Bell Journal*. Both Shannon and Weaver point out the necessity of distinguishing information from meaning; see *The mathematical theory of communication* 3 and 99. See also E. Colin Cherry, A history of the theory of information, *Proc. Inst. Electr. Engineers* 98.383 (1951); Wilson, *Psycholinguistics* 46; Hockett, review of Shannon and Weaver, *Language* 29.89–90 (1953); Miller, *Language and communication* 41.

message regardless of its information content, this is seen to be a false identification.

Some unsolved problems. Full of insights as it is, the three-level sentence-generating conception of grammar described above, like any useful scientific theory, has given rise to a host of new problems. But one of its most powerful features is the possibility which it provides of giving an exact formulation of a number of difficult theoretical questions.

TECHNICAL DIFFICULTIES. First there are innumerable internal 'technical' problems demanding solution. While it does not seem too difficult to state precisely the assumptions and definitions required to erect a rigorously formed level of phrase-structure for kernel sentences and to describe exactly the notions of grammatical category, constituent, the representing relation holding between any analysis and the utterance, and related grammatical ideas, an exact formulation of the level of grammatical transformations is by no means so simple. Before we can say unequivocally just what a transformation is and just how it enters into a grammar, it will be necessary to formulate rigorously an algebra of transformations.[43]

In particular, transformations will have to be so formulated that the transform is provided with a constituent structure which is capable of entering another following transformation as argument, since some sentences will be generated by the use of more than one transformation. The constituent structure of a kernel sentence is derived by successive expansions in a branching-diagram or derivational tree in such a manner that at every step, i.e. after the application of every rule, any constituent of the resulting representation can be identified as a derived and expanded instance of some more general grammatical category in its tree. But a transformation takes as argument a whole constituent structure, specified by its derivational tree, and converts it by means of additions and subtractions of elements into a new constituent structure, and the elements of the new structure are no longer direct expansions of previously derived elements. Some other way, then, will have to be found to specify the grammatical status of the transform elements.

Consider, for example, the case of an interrogative passive sen-

---

[43] A good start has already been made in this direction in Chomsky's *The logical structure of linguistic theory*, Chap. 8 (cf. fn. 1).

tence, derived by means of two successive transformations from an active assertion:

John hit Bill (passive)→ *Bill was hit by John*
Bill was hit by John (question)→ *Was Bill hit by John?*

For the second or question transformation to apply properly, we must be able to recognize automatically that *Bill* is a subject noun-phrase (NP) of the intermediate sentence. This could be specified by the rule that any transform element derived from a NP in the argument shall be a NP in the transform. But this cannot be generalized into an exhaustive rule because of cases like the following.

Suppose that we have an active, affirmative assertion, the subject of which is a conjunction of two genitives. Each genitive must first be obtained by means of some transformation of a kernel sentence, the two must then be joined by means of the conjunction transformation, and then the conjunction must be inserted into the subject position of a kernel sentence by means of still another transformation. Thus:

Britain has an offer (Nom.$_1$)→ *Britain's offer*
America refuses (Nom.$_2$)→ *America's refusal*

Britain's offer
America's refusal } (Conj.)→ *Britain's offer and America's refusal*

It caused some surprise
B's offer and A's refusal } (Subj.)→ *Britain's offer and America's refusal caused some surprise*

Now for the last transformation to apply correctly it is necessary first to have designated the constituent *Britain's offer and America's refusal* as a noun phrase (NP). We might say that it received this status as NP from the NP status of the two underlying constituents from which it was formed. But now this NP status must itself have been established; in this case, it is not possible to derive the NP status of *Britain's offer* or of *America's refusal* from the underlying constituent from which each was transformed, since these underlying forms themselves are not NPs but sentences. Therefore the identity of the transform as a NP must come from elsewhere.

The only other source for the derived constituent structure of transforms, other than the phrase structure of the representations of which they are the transforms, would be comparison with appropriate kernel sentences. If it were possible to state rigorously that *Britain's offer* HAS THE SAME STRUCTURE AS a kernel sequence like *this offer*, we could automatically derive the NP status of *Britain's offer and America's refusal* from the known NP status of *this offer and this refusal*.

This further step, however, introduces a new problem: how to state the meaning of 'has the same structure as'. This might be accomplished if it were possible to establish some set of fundamental categories, such as NP, VP, A (adjective), in terms of which such a comparison with kernel sentences could be made automatically.

Another internal technical problem which awaits exact solution is entailed by the establishment of a grammatical theory upon the notion of grammaticalness of sentences. It is necessary to establish some scale of grammaticalness along which every utterance will lie and which will correspond well to our intuitive feelings about how sentences are construed, and which, furthermore, will be automatically derivable from the general theory of language or from the grammar of each particular language. This is to say that a grammar must explicate our notion that certain structures, while very bizarre, are nevertheless not completely excluded by the pattern of the language, and that certain ones are less excluded than others and perhaps even by a specifiable degree. This question may very well be related to the establishment of the fundamental categories mentioned above.

When one attempts to state exactly and economically in all their great detail the rules for some real natural language, it becomes quite clear that an immediate-constituent or phrase-structure grammar for all the sentences cannot be given without introducing extremely unnatural repetitions of many ad-hoc rules on the one hand, or on the other restating the entire grammar in a much simpler form by the use of grammatical transformations. There is as yet, however, no rigorous proof that a phrase-structure grammar of a natural language is inherently impossible. While the great simplicity permitted by the introduction of transformations is sufficient reason to accept this theory of grammar, it is at least intellectually unsatisfying not to have such a proof, especially when a corresponding proof can be supplied so easily for certain very simply constructed symbolic languages having some of the same properties as natural language.

By now the reader has no doubt come to appreciate the magnitude of the technical problems involved. There is certainly no cause for discouragement here, for there are several clear programs for research in this area of grammatical theory from which success can be expected. Nor is any incompleteness in the specification of the algebra of transformations a reason to halt practical grammar writing; on the contrary, it is only by writing out the myriad details of real grammars that such problems can be solved.

RECURSIVE SELECTIONS. In the treatment of any one language there is also a large number of specific analytic problems involved that may be solved in various ways, no one of which is entirely satisfactory. This sometimes implies that there may be more devices for generating sentences in a grammar than have been discovered so far.

As an example, we may note that there does not seem to be any one completely natural way to generate noun-noun compounds in English. Just as in the case of the genitive construction, there are strong selection rules determining which particular combinations of noun with noun can occur. The genitive combinations seem for the most part to be directly relatable to one or more kernel sentences and can be derived easily by means of a small number of transformations, thus:

John has a car → John's car
John is safe → John's safety
John flies → John's flight
(but: *a week's wages, Verdi's Aida, for John's sake*)

But compound nouns are much more difficult to relate to kernel sentences, except for certain types, such as:

a brush for hair → a hair brush
a tax on gasoline → a gasoline tax
a blow to the body → a body blow
a man in the service → a service man

No general rule can be given for these because of the failure of others:

*a book for cooking ≠ *a cooking book*
*an opinion on politics ≠ *a politics opinion*
*a road to success ≠ *a success road*
*a face in the window ≠ *a window face*

Furthermore, we must take account of the fact that compounding is indefinitely recursive and is productive:

jet engine replacement parts depot =
$$[(jet + engine) + (replacement + parts)] + depot$$
Suez Canal crisis

Therefore compounds cannot simply be entered in the lexicon. But it is also not convenient to permit this type of recursion to occur in the kernel-generating phrase-structure, especially since all but the

very weakest sort of recursions seem to be best handled as transformations. On the other hand, if they are generated elsewhere, all the
selections between the members of the compound will have to be
stated twice, once for the kernel sentences containing corresponding
N+Prep+N, and again for the compound N+N.

Exactly the same problem is encountered also in Turkish. It is
compounded there by the fact that there is no convenient source from
which to derive not only compound nouns but also genitives. In Turkish, simple affirmative statements corresponding to English sentences
with the verb *have* are themselves construed with a genitive. Furthermore, in both languages genitive constructions are recursive like compounds and are therefore best introduced by a transformation.

It does not seem likely that this type of difficulty is confined to
English and Turkish. If a satisfactory solution cannot be found within
the type of grammatical framework described by Chomsky, there are
two alternatives: either there is still another device in language, not
yet described, which contributes new structures in the derivation of
sentences, or else language is not quite so neatly compartmentalized
as it would seem to be at first glance, and perhaps the kernel-
generating phrase-structure level is in fact strongly recursive.

PHONEMIC GRAMMAR. In addition to certain algebraic problems
there are also many difficulties with the comprehensiveness of the
theory of language involved. No attempt has been made here to solve
all the different kinds of problems inherent in the study of language;
a number of what may be truly grammatical problems are left almost
untouched by this treatment. For example, we might demand of a
useful grammatical theory that it explicate the following apparently
universal behavior of speakers of languages: even in the presence of
noise, a native speaker is able to identify correctly with a high degree
of success single monosyllables spoken by a second native speaker.
One can hardly call upon the grammatical redundancy of the language to explain this behavior; clearly there is something in the
sounds themselves which the hearer can identify and classify properly,
and this something must vary widely from language to language,
since, in general, a person cannot perform very well in such an experiment if he listens to a foreign language.

Since the kind of rules required by the sentence-generating machine
that Chomsky describes may be so written that morphemic representations of utterances may be converted quite simply into phonemic

and then phonic sequences, the conditions imposed upon such a grammar never entail any description of this sound structure adequate to account for the phonetic behavior mentioned. Nor is there any motivation in such a grammar for describing constraints on the phonemic constituency of syllables or clusters, although all the machinery necessary for a description of phonemic immediate-constituent structure is available. Also nothing is said in such a grammar about the validation of any proposed phonetic framework in terms of which phonemic systems may be analyzed, such as a system of distinctive features. It seems quite possible that phonemic systems, syllable structure, phoneme syntax (sometimes called 'phonotactics'), and other lowest-level constraints may be describable only in terms of an independent 'phoneme grammar', and that the primacy of the phonemic units is just the fact that the phonemic and syntactic grammars, the former 'looking up' from the phonetic substance, the latter 'looking down' from phrase-structure, adjoin at this level and share precisely these units.

SUPRASEGMENTALS. One currently confused issue about which this conception of grammar has as yet little to say is the question of the suprasegmental phonic elements in the sentence, the stresses, pitches, junctures, features of vowel harmony, etc. There is little doubt but that many suprasegmental features will have to be incorporated directly into the syntax (rather than, say, into the proposed 'phonemic grammar'), and since they tend to have rather extended scope of application over many sentence elements, it is not clear as yet just how they may be introduced into a grammatical description without the construction of some new kind of rules. It seems reasonable, for example, to treat a sentence intonation in English as a kind of morpheme selected in the development of a sentence at a high level in the grammar, in fact, a morpheme which may even undergo the same grammatical transformations as the segmental morphemes. Thus, one might introduce question intonation in the same transformation which inverts subject and verb for yes-no questions, and then, since question-word questions may be produced by a further transformation of yes-no questions, this latter transformation would then merely re-invert the intonation to yield the assertion contour used with this second type of question. In Turkish, on the other hand, the yes-no type of question employs a special affixed morpheme and normal assertion intonation, while the transformation used to introduce an interrogative could also yield the question intonation employed with this kind of question.

ANALYSIS AND SYNTHESIS. It must be emphasized also that while this type of grammar has been constructed to permit the automatic generation of all sentences, there is, of course, no provision for correctly analyzing any given utterance in the presence of the grammar. This might not seem a serious drawback if it were not for the fact that an adequate linguistic theory ought to explain somehow the ability of the hearer to understand utterances as they are received in context, without assuming an impossibly lengthy process of trial and error.[44] Just as the enormously involved structural complexity and interrelatedness of a natural language seldom leave the analyst in doubt when he is confronted with apparently alternative solutions, so too the convergence of numerous interconnected redundancies in the chain may force unique identifications of structure on the native hearer.

MORPHEMICS. Another difficulty, similar to that mentioned in the section on phonemic grammar, is the lack of motivation in such a grammar to provide a detailed description of much of derivative morphology. That part of the morphological structure of a language which is directly involved in the syntax (that is, largely, the inflectional morphology and bases, or morphological heads), will all be introduced in the course of generating the sentences. But once the sentence has been synthesized as a sequence of such morphemes, there is no natural reason to describe the internal structure of words before mapping the morphemes directly into phonemic sequences. It may be that a more adequate specification of the measures of simplicity to be used in judging the excellence of grammars would require an incorporated analysis of words, and therefore of derivational morphemes not yet introduced in the syntax. For example, in English we might permit the derivation of adjectives from nouns within phrase structure, since so many nouns can be correlated with an adjective (*child-ish, mudd-y, fam-ous, use-ful, wood-en, glob-al, telegraph-ic, etc.*), but there does not seem to be much motivation for generating verbs, such as *per-ceive, con-ceive, re-ceive, de-ceive, etc.*, from 'mor-

---

[44] This is not the same question as that of a discovery procedure, which concerns the automatic generation of grammars. This is the weaker notion of automatic generation of the constituent structure of a given sentence, assuming the grammar.

phemes' *re-, per-, etc.,* even though they are correlated with nouns in *-ception,* adjectives in *-ceptive,* and severe constraints on phoneme sequences within words.

VALIDATION. Finally, we must note that the entire theory of grammar proposed in Chomsky's *Syntactic structures* has been used in the description of only portions of very few languages, though work on discourse analysis has indicated at least tentatively that grammatical transformations will be equally pertinent to a description of many widely varying linguistic structures. Several very limited problems in German, Turkish, and Winnebago have been stated in these terms, and Chomsky himself has worked on Hebrew grammar. But to date the only extensive research on tri-level sentence-generating machines has been with English. Much more cross-lingual validation will be required.

Another opportunity for validation is provided by the rather strict ordering of rules required by such grammars and the concomitant implication of a scale of centrality or generality among syntactic structures. Thus, it is shown that interrogative-word questions must be derived from yes-no questions in English, but not vice versa. If now we should find that English-speaking children generally learn to use the former only after having mastered the latter type, this grammatical fact will provide an explication for the ordering in the learning process. But if children tend to learn in the opposite or in random direction, the ordering among the structures in the grammar will be rather difficult to explain.

Wider implications. In conclusion we take note briefly of several further implications of Chomsky's theory of grammar.

COMMON KERNEL. First of all, this theory permits the definition of a special set of sentences for every language—namely, those sentences derivable by the largely nonrecursive phrase-structure level of the grammar, the kernel sentences. All other sentences, derived by the application of grammatical transformations to kernel sentences, may be considered to be more complex; and it may very well be that the kernel always contains only simple, active, declarative, indicative statements. Just as two disparate texts, after having been subjected to discourse analysis, may be found to be quite similar or even identical in their kernel sentences, so too, many languages, though superficially divergent, may prove to be very similar if compared in their kernel sentences only. In fact, such a comparison may help in the explication of the notion of genetic family; for now, with the help of a more articulated grammar, languages may be compared structurally in the algebras which appear in their grammars.

MACHINE TRANSLATION. Another quite different area in which Chomsky's conception of grammar may prove to be of the utmost importance is the field of machine translation. We speak now no longer of machines as algorithmic schemata, but as concrete mechanical devices, in particular, computers which will automatically translate texts written in one language into corresponding texts in another. It may prove possible, by validating some theory of grammar, to demonstrate that machine translation—or more precisely, an exact solution to the problem of machine translation—is inherently impossible.[45] On the other hand, it may be quite feasible to construct a best approximation to a perfect translator by building separately three different kinds of device, one corresponding to each of the three levels of linguistic structure, once the algebra of the three levels is clearly understood. In this way we may circumvent the discouraging problems involved in any scheme which attempts merely to render more sophisticated an essentially word-for-word type of translation system.

LEARNING THEORY. Perhaps the most baffling and certainly in the long run by far the most interesting implications of Chomsky's theories will be found in their cohesions with the field of human psychology. Being totally incompetent in this area, I shall allude to only one possible consideration, but one which I find extremely intriguing. If this theory of grammar which we have been discussing can be validated without fundamental changes, then the mechanism which we must attribute to human beings to account for their speech behavior has all the characteristics of a sophisticated scientific theory. We cannot look into a human speaker's head to see just what kind of device he uses there with which to generate the sentences of his language, and so, in the manner of any physical scientist confronted with observations on the world, we can only construct a model which has all the desired properties, that is, which also generates those sentences in the same way as the human speaker. If the model has been rendered maximally general, it should predict correctly the human speak-

---

[45] It already seems quite likely that no finite automaton, such as an electronic computer, will be adequate to generate the nested and recursive properties of natural language.

er's future linguistic behavior. We may then attribute the structure of this model to the device in the human head, and say that we understand human speech behavior better than before.

Now it might be objected that the particular structure of our model was entailed, at least in part, by the imposition of a simplicity criterion, and there is no reason to believe that the human speaker is subject to that restriction. We must keep in mind, however, that simplicity in this context is intended in the same sense as in connection with any scientific theory. If we were omniscient and could predict correctly every future event, science would consist merely of a list of those events. In the absence of such universal knowledge we must construct models for the behavior of the world which will account exactly for all data known to date, and then, by rendering them maximally general, hope that they will also predict correctly the observations yet to be made. This is done by choosing among all the alternative models which will account for a given set of known data that model which is maximally simple and elegant—that is, general. We may then attribute the structure of our model to the world itself, until some new and unpredicted datum forces us to change our model —that is, to change our conception of how the world is really constructed. Granting that this so-called scientific method is valid, it is not too much to assume that human beings talk in the same way that our grammar 'talks', provided the grammar has been constructed as an adequate and maximally general model for that speech behavior.

While admitting that all of the physical data necessary for the construction of a scientific theory must somehow be contained in the observations available to the scientist, we must not suppose that a theory can be constructed by means of a simple process of induction from the data.[46] A zoologist, observing that each individual specimen of lizard contains a three-chambered heart, may by simple induction generalize these observations to the universal rule that all lizards are characterized by having a three-chambered heart; each specimen contains in its directly observable physical structure an instance of the general rule. But the construction of a scientific theory like the electron theory of chemical valence cannot be accounted for by any such simple inductive reasoning. One cannot observe individual instances of electrons in atoms from which to generalize atomic structure. In

[46] Hempel 23–24, 32–39 (cf. fn. 6 above).

the construction of a theory very abstract concepts and models must be postulated and then verified against the data in question. We say that atoms have such and such electrons only because in this way it is possible to account simply and correctly for the observed valences. And when these postulated entities turn out later also to account for many other kinds of observations, such as the photoelectric effect, we are that much more sure that our model does reflect reality. Finally, the more complex the interrelationships among the elements of the model must be in order to have the desired properties, the more unlikely it becomes that an alternative model, yet to be constructed, will ever excel it.

Now the grammar of a natural language has precisely this character. It is a postulated structure containing highly abstract concepts used to account for a speaker's generation of the grammatical sentences of his language. It contains many entities which are not directly observable in the physical structure of any one sentence but which must be hypothesized as a source from which many different sentences may be derived.

For example, there is nothing in the directly observable structure of interrogative sentences that would associate yes-no questions with *wh*-questions. Rather, the latter are more clearly seen to be variants of relative clauses. The simplest way to connect them all up is to assume that yes-no questions are derived from assertions by means of a question transformation which reverses the order of the subject NP and the finite verb. The relative clause is then derived from those same assertions by means of another, a *wh*-transformation, which also reverses order, but only for a noninitial NP, and then adds *wh*- to the NP. Finally, the *wh*-questions are derived by means of this same *wh*-transformation, but this time from yes-no questions, rather than from assertions. These transformations apply BEFORE those which append the affix to the finite verb (the affix is first introduced in the same position before the finite verb as the auxiliary verbs) and which introduce *do* to carry any unattached affix, and the morphophonemic rules which produce *who* and *what* from *wh*- plus $NP_{animate}$ and $NP_{inanimate}$, etc.

Assertion: NP_1 + Affix + VP + NP_2 (affix)→ NP_1 + VP + Affix + NP_2 (morphoph.)→ *John* + *saw* + *Bill* (.)
Yes-no question: NP_1 + Affix + VP + NP_2 (question)→ Affix

+ NP₁ + VP + NP₂ (affix)→ *do* + Affix + NP₁ + VP + NP₂ (morphoph.)→ *Did + John + see + Bill (?)*

wh-relative on subject: NP₁ + Affix + VP + NP₂ (*wh-*)→ NP₁ + Affix + VP + NP₂ → *wh* + NP₁ + Affix + VP + NP₂ (affix)→ *wh* + NP₁ + VP + Affix + NP₂ (morphoph.)→ *who + saw + Bill (,)*

wh-relative on object: NP₁ + Affix + VP + NP₂ (*wh-*)→ NP₂ + NP₁ + Af + VP → *wh* + NP₂ + NP₁ + Affix + VP (affix)→ *wh* + NP₂ + NP₁ + VP + Affix (morphoph.)→ *whom + John + saw (,)*

wh-question on subject: Affix + NP₁ + VP + NP₂ (*wh-*)→ NP₁ + Affix + VP + NP₂ → *wh* + NP₁ + Affix + VP + NP₂ (affix)→ *wh* + NP₁ + VP + Affix + NP₂ (morphoph.)→ *Who + saw + Bill (?)*

wh-question on object: Affix + NP₁ + VP + NP₂ (*wh-*)→ NP₂ + Affix + NP₁ + VP → *wh* + NP₂ + Affix + NP₁ + VP (affix)→ *wh* + NP₂ + *do* + Affix + NP₁ + VP (morphoph.)→ *Whom + did + John + see (?)*

This derivation shows how *wh*-questions receive their 'interrogativeness' from yes-no questions, of which they are transforms. No amount of simple generalization or induction could have yielded such an elegant result.

We come now to the point of this lengthy discussion of induction versus theory construction. Though it is possible, it is certainly not an easy task for a psychologist to explain the mechanism by means of which a child, confronted with a vast and perplexing array of different stimuli, manages to learn certain things which can be generalized by induction from repeated occurrences. We would not ordinarily suppose that young children are capable of constructing scientific theories. Yet in the case of this typically human and culturally universal phenomenon of speech, the simplest model that we can construct to account for it reveals that a grammar is of the same order as a predictive theory. If we are to account adequately for the indubitable fact that a child by the age of five or six has somehow reconstructed for himself the theory of his language, it would seem that our notions of human learning are due for some considerable sophistication.

Some Issues in the Theory of Grammar*

HILARY PUTNAM

Introduction. Although this symposium is devoted to problems in the field of mathematical linguistics (a peculiar field, in that some of its leading experts doubt its existence), in my paper I am not going to attempt to prove any theorems or state any results. Rather, I shall take advantage of my privilege as a philosopher and devote myself to a survey of work done by others in the area and to a discussion of issues raised by linguists concerning the work done in this area. There are, in addition to the difficult technical problems, whose existence everyone acknowledges, also very serious conceptual difficulties, as is shown by the fact that Chomsky's book *Syntactic structures,* which is regarded by some as a foundation-stone for this kind of activity, has been described by no less an authority than Roman Jakobson as an *argumentum a contrario*[1] showing the impossibility of the whole enterprise.

What I want to do first is to provide, so to speak, a conceptual setting for the kind of work that Chomsky is doing. I believe that the conceptual setting I will provide is one that will be acceptable to Chomsky himself—but this, of course, is not vital. The interpretations of a scientific theory most acceptable to the scientist himself may often be the least tenable ones, and so we shall worry about finding an interpretation or conceptual setting, for the theory of grammars which seems to us to be correct, not necessarily one which some particular linguist will ratify.

In particular, I propose to connect the theory of grammars with a program in linguistics initiated by Paul Ziff and presented by him in his forthcoming book, *Semantic analysis.* Ziff is concerned of course not only, or even primarily, with questions of grammar, but with questions of meaning. Even if most linguists, however, are not yet primarily or very deeply concerned with semantical questions, it seems to me fairly obvious that at some not very distant date, lin-

* Reprinted with the permission of the author and the American Mathematical Society from the *Proceedings of the Twelfth Symposium in Applied Mathematics* © 1961 by the American Mathematical Society.

[1] In *Boas' view of grammatical meaning,* American Anthropologist vol. 61 (1959), pp. 139–45.

guistics must begin to deal with these questions much more extensively than it is doing today, and that programs in grammar are to be judged to some extent at least, by the way in which they fit into reasonable programs for linguistic investigation as a whole—that means, in the long run, into programs for investigating not only grammatical but also semantical aspects of natural languages.

I. On understanding deviant utterances. The main concept with which Ziff works is the concept of a *deviant* sentence (or, as he prefers to say, "deviant utterance"). By a deviant sentence, he means any sentence which deviates from any linguistic regularity whatsoever, where by a linguistic regularity we may understand either an inductively certifiable generalization concerning the observable behavior of informants, or a projection introduced by the linguist for reasons of systematic simplicity, that is to say an idealization of some sort. I shall assume here that some degree of idealization is inevitable in linguistic work, and I shall also assume that the question of how much idealization is legitimate is one that has no general answer. What one has to answer in a specific case is whether the idealizations made by a particular linguist in a particular context were or were not too severe.

Now, the regularities from which a deviant sentence deviates may be sometimes grammatical regularities or sometimes semantical regularities. The sentence "She goed home." we would all presumably classify as deviant, and presumably there would be no hesitation in classifying the deviation as a deviation at the level of grammar. The sentence "The star by which seafarers normally steer is graceful." is also deviant, but at a more subtle level. What is deviant about this sentence is that the word "graceful" ordinarily has to do with form and motion, and a star does not have form or motion. This kind of deviation is obviously at the level of semantics.

Two things should be noticed at once: First, some linguists believe that they can do without any notion of linguistic deviation, but this is a mistake. If one recognizes linguistic regularities at all, then one must recognize actual or possible deviations from those regularities. Now then, a grammar of a language is nothing but a statement of certain supposed linguistic regularities. Anyone who writes a grammar of any natural language is therefore automatically classifying certain sentences as non-deviant, and by implication, certain others as deviant. Secondly, some linguists claim that any sentence, which could under any circumstances, no matter how far-fetched, be "passed" by an informant, is non-deviant. This may be a nice theoretical position, although I shall argue against it in a moment; but it should be observed, that even if it were the correct theoretical position, it is a position that no linguist actually conforms to in practice. I am quite sure that the very linguists who claim that any sentence that an informant might conceivably use is non-deviant, will in writing a grammar of any language whatsoever automatically rule out, by implication at least, many sentences that informants might employ. For example, Joseph Applegate once reported to me an amusing conversation with another linguist who had somewhat rashly claimed that an English speaker would under no circumstances understand a sentence in which the verb "sneezed" was used as a transitive verb. Within a very few minutes in the same conversation he had succeeded in tricking the other linguist into herself using the somewhat "exotic" sentence: "Pepper doesn't sneeze me." Now then, this is extremely amusing, and it does establish a point: Namely, that no matter how deviant a sentence may be it is extremely unwise to say that there are no circumstances under which a speaker of the language might produce or a hearer of the language might construe it. But this example should not be taken as making the quite different point that the sentence "Pepper does not sneeze me." is non-deviant. I shall argue this below. For the moment I only make the weaker claim that even if a linguist when arguing linguistic theory claims that, for instance, "Pepper does not sneeze me." is non-deviant; when *writing* a grammar of English, he is very likely to inadvertently contradict his own philosophy of linguistics by ruling out this very sentence. He may not rule it out explicitly by calling it ungrammatical; in fact, he may not use the term "ungrammatical" at all. But that does not matter. If he gives rules for producing grammatical sentences of English and these rules have the feature that they would never produce the sentence just mentioned, then we may obviously say that he has ruled out the sentence just mentioned by implication. It is clear, in fact, that the only way in which one could avoid ruling out any sentences of the form exhibited by "Pepper does not sneeze me." as deviant, would be by writing a grammar of English in which every verb was allowed to be used as a transitive verb. And even if one did that, it wouldn't help! For presumably, unless the grammar is the one-sentence grammar which says "Any finite sequence of English words is a sentence.", then there must be *some* finite sequences of English words which, by implication at least, are ruled out as deviant and I will here and now guarantee to find situations under which informants would produce some of these sentences and hearers would understand some of them. In short, if someone says, "Why isn't this a reasonable program for linguistic theory: to write a grammar of, say, English which predicts all and only those sentences which English speakers might conceivably use or English hearers might conceivably understand?", the answer is two-fold. First, that a grammar in this sense would not resemble any grammar ever written by any linguist (and I include linguists who claim that the program just alluded to is *their* program) and secondly, that the program would either be trivial or impossible of execution. It would be trivial of execution if one took the standpoint that for any finite sequence of English words not exceeding a certain length there are some circumstances under which that sequence might be employed; then one gets the one-sentence grammar alluded to before. In fact, one can write a single one-sentence grammar for all natural languages at once on this view! If one, however, interprets more narrowly the notion of a sentence that an English speaker might use or an English hearer might understand, then, I think two things are going to happen: namely, some degree of arbitrariness is going to creep in (e.g., one linguist will count "Pepper does not sneeze me." as a sentence that an English speaker might use, and another will reject it), and secondly, arbitrariness or no arbitrariness, no one will succeed in carrying out the task. This prediction is not as daring as it might seem, for it takes only a moment's reflection to see that the program we have just been criticizing is the program of doing wholly without idealizations in linguistic theory; and no science, whether it be a life science or a physical science, has ever managed to take a single step without the very liberal use of idealizations. Even those linguists, and they are fortunately few, who have an exaggerated confidence in the powers of such statistical techniques as multiple-factor analysis, forget that multiple-factor analysis is itself one of the most ingenious idealizations ever introduced into the empirical sciences.

Let me assume, then, that our objective is going to be to set down some system of linguistic regularities characterizing some aspects of a particular natural language, and that we are going to be willing, indeed eager to idealize and "oversimplify" to some extent. To put it another way, we will be worried about the criticism that someone has produced a better description of the same language than we have, but not worried about the criticism that our description is not ideal in the impossible sense of conforming exactly to the exact behavior of every hearer and speaker.

There are now two questions which face us corresponding to the two classes we have distinguished: deviant and non-deviant. These are, what to say about the non-deviant sentences, and what to say about the deviant sentences. The former problem is the problem of showing how the non-deviant sentences are built up, what their composition is, how their meaning is determined by their composition, *et cetera*. This is the problem which, at the grammatical level, occupies Chomsky in his *Syntactic structures,* and which occupies Ziff at the semantical level in *Semantic analysis.*

Important and seemingly insuperable as this problem is, I wish to neglect it here and to focus attention on a different problem, namely the problem of what to say about the deviant sentences. One thing we might do, of course, is to say nothing about them. We might take the standpoint that to call a sentence deviant is to say "Let's forget about it. Linguistic theory does not have to deal with this." But if this were our standpoint then I would be inclined to sympathize with all the linguists who dislike such notions as "deviant", "ungrammatical", and so forth. Shutting one's eyes to the very empirical facts one is supposed to be trying to account for is not good scientific practice; and this is presumably what the people who make the unrealistic proposal that we should count every sentence ever heard as non-deviant, have in mind. Indeed, as Ziff repeatedly emphasizes, since a great deal of the discourse most commonly used and especially the discourse of greatest conceptual importance, discourse of innovators in every field—in science, in politics, in moral life, in philosophy—consists of deviant sentences, to reject the problem of accounting for the use and the understanding of deviant sentences is to reject one of the most interesting problems in linguistics. Thus, Ziff proposes as a program for linguistics, not merely to provide a description of the non-deviant sentences of a language, but to go on, using that description as a base, and to try to account for the various kinds of deviancy in terms of meaning, function, structure, and so forth. This program is only stated as a program in *Semantic analysis,* which focuses attention mainly on non-deviant sentences; however, Ziff, since the completion of *Semantic analysis,* has been working extensively on a theory of the way in which we understand deviant utterances.

The details of this theory need not concern us here, but I will give one or two very simple examples in order to illustrate what is meant by accounting for the way in which we understand deviant sentences, and to show the role played by the notion of a deviant sentence in the account. The first example is the Dylan Thomas line, "A grief ago I saw him there." Clearly, "grief" is being used figuratively here. But what exactly does it mean to say that a word is being used figuratively? A plausible account might be along somewhat the following lines: The hearer, on hearing the sentence, "A grief ago I saw him there.", immediately recognizes that the sentence he has just heard is deviant. He then proceeds to find a similar sentence which is non-deviant from which the given sentence may be, in some sense or other, derived. One such sentence would be, "A moment ago I saw him there."; another would be, "A year ago I saw him there."; another would be, "An age ago I saw him there."; and so forth. Notice that the substitution of a single word for the word "grief" is capable of turning the sentence, "A grief ago I saw him there." into a non-deviant sentence; and notice, moreover, that all the words that we have so far substituted in order to regularize this sentence have this semantical feature in common: that they are measures of time. This accords with the natural, informal explanation of the line: namely, "Grief is being used as if it were a measure of time." Notice what we have done here: Although we call the sentence, "A grief ago I saw him there." a deviant sentence, this does not mean that it is in any sense a bad sentence, or that Dylan Thomas ought not to have used it. The term "deviant" is obviously a technical term which has an explanatory, and not a valuational, function. Calling the sentence deviant is also not to say that it is a freak, that it is something that transcends all possibility of linguistic explanation. On the contrary, calling it deviant is an essential part of the explanation.

"But then," the reader may object, "if you are going to recognize this sentence as a "good" sentence, if you are going to try to account for it, why call it deviant at all? Why not just modify your grammar so that the word "grief" can occur in any position in which a measure of time can occur?" This proposal, however, leads us right back to the blind alley of rejecting all idealizations. A more reasonable proposal is this: We first rather stringently, perhaps over-stringently rule out all but certain privileged uses of the word "grief" as deviant. We then frame a definition of the word "grief" which covers the remaining non-deviant uses. Notice that this is possible precisely because we have been so stringent in what we are willing to accept as non-deviant uses. The lenient standpoint which counts all possible uses on a par has as one of its many disadvantages that it makes the framing of ordinary dictionary definitions either impossible or untestable. The framing of an adequate dictionary definition of the word "grief" is impossible if the definition is supposed to account for all uses of the word "grief", and all uses count as equally good. Try to think of a definition of the word "grief" that would be reasonable in a dictionary and that would fit the use of "grief" both as a mood or feeling and as "a measure of time." On the other hand, if we retain the usual dictionary definitions and also count all uses on a par, but simply say that a definition need not agree with the uses of the word of which the definition is a definition—then it becomes wholly unclear what the function of a definition is, or how one definition might be said to be correct and another might be said to be incorrect. All of these matters have been taken up at much more length in the book by Ziff I have mentioned, and I will not discuss them further here.

Moreover, it will be noticed that the program of first accounting for the regularities which are represented by a distinguished set of non-deviant uses, and then trying to account for a much wider set of deviant uses by regarding these as in some sense derived from the non-deviant uses, fits the ancient and intuitive distinction between literal and figurative uses of a word.

Finally, and this is the most important point, notice that the recommendation that we draw no distinction between the use of "grief" in the sentence, "A grief ago I saw him there.", and the sentence, "She was in a state of grief."—while it sounds ever so much more lenient and non-discriminatory than the Ziffian approach—in fact, gives one not the slightest hint of a procedure for explaining the Dylan Thomas line in question. On the other hand, the discriminatory procedure of beginning with the idea that the sentence is deviant actually gives us a method not of rejecting the sentence but of understanding it. Namely, we have the procedure (this, of course, is a procedure only for a very simple class of deviant sentences) of trying to find a non-deviant sentence from which the deviant sentence in question may be derived by a one-word substitution and then of seeing the meaning associated with the whole class of relevant one-word substitutions. This was the technique we used above, and, of course, this particular sentence is a very good one for this particular technique.

Classifying a sentence as deviant can often be the most useful first step in analyzing it in terms of what it deviates from, and how and why. Following Fodor[2], we might go further and, for example, introduce the notion of standard deviations from standardness, uniform mechanisms for producing and understanding whole classes of deviant sentences, e.g., irony.

In the present connection, I should like to take up an argument of Jakobson's against Chomsky's work. Jakobson contends[3] that certain sentences that are ruled out by Chomsky's description of English, for example, "Ideas are green.", are perfectly regular, non-deviant sentences. His view is that the sentence, "Ideas are green." is simply a false sentence. Now then, one should never call a sentence ungrammatical or even deviant at a semantical level if the only thing wrong with it is that it happens to be false. But I think that there is something decidedly wrong with the view that such sentences as "Ideas are green.", or "Virtue swims.", are *merely* "false".

I don't want to go into this issue at length, simply because it has been discussed for so many years by so many philosophers; but let me, as it were, allude to some of the results of the philosophic debate. In the first place, philosophers have found it useful to distinguish between a sentence-type or sentence on the one hand, and the various acts that could be performed with sentences of that type on the other, e.g., statement-making. As soon as one draws this distinction one is inclined to be unhappy with the notion of a *false sentence*. If a sentence had the feature that every token of the type could be used to make one and only one statement, and that statement had a clear truth-value—if it was always truth or always falsity—then one might understand the locution "This sentence is false." as short for "The statement that one would be making, if one employed a token of this type in order to make a statement, would be false." But the fact is that there are very few, perhaps no, sentences in English which can be used to make one and only one statement.

Moreover, I think the sentence "Ideas are green." is clearly *not* such a sentence. If one uttered the sentence "Ideas are green." one would probably be taken not to be making a statement at all, but to be doing something else—for instance, telling a joke, interrupting a conversation, *et cetera*. Try it and see! Linguists and philosophers

[2] In *Some uses of "use"*, Princeton Doctoral Dissertation, 1960.
[3] Op. cit., pp. 144–45.

are too prone *not* to make such simple experiments as this one. But I am quite serious. Try to use the sentence "Ideas are green." to make a statement, and see what reaction you get from your hearers. You may, in your own opinion, succeed in using the sentence "Ideas are green." to make a statement, but I doubt whether you will be taken as having made a statement by the people who listen to you. Giggles, rather than dissent, are likely to be the reaction you will face; and giggles, be it remembered, are the normal reaction when it is believed that someone, when uttering a sentence in a statement-making tone of voice has not made a statement and has not really in fact intended to make a statement.

But suppose we grant that, in some far-fetched circumstances perhaps, the sentence "Ideas are green." might be employed to make a statement. Jakobson says that the statement would be a false one—but how does he know? Presumably he thinks that there is only one statement that the sentence "Ideas are green." could plausibly be used to make, and that the statement is clearly false; but I would think, and many philosophers would agree with me that a) there is no statement that the sentence "Ideas are green." could plausibly be used to make, and b) there are a number of statements that the sentence "Ideas are green." could implausibly be used to make, and, of the latter, some are probably true and some are probably false.

Note that it would do no good to say in an authoritative tone of voice that when one says the sentence "Ideas are green." is false, one is assuming of course, that the sentence "Ideas are green." is being used to make one particular statement, namely the statement *that ideas are green.* For saying, with no contextual clue to help the hearer out, "When I say 'ideas are green', I *mean* ideas are green", is not saying what you mean at all. If someone says, "Well just consider the context of philosophic discussion. Suppose one asserted as an abstract truth, 'Ideas are green' he would have made a false statement, wouldn't he?" My position is that he wouldn't have made any statement that I understand at all.

But I don't wish to rest my case on the sentence-statement distinction just alluded to. Let me assume for the sake of argument that Jakobson is right; that there is, considered in the abstract, such a statement as the statement that ideas are green, and that this statement is clearly false. Does it follow that when we reject the sentence "Ideas are green." as deviant, we are rejecting it *merely* because it's "false"? Not at all! For suppose that my necktie is not green and consider the two sentences "Ideas are green." and "My necktie is green." Both are "false", but it is quite clear that the two sentences must be "false" in different ways. Traditional philosophers distinguished the two kinds of "falsity" as *a priori* falsity and *a posteriori* falsity. That is, "My necktie is green." is contingently false; on the other hand, the "statement" "Ideas are green." must, if it has a truth value at all, be *a priori* false. This distinction is, however, all we need to justify calling the sentence "Ideas are green." a deviant sentence, for as soon as we have the distinction between *a priori* and contingent falsity, we can ask, "What is the characteristic of the nouns N, such that 'N's are green.' is not *a priori* false or nonsense?" The characteristic would presumably be that these are the so-called concrete nouns. This might be rendered by saying that the phrase "are green" "takes" a concrete subject; and saying that the sentence "Ideas are green." deviates from a linguistic regularity by employing with the phrase "are green" a subject that the phrase does not "take".

Thus the sentences "Ideas are green.", "Virtue swims.", "Golf plays John.", and so forth deviate from statable linguistic regularities, at least at the level of semantics. Moreover, this is so independently of whether one regards them as "false" or not. Showing that they are deviant may involve methodological problems; but these problems (of justifying a description of a language) arise even at the level of grammar.

II. The line between grammar and semantics. So far, the only question we have considered is the question whether a sentence is deviant or non-deviant. Given that a sentence is deviant, we have not raised the further question whether it should be called grammatical or ungrammatical. But this question can no longer be postponed; for the job of a grammar is not to rule out all deviant sentences— e.g., a grammar should not rule out the sentence "The star by which seafarers normally steer is graceful."—but to rule out only those deviant sentences whose deviancy is in some sense grammatical deviancy. But how are we to tell whether a given case of deviancy is grammatical or semantical?

A position that I have heard linguists put forward is that there are two sharply different kinds of deviancy, grammatical deviancy and semantical deviancy, and that very little is grammatically deviant. That is to say, most of the sentences we have been calling deviant are deviant, but deviant for reasons that should be called semantical and not grammatical.

A few examples may make the dispute clear. These linguists would for example reject the category "animate noun" as a permissible grammatical category, although they would of course admit it as a potential semantical category. Now, suppose a Frenchman says, referring to a table, "She is red," or, to put more of the context into the sentence itself, suppose he says, "George gave me a table and I saw at once that she was red and had four legs." Chomsky would say that this sentence is ungrammatical because the pronoun "she" does not agree with the inanimate noun "table". These linguists, on the other hand, would maintain that the sentence in question is grammatical, simply because they have no basis for calling it ungrammatical. One wonders how they would deal with such languages as German and French, where questions of gender have long been regarded as grammatical questions: Would they proceed the same way, or would they have one policy for English and another for French, and if so, on what basis? Their position, as I gather it, is that it is only features that are arbitrary, that have nothing to do with meaning, that are properly called grammatical. However, I agree with Jakobson and with Boas, that there do not appear to be any arbitrary features in a language in the sense indicated. For example, if one says that it is arbitrary that we say "She is here." and not "Is she here.", the obvious answer is that while it may be arbitrary in some absolute sense, in the context of English it is not arbitrary; we use one when we want to make a statement and the other when we want to ask a question. Notice that if we agree that the categories "abstract" and "concrete" should be prohibited in grammar, then on exactly the same grounds we should prohibit "masculine" and "feminine" on the one hand, and "indicative" and "interrogative" on the other.

There is, of course, an absolute sense which one has a vague feeling for but which one has difficulty putting into words, in which one is tempted to say that word-order in English *is* arbitrary; that is to say, the conventions determining *which* word-order is declarative and which is interrogative could conceivably have been reversed without, as far as we can see, impairing the functional efficiency of the language. The trouble is that in this absolute sense, if it can be made sense of at all, semantical features are just as arbitrary as syntactical ones. Any word might, after all, have meant something different from what it does mean.

Without prolonging this dispute any further, let us just say this: that adding a category to our grammar has mainly the function of enabling us to state more regularities. If these regularities seem to pertain to a very small class of sentences we will in general be unhappy at calling them grammatical regularities; if they pertain to a great many sentences, or to the use of important morpheme classes, e.g., the pronouns or the articles, then it will seem more conventional to call them grammatical regularities. On this view, exactly where we should draw the line between semantics and grammar is a matter of convenience, and not a genuine theoretical question at all.

III. Independence of meaning. An issue that we can hardly bypass, if only because it has generated so much controversy, is the issue between those who assert and those who deny that grammar can be done "independently of meaning". Among American linguists, Zellig Harris was the first I know of to emphasize this claim. On the other hand, Jakobson claims in the article alluded to above that Chomsky's monograph is a "magnificent *argumentum a contrario*" on this very point, and speaks optimistically of a pending "hierarchy of grammatical meanings".

As a preliminary to taking a look at this vexed question, let me consider a somewhat parallel (if irrelevant-sounding) question: "Can one discover a man's occupation without seeing him at work?" The answer is obviously "yes"—one can, for example, put the question "What do you do for a living?" But even if this is ruled out as "cheating", the answer is not necessarily "no". Sherlock Holmes, as we all know, could discover an enormous number of things about someone—not just his occupation—from the most irrelevant seeming clues. So the proper answer to the above question is (roughly): "It depends on how good a detective you are."

Coming to language: it is apparent that the question: "Can one discover the phonemes (morphemes, form-classes, etc.) of a language without learning the language (learning the meaning of any form, learning that any two forms are synonymous)?" is quite parallel to the occupation question, and it seems evident (to me, at least) that the immediate answer is the same: "It depends on how good a detective you are."

Thus, some linguists apparently maintain (at least when they are arguing this question) that one cannot discover the phonemes of a language without learning the meanings of the forms in that language (or at least learning that certain pairs are pairs of non-synonymous expressions). I am sure that these very same linguists, however, would not be surprised (provided the statement were not connected with this "controversy") to hear that some linguist had inferred the phonemes of a language X from the way the X-speaker spoke English (*a fortiori*, without learning X). One would, of course, regard this as an amazing "*tour de force*", but not as impossible in principle. But if someone could conceivably do this as a *tour de force*, why might he not do it repeatedly, and even train graduate students in the art. (Cf. the accomplishments of Pike in establishing rapid comprehension of portions of an alien language. These would count as an individual *tour de force*—except that Pike has repeated the "TRICK" on many occasions, and has taught it to some of his students.) Finally, why might one not even "mechanize" such a trick, by reducing it to say a standardized test of some kind that could be administered by a properly trained clerk (or a machine)?

Again, if there is nothing inconceivable in the idea of someone's inferring the phonemes of a language from the way the speaker of that language speaks a different language, why might not a list of nonsense syllables take the place of the different language? I am not saying that any of these procedures is practicable today or will ever be practicable, but only that no issue of principle is involved. Every linguist believes that phonemics have an "obligatory" character, and that the phonemics of one's native language influence the way one speaks (in the overwhelming majority of cases) even when one is speaking a different language, reciting (or making up) nonsense syllables, etc. But then how on earth could it be impossible in principle to discover the phonemes of an alien language except in one way?

Viewed in this light, Harris' methods do not appear so surprising. Harris discovers the phonemes of a language in roughly the following way: the linguist recites a sequence of expressions, e.g. "cat, cat, cad, cab, cab, cad", and the informant describes what he heard. If the informant says: "you said A twice and then B and then C twice and then B" (where A, B, C in the above example would be cat, cad, cab as pronounced by the informant, or approximations thereto) then one would conclude (tentatively, of course!) that b, c, t were allophones of different phonemes in the alien tongue. On the other hand, if the informant says: "you said A three times and then B twice and then A again" (where A is cad or cat or something intermediate, and B is cab) then one would be pretty sure that b, d were allophones of different phonemes and d, t were allophones of the same phoneme in the alien language. (Harris would normally use expressions in the alien language itself in this test, but the test might conceivably "work" with nonsense syllables, in which case one would have the possibility envisaged in the preceding paragraphs.)

Coming to morpheme boundaries, Harris again uses "structural" methods, instead of relying on such notions as "shortest meaningful unit". I will not describe these methods in detail, but they depend roughly on the counting of "exclusions"—that is, sounds that cannot occur immediately after certain initial segments of sentences, e.g., all sounds except "t" are excluded after the initial segment "Isn't that a daguerreo-". These exclusions are exclusions "going from left to right". Similarly one can count exclusions "going from right to left" —that is, sounds that cannot occur immediately before certain terminal segments of sentences (e.g., "h" is excluded immediately before "-ing". Then (Harris finds) morpheme boundaries can be identified as local minima in the number of exclusions which are minima counting both from left to right and from right to left. This test not only does not "depend on meaning", but seems more successful than any test that *does* "depend on meaning" that I know of.

But why should all of this evoke argument among linguists? I don't mean, why should Harris' methods in particular evoke argument (anybody's methods naturally evoke argument, in any science)—perhaps these particular methods don't work; I mean, why should there be argument that methods of this kind *can't* work in principle? Why couldn't there be a linguistic counter-part of Sherlock Holmes?

I suppose what is bothering Harris' opponents is this: the notions "phoneme" and "morpheme" have been conventionally defined in terms of semantical notions; hence any method of discovering what the phonemes/morphemes of a language are must utilize semantical information. But this is a non-sequitur! (Just as it would be a non-sequitur to conclude from the definition of "occupation" as the way a man makes his living, that one cannot *discover* a man's occupation unless he is engaged in working.) Language is doubtless learned when its various parts are performing their various semantical functions; but once one has learned the segmentation of one's language into parts, one may "give away" this segmentation in other apparently irrelevant contexts, just as one may give away anything else one knows.

Of course, I should not like to give the impression that I believe Harris to have found a procedure whereby one cannot fail (in principle) to discover the phonemes or morphemes of a natural language. Harris and his opponents both seem to think that linguistics can provide uniform discovery procedures. I agree with Chomsky that whether one uses "semantical information" about a language or not, the objective of a uniform procedure for discovering the correct description is as utopian in linguistics as in any other natural science. And that is yet another reason for finding the pseudo-issue of "independence of meaning" not very interesting; it depends too fundamentally on the misconception that the task of linguistic theory is to eliminate the theorist altogether, not just to provide him with useful tools (tests, procedures, etc.).

IV.   The autonomy of grammar. An issue closely related to the one discussed in the preceding section is this: Is it possible to define the fundamental concepts of grammar, e.g., "morpheme" "phoneme" in non-semantical terms? Although this issue *is* closely related to the one discussed in the preceding section, it is important to realize that two distinct issues are involved. In the preceding section we were discussing the feasibility of discovery procedures in linguistics which do not require any semantical information, as input. In this section we are discussing the way in which certain fundamental concepts in linguistics should be defined. Unfortunately, a great deal of confusion seems to be rife in linguistic circles as to the difference between these two issues.

Chomsky seems inclined to the view that the fundamental concepts of structural linguistics can be defined without employing any semantical notions, and this is perhaps what he means when he speaks of the autonomy of grammar. On the other hand, it should be realized that even if Chomsky is wrong, his work cannot possibly be taken as an *argumentum a contrario* against the thesis of the autonomy of grammar, simply because Chomsky does not, in fact, define the fundamental concepts of structural linguistics at all. He takes them as primitive or undefined notions in his entire work. Indeed, it is just this that makes Jakobson's attack on Chomsky so puzzling. Many of Jakobson's criticisms are to the effect that certain sentences are being ruled out by Chomsky as ungrammatical merely because they are false or somehow absurd on the basis of their meaning. But this would seem to indicate, not that Chomsky is placing too little reliance on meaning but too much reliance on meaning. If anything, the charge should then be that Chomsky's work is an *argumentum a contrario* against the possibility of basing a grammar on certain fundamental semantical notions, e.g., truth and falsity. Certainly it is not an *argumentum a contrario* against the thesis that there exist nonsemantical discovery procedures in linguistics, because Chomsky refrains from talking about discovery procedures at all, except to express a pessimism (which I share) with respect to the possibility of finding useful uniform discovery procedures, whether or not one uses semantical information; and, as just remarked, Chomsky does not define the fundamental notions "phoneme", "morpheme", "noun", "verb", etc. at all; rather, he models his grammar exclusively on a hypothetico-deductive system in which certain terms are taken as "primitives". But Chomsky's work aside, we are left with the question of just how, if at all, to define such notions as "phoneme" and "morpheme".

Before saying something about this question, however, let us first consider what might be meant by the distinction between semantical and syntactical notions, as applied to a natural language. I wish to suggest that we might take the fundamental syntactical notion to be the notion of structural identity. We might say that two sequences of phones in a natural language are structurally identical if a speaker of the language counts them as the same expression and otherwise structurally non-identical. Of course, this raises a number of problems: It is not crystal clear what it means to say that a speaker of a natural language counts two phone sequences as the same expression, apart from contexts in which we have available a bilingual informant who is willing to make explicit metalinguistic statements, at least of a very simple kind ("You said the same word twice!"), and a linguist who is willing to rely on such explicit metalinguistic statements. If we ask for characterization of what it means to say that an informant counts two phone sequences as the same, where the informant is a speaker of only one language *x*, and the characterization is to be wholly behavioral, and not to refer to dispositions to make certain kinds of explicit metalinguistic statements about *x*, then we shall probably not be able at present to say very much. Moreover, even if we succeed in thinking of a number of things that we might call "symptoms" of the disposition to count two phone sequences as the same expression, it would still be a mistake to think that one could arrive at an explicit definition of this disposition in terms of such symptoms. I will not go into this last point any further, since to do so would take us afield into the familiar controversy pro and con operationalism. Instead I will just remark that here we are reminded that linguistics is after all a social science and that its fundamental concepts have the same kind of dispositional and human character as do the fundamental concepts of any other social science.

Another less serious problem that we must face is this: What if someone says that the relation of structural identity, as defined above, is a semantical notion and that therefore syntax, as the study of the properties of phone sequences that are invariant under this relation, is a branch of semantics? This problem is not serious because it is obviously purely verbal. Of course, one can "prove" that syntax is not autonomous by defining the terms "syntax" and "semantics" so that syntax becomes *by definition* a part of semantics. But no useful object is thereby gained. I would propose, guided admittedly by the usual practice in formal languages, to take as the fundamental notions of semantics the notions of truth and synonymy; and my thesis is that the relation of structural identity of expressions is more basic than the notions of semantics in two senses: the latter notions seem to presuppose the former notion; and the notion of structural identity is, I believe, not definable in terms of the semantical notions referred to.

Assuming that the notion of structural identity and non-identity is an acceptable one, however, we are part of the way to the notion of a phoneme. Namely, the notion of a contrasting pair may now be defined. Two structurally non-identical phone sequences A and A' are a contrasting pair, if A is identical with A' except that A' contains one occurrence of a phone P', where A has one occurrence of a phone P. In this case we shall also say that P and P' are verifiably non-equivalent phones. Now then, if the complementary relation, the relation of *not* being verifiably non-equivalent phones, were only an equivalence relation, we should have the full notion of a phoneme. Namely, the phonemes would be just the equivalence classes generated by this equivalence relation. Unfortunately, and this is what makes the notion of a phoneme a somewhat difficult one, although it is obviously based on the relation of not being verifiably non-equivalent phones, the relation which holds between two phones if and only if they are allophones of the same phoneme *is* to be an equivalence relation. What one does in practice is to seek the biggest relation which *is* an equivalence relation and whose complement includes the relation of verifiable non-equivalence alluded to above. But in general there is no unique such biggest relation, and thus there is some degree of arbitrariness in the classification of the phones of a language into separate phonemes. What this goes to show, however, is not that the notion of a phoneme is fundamentally a semantical one, but that it is to some extent a defective one; or to put it better, that it should be relativized not just to a language but to a particular description of a language.

To sum up: The classification of phones into phonemes is a somewhat artificial classification which is based on deliberately ignoring the fact that the complement of the verifiable non-equivalence relation is not an equivalence relation. But this classification, artificial though it may be, is by our lights a purely structural matter. Phonemics, then, is autonomous in Chomsky's sense. When we come to the notion of a morpheme, however, it is more difficult to know what to say. Speaking for myself, I should say that I have never seen a satisfactory definition of this concept in either semantical or nonsemantical terms. Also, I am not satisfied with Chomsky's idea of taking the concept as primitive. The trouble with modeling linguistic theory on the notion of a hypothetico-deductive system is that the model does not seem a particularly reasonable one. A hypothetico-deductive system is a reasonable model for a physical theory in which one is inferring unobservable entities from observable entities. But I don't think that Chomsky wants to say that morphemes are inferred entities, and if he does want to say this, then *I* want to say that I find myself very unclear as to the alleged nature of these inferred entities and as to the nature of the supposed inference to their existence. Sometimes Chomsky writes as if he held both the view that a hypothetico-deductive system is a reasonable model for a physical theory and the view that the primitive terms in such a system need not be supposed to refer to anything. On this view, scientific theories are, so to speak, merely computational devices. I don't know whether I do Chomsky an injustice or not in ascribing this view to him. But I do know that I do not find it an acceptable philosophy of science for physics, and I should be extremely suspicious of the view that it was an acceptable philosophy of science for any one of the social sciences, including linguistics.

Another possible way out would be this: We might say that the morphemes of a language, relative to a particular grammar, are the shortest phone sequences which are assigned to phrase-structure categories in that grammar. Besides bringing in a host of new undefined terms, e.g., phrase-structure categories, this proposal would have the drawback of relativizing the notion of morpheme to a grammar. This relativization goes against the very deep-seated intuitive feeling that a language does have natural building blocks, no matter how difficult it may be to make this concept of the natural building-block precise, and that the morphemes are they.

Yet another proposal, which is extracted not so much from Chomsky's work as from discussions with Chomsky, might be to first relativize the notion of a morpheme to a grammar, in the way just proposed, and then to say that the "real" morphemes in a language are to be identified with the morphemes according to a simplest grammar of that language. This last proposal seems to have two objectionable features: First, that it is by no means clear that there is such a thing as a well-defined simplest grammar of a natural language, and secondly that if there is such a thing, then there may be two simplest grammars A and B which do not segment the language into building-blocks in the same way. If this last eventuality—the possibility of two non-isomorphic simplest descriptions of a natural language—is not really a possibility, then the reason it is not really a possibility must be that a natural language really has a set of fundamental building-blocks in some sense which has nothing to do with descriptions of that language. But then we should try to make that sense clear, and not go the long way around via talk about all possible theories and via employment of the catch-all term "simplicity".

I am not recommending that we abandon the concept "morpheme"; I think the vague characterization of the morphemes as the smallest units that belong to phrase-structure categories is enough to go on for the time being. On the other hand, further attempts to provide a foundation for the notion are clearly in order. To put it bluntly, I feel that there are a great many things here that are presently not *understood,* and that it will take more insight into language structure as a whole before we are able to say in precisely what sense a language has natural building-blocks.

V. **The grammatical sentences of a language are a recursive set.** In this section I should like to present evidence of several kinds for the view that the grammatical sentences of a natural language, under a mild idealization, form a recursive set. The following facts seem to me to point in this direction: (1) The self-containedness of language. By the self-containedness of language, I mean the fact that speakers can presumably classify sentences as acceptable or unacceptable, deviant or non-deviant, *et cetera,* without reliance on extra-linguistic contexts. There are of course exceptions to this rule, but I am more impressed by the multiplicity of non-exceptions. I imagine, for example, that if I were on any number of occasions presented with a *list* of sentences and asked to say which ones I thought were grammatical and which ones I thought were ungrammatical, I would on each occasion and without any information on the supposed context of use of the individual sentence classify "Mary goed home" as an ungrammatical sentence, and "Mary went home" as a grammatical sentence. This act of classifying sentences as grammatical or ungrammatical seems to be one I can perform given no input except the sentences themselves. In short, it seems that in doing this job of classifying I am implicitly relying on something like an effective procedure.

In this connection, I am of course relying on certain very general hypotheses as to the character of the human brain. To be specific, I would suggest that there are many considerations which point to the idea that a Turing machine plus random elements is a reasonable model for the human brain. Now, although the idea that random elements are a part of the human brain is important in the life sciences in a great many contexts, the present context is one in which the role of the random elements should be left out, at least for purposes of idealization. Even if it is true, that given a list of sentences to classify as grammatical or ungrammatical, my behavior would be to a tiny extent random, e.g., one time in a hundred I might classify "Mary goed home" as grammatical instead of as ungrammatical, this is a fact which we wish to leave out in our idealization. In other words, we wish to pretend that the classifier, if he will classify a sentence as grammatical on one occasion, will classify it as grammatical on any occasion. With this idealization in force, it seems to me that we are in effect committed (at least if we have the over-all mechanistic view of the brain that I do) to viewing the classifier as simply a Turing machine.

Even if the classifier is a Turing machine, however, it does not follow that the set of grammatical sentences is recursive. This only follows if the classifier is a Turing machine without input; or more precisely, without input other than the individual sentence that he is classifying. That the individual sentence that he is classifying may be regarded as the sole relevant input, amounts, however, to saying just that if a sentence is counted as grammatical, then it will be counted as grammatical even if presented on a different occasion, and even if different sentences have been previously presented; and this seems, if not exactly true of actual classifiers, at least a reasonable idealization. This, of course, is just what I mean by the self-containedness of language.

(2) A second argument supporting the view that the classification of sentences as grammatical and nongrammatical is something effective or mechanical (and hence that the set of grammatical sentences is recursive, at least if we assume Church's thesis) is the usability of nonsense sentences. As Chomsky has pointed out, one can perfectly well ask a classifier to look through a list of nonsense sentences and to say which ones are grammatical and which ones are ungrammatical. Here again it seems to be very much the case that the relevant input is simply the sentence being classified and that, moreover, the features of the sentence being classified that are relevant are almost certainly purely structural. Jakobson has pointed out that so-called grammatical nonsense sentences can often be construed, but I feel that we may neglect this in the present context. Even if it is true that after some minutes of reflection I can succeed in construing the sentence "Colorless green ideas sleep furiously." I feel very certain that I do not tell that it is grammatical by first construing it in the manner suggested in Jakobson's paper.

(3) A third consideration supporting the view that the classification of sentences into grammatical and ungrammatical is a machine-like affair is the teachability of grammar and the relative independence of intelligence level of this skill. Even a person of very low-grade intelligence normally learns both to speak his particular dialect grammatically and to recognize deviations from grammaticalness. It is important, of course, in connection with this point, not to confuse the grammar of the particular dialect with "grammar" in the high-school sense, that is to say, the grammar of the prestige dialect. I am well aware that people belonging to lower-income groups often speak "ungrammatically" (that is to say, they speak their own dialect perfectly grammatically, but speaking their own dialect is what is usually called "speaking ungrammatically"). My point is that a moron whose parents happen to speak the prestige dialect may have serious vocabulary deficiencies but he rarely has grammar deficiencies. He too learns to speak the prestige dialect, and to feel that there is something wrong with sentences that deviate from the grammatical regularities of the prestige dialect, even if he does not have the ex-

tremely complicated skill (parsing) which is required to say what is wrong. But an ability of this kind, which can be acquired by practically anyone or which can be utilized by practically anyone independently of intelligence level, is almost certainly quasi-mechanical in character.

I am willing to grant that no one of the considerations cited above is by itself decisive; but it seems to me that the collection of these facts—the self-containedness of language, the usability of nonsense sentences, and the relative universality of grammar intuitions within a dialect group, taken together support the model of the classifier as a Turing machine who is processing each new sentence with which he is provided according to some mechanical program. To accept this idealization, however, is just to accept the following model of grammar: that the grammatical sentences under consideration are a recursive set.

Accepting this idealization makes it legitimate to seek recursive function-theoretic structures which could serve as models for grammars. In Chomsky's book *Syntactic structures* a number of such models are examined and found too narrow. In particular, a widely used model, phrase-structure grammar, is found by Chomsky to be over-restrictive since it rules out certain extremely convenient types of rules. For example, the following very simple rule, which would seem to be a legitimate kind of linguistic rule, is not a phrase-structure rule. If S_1 and S_2 are grammatical sentences, and S_1 differs from S_2 only in that x appears in S_1 where y appears in S_2, and x and y are constituents of the same type in S_1 and S_2, respectively, then S_3 is a sentence, where S_3 is the result of replacing x by x *and* y in S_1.

To make an analogy with formal languages, we may say that phrase-structure grammars employ rules that correspond to axiom schemata in, say, the propositional calculus. On the other hand, a transformational rule like the familiar rule that "any formula of the form $(x)A \supset A'$ is to be an axiom, provided A' is like A except for containing free y wherever A has free x" already goes beyond the bounds of phrase-structure grammar. And Chomsky is, in effect, proposing that structural grammars may legitimately use rules that are modeled on the last-cited rule, and not just on axiom schemata.

I find the examples that Chomsky gives of transformations in English extremely convincing. (I mean his examples of permissible kinds of linguistic rules. There may be empirical objections to certain of them as statements about English.) However, Chomsky's general characterization of a transformational grammar is much too wide. It is easy to show that any recursively enumerable set of sentences could be generated by a transformational grammar in Chomsky's sense. Since, however, the whole motive for seeking transformational grammars was to reflect the character of natural languages and since the fundamental insight, if it is an insight, on which transformational grammars are based is the insight that the set of sentences in a natural language is a recursive set, then transformational grammars should be characterized in such a way that this feature is "built in".

In short, I think Chomsky has convincingly set the problem for theory of grammars—namely, the problem of delimiting a class of transformational grammars which is wide enough to include all the grammars we will ever want to write as grammars of natural languages, but not so wide as to include any grammar for a non-recursive language (that is, for a language in which the set of grammatical sentences is not recursive). This problem appears, however, to be extremely difficult. In closing I shall make a few remarks about the direction in which one might seek for a solution.

VI. The problem of characterizing transformational grammars. The transformations employed by Chomsky in *Syntactic structures* mostly have the property that the product is longer than the datum. (1) It might be possible, without altering the resultant set of "terminal strings" (grammatical sentences yielded by the grammar) to rewrite the grammar so as to use *only* rules with this property (let us call them "cut-free" rules). Then (as is easily verified) the set of terminal strings would always be recursive.

The above suggestion (1) seems unattractive, however, since using only cut-free rules, even if it can be done (and it is not known whether or not it can be) involves *complicating* the statement of the grammar, and the main argument for admitting "transformations" in the first place was the resultant simplification.

(2) One might impose two restrictions on all grammars for natural languages: (a) that not more than n_1 words may be deleted in a deletion-transformation; and (b) that not more than n_2 deletion-transformation may occur in the derivation of a terminal string, where n_1, n_2 are constants depending on the language. However, the second restriction seems *ad hoc* and unattractive. (The first restriction can usually be met in a natural way, e.g., by confining deletions to cases

of the form "preposition + pronoun.") It seems to me that it would be quite natural and important to seek to prove a theorem of the form: *Whenever one can derive σ in L* (where σ is a variable over terminal strings and *L* is some language), *one can find a* derivation (of the same string σ) *which does not use more than n_2 deletions* (where n_2 may depend on *L*); but this is quite different from making a restriction on the number of deletions part of the definition of a derivation. However, there is no hope of proving a theorem of this kind for all *L*'s which possess a transformational grammar, unless one first has a suitable definition of "transformational grammar." This, then, is a significant (and probably very difficult) open question: to define "transformational grammar" in a way which (i) wide enough for all linguistic purposes; (ii) free of "artificial" clauses like the one restricting the number of uses of deletion in a derivation; and (iii) such that a "cut-elimination" theorem will be forthcoming about all *L*'s with a transformational grammar. Unfortunately, I have no idea how to solve this problem.

Methodological Reflections on Current Linguistic Theory*

W. V. QUINE

I want to make some broadly methodological remarks on a variety of issues. To begin with I'll talk of *rules,* and dwell a while on the distinction between *fitting* and *guiding.*

Imagine two systems of English grammar: one an old-fashioned system that draws heavily on the Latin grammarians, and the other a streamlined formulation due to Jespersen. Imagine that the two systems are *extensionally equivalent,* in this sense: they determine, re-cursively, the same infinite set of well-formed English sentences. In Denmark the boys in one school learn English by the one system, and those in another school learn it by the other. In the end the boys all sound alike. Both systems of rules *fit* the behavior of all the boys, but each system *guides* the behavior of only half the boys. Both systems *fit* the behavior also of all us native speakers of English; this is what makes both systems correct. But neither system guides us native speakers of English; no rules do, except for some intrusions of inessential schoolwork.

My distinction between fitting and guiding is, you see, the obvious and flat-footed one. Fitting is a matter of true description; guiding is a matter of cause and effect. Behavior *fits* a rule whenever it con-forms to it; whenever the rule truly describes the behavior. But the behavior is not *guided* by the rule unless the behaver knows the rule and can state it. This behaver *observes* the rule.

But now it seems that Chomsky and his followers recognize an intermediate condition, between mere fitting and full guidance in my flat-footed sense of the word. They regard English speech as in some sense rule-*guided* not only in the case of the Danish schoolboys, but also in our own case, however unprepared we be to state the rules. According to this doctrine, two extensionally equivalent systems of grammatical rules need not be equally correct. The right rules are the rules that the native speakers themselves have somehow implicitly

* Reprinted by permission of the author and publisher from Davidson and Harman, eds., *Semantics of Natural Language,* D. Reidel Publishing Co., Dordrecht-Holland, 1972, pp. 442–54.

in mind. It is the grammarian's task to find the right rules, in this sense. This added task is set by demanding not just any old recursive demarcation of the right totality of well-formed sentences, but rather a recursive demarcation of the right totality of trees. The trees used to be mere *ad hoc* scaffolding by the aid of which the grammarians, each in his own way, contrived to specify the objective totality of well-formed sentences. According to the new doctrine, the trees are themselves part of the objective linguistic reality to be specified.

We have all known that the native speaker must have acquired some recursive habit of mind, however unconscious, for building sentences in an essentially treelike way; this is evident from the infinitude of his repertoire. We can all go this far with Postal when, in his review of Dixon, he writes:

> The claim that there are linguistic rules is simply the claim that in-
> dividuals know their language and have not learned each of its sen-
> tences separately.[1]

His word 'claim', even, seems ill suited to anything so uncontroversial. What is more than trivial, in the new doctrine that I speak of, is rather the following: it imputes to the natives an unconscious preference for one system of rules over another, equally unconscious, which is extensionally equivalent to it.

Are the unconscious rules the same, even, from one native speaker to the next? Let us grant that the generated infinitude of well-formed sentences is itself the same for two natives. There may then seem to be a presumption of sameness of generating rules—just because any appreciably different but extensionally equivalent system of rules is apt to be prohibitively complex and artificial. However, this suggestion gets us nowhere. Insofar as it is true, the grammarian can just follow his old plan, after all, of settling for *any* system of rules, naturally the simpler the better, that demarcates the right infinite set of well-formed sentences. If the new doctrine of the grammarian's added burden has any content, it owes it to there being appreciably unlike and still comparably manageable systems of rules for generating the same infinite totality of well-formed sentences. From experiences with axiom systems in mathematics, incidentally, we can easily believe in the existence of such alternatives. In my parable of the Danish schoolboys I have already assumed the existence of just such alternative systems for English; though it should of course be said,

---

[1] Paul Postal, review of Dixon, *Language*, 84–93, specifically p. 88.

if we are to be fussy about the facts, that Jespersen's grammar and that of the old-fashioned textbooks really fall short of extensional equivalence at some points.

We see then that the new doctrine of the grammarian's added burden raises the problem of evidence whereby to decide, or conjecture, which of two extensionally equivalent systems of rules has been implicitly guiding the native's verbal behavior. Implicit guidance is a moot enough idea to demand some explicit methodology. If it is to make any sense to say that a native was implicitly guided by one system of rules and not by another extensionally equivalent system, this sense must link up somehow with the native's dispositions to behave in observable ways in observable circumstances. These dispositions must go beyond the mere attesting to the well-formedness of strings, since extensionally equivalent rules are indistinguishable on that score. It could be a question of dispositions to make or accept certain transformations and not others; or certain inferences and not others.

Certainly I have no quarrel with dispositions. Nor do I question the notion of implicit and unconscious conformity to a rule, when this is merely a question of fitting. Bodies obey, in this sense, the law of falling bodies, and English speakers obey, in this sense, any and all of the extensionally equivalent systems of grammar that demarcate the right totality of well-formed English sentences. These are acceptably clear dispositions on the part of bodies and English speakers. The sticking point is this Chomskian midpoint between rules as merely fitting, on the one hand, and rules as real and overt guides on the other; Chomsky's intermediate notion of rules as heeded inarticulately. It is a point deserving of close methodological attention.

Ironically these same linguists have expressed doubt about the relatively clear and humdrum notion of a disposition to verbal behavior. Chomsky writes:

> Presumably, a complex of dispositions is a structure that can be represented as a set of probabilities for utterances in certain definable "circumstances" . . . But it must be recognized that the notion "probability of a sentence" is an entirely useless one . . . On empirical grounds, the probability of my producing some given sentence of English . . . is indistinguishable from the probability of my producing a given sentence of Japanese.[2]

[2] Noam Chomsky, 'Quine's Empirical Assumptions', *Synthese* 19 (1968) 53–68, specifically p. 57.

I am puzzled by how quickly he turns his back on the crucial phrase "in certain definable 'circumstances'." Solubility in water would be a pretty idle disposition if defined in terms of the absolute probability of dissolving, without reference to the circumstance of being in water. Weight would be a pretty idle disposition if defined in terms of the absolute probability of falling, without reference to the circumstance of removal of support. Verbal dispositions would be pretty idle if defined in terms of the absolute probability of utterance out of the blue. I, among others, have talked mainly of verbal dispositions in a very specific circumstance: a questionnaire circumstance, the circumstance of being offered a sentence for assent or dissent or indecision or bizarreness reaction.

Chomsky's nihilistic attitude toward dispositions is the more puzzling in that I find it again in the newspaper account of his recent lectures in England, despite an intervening answer of mine[3] to the earlier statement. I seem to detect an echo of it also in a footnote in Postal's review of Dixon.[4] This rejection of dispositions would be bewildering by itself. It is doubly so when contrasted with the rather uncritical doctrine just previously considered—the doctrine of unconscious preferences among extensionally equivalent grammars. I'd like to think that I am missing something.

Now some more remarks on the task of the grammarian. What I have said suggests, too simply, the following notion of the grammarians' classical task: that it is the task of demarcating, recursively and in formal terms, the infinite totality of the well-formed strings of phonemes of the chosen language. It would seem from my remarks up to now that this is the basic or classical task, which, then, is added to if one insists further on some distinction between right and wrong rules, right and wrong trees subtending this same superficial mass of foliage. The trouble with thus stating the basic or classical task is that it presupposes some prior behavioral standard of what, in general, to aspire to include under the head of well-formed strings for a given community. What are the behavioral data of well-formedness? Passive observation of chance utterances is a beginning. The grammarian can extrapolate this corpus by analogical construction, and he can test these conjectures on an informant to see if they elicit only a manifestation of bewilderment. But of course the grammarian

[3] W. V. Quine, 'Replies', *Synthese* 19 (1968) 264–321, specifically p. 280.
[4] Paul Postal, *op. cit.*, note 12.

settles for no such criterion. Traditionally, at any rate, the grammarian has accepted wide ranges of sentences as grammatical which an informant would reject as bizarre. I think of sentences such as Carnap's example, 'This stone is thinking about Vienna.'

A more realistic characterization of the grammarians' classical task is an open-ended one. He does not have a prior behavioral criterion of well-formedness; he just has some sufficient behavioral conditions. Strings heard from natives count as well-formed, at least provisionally. So do sentences which, when tried on an informant, elicit casual and unbewildered responses. What I then picture the grammarian as doing is to devise as simple a formal recursion as he can which takes in all these confirmably well-formed strings and excludes all strings that would bring really excessive bizarreness reactions. He rounds out and rounds off his data. Sometimes of course he will even reject a heard string as ill-formed, thus rejecting a datum, if he can appreciably simplify his system in so doing; but it would be regrettable to do much of this.

In this somewhat melancholy version of the grammarian's task, I have held Chomsky's doctrine in abeyance. Chomsky believes that the linguistic community itself has a sense of grammaticality which the grammarian can and should uncover; that grammaticality is not just the grammarian's rounding off of performance data. Up to a point I agree; the native's disposition to bizarreness reactions is an implicit sense of grammaticality of a sort. But Chomsky would of course credit the native with a full and precise sense of grammaticality, this being of a piece with the native's purported fund of tacit rules—the native's purported bias even among extensionally equivalent grammars. Now this doctrine is interesting, certainly, if true; let me only mention again the crying need, at this point, for explicitness of criteria and awareness of method.

An attitude that is closely linked to this doctrine is a readiness to recognize linguistic universals. The problem of evidence for a linguistic universal is insufficiently appreciated. Someone says, let us suppose, that the subject-predicate construction occurs in all the languages he has examined. Now of course all those languages have been translated, however forcibly, into English and *vice versa*. Point, then, in those languages to the translations of the English subject-predicate construction, and you establish the thesis; the subject-predicate construction occurs in all those languages. Or is it imposed by translation? What is the difference? Does the thesis say more than that basic

English is translatable into all those languages? And what does even this latter claim amount to, pending some standard of faithfulness and objectivity of translation?

To make proper sense of the hypothesis that the subject-predicate construction is a linguistic universal, we need an unequivocal behavioral criterion of subject and predicate. It is not enough to say that if we take these and these as subjects and those and those as predicates then there are ways of so handling the rest of the language as to get general English translations. The trouble is that there are extensionally equivalent grammars. Timely reflection on method and evidence should tend to stifle much of the talk of linguistic universals.

Insofar, on the other hand, as one is prepared to impute to the native a specific and detailed though inarticulate grammatical system, one is apt to conceive of the notions of subject and predicate and similar notions as objective and as unequivocally apprehended by the native himself. To conceive of them thus is no more of a strain, surely, than to suppose that the native favors one of two extensionally equivalent grammars over another. In all this there is no folly, I feel sure, that conscientious reflection on method and evidence cannot cure; but the cure is apt to take time.

I think it is instructive, before leaving this topic, to fit an idea of Geach's into the picture. Besides singling out the well-formed strings, Geach argues, our grammar must distinguish between proper and spurious components of well-formed strings. One of his examples of a spurious component was 'Plato was bald' in the context 'The philosopher whose most eminent pupil was Plato was bald.'[5] This demand is reminiscent of Chomsky's demand that the grammarian show how to generate not only the well-formed strings but the right trees. Yet Geach is not committed to finding a bias in the native community between extensionally equivalent grammars. I expect Geach's demand is reconcilable even with the humdrum view of the grammarian's task as the task merely of generating the well-formed strings; for the thing that Geach demands, the marking of the proper components of each well-formed string, would doubtless be a valuable auxiliary to the rules for generating further well-formed strings. The same case can be made, more generally, for Chomsky's insistence that the grammarian's proper product is the whole tree rather than just the well-formed strings that it issues in. The argument is simply that

[5] Peter Geach, 'Logical Procedures and the Identity of Expressions', *Ratio* 7 (1965) 199–205, specifically p. 201.

rules for generating further well-formed strings (and trees) can then be formulated in terms of past trees and not just past well-formed strings. This is a strong argument, and it does not depend on any obscure doctrine to the effect that the natives tacitly prefer one system of grammar to another that is extensionally equivalent to it. It would be well to sort out these motives and benefits and see whether the obscure points of doctrine might not be cheerfully dropped.

Such an inquiry could, I suppose, convince us that there is indeed an unarticulated system of grammatical rules which is somehow implicit in the native mind in a way that an extensionally equivalent system is not. For me such a conviction would depend in part upon clarification of criteria.

To get down more nearly to cases, suppose again a language for which we have two extensionally equivalent systems of grammar; two extensionally equivalent recursive definitions of well-formed string. According to one of these systems, the immediate constituents of a certain sentence are '*AB*' and '*C*'; according to the other system they are '*A*' and '*BC*'. The enigmatic doctrine under consideration says that one of these analyses is right, and the other wrong, by tacit consensus of native speakers. How do we find out which is right?

An unimaginative suggestion might be: ask the natives. Ask them, in their language, whether the real constituents of '*ABC*' are '*AB*' and '*C*'. Does this pose an embarrassing question of translation? Well, then let the native language be English. The essential problem remains; we do not really understand our own English question. We are looking for a criterion of what to count as the real or proper grammar, as over against an extensionally equivalent counterfeit. We are looking, in the specific case, for a test of what to count as the real or proper constituents of '*ABC*', as against counterfeit constituents. And now the test suggested is that we ask the native the very question which we do not understand ourselves: the very question for which we ourselves are seeking a test. We are moving in an oddly warped circle.

Better and more imaginative suggestions may be forthcoming for determining, less directly, what to regard as the real constituents of '*ABC*' from the point of view of tacit native grammar. I suggested some time ago that it could be a question of dispositions to make or accept certain transformations or inferences. But I want now to make use of the unimaginative suggestion as a point at which to take off on a tangent, leaving at last this whole question of a native bias toward one of two extensionally equivalent grammars.

The unimaginative suggestion was: ask the natives. The same question, and the same warped circle or one very much like it, are encountered from time to time in semantics. People like me challenge the notion of synonymy and ask for a criterion. What is synonymy? How do you tell whether two expressions are synonymous? Ask the natives. This essentially was Arne Næss's answer some decades ago, as I analyze it.[6] Moreover he suited the action to the word, disseminating questionnaires and claiming significantly uniform results. This was also essentially the answer more recently of Fodor and Katz,[7] as I analyze it; and I have sensed suggestions of it in Chomsky. Now a reason for pausing over this oddly warped circle is that an empirical investigation, however odd, that yields uniformities has a claim to attention. Grant for the sake of argument that Næss's questionnaire on synonymy yielded statistically significant uniformities; what do they mean? Do they show that Næss's laymen are pretty much alike on the score of their synonymy pairs, obscure though it be to us wherein synonymy consists? Do they show something also, or instead, about how Næss's laymen use the obscure word 'synonymy' or its paraphrases? Separation of these components presents an odd problem.

Essentially the same question is raised outside linguistics by work of Smith Stevens on subjective magnitudes.[8] For years he gathered subjective testimony of the pitch and loudness of sounds: whether this was twice as high as that, or half again as loud as that. He plotted these findings against the physical frequencies and volumes, and came out with significant correlations—not linear, but logarithmic. Significant, but of what? Was it uniformity of error in his subjects' effort to estimate physical frequency and volume? Or was it uniformity of subjective experience, coupled with uniformity of meaning attached to enigmatically subjective expressions like 'twice as high' and 'half again as loud'? Or did the subjective experience vary from subject to subject, while the meaning attached to the subjective expressions varied in a compensatory way? The uniformities surprise me and I

[6] Arne Næss, *Interpretation and Preciseness,* Dybwad, Oslo, 1953.

[7] Jerry Fodor and Jerrold Katz, 'The Structure of a Semantic Theory', *Language* 39 (1963) 170–210.

[8] S. S. Stevens, 'On the Psychophysical Law', *Psychological Review* 64 (1957) 153–81.

am prepared to find them instructive, but I am at a loss to sort them out. It is the same warped circle.

Turning back to synonymy, or to the semantical notion of analyticity which is interdefinable with synonymy, I might mention also a questionnaire experiment which avoided the warped circle. Apostel and others[9] in Geneva compiled various lists of sentences. One list contained only sentences that the experimenters regarded as analytic. Other lists had varied and irrelevant motifs. Subjects were given these lists, untitled, and were asked to sort various further sentences into the appropriate lists. The experiment, much the same as one proposed more recently by Katz,[10] sought evidence of a felt similarity among analytic sentences, without benefit of title. The outcome was reported as at best indecisive.

A controversy over semantical notions has simmered for twenty years. Some of us have criticized these notions as insufficiently empirical. Others have defended the notions without improving them. Their defense has been visibly motivated by a sense of the indispensability of these notions in various applications. We would have been spared much of this rearguard action if the defenders of semantical notions had taken the criticism of these notions to heart, and sought seriously to get along without them. In one, certainly, of its most conspicuous applications the notion of synonymy is not needed; namely, in the definition of the phoneme. According to the familiar definition, what shows that two sounds belong to distinct phonemes is that the substitution of one for the other changes the meaning of some expression. Surely, however, meaning enough for this purpose is afforded by the innocent and uncontroversial notion of stimulus meaning.

The behavioral definition of stimulus meaning is as follows, nearly enough: the stimulus meaning of a sentence, for a given speaker, is the class of all stimulatory situations in the presence of which he will assent to the sentence if queried. Stimulus meaning is at its best among observation sentences. The behavioral definition of an observation sentence is as follows: an observation sentence is a sentence whose stimulus meaning is the same for just about all speakers of the language. Examples: 'It is raining', 'This is red', 'This is a rabbit'.

---

[9] L. Apostel, W. Mays, A. Morf, and J. Piaget, *Les liaisons analytiques et synthétiques dans le comportement du sujet*, Presses Universitaires, Paris 1937.

[10] Jerrold Katz, 'Some Remarks on Quine on Analyticity', *Journal of Philosophy* 64 (1967) 36–52.

Sameness of stimulus meaning is no appreciable approximation to the general notion of synonymy to which semantics has aspired. Within observation sentences, however, sameness of stimulus meaning is synonymy enough. For distinguishing phonemes, consequently, it is enough; for surely, if two sounds belong to distinct phonemes, the meaning of some observation sentences will be changed by the substitution.

For that matter, phonemes can also no doubt be distinguished by appealing merely to well-formedness of expressions; by appealing, that is, to the capacity of a string of sounds to occur in the native stream of speech. Presumably, if two sounds belong to distinct phonemes, the substitution will render some coherent string of sounds incoherent. This way of defining the phoneme was proposed by Anders Wedberg,[11] and was already implicit, I think, in Zellig Harris. I wanted to bring in the definition in terms of stimulus meaning, however, as an example of how stimulus meaning can sometimes do the work that is desired of meaning or synonymy.

I turn, for the remainder of my remarks, to the notion of deep structure and its relation to logical analysis. Take, first, logical analysis. What do we do when we paraphrase a sentence by introducing logical symbols for truth functions and quantifiers? In principle it is the same as when in highschool algebra we were given some data about rowing up and down a river; we paraphrased the data into algebraic equations, with a view to solving these for the speed of the river. In principle it is the same also as programming a computer.

I find the phrase 'logical analysis' misleading, in its suggestion that we are exposing a logical structure that lay hidden in the sentence all along. This conception I find both obscure and idle. When we move from verbal sentences to logical formulas we are merely retreating to a notation that has certain technical advantages, algorithmic and conceptual. I mentioned the analogy of the computer; but essentially the same thing is happening in a more moderate way when in natural history we switch to the Latin binomials for genera and species, or when in relativity physics we paraphrase our temporal references into a spatial idiom using four dimensions. No one wants to say that the binomials of Linnæus or the fourth dimension of Einstein or the binary code of the computer were somehow implicit

[11] Anders Wedberg, 'On the Principles of phonemic Analysis', *Ajatus* 26 (1964) 235–53.

in ordinary language; and I have seen no more reason to so regard the quantifiers and truth functions.

What now of deep structure? If we believe that native speakers have a detailed though inarticulate grammatical system, specific even as between extensionally equivalent systems, then certainly we believe that deep structure, whatever there may be of it, is there to be uncovered. How to tell whether we are getting it right, whether we are matching the inarticulate native analysis or just carving out an extensional equivalent, is a methodological question that I have mentioned already.

If on the contrary we hold every grammar to be as authentic as every extensionally equivalent grammar, and to be preferred only for its simplicity and convenience, then deep structure loses its objectivity but need not lose its place. Deep structure, and the transformations to and from it, might still qualify as auxiliaries to the simplest and most convenient system we know for demarcating the class of well-formed strings. They would stay on in this role just as the trees would stay on, and Geach's discrimination of proper and improper ingredients.

Thus conceived, the grammarian's deep structure is similar in a way to logical structure. Both are paraphrases of sentences of ordinary language; both are paraphrases that we resort to for certain purposes of technical convenience. But the purposes are not the same. The grammarian's purpose is to put the sentence into a form that can be generated by a grammatical tree in the most efficient way. The logician's purpose is to put the sentence into a form that admits most efficiently of logical calculation, or shows its implications and conceptual affinities most perspicuously, obviating fallacy and paradox.

These different purposes, the grammarian's and the logician's, are not in general best served by the same paraphrases; and for this reason the grammarian's deep structure is not to be identified with logical structure, suggestive though the one may be for the other. I have two major examples in mind to bring out the divergence.

One example is the elimination of singular terms other than variables. Let 'a' represent such a singular term—perhaps a proper name, perhaps a complex singular term—and let 'Fa' represent a sentence containing it. We can paraphrase 'Fa', to begin with, as '$(\exists x)(Fx.a{=}x)$'. In this way all singular terms, other than simple variables such as the '*x*' here, can be confined to one specific manner of occurrence: occurrence to the left of '='. Then, as a next step, we can reckon this identity sign to the singular term as an invariable suffix, thus re-parsing the singular term as a general term or predicate.

The advantages of this transformation are specific and limited. Laws of logic become simplified, through not having to provide for the instantiation of quantifications by terms other than variables. The simplification is the greater for the fact that the instantiations thus avoided were ones that depended awkwardly on existence assumptions. Certain gains in philosophical clarity ensue also. Variables, rather than names, come to be seen as the primary avenue of reference. Little puzzles about names that fail to name anything are swept aside.

This elimination of singular terms is not all good, however, even for logic and mathematics. Inference moves faster when we can instantiate quantifications directly by names and complex singular terms, rather than working through the variables and paraphrases. And complex singular terms are in practice vital for algebraic technique. An algebraist who was not free to substitute complex expressions directly for variables, or to substitute one side of a complex equality directly for the other, would soon give up.

The important point thus emerges that logical analysis itself—better, logical paraphrase—may go one way or another depending on one's specific logical purpose. The image of exposing an already present logical structure by analysis is a poor one. And when our interest turns to English grammar, again we are bound to find that the elimination of singular terms is to no purpose. Surely it yields no deep structure that would help to simplify an account of English grammar. Thus take the distinction between the referential and the non-referential use of singular terms. Work of Geach[12] and Strawson[13] suggests that this distinction is vital to an appreciation of English; but the logical paraphrase obliterates it utterly.

In my view the logical structure and the deep structure, or let me say the logician's paraphrases and the grammarian's paraphrase, differ not in kind but in detail and purpose. They differ in the same sort

[12] Peter Geach, *Reference and Generality*, Cornell University Press, Ithaca, N.Y., 1962.
[13] P. F. Strawson, 'Singular Terms and Predication', *Synthese* 19 (1968) 97–117.

of way that the logician's two paraphrases differ from each other: one the austere and pellucid paraphrase containing no singular terms but variables, and the other the algorithmically efficient paraphrase bristling with complex singular terms.

The elimination of singular terms was one example of the difference between paraphrasing for logic and paraphrasing for grammar. Now the other example I have in mind is the treatment of time as a fourth dimension. A while ago I referred this to physics, but it is vital equally for logic and philosophy. A logic of tense is a towering triviality which we have no excuse to put up with if our concern is merely with the scientific use of language rather than with the scientific study of it. We program language into the simple neo-classical logic of truth functions and quantifiers, by eliminating tense and treating times on a par with places. The resulting simplification of formal logic may be sensed from this example, which I have used before: George V married Queen Mary; Queen Mary is a widow; therefore George V married a widow. We cease to have to provide against this kind of thing, among others.

Philosophical clarification ensues as well. Thus consider the following puzzles. How can things be related that do not coexist at any one time? How can a variable range now over things that no longer exist? or range ever over things that never coexist? How can a class have members that never coexist? How can a class, which is an abstract object, be said to change, as it must when its members change or cease to exist? We make a clean sweep of all such puzzles by dropping tense and treating all past, present, and future bodies as four-dimensional substances tenselessly scattered about in spacetime.

This is a paraphrase which, we see, works wonders for logic, philosophy, and physics as well, but presumably is not wanted for English grammar. A deep structure without tense seems unpromising, at any rate, as a means of simplifying a grammatical account of an Indo-European language. Here again, evidently, is a wide divergence between the structure that the logician is after and what the grammarian wants under the head of deep structure. And yet, reading Postal's typescript 'Coreferentiality and physical objects,' I begin to wonder whether the four-dimensional view might be useful sometimes in grammar too.

My previous example, the elimination of singular terms, spoke for pluralism not just as between logical structure and grammatical deep structure, but within logical structure; one logical paraphrase served one logical purpose, another another. Perhaps now there is a case also for pluralism within grammatical deep structure: one paraphrase might serve one grammatical purpose, another another. A paraphrase into the tenseless idiom of four dimensions might play an auxiliary role in connection with some grammatical twists, while a different deep structure, retaining tense, might still be exploited for other grammatical ends. So let me conclude with a plea against absolutism.

The Underlying Structures of Sentences Are the Primary Units of Immediate Speech Processing*[1]

T. G. BEVER,[2] J. R. LACKNER,
and R. KIRK

Two studies of the subjective location of clicks in spoken sentences indicate: (1) within-clause phrase structure boundaries do not significantly affect the segmentation of spoken sentences; (2) divisions between underlying structure sentences determine segmentation even in the absence of corresponding explicit clause divisions in the surface phrase structure. These results support a model of speech processing according to which listeners actively segment and organize spoken sequences into potential underlying syntactic structures.

According to Wilhelm Wundt, a sentence has two simultaneous psychological levels of organization. At the surface level the associative phrase relations are indicated by the order of the words in a sentence. At a deeper level the "logical" relational concepts, "subject," "predicate," and "object," express the internal relations among the words and phrases of a sentence. The actual order of the words in a sentence does not always correspond to or directly reveal the underlying relations. For example, in corresponding active and passive sentences the underlying relations are the same although the word orders differ:

> In the two sentences, *Caesar crossed the Rubicon,* and *the Rubicon was crossed by Caesar* . . . , the acting person ("subject") is in both cases, Caesar. But he is the topic of the statement only in the first and not in the second sentence [1900, p. 268].

The implications for behavior of this two-level syntactic analysis

* Reprinted by permission from *Perception and Psychophysics* 5 (1969), pp. 225–34.

[1] This work was supported by NDEA, AF 19 (628) 5705 to M.I.T., Grant No. SD-187 Department of Defense Advanced Projects Agency to Harvard University and NIMH No. PO1-MH 12623 Harvard University, and by the Harvard Society of Fellows. We are indebted to H. L. Teuber, P. Rosenbaum, R. Hurtig, V. Valian, and H. Savin for advice on this manuscript.

[2] Address: Department of Psychology, Rockefeller University, York Avenue and East 66th, New York, N.Y. 10021.

of sentences were not lost on Wundt. For him, the relations were not only logical but also psychological:

> The logical and psychological (domains) are not two things in opposition whose parts are separated, rather the logical relations among the words in the sentence are fundamentally *psycho*logical relations: logic has only abstracted them from the psychological process of thought in order to explore them according to their particular laws, carried back to a form as perfect as possible [1900, p. 262].

The logical relations in speech perception provide the basis for an active "apperceptive" synthesis of separate units in speech perception.

> . . . Relations of (this) type are . . . those which can occur between the mental concepts and their own component elements: the apperceptive relations. The intuition of activity . . . accompanies (these relations) not simply as one of the resultant effect of the relations, rather the activity precedes (the logical) relations; accordingly the relations themselves are conceived as coming into existence with the assistance of attentional processes. In this sense we view (the internal logical relations of stimuli) as *active* experiences [1877, pp. 291–92].

Wundt's analysis of underlying sentence relations and his claim that perceptual processes include the active synthesis of such apperceptive relations combine to present a particular view of sentence processing; listeners actively organize speech into segments defined in terms of underlying "logical" sentential relations. In this paper we present evidence that supports this view of the behavioral segmentation of speech.

Recently the distinction between the actual order of words in sentences and their underlying logical relations has been rediscovered and expanded in linguistic theory. Current transformational grammar also represents the insight that there are two levels of syntactic analysis for each sentence. The level of "surface phrase structure" describes the hierarchical phrase structure associations among adjacent words and clauses. The two example sentences mentioned by Wundt would be represented at this level as in Fig. 1. Each branching "node" of the phrase structure tree corresponds to a phrase structure "constituent." Each constituent corresponds to an association among the words and phrases that it contains. For example, in the first sentence

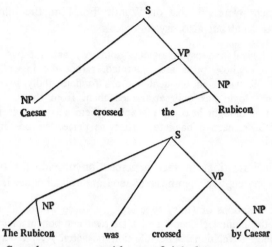

Fig. 1. Sample sentences with superficial phrase structure trees.

the structure represents the fact that the words "the" and "Rubicon" are more closely related than the words "crossed" and "the."

The level of "underlying phrase structure" represents the "logical" relations which the words bear to each other. For instance, Wundt's two examples would be analyzed as having the same underlying phrase structure represented in the tree diagram in Fig. 2.[3]

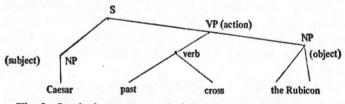
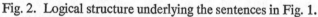

Fig. 2. Logical structure underlying the sentences in Fig. 1.

[3] For clarity of exposition we have labeled explicitly the particular logical functions of the phrases "subject," "predicate," and "object." As Chomsky (1965) has pointed out, these labels are redundant with the actual configuration of the underlying phrase structure tree. Throughout this chapter we shall refer to such internal abstract structures as "underlying structure sentences." Such terminology does not assert that the underlying structure is composed of *actual* pronounceable sentences; rather, the term "underlying structure sentences" in this chapter refers to an abstract unordered hierarchical and functional set of relations among the actual phrases included within exactly one expansion of "S" in the underlying phrase structure.

In addition, current grammar specifies "transformational rules," which express the relation between the two levels of analysis.[4] Thus, every sentence has an underlying logical phrase structure, an apparent phrase structure, and a set of rules which derive the latter from the former. To "know" a language is to know a grammar which specifies all the possible underlying logical structures and the set of transformational rules which produces all the possible apparent phrase structures from them.

A great deal of attention has been given to the "psychological reality" of the structures and rules postulated in transformational grammars. The most notable success has been to show that the form in which sentences are understood and memorized corresponds closely to the logical structure underlying them.[5] Thus, any model for speech perception proposed in this tradition includes a device which isolates the logical structure corresponding to each lexical sequence.

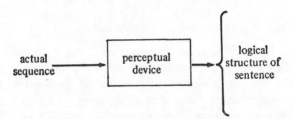

For such a perceptual device to operate efficiently, the actual sequence of words in a speech utterance must be segmented into those subsequences which correspond to a full sentence at the underlying structure level. For example, if one hears the sequence represented phonetically in Sentence 1, one must decide that it has two distinct sentence structures corresponding to it at the underlying structure level, and not more nor less.

[4] For example, a "transformation" attaches the tense marker to the verb to yield in the surface phrase structure the simple declarative sentence: CAESAR CROSS + past the RUBICON. The passive construction is described by application of a general "passive" rule which reorders the subject and object to produce the sequence: The RUBICON − past − BE + past participle CROSS by CAESAR, which is transformed ultimately into The Rubicon Be + past cross + participle by Caesar. See Chomsky (1965) for a general discussion, and Bever et al (1963) for a discussion of the affix-movement and passive transformations in relation to psychological issues.

[5] Cf. Miller (1962), Mehler (1963), and Mehler and Bever (1967).

(1)   δaboylaiksgerlzgerlzluvboyz (i.e., the boy likes girls; girls love boys)

Failure to find the correct basic segmentation into sequences which do correspond to underlying structure sentences could impede comprehension. If a listener assumed that the second instance of "girls," above, was actually a spurious repetition, then he would be faced with finding an underlying structure for the following: *The boy likes girls love boys.* The problem is that this sequence has no single underlying syntactic structure.

There is no known automatic procedure which insures the proper segmentation of actual sequences. In cases like Sentence 1, however, segmentation strategies which separate underlying structure sentences in a discourse can utilize contextual, semantic, and pronunciation cues. The segmentation problem is much more complex for sentences embedded within other sentences. For example, consider Sentence 2a:

(2a)   When he left everybody grew sad.

This has two deep structure sentences, each one corresponding to one of the "clauses" in the apparent sequence: "when he left, everybody grew sad." We shall represent this structural division into clauses at the surface structure level with parentheses, "()," and the corresponding underlying structure segmentation with brackets, "[]," e.g.,

(2b)   ([When he left]) ([everybody grew sad])

If the wrong perceptual segmentation were attempted then correct perceptual analysis of the sentence would become impossible. For example, the listener might initially segment the first four words into a potential underlying structure sentence ("when he left everybody . . ."), but would then have two words left over ("grew sad") with no derivations from an underlying structure sentence.

A recent series of experiments has suggested that an initial strategy of speech perception segments together those lexical sequences which potentially correspond directly to underlying structure sentences (Fodor & Bever, 1963; Garrett, Bever, & Fodor, 1966; Bever, Fodor, & Garrett, 1966). Ss report the location of a single click in a sentence as having occurred closer to the point between two clauses than its objective location. For example, Fodor and Bever (1963) found that in Sentence 3 a click objectively located in "yesterday" or in "the" was most often reported as having occurred between those two words. Fodor and Bever argued that the systematic displacement of the click towards the point between clauses showed that the clause had relatively high psychological coherence, since it "resisted" interruption by the click.

(3) ([Because it rained yesterday]) ([the picnic will be cancelled])

Several experiments have shown that this systematic effect of the syntactic segmentation is not due to actual pauses or cues in the pronunciation of the sentence. Garrett, Bever, and Fodor (1966) used materials in which the exact identical acoustic sequence was assigned different clause structures depending on what preceded. Consider the sequence ". . . eagerness to win the horse is quite immature." If it is preceded by "your . . ." then the clause break immediately follows "horse." But if that sequence is preceded by "In its . . ." then the clause break immediately follows "win." The authors recorded the sequence with one initial sequence or the other and tested Ss ability to locate clicks in the different sentences. The results showed that the clause structure assigned each sequence affected the subjective location of the clicks. In a second study,[6] Abrams, Bever, and Garrett found similar results with sentences constructed by splicing words from a random list.

Scattered through the materials in these experiments were sentences which did not consist of two entirely separate clauses in the surface structure, but which had one clause embedded within another. For example, in Sentence 4a, there are two underlying structure sentences, but they are not literally reflected in the actual utterance as two distinct uninterrupted sequences.

(4a) ([The man ([who nobody likes]) is leaving soon])
(4b) ([Nobody likes the man ([who is leaving soon])])

Nevertheless, Fodor and Bever found that the extremes of the embedded clauses (e.g., Sentence 4a) are as effective in "attracting" the subjective location of clicks as they are in sentences with two distinct clauses (e.g., Sentence 4b). In some cases in the previous experiments, two underlying structure sentences corresponded to a sequence

[6] Abrams, K., Bever, T. G., & Garrett, M. Syntactic structure modifies attention during speech preception and recognition.

in which the division into two clauses was even less obvious in the actual structure. Consider Sentence 5a:

(5a) ([[The reporters assigned to George] drove to the airport])
(5b) ([The reporters ([who were assigned to George]) drove to the airport])

The sequence ". . . assigned to George . . ." does not have the same intuitive distinctiveness as a clause in the surface structure of Sentence 5a as in Sentence 5b. Nevertheless, sentences in which the surface structure does not obviously reflect the underlying structure, like Sentence 5a, were found to affect the subjective location of clicks (e.g., clicks were displaced perceptually to the point following "George"). In certain cases one underlying structure sentence was so completely embedded within another that there was no trace of an explicit clause boundary in the apparent structure, as in Sentence 6 (taken from Garrett, Bever, and Fodor).

(6) ([[Only the metropolitan district of Hamburg] was leveled by the war])

In this sentence the point between "Hamburg" and "was" was found to be effective in attracting subjective click location even though this point is not a break between clauses in the surface phrase structure.

These data suggest that an early step in the organization of a string of words is to isolate those sequences in the surface order which correspond to underlying structure sentences. This strategy justifies the following experimental prediction for the subjective location of clicks:

H1: *Errors in location of clicks presented during sentences are towards those points which correspond to divisions between underlying structure sentences.*

This hypothesis received initial confirmation through the experiments described above. However, most of the results in the preceding experiments do not bear specifically on this hypothesis and are also subject to several orthogonal interpretations.

First, it might be the case that *any* phrase structure division marked in the surface phrase structure division of sentences has an effect on the click location. This was specifically claimed by Fodor and Bever (although they had examined primarily the effect of breaks between explicit surface structure clauses). Therefore, the previous experimental results also support the following hypothesis:

H2: *Errors in location of clicks presented during sentences are to-*

ward every surface phrase structure division, including those within clauses.

The points in a sequence which correspond to divisions between the underlying sentences usually are also the largest phrase-structure divisions in the surface structure: it would be expected on H2 that these divisions would have maximum effect in attracting the subjective location of a click.

Second, most of the sentences in the previous experiments had an underlying structure division which was directly reflected in the surface phrase structure by an explicit clause division. That is, in general, the previous experiments would also support the following hypothesis:

H3: *Errors in location of clicks presented during sentences are only towards those points at which an underlying structure sentence division coincides with an explicit clause division in the surface structure.*

This paper presents two studies designed to explore these alternative hypotheses. First, we will examine the perceptual effect of within-clause surface phrase structure divisions, and show that these structural breaks do not reliably affect subjective click location. Second, we will present a study in which the sentences are carefully balanced for surface phrase structure, length, and other superficial features, but are systematically varied for the position in the actual sequence which corresponds to the division between two underlying structure sentences. In this experiment the division between the underlying sentences does attract clicks despite the lack of correlated divisions in the surface phrase structure. Thus, this paper supports Hypothesis H1, that a basic strategy of speech processing is actively to organize speech stimuli in terms of their underlying "logical" syntactic structure.

EXPERIMENT 1

English grammar defines a distinct surface phrase structure for each sentence. The surface phrase structure represents how the adjacent words are grouped together into "immediate constituents." We can define two types of immediate constituents, those which are clauses (i.e., directly derived from underlying structure sentences) and those which are "minor" phrases within clauses. For example, in Sentence 7 there are two main clauses, made up of the first 4 words and the last 10.

(7) ([When he stood up]) ([my son's book fell from the low and small table])

Within each clause, there are smaller phrase groupings; for example, in the sequence, "he stood up . . . ," the second two words are more closely grouped together than the first and the second words. This is called a "right-branching" structure since the phrase structure branches to the right. In contrast, ". . . my son's book . . ." has a left-branching structure which groups the first two words more closely than the second two. Finally, the sequence "low and small" has an intermediate ("ternary") structure since the first two words are as closely grouped together as the second two words. (See Fig. 3 for a surface phrase structure tree diagram of this sentence.)

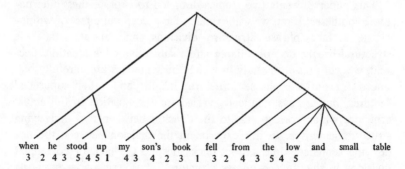

Fig. 3. Sample sentence with surface phrase structure tree and phrase structure depth indicators (Experiment 1).

Fodor and Bever claimed that the phrase is the perceptual unit of speech including "minor" phrases. However, in their study and in the other studies quoted above, the surface phrase-structure/clause-breaks studies usually corresponded to divisions between underlying sentences. The present experiment was undertaken to clarify whether or not "minor," within-clause phrase-structure breaks in the surface structure do affect click location. To investigate this we studied the perception of clicks in sentences in which the minor surface phrase structure within each clause differed systematically without associated differences in the underlying syntactic structure.

Stimulus Materials

Twenty-five English sentences, 12 words in length, were recorded with a normal subdued intonation. Each sentence was categorized as having a surface structure clause break after the 4th, 5th, 6th, 7th, or 8th word. The two words following the clause break of each sentence were monosyllables. The within-clause phrase structure was varied so that there were roughly the same number of left-branching, right-branching, and ternary-branching within-clause constituents immediately preceding and following the clause breaks (see Appendix 1).

The set of 25 stimulus sentences was recorded onto a master tape and five different orderings of this set were prepared from the master tape. Clicks were then placed on the other track simultaneous with each of the 125 resulting copies. For each sentence a click was placed in one of five positions relative to the clause break. The positions used were the major clause break itself, the middle of each of the two words immediately preceding the major break, and the middle of each of the two words immediately following the major break.[7] Each consecutive fifth of the five orders of stimulus sentences was balanced with respect to click placement relative to the clause break. In addition, each fifth of the five orders was balanced with respect to the positions of the clause break of the sentences. (See Fig. 4 for an outline of the design of the materials.)

The experimental procedure was the same as in Fodor and Bever. After each stimulus sentence, the S wrote down the sentence and indicated with a slash the position in the sentence at which he heard the click. Thirty Ss heard each experimental order. An equal number of Ss heard all the sentences in the right ear and the clicks in the left ear and vice versa. Ss were Harvard Summer School undergraduates who volunteered for paid participation in the experiment.

---

[7] Placing the click in sentences was achieved by disengaging the transport mechanism of the tape deck and manually moving the tape across the playback head until the desired position was located. Using the same procedure the accuracy of all the locations was then judged independently by the three authors.

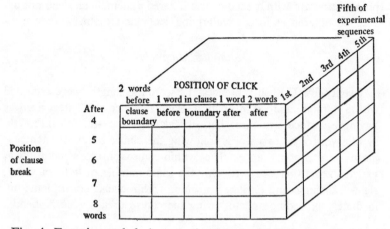

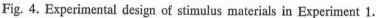

Fig. 4. Experimental design of stimulus materials in Experiment 1.

Results

The 150 Ss yielded 3704 click location responses of which 65.4% were errors; 46 responses were lost, usually due to a S's failure to indicate where he thought the click had occurred.

There were two main results: (1) Surface phrase-structure boundaries between clauses subjectively attracted interrupting clicks. (2) Surface phrase-structure boundaries within clauses had no consistent effect on the subjective location of clicks.

We first tested the prediction that clause boundaries would attract click location, to verify that our Ss and experimental techniques replicated the previous findings. For each click position relative to the break we compared the number of errors which went towards or into the clause break with the number of errors an equal distance away from the clause break. For example, a response to a click objectively in the word, "son's," in Sentence 7 that placed it in "my" was counted as confirming the clause-break hypothesis, while a location response in "book" was counted as disconfirming the response.[8] Of the error

---

[8] Responses larger than the distance between the objective click position and the clause break did not figure in this analysis. Thus, for example, a response to a click objectively in "son's" in Sentence 7, which placed the click in the word "low" or the word "up," would not be counted. In all, 27.9% of the error responses were excluded from this analysis because they were too large in one direction or the other.

responses, 77% confirmed the hypothesis that the clause boundary attracts subjective location of clicks. This result was significant by sentence (p < .001).

Phrase-structure divisions within clauses were not effective in attracting click errors. We tested this by assigning each position within words and between words a number which corresponds to the number of constituents which that point in the sentence interrupts. For example, the different points in Sentence 7 would have been assigned phrase-structure depths indicated in Fig. 3 (only those points less than four syllables and spaces to either side of at least one actual click placement were included in this analysis. Appendix 1 presents the surface phrase-structure analyses we used).

Each location error was first measured for the number of syllables and spaces it spanned. (Spaces between words were counted as one-half syllable in duration.) For each error size we examined the prediction that more errors would be into the position which interrupts fewer immediate constituents (e.g., has a lower number in the above analysis). For example, this predicted that more location errors of one-half syllable to a click objectively in "stood" would precede "stood" than follow it; a location error of one syllable was predicted to go into the word, "he." Errors into the clause break, or an equal magnitude away from the clause break were not included in this test, since we had already shown that the clause break does attract clicks.

There were 194 effective predictions governing the relative number of location errors of one-half to two syllables in size.[9] Of those,

[9] Ideally, 400 within-clause phrase structure predictions could be made for the four error magnitudes in 25 sentences and five click positions. (Four error magnitudes × 25 sentences × 5 click positions = 500 predictions- 100 cases which involve the major clause break, e.g., errors of one-half syllable to clicks objectively in the word immediately before or after the clause break.) However, in many cases the prediction could not be tested either because the two points in the sentence had an equal phrase structure depth, or there were no errors made into either position. There was an interaction with error magnitude; errors of one-half syllable confirmed the within-clause phrase structure hypothesis more than the larger errors (see Table A—Location error distribution according to magnitude).

Table A

½	1	1½	2	error size in syllables
52%	41%	33%	36%	% confirming within-clause phrase structure prediction

For the errors of one-half syllable there was a strong interaction with the only 41.5% confirmed the within-clause phrase-structure hypothesis. In a reanalysis of our data M. Garrett [details reported in Garrett & Bever (in press)] found that the minor surface structure configuration weakly predicted the *direction* of small location errors (p < .10, two-tail) but not the specific location. Garrett also examined the correlation of the accuracy of clicks located at a break and the number of minor phrases which terminate or begin at that break. All correlations were low and nonsignificant (less than .2).

The failure of the surface phrase-structure predictions to be confirmed in general, leaves open the possibility that the underlying structure configuration of the sentences could account for the location errors, even in the absence of associated surface-structure clause breaks (H1). Although the stimuli in this experiment were not specifically designed to test H1, the underlying structure organization of a sentence coincided with surface order in some of the sentences. Consider Sentence 8 for example:

(8) ([The inexperienced pilot lost his breath]) (since [the plane dove [too fast]])

In the above sentence there are phrase-structure divisions which are not clause divisions but which nevertheless correspond to divisions between sentences in the underlying syntactic structure (marked with a square bracket). Of the 11 divisions of this sort which occurred in our materials, 8 attracted relatively more clicks (compared with the surface phrase-structure divisions an equal distance away for all error magnitudes), and 3 attracted relatively fewer clicks. To compare the attractive force of the underlying structure divisions, we categorized the within-clause structure analyses into those in which an underlying structure break coincided with the deeper break in the within-clause surface structure and those in which it did not. Of the 23 predictions in which the deeper surface structure break coincided with an underlying structure division, 20 confirmed the original within-clause surface-structure prediction. Of the 51 cases in which the predicted within-clause break did not coincide with an underlying structure division, only 19 confirmed the within-clause phrase-

---

objective location of the click and the tendency to confirm the within-clause phrase hypothesis. One-half syllable errors in response to a click located objectively in the clause break confirmed the within-clause phrase-structure hypothesis 23%; one-half syllable errors in response to a click located objectively two words before or after the clause break confirmed the within-clause phrase-structure hypothesis 71%.

structure prediction. In nine instances the underlying structure-break prediction conflicted with the within-clause phrase-structure prediction; i.e., the shallower break in the surface structure corresponded to an underlying structure division between underlying sentences. In eight of these nine instances, the prediction based on the underlying structure was confirmed. Finally, in the four cases in which the within-clause phrase structure made no relative prediction, predictions based on the underlying structure were confirmed.

EXPERIMENT 2

The preceding results suggest that within-clause phrase structure has no consistent effect on click location. They also indicate that the most effective structural division governing errors in click location is the point corresponding to the division between sentences in the underlying structure. However, the stimuli in Experiment 1 were not critically designed to test this hypothesis, so the following experiment was also carried out.

Materials

Six sets of three sentences each were constructed in which the position of an underlying structure break was varied, while surface structure was held constant. The major variable in each set of sentences was the type of verb and complement clause. In one set of sentences the entire complement sentence is the direct object of the main verb ("nounphrase complement verbs"); in a corresponding set of sentences the subject of the complement clause is itself the direct object of the main verb ("verbphrase complement verbs").[10] Consider, for

[10] See Rosenbaum (1967) for a justification of these underlying structure analyses. The potential clause boundaries after the object nounphrase in the surface structure (deriving from the underlying structure sentences) are deleted in all three types of complement sentences. A crucial test is the fact that reflexivization cannot extend across a clause boundary, but it can extend to *all* of the complement sentences. That is, while Sentence a is ungrammatical, Sentences b, c, and d are all fully grammatical. Thus, the linguistic evidence indicates that neither Sentence b (Type 1) nor Sentence c (Type 2) nor Sentence d (Type 3) have clause boundary following the object nounphrase in the surface structure.
  (a) *John cried when himself was seen
  (b) John can't bear himself to be seen
  (c) John can't bear himself being seen
  (d) John can't force himself to be seen

example, these three sentences (excluding surface structure clause divisions):

(9) Type 1—nounphrase complement
$[_1$The corrupt police can't bear $[_2$the criminals to confess$]_2]_1$

Type 2—nounphrase complement
(a) $[_1$The corrupt police can't bear $[_2$the criminals' confessing$]_2]_1$
(b) $[_1$The corrupt police can't bear the criminals' confessing$]_1$

Type 3—verbphrase complement
$[_1$The corrupt police can't force the criminals $[_2$to confess$]_2]_1$

In the first type of sentence the entire embedded complement clause is the logical object of the main verb ("bear"); the underlying structure sentence corresponding to "the criminals confess" is directly reflected in the actual word order. In the second sentence type there are two possible underlying structures: (a) one identical to Type 1, and (b) one in which the object of the main verb ("bear") is the gerund itself (e.g., the object is "confessing" as in "They can't bear the criminals' confessing because of its maudlin style"); thus, in analysis Type 2b the actual sequence does not directly reflect an underlying structure sentence. In sentence Type 3 the subject of the embedded complement sentence is simultaneously the object of the main verb. Thus, in sentence Type 3 the surface order represents two distinct underlying structure sentences which overlap in the surface order. (The underlying structure configurations are outlined in Fig. 5.)

Our general hypothesis (H1) is that the basic unit of immediate speech processing is any sequence which corresponds to a "sentence" (single expansion of "S") at the level of underlying structure. This general hypothesis motivates two specific predictions for the subjective location of clicks in sentence Types 1, 2, and 3.

P1: Clicks in "verbphrase complement" sentences (i.e., with verbs like "force") will be located subjectively between the verb and following noun less often than in sentences with "nounphrase complement" (i.e., with verbs like "bear").

P2: Clicks in nounphrase complement verbs with gerund object (e.g., "the criminal confessing") will be located subjectively between

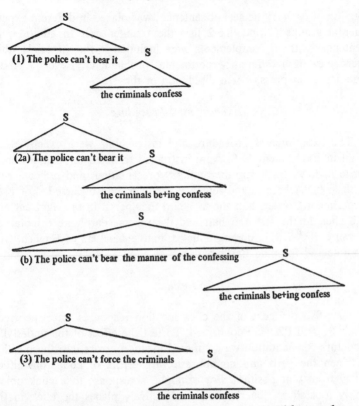

Fig. 5. Underlying syntactic structures for sentences with complement verbs (within-clause phrase structure is omitted). (Experiment 2)

the verb and noun less often than for the same verbs with sentence object (e.g., "the criminal to confess"). This prediction follows from the fact that Type 2 sentences have two potential underlying structure analyses; one similar to Type 1, and one not similar to Type 1.

To control for any possible differences in pronunciation of the three versions, six sentences were constructed by cross-splicing different parts of one sentence onto another. For example, the sequence "the corrupt police can't bear . . . ," originally recorded as part of Type 1, was spliced onto ". . . the criminals' confessing," originally recorded as part of Type 2. Clicks were placed either in the main verb or in the middle of the following nounphrase. This yielded six experimental sentences from each set. A different experimental version of each of the sets of sentences was placed in different experimental groups (Appendix 2 lists these sentences). In addition, 12 sentences without complements were included in the materials [they were part of a different experimental problem, cf. Bever, Lackner and Stolz (in press) for a discussion of these].

Experimental Procedure

The experimental procedure and instructions were exactly those used in Experiment 1. Ss were instructed to listen to each sentence, write it down following the auditory presentation, and indicate with a slash "/" where in the sentence the click had occurred. For each experimental order, half the Ss heard the speech in the right ear and the click in the left and half had the reverse earphone orientation. Ss were 160 M.I.T. undergraduates, native speakers of English, who volunteered for paid participation.

Results

Sixty-five per cent of the click location responses were incorrect. Both P1 and P2 were confirmed. To test the effect of the underlying structure segmentation we compared location errors into the position between the verb and nounphrase with errors of equal magnitude away from that position. For example, a response to a click objectively located in "bear," which subjectively places the click in the break between "bear" and "criminals," would count as attracted into the critical verb-nounphrase sequence, while a location placed immediately preceding the verb would count as repelled out of the sequence.

This analysis confirms the predictions based on the underlying structure (see the means in Table 1). The structure which attracted clicks most strongly into the middle of the complement verb/nounphrase sequence was the nounphrase complement sentences, Type 1. The least effective break was in the sentence with verbphrase complements, Type 3. The structure ambiguous as to whether or not there is an underlying structure division after the verb, Type 2, received an intermediate proportion of errors into the verb/nounphrase sequence. These results were consistent by sentence: sentence Type 1 received a larger proportion of errors into the verb/nounphrase sequence than the corresponding sentences for Types 2 and 3 for all six triplets of sentences (p < .02 by sign test, one-tail). These results are equally true of spliced and nonspliced versions of the sentences and were also significant by S. Two Ss (one heard speech in the left ear and click in the right ear, one in the reverse orientation) were selected randomly from each experimental group (16 groups). A significant majority of these had more errors intruding into the verb/nounphrase sequence for sentence Type 1 than for Type 3 (p < .001 by sign test, one-tail), more for Type 1 than for Type 2 (p < .02 by sign test, one-tail), and more for Type 2 than for Type 3 (p < .02 by sign test, one-tail).

The confirmation of P1 is largely due to differences in the location of clicks objectively in the verb. Table 1 presents the results for the

Table 1

Proportion of Location Errors of Equal Magnitude into Position between Verb and Nounphrase in Experimental Sentences. Experiment 2

	Click objectively in the verb	Click objectively in the following noun	Mean
(1) Nounphrase verb and object complement sentence (Type 1)	.8	.8	.8
(2) Nounphrase verb and object complement gerund (Type 2)	.7	.7	.7
(3) Verbphrase verb and object complement sentence (Type 3)	.4	.7	.6

sentence structures organized by objective click location. For all six sets of sentences, the subjective location of clicks objectively in the verb accounts for more of the difference between structures in Types 1 and 3 than does the subjective location of clicks objectively in the following nounphrase (p < .02 by sign test, two-tail). Similarly, the responses to clicks objectively in the verb accounts for more of the difference between Types 2 and 3 than do the responses to clicks objectively in the nounphrase for five out of six sets of sentences (p < .04 by sign test, two-tail). Finally, the clicks objectively in the verb and nounphrase contribute equally to the difference between Types 1 and 2. That is, when the verbs between two structure types differ (as between Types 1 and 3 or Types 2 and 3), the errors in the response to the clicks in the verb differ more than to the clicks in the following nounphrase. When the verbs are the same (as in Types 1 and 2) the in-verb and in-noun clicks contribute equally to the differences between the types. Thus, the main variable which determines the differences in subjective click location is the syntactic type of verb in which the click actually occurs.[11]

These results indicate that the syntactic division which affects subjective click location is the point in a sentence which corresponds to a division between "sentences" in the underlying syntactic structure. Current linguistic theory indicates that there is no basis for distinguishing the surface phrase structure of a verbphrase complement sentence like Type 3 from that of a nounphrase complement sentence like Type 1 (see Note 10). Thus, the marked differences in subjective click location must be due only to the underlying structure organization.[12]

[11] Clicks objectively in the verb contribute as much to the difference between structure Types 1 and 2 as do the responses to clicks objectively in the following nounphrase. This is somewhat surprising, since through the verb, sentence structure Types 1 and 2 are identical. How can the fact that a gerund (as opposed to a complement sentence) will follow the verb have an effect on the perception of a click coincident with the verb? The answer lies in the possibility that the mechanism of locating clicks in speech following the sentence is not only immediately perceptual, but also takes into account some of the stimulus which follows the click. Thus, after hearing the entire sentence (or a large part of it), the presence of a complement or gerund construction can affect the placement of clicks objectively preceding it (cf. Abrams, Bever, & Garrett; Bever, Lackner, & Stolz, for brief discussions of the behavioral nature of the location of clicks in sentences). In this paper we assume that the interaction of click location and speech segmentation is "immediate," without attempting to decide how much of the effect is due to "perceptual" processes and how much to "short-term memory."

[12] However, some linguistic analyses of the complement sentences might provide differences in surface phrase structures that could account for some of the results. If there were a distinction in the phrase structure which would differentiate the two types of sentences in the surface structure it would be the presence of an "S"-node in the surface phrase structure of Type 1 and the absence of an "S"-node in Type 3. But even if there were a difference in the surface phrase structure it would still be the case that the potential difference would only be the extent of one phrase structure node; we found in Experiment 1 that differences of several phrase-structure nodes have little effect on click placement, unless one of the nodes coincides with a division between underlying sentences. At the very least the difference between structures like Type 1 and those like Type 3 in their effect on click location is a systematic confirmation of the results found in Experiment 1; if there is a difference of one node in the surface phrase structure, it is effective only if it coincides with a deep structure division. Furthermore, it would be difficult to motivate the intermediate effect of sentences of Type 2 by appeal to surface structure differences.

As in previous experiments, there was a significant asymmetry in average click location correlated with earphone orientation. The average subjective location for the six critical sentences was −.08 syllable relative to the objective position of all clicks for Ss who heard the click in the left ear and the speech in the right ear. The average response for S with reverse earphone orientation was +.01 syllables. This difference was significant by sentence (p < .02 two-tail by sign test, two-tail for the unique sentences; in the experiment, a given S contributed data for only six sentences, but never more than one response to any given sentence, so a sign test was justified).

Discussion

The two experiments in this paper were designed to refine the earlier findings concerning the effect of segmentation on the subjective location of clicks in speech. Previous results had indicated that explicit clause boundaries marked in surface phrase structure as well as underlying logical phrase structure, correspond to boundaries of processing units. However, there were three interpretations which were consistent with those results: (H1) any surface phrase-structure break which corresponds to a division between underlying structure sentences is an effective unit; (H2) all surface phrase-structure divisions correspond to units and the "larger" the division in the surface phrase structure (in terms of the number of nodes it separates) the larger the effectiveness of the sequence bounded by that break; and (H3) only underlying structure sentences which appear as separate clauses in the surface structure are effective units.

In Experiment 1, we systematically varied the surface depth of the phrase-structure breaks within clauses to make it possible for a small effect to appear. We found no reliable tendency for the proportion of errors into a within-clause break to correspond to the relative depth of that break. Furthermore, Garrett and Bever (in press) examined the results from Experiment 1 and found no correlation between the effectiveness of a clause break and the number of phrase-structure units which end at a particular clause. In a different experiment, Bever, Lackner, and Stolz (in press) found no differences in the effect on click location of three kinds of within-clause structures: adjective-noun ("red ball"), verb-object ("hit ball") and subject-verb ("ball hit").[13] Recently, Bever, Fodor, and Garrett [(1966) discussed in Garrett & Bever (in press)] investigated the relative effectiveness of pairs of surface structure transitions which were superficially quite similar, but which differed by having or not having an "S" node in the surface phrase-structure tree. Consider the two examples in Sentence 11:

(11a) They watched [the light turn green]
(11b) They watched the light green car

The relevant difference between the two structures just after the verb is the presence of an additional node in the surface structure of sentence 11a. Bever et al found that this difference of a single node had a profound effect on the pattern of errors in click placement (i.e., more clicks intruded into the main verb nounphrase sequence in Sentence 11a). Together with the negative results from Experiment 1 in this chapter, these findings support the following initial conclusion: a relative increase in the number of surface structure nodes defines a unit of immediate processing *only* if the increase is related to an underlying sentence-node in the logical structure. Thus, Hypothesis 2 above is not correct.

All the further evidence supports Hypothesis 1 and simultaneously invalidates Hypothesis 3. Bever et al had previously found a tendency (nonsignificant) for sequences with nonapparent divisions between underlying structure sentences to be more effective in "attracting" clicks than structures which did not correspond to underlying structure divisions. As pointed out in the introduction, several sentences in the previously published click-location experiments did not have explicit clause breaks in the surface structure, but nevertheless attracted clicks to points corresponding to underlying structure divisions. This finding was also supported by the 11 instances in Experiment 1 in which divisions between underlying structure sentences are not reflected in clause divisions in the surface structure, but nevertheless attracted clicks. Finally, Experiment 2 in this paper indicates systematically the effectiveness of divisions between underlying structure

---

[13] In their experiment they controlled for possible differences in pronunciation by using sentences produced by cross-splicing, and they systematically varied the transitional probability (TP). Although TP did affect the relative placement of clicks, these differences in the within-clause phrase structure depths did not.

sentences in the absence of explicit division into obvious clauses in the surface phrase structure.

These results demonstrate that immediate segmentation of sentences is responsive to underlying structure sentences. However, there are various difficulties with each of the experiments we have presented. It is not clear whether all underlying structure divisions have an effect on perceptual segmentation, or whether this effect is limited to those underlying structure sentences whose relations are reflected in terms of adjacencies or particular "canonical" orders in the surface structure. For instance, in the examples below, it is not clear that both the first and second sequences will be treated as processing units. Both derive from the same underlying structure "sentences" (*my steak BE rare, my steak BE tender*) but only the first reflects this in the surface structure by having the shared noun come first rather than last.

(12a) I like my steak rare and tender
(12b) I like my rare and tender steak

In addition, there are several methodological difficulties which might account for the failure of recent experiments to show an effect of within-clause phrase structure on click location. Perhaps the effects of within-clause structure are masked by the proximity of large between-clause breaks in our materials. Support for this hypothesis is suggested by the fact that errors of half syllable do show within-clause phrase structure effects for clicks located two words before or after the major clause break, while clicks which are objectively closer to the break and errors which are larger do not show any effect (see Note 9). Also, while minor breaks do not appear to "attract" click location errors, it might be that they could effect the actual number of errors—that is, a click located in a relatively deep phrase-structure break might be more accurately located than a click in a relatively shallow break.

It would be surprising if minor phrase structure had no effect on segmentation at all: even according to the view that underlying structure organization is psychologically primary, a listener must isolate the major segments in a sequence. (This is at least logically prior to determining their deep structure relations.) Therefore, we expect that a more sensitive measure of perceptual segmentation will reveal effects of the major segments organized in the deep structure, such as "subject nounphrase," "object nounphrase," and so on.

It is our general view that a primary part of immediate speech processing is the isolation of underlying structure sentence-units. This does not mean that no other features of actual sentences can induce segmentation. For example, Garrett (1965) found that an introduced pause attracts clicks; Bever, Fodor, and Garrett found that a clause boundary obvious in the surface structure is more effective in "attracting" clicks than an implicit boundary. It is clear as well that major acoustic features can guide perceptual segmentation in the absence of structural divisions, e.g., sequences surrounded by major pauses in the signal, or extremely long sequences without internal structure can be treated as perceptual units (e.g., long proper names). In addition, listeners can attend to the surface structure of sentences to isolate minor differences in stress as aids to disambiguating certain kinds of phrases. Thus, our view that the underlying structure analysis of speech is a primary basis for segmentation describes what we ordinarily do, but does not restrict what we *can* do.

Coda: The Integration of Perceptual Segmentation with Specific Lexical Knowledge

In a recent series of papers, Fodor and Garrett (1967) and Fodor, Garrett, and Bever (1968) suggested that listeners actively use their knowledge of the underlying structure potentialities of particular lexical items in sentence comprehension. They supported this view by showing that sentences whose verbs have several underlying structure possibilities (e.g., Sentence 13a) are more complex than structurally identical sentences whose verbs have only one underlying structure possibility (e.g., Sentence 13b). This claims that it is not only the actual, realized structure of a sentence which determines its complexity, but also the structural potentialities of the individual lexical items.

(13a) John *believed* Bill
(13b) John *punched* Bill

The differences between the three types of sentences in Experiment 2 were primarily due to effects on the clicks objectively located in the main verbs. This indicates that specific lexical knowledge of the verb itself is used as a guide in the segmentation of underlying structure sentences as well as in the apprehension of their structure.

The immediate influence of the verb type on segmentation suggests that listeners are sensitive to the potential underlying structure organizations which can follow a particular verb and guide their perceptual segmentation in terms of the expectancy that an underlying structure sentence division is about to occur. Consider the underlying structural possibilities of the following sample verbs:

		Example completion	Syntactic type
nounphrase complement:		(a) the criminals ····	direct object
		(b) the criminals	
		to confess	complement sen-
		···· confessing	tence objects
the corrupt police can't *bear* ...		's confessing	
		(c) the criminals' ···· confessing	gerund object
		(d) to confess ······	complement or gerund in which
		confessing ······	the logical subject is the same as that of the main verb
verbphrase complement:			
the corrupt police can't *force* ...		(14e) the criminal (to ·· confess)	direct object followed optionally by a complement clause

Thus, a verbphrase complement verb (like "force") *must* be followed immediately by a direct object; this knowledge can be used to predict that a new underlying structure sentence cannot begin immediately following the verb, so segmentation is not established at that point. On the other hand, most of the potential constructions following a nounphrase complement verb (like "bear") begin a new underlying structure sentence. It is our hypothesis that listeners use this knowledge of the possible structures that follow nounphrase complement verbs to establish a segmentation at the point following the verb, *as they hear it*. In contrast, as listeners hear verbphrase complement verbs they know (intuitively) that a direct object must follow the verb, so they do not establish segmentation of an underlying structure sentence break immediately following the verb. Thus, in Experiment 2, the verb type was the primary determinant of the pattern of errors to clicks objectivity in the verb. This interpretation is also consistent with the finding in Experiment 2 that the pattern of errors to clicks objectively in the following nounphrase is uniform across all structure types. In all three constructions the nounphrase coincides with the subject of an underlying structure sentence, regardless of its relation to the preceding verb. Consequently, as listeners hear the nounphrase, they establish segmentation of a new underlying structure sentence. Therefore, all clicks objectively located in the nounphrase have an equal (higher than random) tendency to be subjectively located as immediately preceding the nounphrase.

A general picture of speech processing emerges from these studies. As we hear a sentence, we organize it in terms of underlying structure sentences, with subjects, verbs, objects, and modifiers. In this process we ignore structural features which are not immediately useful to the discovery of the sentence's potential underlying structure (e.g., we ignore many details of surface phrase structure.) Rather than recapitulating the *full* grammatical derivation brought out in the linguistic analysis of a particular sentence, the underlying structure segmentation of sentences and organization within sentences is projected immediately and directly from the structural potentialities of the words in a sequence. It is in this way that the "logical structure" which Wundt considered fundamental to the perception of sentences is actively reflected in the immediate processing of speech stimuli.

APPENDIX 1: THE SENTENCES USED IN EXPERIMENT 1,
WITH SURFACE PHRASE STRUCTURES INDICATED BY
PARENTHESES

(Hiding ((my friends) hat)) ((the small girl) (laughed (at (his strange predicament))))

(John (ran (quite fast))) but ((we) (caught him (in (the narrow alley))))

(When ((he) (stood up))) (((my son's) book) (fell (from (the low table))))

(After (a few tries)) ((the boy) (beat (his father) (at (Chinese checkers))))

(The boy and girl) ((won and lost) (at cards) (during (the afternoon)))

(They) (fought (tooth and nail))) (to get (past (the huge angry crowd)))

(By (making (his plan) known)) (Jim) (brought out) (the (objections (of everybody)))))

((In order (to see out)) ((the small child) ((pushed up) (the windows)))

(To determine ((the tree's age)) ((those boys) (asked (the old (forest ranger))))

((In addition) (to (his wives))) ((the prince) (brought ((the court's) only dwarf)))

((The inexperienced pilot) (lost (his breath))) (since ((the plane) (dove (too fast))))

If (you (did ((call up) Bill))) (I (thank you (for (your trouble))))

(The guard) (took ((your aunt's) (purse ((in which) (she (had (ten dollars)))))))

(They) (asked (the mean old man) (to be kind (to (his dog))))

(Since ((she) (was free (that day)))) ((her friends) (asked her (to come)))

(When ((the new minister) ((called up) Fred))) ((the plan) (was (discussed thoroughly)))

((Any student) (who (is (bright but young)))) (would not have (seen it))

(That ((the matter) was ((dealt with) fast))) (was (a shock) (to Harry))

(That ((a solution) (could not be found))) (seemed (quite clear) (to us))

(After ((the dry summer) (of (that year)))) ((most crops) (were (completely lost)))

((The boy) (who was (waiting (in (the hall))))) (is (a new student))

((The lawyer) (who (couldn't (decide (what (to do)))))) ((sat down) (in disgust))

((Not quite all) (of (the (brand new) chairs))) ((were shipped) (that day))

(Because (coffee (spilled on (her (sky blue) dress)))) (she (went home early))

(The entire (skiing party)) (feeling (nice and warm)) (laughed and sang loudly)

APPENDIX 2: SENTENCE TRIPLES WITH DIFFERENT
SYNTACTIC STRUCTURES USED IN EXPERIMENT 2

(1a)   The general preferred the troops to fight against the advancing enemy.
(1b)   The general preferred the troops' fighting against the advancing enemy.
(1c)   The general defied the troops to fight against the advancing enemy.

(2a)   The little girl hated her mother to cook her some cauliflower.
(2b)   The little girl hated her mother's cooking her some cauliflower.
(2c)   The little girl told her mother to cook her some cauliflower.

(3a)   The shopkeeper desired John to pile some boxes in the corner.
(3b)   The shopkeeper desired John's piling some boxes in the corner.
(3c)   The shopkeeper directed John to pile some boxes in the corner.

(4a)   The teacher wanted the guilty boy to inform on his classmates.
(4b)   The teacher wanted the guilty boy's informing on his classmates.
(4c)   The teacher tempted the guilty boy to inform on his classmates.

(5a)   The corrupt police can't bear criminals to confess very quickly.
(5b)   The corrupt police can't bear criminals' confessing very quickly.
(5c)   The corrupt police can't force criminals to confess very quickly.

(6a)   The prophet will like the people to renounce their indifference.
(6b)   The prophet will like the people's renouncing their indifference.
(6c)   The prophet will cause the people to renounce their indifference.

REFERENCES

BEVER, T. The cognitive basis for linguistic structures. In J. Hayes (Ed.), *Language and cognition*. Englewood Cliffs, N.J.: Prentice Hall, in press.

BEVER, T., LACKNER, J., and STOLZ, W. Transitional probability is not a general mechanism for the segmentation of speech. Journal of Experimental Psychology, in press.

BEVER, T., FODOR, J., and GARRETT, M. The perception of language and gestalt principles. Paper presented at the International Congress of Psychology, Moscow, 1966.

BEVER, T., KIRK, R., and LACKNER, J. An autonomic reflection of syntactic structure. Neuropsychologia, in press.

CHOMSKY, N. *Aspects of the theory of syntax.* Cambridge: M.I.T. Press, 1965.

FODOR, J., and BEVER, T. The psychological reality of linguistic segments. Journal of Verbal Learning & Verbal Behavior, 1965, 4, 414–20.

FODOR, J., and GARRETT, M. Some syntactic determinants of sentential complexity. Perception & Psychophysics, 1967, 2, 289–96.

FODOR, J., GARRETT, M., and BEVER, T. Some syntactic determinants of complexity. II. Verb structure. Perception & Psychophysics, 1968, 3, 453–61.

GARRETT, M. Syntactic structures and judgments of auditory events. Unpublished doctoral dissertation, University of Illinois, 1965.

GARRETT, M., and BEVER, T. The perceptual segmentation of sentences. In T. Bever and W. Weksel (Eds.), *The structure and psychology of language.* New York: Holt, Rinehart & Winston, in press.

GARRETT, M., BEVER, T., and FODOR, J. The active use of grammar in speech perception. Perception & Psychophysics, 1966, 1, 30–32.

JOHNSON, N. The psychological reality of phrase structure rules. Journal of Verbal Learning & Verbal Behavior, 1965, 4, 469–75.

ROSENBAUM, P. *The grammar of English predicate complement constructions.* Cambridge: M.I.T. Press, 1967.

WUNDT, W. *Die Sprache. II.* Leipzig, 1900.

WUNDT, W. *Grundriss der Psychologie.* Leipzig, 1897.

The Psychology of Language and Structuralist Investigations of Nativism

THOMAS G. BEVER

The existence of conceptual distinctions is one of the strongest arguments against the empiricist's proposal that all knowledge derives from sensory impressions. For example, the distinction between analytic and synthetic truths is inexplicable solely as the result of experience, since the concept of something that is true in all possible instances cannot be derived from a finite number of environmental impressions. Thus, such concepts are often at the heart of nativists' claims that certain aspects of knowledge are inborn, at least in the sense that they are based on a biological predisposition. A frequent empiricist reply concerning such categories of knowledge as analytic truths is to deny their existence: analytic truths are interpreted simply as "extreme" cases of factual truths—thus humans do not have "knowledge" of the analytic-synthetic distinction since the distinction does not exist.

One might claim that it is sufficient for the nativist to argue that humans *believe* that they have such knowledge, since the nativist and empiricist can be viewed as arguing about the kinds of knowledge that people think they have. However, once a presumptive nativist takes this step he/she can be accused of trying to account for the existence of delusions, including inconsistent beliefs, and hence for the "knowledge" of *anything*.

What is needed to make sense of such a mess is a theory of analyticity with consequences beyond enumeration of the allegedly analytic statements. Such a theory could in principle be tested and ultimately stand or fall on the weight of accumulated evidence. The analytic/synthetic distinction could be shown to be necessary not merely to account for the apparent fact that some people believe it exists, but also to account for other phenomena as well. A formal theory of analyticity has been proposed in conjunction with modern linguistic theory[1]—basically, analytic sentences are those which are true (or false) by virtue of the formal definitions of their components and the rules for combination. Unfortunately, there are no clear ap-

[1] Katz (1972).

plications of this definition to other empirical phenomena. This is not to claim that the formal distinction is false. However, a theory of empirical extensions is needed to enmesh the analytic/synthetic distinction in a variety of phenomena that can be explained only by appeal to that distinction. In short, what is missing is a theory of semantic *performance,* a theory of how we use the distinctions we know.

The most obvious aspect of how we use meanings in behavior is their role in referring expressions. It is often thought that the most salient phenomenon to start with in the study of reference is the reference of isolated words, usually concrete nouns. There is something appealingly simple about the use of the expressions "triangle" or "red cow" in the presence of a triangle or red cow: surely, it is thought, the understanding of the mechanisms of reference must start with these simple cases, and move to more complex ones. However, this approach is not the one taken by current linguistic theories, for several reasons. First, it is not at all obvious that behavioral data bear out the claim that simple nouns are commonly used to refer; how often is it that one's conversational acquaintances come out with "triangle" or "red cow" as complete utterances? As far as behavior is concerned we would appear to think verbally and talk in utterances that contain or imply predicates, as in "that is a ——." We simply do not go around naming objects in automatic response to their presence (or absence). Rather we seem to use the names of objects primarily to predicate properties of them.

The second reason for rejecting the claim that simple nouns hold the key to the study of reference is formal—within the current theory of linguistic study, the relevance of a meaning of a word is mediated by its effect on the meaning of an utterance which minimally contains a predicate—that is, words alone do not have all the information that gives an utterance its meaning; rather, words are components which combine according to their structural relations in an utterance to give it meaning. Thus we must start the study of reference with the referential properties of structured utterances, not single words.

It may seem odd to use a theoretical position about the nature of meaning as partial justification for a decision about how to approach the study of reference. However, this is merely to make explicit the kind of *a priori* consideration which underlies the claim that the use of simple nouns is the paradigm case of reference—that claim has no apparent empirical support except the fact that children are alleged to use single concrete nouns as an early form of utterance. But *that* fact is relevant to the study of reference only if we accept the view that a child's manifest behavior reveals what is psychologically basic; such a view is clearly consistent primarily with an empiricist position (in combination with an operationalist assumption that internalized structures in adults make use only of what was once external in children's behavior). Hence the claim that simple nouns are basic to reference was itself a claim rooted in a theory of knowledge.

The upshot of the considerations thus far is that to provide convincing data on the existence of categorical distinctions of linguistic knowledge we must turn to the study of the use of utterances that contain predications. A similar conclusion was based on laboratory attempts to determine the minimal unit of speech perception.[2] This research started with the possibility that speech is perceived as a series of individual sounds (phonemes), strung together into an utterance, just as pearls are strung in a necklace: since there is a small number of such sounds, learning to understand utterances could be accounted for in an empiricist model. However, it was discovered that the perception of sounds in isolation was far worse than when they were combined into words; it was further discovered that the perception of words in isolation is worse than when the same words are put together into a sentence; this effect is true even when one controls for the fact that words in normal sentences impose mutual constraints. The psychological basis for such phenomena was unclear, but it left the psychological study of language with the problem of defining what a *sentence* is, since at least that "high" a level of analysis seemed to be required to account for the perception of utterances. This presented a deeply disturbing puzzle for an empiricist theory of behavior—since there appears to be no psychologically interesting upper limit on the number of sentences (or potential utterances) (unlike the number of phonemes or words) one must appeal to knowledge that cannot be defined purely as a function of limited experience.

Chomsky[3] proposed that a grammar meet this problem directly: it is to be an account of the finite system of knowledge that defines the arbitrarily large set of sentences in a language. In traditional psy-

[2] This line of research is associated with the work of G. A. Miller. See Miller (1951) and (1967) for representative reviews.
[3] Chomsky (1957).

chological terms the grammer defines the "generalization space" which is implied by linguistic knowledge. Psychologists, including empiricists, had come to accept the notion that responses to inexperienced cases can occur on the basis of "generalization" from experienced cases. For example, if I am trained to raise my hand one foot when I hear a 100cps tone and three feet when I hear a 150cps tone, I probably will raise my hand somewhere between one and three feet upon hearing a 125cps tone (if I do anything at all). There appears to be an arbitrarily large number of such "learned" tone-hand-height relations. Such novel, untrained responses are explained by recourse to the assumption that I have defined a tonal dimension and related it to a hand-raising one in a monotonic fashion. This notion requires that I have such simple dimensions in my sensory and motoric repertoire and can relate one dimension to another. The availability of such psychological dimensions of knowledge has not been taken as grossly inconsistent with empiricism, since they appear to be firmly rooted in physically interpretable dimensions. At least we could envision a model of a machine which linked tone and hand height through a mechanical coupling. However, the proposal that a child extrapolates a grammar from a small number of cases is a much greater challenge: there is no obvious physical parameter of any set of known sentences which can predict the other sentences which could occur. Rather the calculus which defines the sentence-space involves formal devices which appear to have no physical basis at all, and thus to be attributable only to structures within the child's mind.

Psychologists can respond to this challenge in a number of ways. First, they may try to show that, in fact, grammar is only deceptively complicated and that it can be learned according to "known" empiricist-operationalist principles of learning. In the case of transformational grammar such attempts must founder at least on the distinction between the inner and outer syntactic form of sentences. The crucial fact is that *no* sentence form represents explicitly its inner form; thus, any theory which requires that inner knowledge be extracted from explicit data cannot explain the existence of a transformational grammar in the human mind.

A second way to meet the challenge posed by a grammar is to deny that the concept of "grammaticality" is meaningful psychologically. The grammatical model assigns certain sequences a derivation which maps their inner form onto their external form via a series of "transformations." The primary empirical reflection of such a model is a speaker's intuition that such a sequence is "acceptable." In addition a few other features that the grammatical model assigns to sequences have been offered empirical interpretations. For example, if the grammar assigns more than one derivation to a sequence, the prediction is made that that sequence is intuitively appreciated as "ambiguous"; various kinds of ungrammaticality are distinguished intuitively as a consequence of the kind of rules that are violated in their (non)generation by the grammar; and so on.

If such intuitions can be shown to be ephemeral, then one can deny that the grammatical model makes behaviorally relevant distinctions. That is, the "linguist's grammar" could be viewed as describing an arbitrary set of distinctions that do not represent real phenomena. This criticism is supported by the fact that intuitions about a sequence cannot literally be about its *grammaticality*, rather they are judgments about its *acceptability*. Many examples of such judgments can be shown to rest on intuitional continua rather than being discrete. For example, the acceptability of the sentence in (1) can be manipulated by the context in which it occurs: if (1) follows (2) it is less acceptable than if it follows (3).

(1) But, the horse raced past the barn fell.

(2) The horse walked past the house with no problem.

(3) The horse that was raced past the house didn't fall.

Thus, there would appear to be no clear way of isolating intuitions about "grammaticality" from other worldly knowledge—hence a "grammar" is an artifact, describing an artificially delimited set of acceptable sentences. *Real* linguistic behavior is on a continuum.

However, the difficulty of obtaining behaviorally pure intuitions that directly bear on a theoretical question is common in psychological research. For example, the page you are now reading is "white" and "rectangular" and will be so judged over a wide range of lighting conditions (including those in which no white light is present) and orientations of the book (including those which present a non-rectangular image to your retina). However, there are conditions under which you may be uncertain about such judgments—if your reading light is red, and the page looks red, you do not know whether that is because the page *is* red or white: there are circumstances under which relatively clear perceptual judgments can be influenced by the context in which the stimuli occur. This has not brought the study of color theory to a halt—rather it has encouraged psychologists to pursue the study of such a theory in a relatively constrained way.

For example, typical primary data were reports of perceived color from subjects sitting in a darkened room, looking through a tube that constrained the visual field. A color theory based on such relatively context-free judgments was developed and ultimately integrated with some natural contextual variables to explain more visual phenomena.

The procedure in the study of language is much the same. There are certain sequence acceptability judgments that are sufficiently clear to warrant the *pre-theoretic* claim that a grammar exists. For example, there is nothing hard to understand or say about the sentences in (4), they simply "are not English" for some reason, and a grammar is sought as the fundamental theory that accounts for such judgments.

(4) In English, article precedes noun

I hope it for to be a nice day tomorrow

White man speak with forked tongue

The fact that other judgments are less clear prompts the linguist to avoid them at first, just as color theorists started with limited data. Once a theory is constructed to account for the clear cases, then one can attempt to extend it to the cases that were originally unclear.

In this sense linguistic science is no different from many parts of human psychology that start with introspective reports as initial data —the main difference is that relatively little attention has been given to the nature of the intuitional processes involved in the collection of grammatically relevant acceptability judgments from native speakers. Roughly, linguistically sophisticated informants are expected to exclude their knowledge that a special context could make almost any sequence acceptable, to exclude semantic likelihood as relevant, and so forth. We will have more than a practical mastery of this process only when we have a deeper theory of the mechanisms of language use. For example, one cannot understand in theoretical terms how to exclude a particular acceptability judgment as irrelevant to grammar and due to perceptual processes unless one has some theory as to how the latter operate. In this regard the integration of linguistics and psycholinguistic research can serve as a model for the investigation of introspective processes in general.

As the theory of introspection emerges, the psychological validity of the transformational grammatical model will be increasingly confirmable. However, psychologists are usually dissatisfied with a theory that explains intuitions alone. They view such data as tainted, perhaps because of a period in the formation of modern psychology when "introspectionism" got out of hand and threatened to drown the field in a swamp of uncontrolled personal intuitions.

Accordingly, the third way to meet the challenge posed by transformational grammar is to examine whether the grammatical model makes true predictions beyond the enumeration of the intuitions it is set up to describe. Hence, the psychologist sought experimental "verification" of the grammatical model in the laboratory: such attempts underlie the formation of modern "psycholinguistics."[4] The experimental studies are of two types—those that sought to establish the reality of the inner forms which a transformational grammar assigns a sentence, and those which attempted to show that the transformational rules which map the inner forms into the outer ones correspond directly to psychological operations. While the former goal succeeded, the latter has failed thus far.

Experiments that demonstrate the "psychological reality" of inner forms of sentences have concentrated on three problems: memory, segmentation, and ambiguity. The methodology closest to linguistic investigation is to demonstrate that relations among sentences which share an inner syntactic form are responded to by subjects in actual "experiments" as more similar than sentences which do not share an inner form. For example, the sentences in (5) are mutually confused in immediate recall with a higher frequency than other types of confusions.

(5a) Harry surprised Max.

(5b) Max was surprised by Harry.

Furthermore, sentences like those in (6)

(6a) They desired the police to forbid loitering.

(6b) They desired the police to quit loitering.

are recalled better when the experimental subject is reminded of what the entire sentence was by being prompted with the noun that appeared most frequently in its inner form: that is, "police" is a more effective prompt in sentences like (6b) than (6a). (In (6b) "police" is the inner subject of both "quit" and "loiter" but in (6a) it is the subject only of "forbid.") Sentences like those in (7) are recalled better than those in (8), allegedly because the forms in (7) are closer outer representatives of the inner organization of the adverbial modi-

---

[4] See Miller (1967) and Fodor et al. (1974) Chapter 5, for reviews. The various empirical studies are not referenced individually.

fiers (modifying the entire main clause of the sentence in (7b) and the main verb only in (7a).)

(7a) The police quickly quit loitering.
(7b) Fortunately the police quit loitering.
(8a) Quickly the police quit loitering.
(8b) The police fortunately quit loitering.

Such demonstrations as these are important because they show that variation in the inner form is involved in how subjects respond to sentences, even when the outer form and meaning are held as constant as possible. This technique figures crucially in experiments showing that sentences are segmented behaviorally according to divisions between complete propositions in the inner form. The differential effect of inner propositional analysis is brought out by contrasting the subjective report of where a brief click occurred in the sentences in (9).

(9a) They desired/the pólice to loiter.
(9b) They defied the pólice/to loiter.

Although the click occurred in the same place in each sentence (on "pólice"), the relative frequency of reports is indicated by the slashes. These points correspond to the junctures between the propositions in the inner form.

These experiments are at pains to control the outer form of sentences and show that variations in the inner form determine aspects of behavior. The ultimate in such control is achieved by the experimental use of ambiguous sentences. For example, the two interpretations of (10a) differ in their inner syntactic form, while the two interpretations of (10b) do not.

(10a) They asked the police to stop loitering.
(10b) They asked the police to stop writing letters.

It has been shown that sentences like (10a) occasion longer comprehension times in certain cases (see pp. 156–57 below), and differ in the ease of recognition of the ambiguity. These behavioral differences in response to the ambiguities in (10a) and (10b) can be attributed to the fact that the grammar differentiates the *kind* of ambiguity in terms of the relation of the inner forms to the outer form.

Such studies demonstrate the psychological relevance of the inner form of sentences that a transformational grammar ascribes to them. However, the studies do not demonstrate that the transformational operations which map an inner form onto an outer one correspond to actual psychological operations. The dominant technique for study of this question has been to examine the relative psychological complexity of sentence pairs which share an inner form and a set of transformations, but in which one sentence has an additional transformation compared with the other sentence. For example, (11b) has a passive transformation but otherwise is structurally identical with (11a); initial experiments showed that sentences like those in (11b) are in fact harder to verify than those in (11a).

(11a) Two precedes three.

(11b) Three is preceded by two.

Such experiments were at first interpreted as demonstrating that every transformational operation corresponds to a psychological one. However, a variety of experimental failures to extend this generalization beyond simple cases combined with clear counterexamples to call the principle into question. For example, all the (-b) sentences in (12)–(17) below involve more transformations than their corresponding constructions in (-a). Yet the constructions in (-b) are psychologically *less* complex.

(12a) That Mary is here surprised Bill.

(12b) It surprised Bill that Mary is here.

(13a) Harry believed of Bill that the doctor saw him.

(13b) Harry believed Bill to have been seen by the doctor.

(14a) The boy that everybody hated since he always said he was right left.

(14b) The boy left that everybody hated since he always said he was right.

(15a) The waiter brought back the order.

(15b) The waiter brought the order back.

(16a) The bucket that was red fell over.

(16b) The red bucket fell over.

(17a) The reporter everyone I met trusts said Thieu will resign.

(17b) The reporter trusted by everyone I met said Thieu will resign.

The upshot of such examples is that there is no unequivocal evidence in favor of the claim that transformations are directly mapped onto psychological operations. Thus the result of the first bloom of transformational psycholinguistics was to establish the psychological relevance of the distinction between the inner and outer forms of sentences, but to leave open the psychological mechanisms that map one onto the other in actual behavior.

This can be viewed in part as a result of the lack of attention given within linguistics to the way in which the formal model of grammar is to be interpreted.[5] Just as the empirical extensions of semantic theory were limited to an initial set of intuitions about meanings, the model of grammar was assigned one primary empirical reflection—"grammaticality": a sequence that is assigned a derivation within the grammar is assigned the property of being "grammatical." Other properties assigned to sequences by the model (ambiguity, sentence relatedness, etc.) appeared to be confirmed since they were based on the distinction between inner and outer forms in the first place. What was disconfirmed was the psychologists' hope that the empirical interpretation of the model would include the claim that the number of transformations in a derivation corresponds to the number of mental operations involved in understanding a sentence.

This negative result leaves us uncertain about whether such a form of behavior as comprehension is a coherent statable function of the grammatical model. This opens the possibility that comprehension involves mental structures that are independent of grammatical ones. Many experiments that failed to demonstrate that comprehension is a simple function of grammar have nevertheless provided information bearing on the structures used in speech perception. The emergence of this theory and its integration with the grammar can serve as a model for a neo-structuralist approach to the study of language.

The problem of the listener is to extract the meaning of an utterance from its outer form. The current studies suggest that listeners do this at a number of levels simultaneously, syllable by syllable, word by word and "clause" by "clause." At each level, listeners alternate between accumulating information and structural hypotheses and assigning a particular analysis. Most attention has been given to the interaction of linguistic structure and perception at the level of the clause, so I shall concentrate on it. The studies have isolated three processes which apply directly to the outer form of a sentence during comprehension; segmentation, erasure and functional labeling.[6]

The process of segmentation groups together as a perceptual unit each part of a sequence that could constitute (or is likely to constitute) a complete underlying structure clause. One way of showing this is to observe the pattern of location errors in response to a click introduced while listening to sentences. A variety of experiments have

---

[5] See Katz and Bever (in press) for a discussion of the distinction in linguistics between a model and its interpretation.

[6] See Bever (1968) and Fodor et al. (in press) Chapter 6.

confirmed that listeners tend to think that the click actually occurred at the boundary between clauses, suggesting that the "perceptual integrity" of the clause "repels" the perception of the click to its boundaries. That the effect is truly caused by the structure contributed by the listener rather than some physical parameter of the signal contributed by the speaker can be shown by using sentences like those in (18) and (19).

(18) His hope of marrying the girl/is impractical.

(19) In her hope of marrying/the girl is impractical.

The linguistic sequence surrounding the click is exactly the same (indeed is a tape-recorded copy) in both cases; but the difference in structure predicts the relative perceived location of the clicks (indicated by the slashes). That the effect is *perceptual* rather than due to memory is shown by the fact that the response pattern is the same when the subject does not have to write out the sentence. To show that it is not due to guessing one can compare the pattern of responses when subjects are in fact guessing—such patterns do *not* show the effect of structure. Thus we can conclude that listeners actively apply their knowledge of the structure of a sequence to segment it as they hear it.

The role of such structural segmentation is reflected in variations in attention—listeners alternate between attending to all external stimulus inputs during a clause and internal processes of organization at the end of a clause. Accordingly, at the ends of clauses attention is weakest for any external stimulus, reaction time to a click is slowest, discrimination is poorest. These effects are reflected physiologically in an unconscious way—the electroencephalic brain response to a click is slower when the click occurs in the last word of a clause compared with the first word. Such results suggest that at the end of a clause listeners are preoccupied with an internal activity that reduces attention (for about 1/10 second) to *all* external stimuli.

Other studies show that this internal activity involves the assignment of an internal organization to the sequence that has just been heard and the erasure of its external form—that is, at such points it is recoded into a more "abstract" level. This is reflected in the fact that listeners can recognize that the word "girl" was in a sentence more quickly if it is presented following (19) than (18). This is due to the fact that the intervening clause boundary in (18) occasioned recoding of the first clause by the listener so that it is harder to extract the information that the acoustic item "girl" occurred. Nevertheless, the semantic information within a clause is retained, as can be shown by the responses to questions following clause closure. Such responses characteristically reveal uncertainty as to the precise external form of the sentence, but show mastery of the semantic information. Another fact demonstrating that the internal organization of a sequence is assigned by the end of a clause is that sentential ambiguity has no effect if the response task follows the clause boundary. Thus, while (20a) takes longer to complete than the corresponding unambiguous fragments (20b) or (20c), (21a) does not take longer than (21b) or (21c).

(20a) They asked the police to stop picking on. . . .
(20b) They asked the police to quit picking on. . . .
(20c) They asked the police to prevent picking on. . . .
(21a) They asked the police to stop picking on us. . . .
(21b) They asked the police to quit picking on us. . . .
(21c) They asked the police to prevent picking on us. . . .

The fact that a clause contains an ambiguity is no longer relevant once the clause boundary is passed, because listeners have chosen one interpretation by that time. However, before the boundary is reached the ambiguity does have an effect because the listener is actively entertaining both meanings implied by each structural interpretation.

The assignment of the structural interpretation to each clause utilizes a set of mapping rules, "perceptual strategies," which assign internal functional relations to the phrases.[7] Such strategies can be viewed as having the effect of "inverse transformations"; they take an external form as input and map it onto a possible internal form. However, there is no evidence that these rules operate in stages that correspond to the operation of transformations. For example, several basic strategies are summarized in (22): clearly they do not correspond directly to transformational operations.

(22a) $(. . . adv_1 \left\{ \begin{matrix} adj \\ adv_2 \end{matrix} \right\} . . .)$ ——→ adv_1 modifies $\left\{ \begin{matrix} adj \\ adv_2 \end{matrix} \right\}$

(22b) N_1, at clause beginning ————→ N_1=actor, of next inflected verb.

Rather, they appear to be a separate set of rules which pair inner and outer sentence forms by mapping the latter onto the former. Since they do not correspond to transformations individually, it is possible

[7] See Bever (1970).

that they operate in a system that is psychologically independent of the grammar.

One source of behavioral evidence supporting this proposal rests on studies of the development of the child's patterns of sentence comprehension. The child appears to go through several stages of perceptual strategies; the first is to use the strategy in (22c)

(22c) .... NV ————→ .... N = actor, V = action.

If one asks the two-year-old child to act out a simple sentence like those in (23) with dolls, the response pattern shows an early tendency to interpret any noun immediately before a verb as the subject of the verb. Around age four the child shifts to a strategy more like that in (22b), which assigns the initial noun the subject relation, regardless of whether it immediately precedes a verb or not. This leads to an actual *decrease* in correct performance on sentences like (23b).

(23a) The cow kisses the horse.

(23b) It's the horse that the cow kisses.

The same developmental pattern occurs in children learning English as a second language—as their over-all conversational ability in English improves, they shift from responding to sentences with a strategy like (22c) to one like (22b). Since the strategies are not based on transformations, such developmental shifts suggest strongly that the system of comprehension emerges at least partially independently of other systems of linguistic knowledge.

In brief, the perceptual system operates something like the following. During a clause listeners assign lexical class information to the words and attempt to find an appropriate deep structure for the sequence—the set of possible deep structures is assigned on the basis of perceptual strategies which map internal relations onto the external sequence. When an internal structure is found, the listener assigns it to the sequence and establishes perceptual closure around it, removing its external form from the focus of attention. It is, of course, true that this general picture of the perceptual process is not precise enough in most cases to allow for critical experimentation and that much research remains to be done. Nevertheless, the main points are well supported—namely that the perceptual system operates in part independently of grammatical knowledge, and that its operation has measurable behavioral effects.

Such facts allow for an elaboration of the distinction between competence and performance which can clarify the psychological basis for intuitions about acceptability. I pointed out above that every acceptability intuition necessarily involves some aspect of behavior, with the result that one can never be absolutely sure that a particular intuition reveals a property of grammatical knowledge and not of some other linguistic system. The interaction of the perceptual system and grammatical system in such judgments exemplifies the theoretical solution to this problem. The basic principle is the following—if a particular acceptability intuition would require increasing the formal power of a grammar, and if another independently motivated mechanism can account for the acceptability intuition, then the phenomenon is classified as due to that mechanism, and not to the grammar. Such cases are characteristically ones in which the unacceptability of a sequence is accounted for by a behavioral system rather than the grammar. Consider (24) for example: the operation of the perceptual strategy summarized in (22b) would categorize the first NVN

(24) *The horse raced past the barn* fell

sequence as a plausible clause, leaving the listener bewildered as to how to deal with the remaining word "fell," thus leading to an intuition that the entire sequence is unacceptable. It is clear how to rule out sentences like (24) in transformational terms—whenever a relative clause on an initial noun is passivized and the past participle of the verb in that clause is homonymous with the simple past, then the relative pronoun and form of "be" may not be deleted from the relative clause. Thus, (25a) is fully acceptable since it maintains the presence of the "that was . . ." (blocking the NVN strategy) and (25b) is acceptable because the verb form "ridden" is not a possible inflected past verb.

(25a) The horse that was raced past the barn fell.
(25b) The horse ridden past the barn fell.

In this interpretation (24) would be unacceptable because it is ungrammatical. However, the statement of such a restriction within the grammar would involve making the transformations in a derivation sensitive to *potential* derivations that the relative clause verb *might* have entered into. This is necessary to check whether the simple past of the verb would sound the same as the past participle. To do this the rule would have to take into account a potential derivation of the verb in a simple past sentence, which involves greater formal power than a grammar that does not require rules to be sensitive to potential derivations. The existence of an independently motivated perceptual theory that can account for the unacceptability of (24) allows the conclusion that (24) is grammatical, but usually unacceptable because of its interaction with the perceptual strategy in (22b).

It should be emphasized that this treatment not only relieves the grammar of unneeded formal power, but also offers an explanation of why the restriction is the way it is. To treat the phenomenon as a grammatical restriction, leaves it described but unexplained. However, treating it as due to the behavioral application of (22b) explains why it is the homonymy of the simple past with the past participle that is at issue—only insofar as that confusability exists, will (22b) apply to the initial part of sentences like (24) and render them unacceptable.

In certain cases we can use the same methodology to demonstrate that an acceptable sequence is in fact *un*grammatical but acceptable because of its comprehensibility. Consider the cases in (26).[8] They suggest that while a noun phrase containing *det not adj* is not acceptable, (26a), (26c), a sequence with *det not* $\left. {un \atop im} \right\}$ +*adjective* is acceptable (26b), (26d).

(26a) *The not happy man sat down
(26b) The not unhappy man sat down
(26c) *The not possible problem upset us
(26d) The not impossible problem upset us

However, cases like (26b) and (26d) are restricted to negative adjectives that meet the conditions in (27).

(27a) The adjective must be a lexical item when separated from the negative prefix *un* + or *im* +
(27b) The separated adjective must be used in the same way in that context
(27c) The separated adjective must *sound* the same in its separated form as in its prefixed combination.

Condition (27a) is demonstrated by the unacceptability of cases like (28a) in which the non-negated form of the adjective is not a separate word (e.g., *"trepid" is not a word).

(28a) *The not intrepid sailor sat down
(28b) *The not unholy roller disgusted us
(28c) *The not impious regent sat down

Condition (27b) is demonstrated by the unacceptability of (28b) (e.g., "holy" in "holy roller" has different meaning than in "unholy roller.") Finally condition (27c) is demonstrated by the unacceptability of a case like (28c) which meets criteria (27a) and (27b),

---

[8] See Langendoen and Bever (1973). They also offer an analysis of the semantic interpretation of the "not un + adj" construction.

but the separated adjective sounds different when it is a distinct lexical item (e.g. "paious," as opposed to "im+peeous").

One could try to incorporate the restrictions in (27) within the grammar. This would involve a partial liberalization of the rule that preposes complex adjective phrases like that in (29a) to produce sequences like (29b).

(29a) The man who was *not very happy* sat down

(29b) The not very happy man sat down

(29c) The man who was *not unhappy* sat down

The liberalized rule would be allowed to apply to sentences like (29c) to yield (26b). The descriptive problem is how to block such a rule from applying to acceptable sequences like those in (30a,b,c) and generating from them the corresponding unacceptable sentences in (27a,b,c).

(30a) The sailor who was *not intrepid* sat down

(30b) The roller who was *not unholy* disgusted us

(30c) The regent who was *not impious* sat down

The restrictions on the preposing rule would allow it to apply just in case the conditions in (27) are met (which is not the case in 30a,b,c). But *all* these conditions require consideration of how a lexical item (the unnegated form of the adjective) *would* be used in *other* sentences. To do this would add formal power to the grammar, which makes this treatment of the phenomena suspect if the acceptability facts can be accounted for in another way.

In fact the phenomena can be accounted for by the perceptual system. On this view the complex adj-preposing rule applies only in cases like (29a), which is easy to state grammatically and which marks (26a) and (26c) as ungrammatical. However, it also marks (26b) and (26d) as ungrammatical without explaining their acceptability. This is explained by the fact that strategy (22a) can easily misapply to such sequences. An initial stage in perceptual processing is to assign lexical class information to the sequence and then to use such strategies as those in (22a) to find potential internal relations for such a sequence. Suppose that in the initial lexical-class analysis of the sentence like (26b) the *un+adj* is treated as a sequence like *adv#adj* in which the *adj* is a separate lexical item; then strategy (22a) would treat the sequence in (26b) roughly like that in (29a), and lead to a similar interpretation for it. Thus the acceptability of (26b) and (26d) is accounted for as due to miscategorizing the *un* and *adj* as separate words. However, the initial miscategorization of un+adj as *adv#adj* is only likely to occur *insofar as the non-negated form of the adjective itself is recognizable in that environment as a separate word with a relevant meaning.* This is just what conditions (27a,b,c) spell out. Thus, we can not only account for the acceptability of such cases by treating them as ungrammatical but acceptable, we can in fact *explain* why the restrictions on acceptability are the way they are.

Such examples demonstrate the way in which the structuralist program for the description of language is evolving. By treating acceptability phenomena as due to the interaction of grammar and other systems of linguistic knowledge we can limit the formal power of each system. A concept like "grammaticality" is thus a *technical* term which refers to a particular formal property that a grammar may assign to a sequence. The role of "grammaticality" in "acceptability" is itself a function of the interaction of the sequence's grammatical status with other systematic attributes, e.g. the sequence's "perceptability." Such theories and their interactions allow us to return to the basic acceptability intuitions and parcel out the different systems of linguistic knowledge that underlie each judgment.

In this discussion I have concentrated on the interaction of grammar with the perceptual system because the latter has received the most independent attention in modern psycholinguistics. However, it is clear that other systems of linguistic knowledge also influence the judgments about sentence acceptability. For example, the unacceptability of (30) is based on an apparent contradiction due to the fact that statements imply intrinsically that they are believed.

(30) Harry is smart but I don't believe it

(31) is a literal request for information that is interpretable as a request for action due to knowledge about conversational interactions.

(31) Why don't you shut the door?

(32) is odd due to knowledge of cultural stereotypes.

(32) Most stewardesses are ugly.

In each case a nongrammatical system (logic, conversational systems, cultural stereotypes) accounts for the facts. This renders the universal grammar free of having to provide the formal mechanisms to account for such phenomena. Each system of knowledge is maximally simplified by this approach—superficially complex behavioral phenomena are interpreted as due to the interaction of different underlying systems of knowledge.

Researchers in most empirical sciences are familiar with such a methodology—for example, simplicity of gravitational description is maintained if the forces of gravity on an object are viewed as interacting with friction between that object and others—in this way effects due to friction are parceled out, and the concept of gravitational force is left uncomplicated and statable. In the case of linguistic science, keeping the formalisms in a grammar as constrained and uncomplicated as possible is not merely a matter of scientific elegance. The more limited such formalisms are the more precise are the claims they make about what the child must extract from his/her environment. Consequently, the stronger are the claims made about constraints on the possible hypotheses the child makes about the structure of the world.

This point brings the discussion back to the bearing of the study of language on theories of knowledge. We began with the relatively simple desire to embed such distinctions as the analytic/synthetic one in a broader range of data in order to strengthen the empirical base for those distinctions which falsify an empiricist theory of knowledge. In the attempt to do this we have found that first we need a theory of reference, since that is the common use to which meaning is put. Sentences appear to be the normal vehicle for reference, so we need a theory of what sentences are (e.g., a grammar); and then a set of theories as to how sentences are used (e.g., a perceptual model). Furthermore, we find that these systems interact in the generation of actual data.

Thus, as the structuralist theory of language description develops and expands its empirical support, two problems for an empiricist theory of knowledge are emerging. First, we may succeed in embedding such distinctions as the analytic/synthetic one in the explanation of such a wide variety of phenomena that its existence cannot be denied. Second, in the course of doing that, we are also demonstrating the empirical validity of the claim that behavior is itself the result of categorically distinct systems of knowledge.

Since this internal differentiation of the sources of behavior is not explicitly displayed for the child, the fact that it is learned constitutes a separate challenge for an empiricist theory of knowledge. It is one thing to emphasize the traditional nativist point that children conceptualize the world in terms of categorical distinctions the external world does not offer. What we can now ask further is why do children parcel out superficially continuous behaviors that adults display to different systems of knowledge; why are these skills acquired in partial separation from each other? Could it be that children simply know *instinctively* what to do?

BIBLIOGRAPHY

BEVER, T. G. "A Survey of Some Recent Work in Psycholinguistics." In W. J. Plath (Ed.), *Specification and Utilization of a Transformational Grammar.* (Contract AF 19(628)-5127), Bedford, Mass.: I.B.M. Corp., 1968.

———. "The Cognitive Basis for Linguistic Structures." In J. R. Hayes (Ed.), *Cognition and the Development of Language,* New York: Wiley & Sons, 1970.

CHOMSKY, N. *Syntactic Structures.* The Hague, Netherlands: Mouton & Co., 1957.

FODOR, J., BEVER, T. G., and GARRETT, M. *The Psychology of Language: Psycholinguistics and Generative Grammar,* New York: McGraw-Hill, in press.

LANGENDOEN, T. and BEVER, T. G. "Can a Not Unhappy Person be Called a Not Sad One." to appear in S. Anderson and P. Kiparsky (Eds.), *A Festschrift for Morris Halle,* New York: Holt, Rinehart & Winston, 1973.

KATZ, J. J. *Semantic Theory,* New York: Harper & Row, 1972.

KATZ, J. J., and BEVER, T. G. "The Fall and Rise of Empiricism." In T. G. Bever, J. J. Katz, and D. T. Langendoen (Eds.), *Integrated Theory of Linguistic Skill,* Chandler Press (in press).

MILLER, G. A. *Language and Communication.* New York: McGraw-Hill, 1951.

———. *The Psychology of Communication: Seven Essays.* New York: Basic Books, 1967.

Excerpts from *Constraints on Variables in Syntax**

JOHN ROBERT ROSS

2.0.   In a paper written for the 1962 Ninth International Congress of Linguists, "The logical basis of linguistic theory" on pp. 930–31, while discussing the relative clause transformation and the question transformation, Chomsky makes the following statement:

> The same point can be illustrated by an example of a rather different sort. Consider the sentences:
>
> (6) (i)   who(m) did Mary see walking toward the railroad station?
>   (ii) do you know the boy who(m) Mary saw walking to the railroad station?
>
> (7) Mary saw the boy walking toward the railroad station.
>
> (7) is multiply ambiguous; in particular it can have either the syntactic analysis (8i) or (8ii)
>
> (8) (i)   NP – Verb – NP – Complement
>   (ii) NP – Verb – NP
>
> where the second NP in (8ii) consists of a NP ("the boy") with a restrictive relative clause. The interpretation (8ii) is forced if we add "who was" after "boy" in (7); the interpretation (8i) is forced if we delete "ing" in (7). But (6i,6ii) are not subject to this ambiguity; the interpretation (8ii) is ruled out, in these cases. Once again, these are facts that a grammar would have to state to achieve descriptive adequacy. (Notice that there is a further ambiguity, where "Mary" is taken as the subject of "walk," but this is not relevant to the present discussion.)
>
> The problem of explanatory adequacy is, again, that of finding a principled basis for the factually correct description. Consider how (6i) and (6ii) must be generated in a transformational grammar for English. Each must be formed by transformation from a terminal string S underlying (7). In each case, a transformation applies to S which selects the second NP, moves it to the front of the string

* I have excerpted these passages from John Robert Ross, *Constraints on Variables in Syntax*. (MIT dissertation, 1967; Copyright © John Robert Ross. All rights reserved.) I hope that this important work will eventually be published in its entirety. G. H.

S, and replaces it by a wh-form. But in the case of (7) with the structural description (8ii), this specification is ambiguous, since we must determine whether the second NP—the one to be prefixed—is "the boy" or "the boy walking to the railroad station," each of which is an NP. Since transformations must be unambiguous, this matter must be resolved in the general theory. The natural way to resolve it is by a general requirement that the dominating, rather than the dominated, element must always be selected in such a case. This general condition, when appropriately formalized, might then be proposed as a hypothetical linguistic universal. What it asserts is that if the phrase X of category A is embedded within a larger phrase ZXW which is also of category A, then no rule applying to the category A applies to X (but only to ZXW).

It is the principle stated in this last sentence which I will refer to as *the A-over-A principle.* In terms of tree diagram (2.1), the principle asserts that all transformations which refer to A must apply to the topmost instance of A in (2.1), not the dominated A, which I have circled.

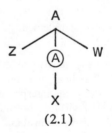

(2.1)

2.1.   Chomsky, in the course of revising the paper quoted above for separate publication as the monograph *Current Issues in Linguistic Theory,* realized that the A-over-A principle was too strong. On page 46, in footnote 10, he gives the examples "who would you approve of my seeing?" "what are you uncertain about giving to John?" and "what would you be surprised by his reading?" where in each case the question word, *who* or *what,* itself an NP, has been moved out of another NP ($[_{NP}$ *my seeing something*], $[_{NP}$ *giving something to John*], $[_{NP}$ *his reading something*]). Other examples of this sort are not difficult to construct, and there are even cases where the relative clause transformation can move either a dominated NP or any one of an unbounded number of NP's which dominate it.

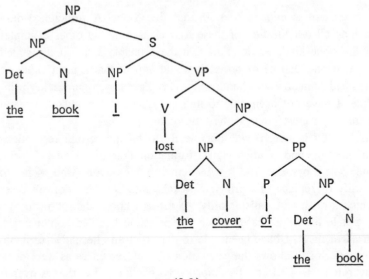

(2.2)

The relative clause rule, when applied to (2.2), will produce either *the book, the cover of which I lost,* or *the book which I lost the cover of,* the second of which would be ruled out by the A-over-A principle. The example can be made more complicated by embedding the NP in ever larger NPs, and as far as I know, this process can be repeated without limit. Thus if the structure underlying (2.3)

(2.3)   The government prescribes the height of the lettering on the covers of the reports.

is embedded as a relative clause into an NP whose head noun is *reports,* the relative clause rule must produce (at least) four relative clauses: *the reports, the height of the lettering on the covers of which the government prescribes; the reports, the lettering on the covers of which the government prescribes the height of; the reports, the covers of which the government prescribes the height of the lettering on; and the reports which the government prescribes the height of the lettering on the covers of.* The problem of how to formulate the relative clause rule so that it will produce all four of these is an important and difficult one which I will discuss in some detail later (cf. § 4.3 below); but for the purposes of the present discussion it is enough to note that the A-over-A principle would exclude all but the first of these four clauses. Many other examples of the same kind, which show that the principle as originally stated is too strong, can be found, so it would appear that it must either be modified somehow, or abandoned and replaced by some weaker principle. I have not been able to find any successful modification, and therefore, I have pursued the latter course.

2.2.   Of course, it was not merely to handle certain restrictions on question and relative clause formation that the A-over-A principle was proposed. And it is incumbent upon anyone who wishes to modify or replace this principle to take into consideration all cases which it dealt with satisfactorily. As far as I know, the following is a complete list of all cases which the principle handled convincingly. In all of these, I have been able to construct an alternative explanation which still allows the generation of such sentences as were demonstrated in § 2.1 to be improperly excluded by the A-over-A principle. For ease of reference, I will repeat here several examples which I have already discussed, so that all cases which seem to support the A-over-A principle are grouped together.

A.   Elements of relative clauses may not be questioned or relativized. Thus, the sentence *I chased* [NP *the boy who threw* [NP *a snowball*] *at our teacher*] can never be embedded as a relative clause in an NP whose head noun is *snowball:* sentence (2.4) is ungrammatical.

(2.4)   *Here is the snowball which I chased the boy who threw at our teacher.

It is easy to see how the A-over-A principle would exclude this: in the source sentence the NP *a snowball* is embedded within a larger NP *the boy who threw a snowball at our teacher,* and the principle dictates that only dominating, not dominated, nodes can be affected by the operation of a rule.

This restriction also applies to elements of reduced relative clauses (i.e., those in which the initial *which is* has been deleted): the NP *bikinis* is impossible to question or relativize in the following sentence: *she reported* [NP *all the girls wearing* [NP *bikinis*]] *to the police.* Thus the following question is impossible:

(2.5) *Which bikinis did she report all the girls wearing to the police?

B. Elements of sentences in apposition to such sentential nouns as *fact, idea, doubt, question,* etc., cannot be questioned or relativized. Thus the sentence *Tom mentioned* [$_{NP}$ *the fact that she had worn* [$_{NP}$ *a bikini.*]] cannot be embedded as a relative clause into an NP whose head noun is *bikini:* sentence (2.6) is ungrammatical:

(2.6) *Where's the bikini which Tom mentioned the fact that Sue had worn?

Once again, it is easy to see how the A-over-A principle can be made use of in excluding this sentence.

C. An extraposed clause may never be moved outside "The first sentence up," as was discussed briefly in § 1.0 [not reprinted here]. Assuming that an approximately correct formulation of the rule for Extraposition from NP is

<u>Extraposition from NP</u>

$$X - \underbrace{[NP - S]}_{NP} - Y \quad \text{OPT}$$

$$\begin{array}{cccc} 1 & 2 & 3 & \Longrightarrow \\ 1 & 0 & 3+2 & \end{array}$$

(1.10)

we see that unless it is somehow restricted, it will have two results when it is applied on the topmost cycle of the structure shown in (2.7).

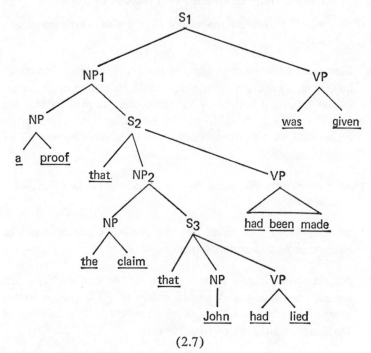

(2.7)

Either S_2 (the subscripts have no systematic significance and are merely inserted as an aid to exposition) could be moved to the end of S_1, which would yield the grammatical sentence (2.8),

(2.8)   A proof was given that the claim that John had lied had been made.

or S_3 could be moved to the end of S_1, which would result in the ungrammatical (2.9),

(2.9)   *A proof that the claim had been made was given that John had lied.

Sentences like (2.9) could be avoided if the A-over-A principle was strengthened somewhat so that if a P-Marker had two proper analyses with respect to the structural index of some transformation, where one proper analysis "dominated" the other, in a sense which is intuitively fairly clear but would probably be difficult to state formally, then the transformation in question would only perform the operations specified in its structural change with respect to the "dominating" proper analysis. Begging the question of how these notions could be made precise, it should be clear that the sequence of nodes [NP S]$_{NP}$ which is immediately dominated by NP$_1$ in (2.7) "dominates," in the intended sense, the sequence of nodes [NP S]$_{NP}$ which is immediately dominated by NP$_2$; so Extraposition from NP could not produce (2.9) from (2.7), if the strengthened version of the A-over-A principle which was sketched immediately above were adopted.

D. In a relative clause structure, , it is not possible to question or relativize the dominated NP^1. This is the case discussed by Chomsky in the passage quoted in § 2.0 above. An example of the kind of sentence that must be excluded is the following: it is not possible to question (2.10) by moving *someone* to the front of the sentence and leaving the relative clause *who I was acquainted with* behind.

(2.10)   He expected [[someone]$_{NP}$ who I was acquainted with]$_{NP}$ to show up.

Thus (2.11) is ungrammatical:

(2.11)   *Who did he expect who I was acquainted with to show up?

In (2.10), if the NP *someone* is to be questioned, the whole NP which dominates it, *someone who I was acquainted with,* must be moved forward with it, yielding (2.12), or, by later extraposition, (2.13)

(2.12)   Who who I was acquainted with did he expect to show up?
(2.13)   Who did he expect to show up who I was acquainted with?

It should be obvious how the A-over-A principle would exclude (2.11).

E. A NP which is exhaustively dominated by a Determiner cannot be questioned or relativized out of the NP which immediately dominates that Determiner. Thus, from (2.14) it is impossible to form (2.15):

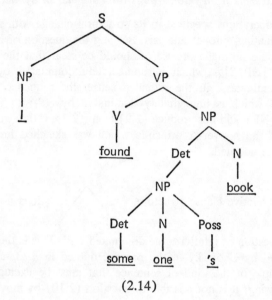

(2.14)

(2.15) *Whose did you find book?

Only (2.16) is possible:

(2.16)   Whose book did you find?

and the A-over-A principle correctly makes this assertion.

F.   An NP which is a conjunct in a coordinate NP structure cannot
     be questioned or relativized. Thus, in (2.17), neither of the
     conjoined NP's may be questioned—(2.18) and (2.19) are both
     impossible.

(2.17)   He will put the chair between$_{NP}$[$_{NP}$[some table]$_{NP}$ and
         [$_{NP}$ some sofa]$_{NP}$]$_{NP}$.
(2.18) *What sofa will he put the chair between some table and?
(2.19) *What table will he put the chair between and some sofa?

Once again, the A-over-A principle will exclude these last two
sentences.

4.1.   *The Complex NP Constraint*
4.1.1.   It is to Edward S. Klima that the essential insight underlying my formulation of this constraint is due. Noticing that the NP

that man could be questioned in (4.3b), but not in (4.3a) (cf. (4.4)), Klima proposed the constraint stated in (4.5):

(4.3) a. I read a statement which was about that man.
　　　 b. I read a statement about that man.
(4.4) a. *The man who I read a statement which was about is sick.
　　　 b. The man who I read a statement about is sick.
(4.5) 　　 Elements dominated by a sentence which is dominated by a noun phrase cannot be questioned or relativized.

If Klima's constraint is used in conjunction with the principle for S-deletion stated in (3.6),

(3.6) *S-pruning:* delete any embedded node S which does not branch (i.e. which does not immediately dominate at least two nodes).

it can explain the difference in grammaticality between (4.4a) and (4.4b), for it is only in (4.3a) that the NP *that man* is contained in a sentence which is itself contained in an NP: when (4.3a) is converted into (4.4b) by the Relative Clause Reduction Rule, the node S which dominates the clause *which was about that man* in (4.3a) is pruned by (3.6).

Although I do not believe it is possible to maintain (4.5), for reasons I will present immediately below, it will be seen that my final formulation of the Complex NP Constraint makes crucial use of the central idea in Klima's formulation: the idea that node deletion affects the potential of constituents to undergo reordering transformations. This hypothesis may seem obvious, at the present stage of development of the theory of grammar, but when Klima first suggested it, when the theory of tree-pruning was much less well-developed than it is at present, it was far from being obvious. In fact, this idea is really the cornerstone of my research on variables.

4.1.2.　　 As I intimated above, however, I find that (4.5) must be rejected, in its present form. For consider the NP *that man* in (4.6): as (4.7) shows, it is relativizable,

(4.6) I read $\left[\,_{NP}[\,_{S}\text{that}\right.$ the police were going to interrogate that man$]_S\left.\right]_{NP}$.
(4.7) the man who I read that the police were going to interrogate

and yet the *that*-clause which contains it would seem to be a noun phrase, as I have indicated in the bracketing of (4.6). Presumably, the approximate deep structure of (4.6) is that shown in (4.8),

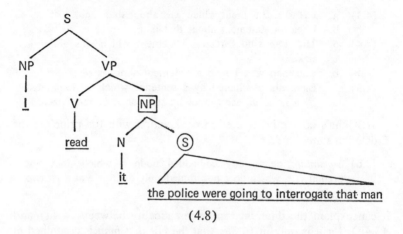

$$(4.8)$$

and unless some way is found of pruning the circled node S or the boxed node NP in (4.8), condition (4.5) will prevent the relativization of *that man*. There is abundant evidence that the first alternative is not feasible:

(4.9)   a.   I read that Bill had seen me.
         b.   *I read that Bill had seen myself.
(4.10)   a.   Evidence that he was drunk will be presented.
         b.   Evidence will be presented that he was drunk.
(4.11)   a.   That Bill$_i$ was unpopular distressed him$_i$.
         b.   That he$_i$ was unpopular distressed Bill$_i$.

The Reflexivization Rule does not "go down into" sentences; thus the fact that (4.9a) is grammatical, while (4.9b) is not, is evidence that *that*-clauses are dominated by S at the time that reflexivization takes place. Similarly, the fact that *that*-clauses may be extraposed, as is the case in (4.10b), indicates that they are dominated by the node S at the time that this rule applies. Finally, the fact that backward pronominalization into *that*-clauses is possible (cf. (4.11a)) also argues that they must be dominated by the node S. So it seems implausible that the circled node S should be deleted by some principle which supplements (3.6), and there is no independent support for such an additional pruning principle in any case. Therefore, the only other way to save (4.5) is to claim that the boxed node NP must be deleted in the process of converting (4.8) into the surface structure which underlies (4.6).

Can the node NP be deleted? In § 3.2 [not reprinted here], I discussed briefly Kuroda's proposal to generalize the notion of tree-pruning in such a way that any non-branching node whose head had been deleted would be pruned. While it is *possible* to propose such a generalized version of (3.6), there is as yet no syntactic evidence which indicates that node deletion *must* prune out occurrences of NP or VP. The complex problems involving case-marking with respect to *amici* and *eius* on the one hand and *meus* on the other, which I discussed in § 3.1.3 [not reprinted here], might be solvable if use were made of some principle of NP deletion, but this has yet to be worked out in detail; and unless some other evidence can be found for NP pruning, invoking it to delete the boxed NP in (4.8) is merely *ad hoc*. For there are many pieces of evidence which show that *that*-clauses are dominated by NP at some point in their derivation.

(4.12) a. That the defendant had been rude was stoutly denied by his lawyer.
        b. What I said was that she was lying.
        c. Bill told me something awful: that ice won't sink.
        d. Muriel said nothing else than that she had been insulted.

That-clauses passivize (4.12a), they occur after the copula in pseudo-cleft sentences (4.12b), after the colon in equative sentences (4.12c), and after *than* in sentences like (4.12d): in all of these contexts, phrases can occur which are unquestionably noun phrases (e.g., *Little Willy, potatoes, flying planes*, etc.), and Lakoff and I argue that the syntactic environments defined by (4.12) can only be filled with noun phrases. If our arguments are correct, then *that*-clauses must be dominated by NP at some stage of their derivation. But it might be claimed that the late rule of *It* Deletion, which deletes the abstract pronoun *it* when it immediately precedes a sentence, could change phrase markers in such a way that the NP node which dominated *it S* would undergo pruning before Question and Relative Clause Formation had applied. Not enough is known about rule ordering at present for this possibility to be excluded, but it should be noted that even if it should prove to be possible to order *It* Deletion before all reordering transformations, thereby accounting for the grammaticality of (4.7) by providing for the deletion of the boxed NP of (4.8), it would still be necessary to explain why there is no difference in grammaticality between (4.13a) and (4.13b),

(4.13) a. This is a hat which I'm going to see to it that my wife buys.
        b. This is a hat which I'm going to see that my wife buys.

After the verb *see* (*to*), the deletion of *it* is optional (in my dialect), and therefore, by the previous argument, while the *that*-clause in (4.13b) might not be dominated by NP, the *that*-clause in (4.13a) still would be. So unless some additional convention for NP pruning could be devised for this case too, (4.5) would not allow the generation of (4.13a). Again, I must reiterate that there is no known evidence for pruning NP under any other circumstances, so the *ad hoc* character of the explanation which is necessitated if (4.5) is adopted is readily apparent.

But there is an even more compelling reason to reject (4.5) than the ones above: as I pointed out in § 2.4.1 above, it is in general the case that elements of reduced relative clauses and elements of full relative clauses behave exactly the same with respect to reordering transformations. This can be seen from the following examples: NP's which are in the same position as *Maxime* in the sentences of (4.14) cannot be questioned (cf. the ungrammaticality of (4.15)),

(4.14) a. Phineas knows a girl who is jealous of Maxime.
        b. Phineas knows a girl who is behind Maxime.
        c. Phineas knows a girl who is working with Maxime.
(4.15) a. *Who does Phineas know a girl who is jealous of?
        b. *Who does Phineas know a girl who is behind?
        c. *Who does Phineas know a girl who is working with?

nor is this possible even after the relative clauses of (4.14) have been reduced (this is evidenced by the ungrammaticality of (4.16)).

(4.16) a. *Who does Phineas know a girl jealous of?
        b. *Who does Phineas know a girl behind?
        c. *Who does Phineas know a girl working with?

It was facts like these which motivated the condition stated in (2.26) above, which I repeat for convenience here.

(2.26)   No element of a constituent of an NP which modifies the head noun may be questioned or relativized.

In light of the facts of (4.15) and (4.16), it would appear that it is the grammaticality of (4.4b) which is problematic, not the ungrammaticality of the sentences in (4.16). And there are parallel facts which have to do with Reflexivization, which I will present in § 4.1.6 below, which also support this interpretation. So condition (4.5), which takes the differences between the sentences in (4.4) to be typical, would seem to be a projection to an incorrect general conclusion from a case where special circumstances obtain. In the next section, I will give some evidence which allows the formulation of a broader-based generalization.

4.1.3.   The sentences of (4.17), which only differ in that the NP object of *believe* has a lexical head noun in the first, but not in the second, differ as to relativizability, as the corresponding sentences of (4.18) show.

(4.17) a.   I believed the claim that Otto was wearing this hat.
         b.   I believed that Otto was wearing this hat.
(4.18) a. *The hat which I believed the claim that Otto was wearing is red.
         b.   The hat which I believed that Otto was wearing is red.

If the analysis proposed by Lakoff and me is correct, the d.c.s. of (4.17a) will be roughly that shown in (4.19):

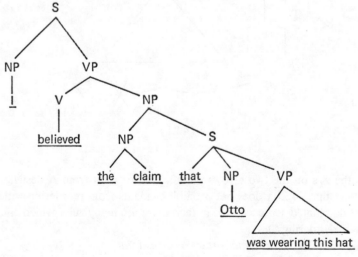

(4.19)

Whether or not we can show it to be correct that abstract nouns followed by sentential clauses in apposition to them have exactly the same $[NP-S]_{NP}$ structure that we argue relative clauses have, it is clear that these constructions are highly similar. Condition (4.20), the Complex NP Constraint, is formulated in an effort to exploit this similarity, to explain the ungrammaticality of sentences like (4.18a) and (4.15) on the same basis.

(4.20)   *The Complex NP Constraint*
No element contained in a sentence dominated by a noun phrase with a lexical head noun may be moved out of that noun phrase by a transformation.

To put it diagrammatically, (4.20) prevents any constituent A from being reordered out of the S in constituents like the NP shown in (4.21),

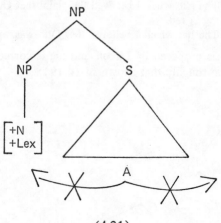

(4.21)

as the X's on the two arrows pointing left or right from A designate. (Note that (4.20) does not prohibit elements from reordering within the dominated sentence, and in fact, there are many rules which effect such reorderings.)

4.2.   *The Coordinate Structure Constraint*

4.2.1.   In § 2.2, in Case F, it was pointed out that conjoined NP's cannot be questioned: this was attested to by the ungrammaticality of (2.18) and (2.19), which I repeat here for convenience.

(2.18) *What sofa will he put the chair between some table and?
(2.19) *What table will he put the chair between and some sofa?

The impossibility of questioning the circled NP nodes in diagram (4.79) can be successfully accounted for by invoking the A-over-A principle,

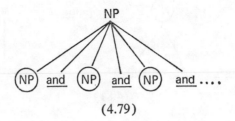

(4.79)

but this principle does not prevent the circled NP nodes in diagrams (4.80) or (4.81) from being questioned or relativized.

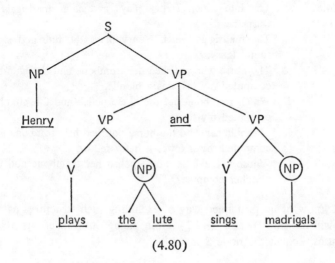

(4.80)

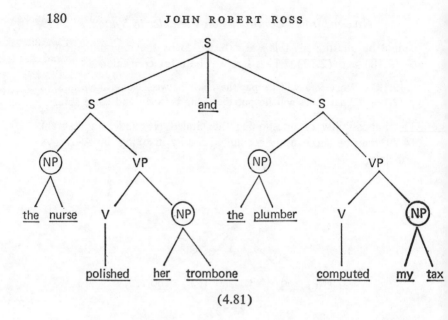

(4.81)

But all of the circled nodes must somehow be restricted from being moved, as the ungrammatical sentences of (4.82) show.

(4.82) a. *The lute which Henry plays and sings madrigals is warped.
        b. *The madrigals which Henry plays the lute and sings sound lousy.
        c. *The nurse who polished her trombone and the plumber computed my tax was a blonde.
        d. *Which trombone did the nurse polish and the plumber computed my tax?
        e. *The plumber who the nurse polished her trombone and computed my tax was a hefty fellow.
        f. *Whose tax did the nurse polish her trombone and the plumber compute?

I know of no principled way of excluding such structures as those shown in (4.80) and (4.81) from being introduced as relative clauses, i.e., at the node S in (4.83),

(4.83)

so it appears to be necessary to add the following constraint to the meta-theory:

(4.84) *The Coordinate Structure Constraint*
In a coordinate structure, no conjunct may be moved, nor may any element contained in a conjunct be moved out of that conjunct.

4.3. *The Pied Piping Convention*

4.3.1. In this section, I will suggest a constraint which can successfully account for the evidence for the A-over-A principle which was presented in case D and case E of § 2.2, and a convention which will provide for the generation of all the relative clauses in the sentences of (4.163). These must all be derived from (4.162), the approximate structure of sentence (2.3), which I have repeated here, for convenience.

(2.3) The government prescribes the height of the lettering on the covers of the reports.

(4.163) a. Reports which the government prescribes the height of the lettering on the covers of are invariably boring.
b. Reports the covers of which the government prescribes the height of the lettering on almost always put me to sleep.
c. Reports the lettering on the covers of which the government prescribes the height of are a shocking waste of public funds.
d. Reports the height of the lettering on the covers of which the government prescribes should be abolished.

It can be seen that if the structure in (4.162) were embedded as a relative clause modifier in a noun phrase whose head noun is *report,* the rule of Relative Clause Formation, as it is stated in (4.135), would only produce the relative clause in (4.163a). If an attempt were made to modify the structural index of (4.135) in such a way

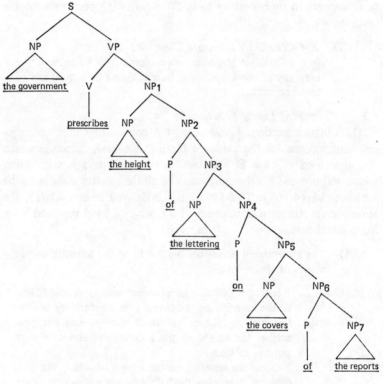

(4.162)

that the new rule would derive either (4.163a) or (4.163b) from (4.162), the revised rule would be that shown in (4.164):

(4.164)

$$W -\left[_{NP}NP - [_sX - \left\{\begin{array}{c} \phi \quad -NP \\ [_{NP}NP\ P - NP]_{NP} \end{array}\right\} - Y]_s\right]_{NP} -Z$$

						OBLIG
1	2	3	4	5	6	7 $\Longrightarrow$
1	2[45]#[3		0	0	6]	7

Condition: 2 = 5

To derive the relative clause in (4.163c), the further complication of the rule shown in (4.165) would be necessary,

(4.165)

$$W -\left[_{NP}NP - [_sX - \left\{\begin{array}{c} \phi \quad -NP \\ [_{NP}NP\ P - NP] \\ [_{NP}NP\ P[_{NP}NP\ P - NP]] \end{array}\right\} - Y]_s\right]_{NP} -Z$$

						OBLIG
1	2	3	4	5	6	7 $\Longrightarrow$
1	2[4 5]#[3		0	0	6]	7

Condition: 2 = 5

and deriving the clause in (4.163d) would entail adding a fourth line to the disjunction inside the braces in (4.165). But since there is no upper bound on the length of a branch consisting entirely of NPs, like NP_1–NP_7 in (4.162), in order to give a finite formulation of this rule, which must be able to generate clauses like those of (4.163) to any desired degree of complexity, either some abbreviatory notation, under which the sequences of terms within the parentheses of (4.164), (4.165), etc. can be collapsed, must be added to the theory of grammar, or some special convention must be. Of these two, the latter is weaker, for to add a new abbreviatory notation to the theory is to make the claim that there are other cases, unrelated to the case at hand, where rules must be collapsed according to the new notation. No such cases exist, to my knowledge, so I propose the convention given in (4.166) as a first approximation to an appropriate universal convention.

(4.166)   Any transformation which is stated in such a way as to effect the reordering of some specified node NP, where this node is preceded and followed by variables, can reorder this NP or any NP which dominates it.

By the term "specified" in (4.166), I mean that node NP, in a branch containing many NP nodes, which is singled out from all other nodes on this branch by virtue of some added condition on the rule in question (such as the condition on the rule of Relative Clause Formation that the NP to be relativized be identical to the NP which the clause modifies, or the condition on the rule of Question that the questioned NP dominate WH+*some*). This convention, then, provides that any reordering transformation which is stated as operating on some NP singled out in some such way may instead operate on any higher NP. Thus the formulation of Relative Clause Formation which was given in (4.135), when supplemented by (4.166), will allow for the adjoining to the front of the sentence of the specified NP_7, *the reports,* or NP_6, *of the reports,* or NP_5, *the covers of the reports,* etc., so that all of the clauses in (4.163) will be generated. That (4.166) is too strong, in that it does not exclude the ungrammatical sentences of (4.167) need not concern us here;

(4.167)   a. *Reports of which the government prescribes the height of the lettering on the covers are invariably boring.

          b. *Reports on the covers of which the government prescribes the height of the lettering almost always put me to sleep.

          c. *Reports of the lettering on the covers of which the government prescribes the height are shocking waste of public funds.

there seems to be a constraint, in my dialect at least, which prohibits noun phrases which start with prepositions from being relativized

and questioned when these directly follow the NP they modify. Thus
(4.168) can be questioned to form (4.169a), but not (4.169b).

(4.168)   He has books by several Greek authors.
(4.169) a.   Which Greek authors does he have books by?
         b. ?*By which Greek authors does he have books?

I will not attempt a more precise formulation of this restriction here:
instead, I will point out two further inadequacies in the formulation
of (4.166).

Firstly, if the structure shown in (4.170) were to be embedded as
a relative clause on an NP whose head noun were *the boy,*

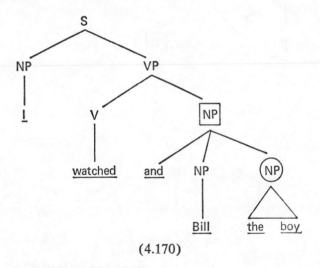

(4.170)

the Coordinate Structure Constraint would not allow the formation
of (4.171):

(4.171) *The boy who I watched Bill and was vain.

However, the circled node NP is dominated by the boxed node NP,
and convention (4.166) would allow this higher node to be preposed,
which would result in the ungrammatical (4.172).

(4.172) *The boy Bill and who(m) I watched was vain.

The ungrammaticality of this sentence indicates the necessity of revising (4.166) in such a way that if an NP dominating the specified

NP is coordinate, neither it nor any higher NP can be moved. I will incorporate such a revision into the final version of the convention, which will be stated in (4.180).

The second inadequacy of (4.166) can be seen in connection with P-marker (4.173)

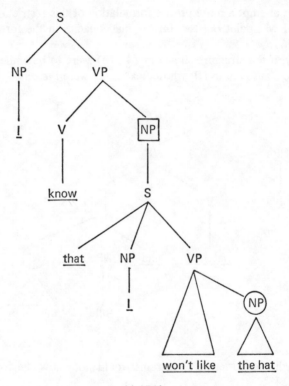

(4.173)

while it is true that the circled node NP can be relativized, as (4.174) shows,

(4.174)   They will give me a hat which I know that I won't like.

once again, (4.166) would allow the preposing of the boxed node NP, and the ungrammatical (4.175) would be produced.

(4.175)   *They will give me a hat that I won't like which I know.

The modification of (4.166) that seems to be required here is that if a branch of a P-marker has an occurrence of the node S intervening between two occurrences of the node NP, only the lower one can be reordered. This restriction does not extend to the node VP, however, as can be seen from the following example.

The approximate structure of the German sentence in (4.176) is that shown in (4.177).

(4.176) Ich habe den Hund zu finden zu versuchen angefangen.
         I   have the dog to find   to try   begun
         "I have begun to try to find the dog."

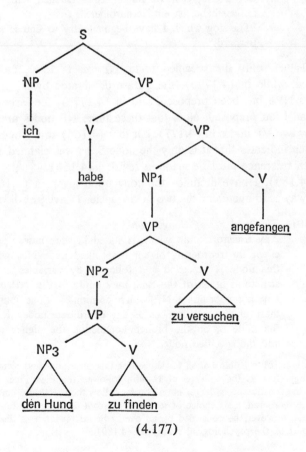

(4.177)

If the structure which underlies (4.177) has been embedded as a relative clause on the subject NP of the structure underlying (4.178),

(4.178)   Der Hund ist ein Bernardiner.
          "The dog   is a   St. Bernard."

the rule of Relative Clause Formation must produce all three of the clauses in the sentences of (4.179).

(4.179) a. Der Hund, den ich zu finden zu versuchen ange-
            fangen habe, ist ein Bernardiner.
        b. Der Hund, den zu finden ich zu versuchen ange-
            fangen habe, ist ein Bernardiner.
        c. Der Hund, den zu finden zu versuchen ich ange-
            fangen habe, ist ein Bernardiner.
            "The dog which I have begun to try to find is a St.
            Bernard."

In (4.179a), only the specified node, NP_3 in (4.177), has been preposed, while in (4.179b), the phrase dominated by NP_2, which contains NP_3, has been preposed, and in (4.177c), the largest NP, NP_1, had been preposed. Note that these three NP nodes are separated by two VP nodes in (4.177), but that (4.166) still is operative. This then indicates that it is only the node S, as was claimed above, to which reference must be made in revising (4.166).

In (4.180), I have modified the convention given in (4.166) in such a way as to overcome the two inadequacies I have just discussed.

(4.180) *The Pied Piping Convention*[1]
         Any transformation which is stated in such a way as to
         effect the reordering of some specified node NP, where
         this node is preceded and followed by variables in the
         structural index of the rule, may apply to this NP or to
         any non-coordinate NP which dominates it, as long as
         there are no occurrences of any coordinate node, nor of
         the node S, on the branch connecting the higher node
         and the specified node.

[1] I am grateful to Robin Lakoff for suggesting this descriptive and picturesque terminology. Just as the children of Hamlin followed the Pied Piper out of town, so the constituents of larger noun phrases follow the specified noun phrase when it is reordered. This choice of terminology from the realm of fairy tales should not, however, be construed by an overly literal reader as a disclaimer on my part of the psychological reality of (4.180).

4.3.2.0.   The convention stated in (4.180) stipulates that any NP above some specified one may be reordered, instead of the specified one, but there are environments where the lower NP may not be moved, and only some higher one can, consonant with the conditions imposed in (4.180). In other words, pied piping is obligatory in some contexts.[2]

4.3.2.1.   For English, and for many other languages, the following constraint, which has the effect of making pied piping obligatory in the stated environment, obtains:

(4.181)   *The Left Branch Condition*
No NP which is the leftmost constituent of a larger NP can be reordered out of this NP by a transformational rule.

In other words, (4.181) prohibits the NP shown in (4.182) from moving along the paths of either of the arrows.

[NP X]$_{NP}$

(4.182)

This constraint accounts for the following facts: if the structure shown in (4.183) is embedded as a relative clause modifier of a NP whose head noun is *boy,* only one output is possible—(4.184a)

---

[2] There are certain nomenclative *Feinschmeckers* who have taken issue with the formulation of this sentence, pointing out that following the original Pied Piper was obligatory for all the children of the town except one, who was lame, so that the phrase "obligatory pied piping" is a case of terminological coals to Newcastle. These critics suggest that since convention (4.180) describes optional accompaniment, such accompaniment should best be dubbed "fellow traveling," or the like, with the term "pied piping" being reserved for cases of mandatory accompaniment, such as those described below.

While the point they make is valid, I have chosen to disregard it, eschewing an exact parallel to the fairy tale in question in the interests of a less elaborate set of terms.

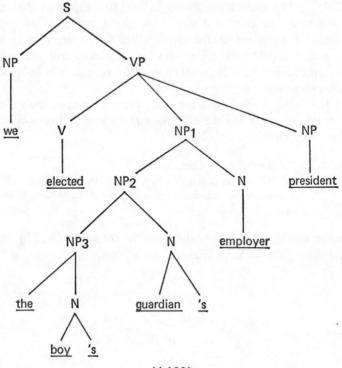

(4.183)

(4.184)   a.   The boy whose guardian's employer we elected president ratted on us.
         b.   *The boy whose guardian's we elected employer president ratted on us.
         c.   *The boy whose we elected guardian's employer president ratted on us.

Sentence (4.184c) is excluded by (4.181), because the rule of Relative Clause Formation has moved the lowest NP, NP₃, from the left branch of NP₁. In (4.184b), it is NP₂ that has been moved from this branch. Since the Left Branch Condition prohibits both of these operations, only the largest NP which (4.180) allows to be moved, NP₁, can be moved to the front of the sentence, and when this happens, (4.184a) is the result.

Parallel facts can be adduced for non-restrictive relative clauses, which differ from restrictives in being preceded and followed by heavy intonation breaks. They derive from coordinate sentences in deep structure, and they are formed by a different rule than (4.135). If commas are inserted into the sentences of (4.184), after *boy* and *investigated,* thus forcing a non-restrictive interpretation of the clauses, their grammaticality is unchanged.

Another rule which is affected by this condition is the rule of Topicalization, (4.185), which converts (4.186a) to (4.186b).

(4.185)

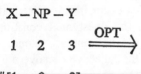

Topicalization

$$X - NP - Y$$

$$1 \quad 2 \quad 3 \overset{OPT}{\Longrightarrow}$$

$$2 \# [1 \quad 0 \quad 3]$$

(4.186) a. I'm going to ask Bill to make the old geezer take up these points later.
b. These points I'm going to ask Bill to make the old geezer take up later.

If rule (4.185) is applied to (4.183), once again it will be seen that only NP_1 can be topicalized, as in (4.187a). If either NP_2 or NP_3 is topicalized, as in (4.187b) and (4.187c), respectively, ungrammatical sentences result.

(4.187) a. The boy's guardian's employer we elected president.
b. *The boy's guardian's we elected employer president.
c. *The boy's we elected guardian's employer president.

A rule that was stated in (3.26), Complex NP Shift, which performs almost the same operation as (4.185), except that it moves the NP in the opposite direction, is also subject to the Left Branch Condition. This rule may apply to (4.183) to move NP_1 over *president* (cf. (4.188a)), but neither NP_2 nor NP_3 can be so moved, as the ungrammaticality of (4.188b) and (4.188c) demonstrates.

(4.188) a. We elected president the boy's guardian's employer.
b. *We elected employer president the boy's guardian's.
c. *We elected guardian's employer president the boy's.

Finally, the Question Rule is subject to the condition: if NP_3 in (4.183) is questioned, it cannot be moved to the front of the sentence alone—pied piping must apply to carry NP$_1$ with it, as (4.189) shows.

(4.189) a. Which boy's guardian's employer did we elect president?

b. *Which boy's guardian's did we elect employer president?

c. *Which boy's did we elect guardian's employer president?

One of the facts which supports the analysis of predicate adjectives which is implicit in diagram (3.25) above is the fact that when adverbs of degree which occur in pre-adjectival or pre-adverbial position are questioned, the questioned constituent, *how,* cannot be moved to the front of the sentence alone, as in (4.190a) and (4.191a), but only if the adjective or adverb is moved with it, as in (4.190b) and (4.191b).

(4.190) a. *How is Peter sane?
         b. How sane is Peter?
(4.191) a. *How have you picked up TNT carelessly?
         b. How carelessly have you picked up TNT?

These facts can be explained by (4.181), if *how* is analyzed as deriving from an underlying NP, and the adjective *sane* and the adverb *carelessly* are dominated by NP at the stage of derivations at which questions are formed. Note also that if the degree adverb *that* in (4.192) is questioned, pied piping must apply to move not only *tall,* but also *a man* to the front of the sentence.

(4.192)   Sheila married that tall a man.
(4.193) a. How tall a man did Sheila marry?
         b. *How tall did Sheila marry a man?
         c. *How did Sheila marry tall a man?

In passing, it should be noted that Case D and Case E of § 2.2, which provide evidence for the A-over-A principle, are special cases of the Left Branch Condition, which will block the derivation of the ungrammatical (2.11) and (2.15).

4.4.   *The Sentential Subject Constraint*

4.4.1.   Compare (4.250a) with its two passives, (4.250b) and (4.250c).

(4.250) a. The reporters expected that the principal would fire some teacher.

  b. That the principal would fire some teacher was ex-
      pected by the reporters.
  c. It was expected by the reporters that the principal
      would fire some teacher.

Noun phrases in the *that*-clauses of (4.250a) and (4.250c) can
be relativized, but not those in the *that*-clause of (4.250b), as
(4.251) shows.

(4.251) a. The teacher who the reporters expected that the prin-
             cipal would fire is a crusty old battle-ax.
         b. *The teacher who that the principal would fire was ex-
             pected by the reporters is a crusty old battle-ax.
         c. The teacher who it was expected by the reporters that
             the principal would fire is a crusty old battle-ax.

How can (4.251b) be blocked? A first approximation would be a
restriction that prevented subconstituents of subject noun phrases
from reordering, while allowing subconstituents of object noun
phrases to do so. But such a restriction would be too strong, as can
be seen from the grammaticality of (4.252).

(4.252) Of which cars were the hoods damaged by the explosion?

The approximate structure of (4.252), at the time when the Question Rule applies, is that shown in (4.253).

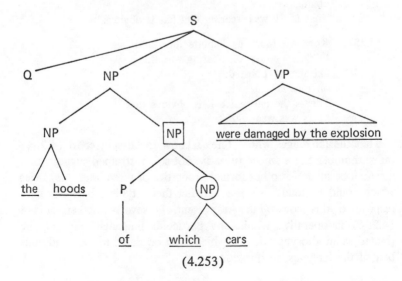

(4.253)

It can be seen that in converting (4.253) to the structure which underlies (4.252), the boxed NP, a subconstituent of the subject of (4.253), has been moved to the front of the sentence, so the suggested restriction is too strong. But there is an obvious difference between (4.252) and the ungrammatical (4.251b): the subject of the latter sentence is a clause, while the subject of the former is only a phrase. The condition stated in (4.254) takes this difference into account.

(4.254)   *The Sentential Subject Constraint*
No element dominated by an S may be moved out of that S if that node S is dominated by an NP which itself is immediately dominated by S.

This constraint, though operative in the grammars of many languages other than English, cannot be stated as a universal, because there are languages whose rules are not subject to it. In Japanese, for instance, although the circled NP in (4.256), which is the approximate structure of (4.255), falls within the scope of (4.254), it can be relativized, as the grammaticality of (4.257) shows.

(4.255)   Mary ga sono boosi o kabutte ita koto
          Mary   that hat   wearing was thing
          ga akiraka da.
          obvious   is
          "That Mary was wearing that hat is obvious."

(4.257)   Kore wa Mary ga kabutte ita koto ga
          this   Mary   wearing was thing
          akiraka na boosi da.
          obvious is hat   is.
          "This is the hat which it is obvious that
          Mary was wearing."

That the languages whose rules I know to be subject to (4.254) far outnumber those whose rules are not so constrained suggests that a search be made for other formal properties of these latter languages which could be made use of to predict their atypical behavior with respect to this constraint. At present, however, whether or not (4.254) is operative within any particular language can only be treated as an idiosyncratic fact which must be stated in the conditions box of the language in question.

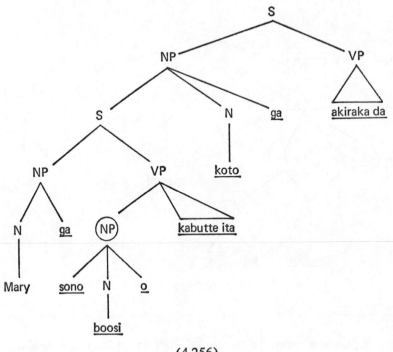

(4.256)

4.4.2. George Lakoff has pointed out to me that on the basis of only the facts considered so far, it would be unnecessary to state the Sentential Subject Constraint, for it is a special case of (3.27), the output condition which makes sentences containing internal [NPS]NP unacceptable. Thus, since (4.251b) contains the internal clause *that the principal would fire,* and since this clause is dominated exhaustively by NP, condition (3.27) would account for its unacceptability. But the two arguments below seem to me only to be accountable for if condition (4.254) is assumed to be operative in the grammar of English.

Firstly, consider sentence (4.258), and its associated constituent structure (4.259).

(4.258)   That I brought this hat seemed strange to the nurse.

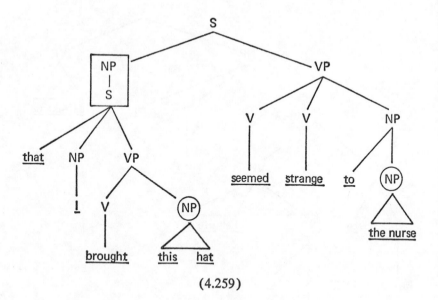

(4.259)

Relativizing either of the circled NP's in (4.259) will produce sentences which are not fully acceptable (cf. (4.260)),

(4.260) a. *The hat which that I brought seemed strange to the nurse was a fedora.

         b. ?The nurse who that I brought this hat seemed strange to was as dumb as a post.

because both relative clauses in (4.260) will contain the boxed NP over S of (4.259) as an internal constituent. Condition (3.27) will be adequate to characterizing both as being unacceptable, but it will not be able to account for the clear difference in status between (4.260a) and (4.260b). The latter sentence is admittedly awkward, but it can be read in such a way as to be comprehensible. The former sentence, however, seems to me to be beyond intonational help. I conclude that (4.260b) should be labeled grammatical but unacceptable, but that (4.260a) must be deemed ungrammatical. To do this, (4.254), or some more general constraint, must be assumed to be operative in English, as well as (3.27).

The second argument for (4.254) concerns the following two sentences:

(4.261) a. I disliked the boy's loud playing of the piano.
            b. I disliked the boy's playing the piano loudly.

Lees gives a number of arguments which show these to be different. I will assume that the derived structure of (4.261a) is that shown in (4.262), and that of (4.261b) is that shown in (4.263).

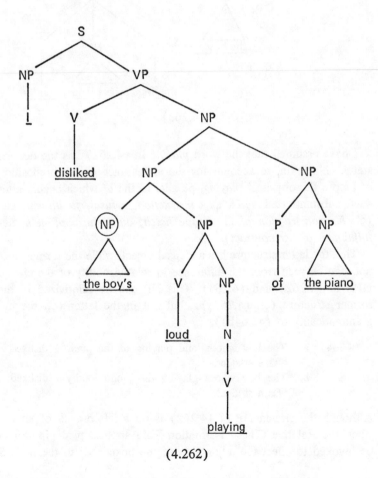

(4.262)

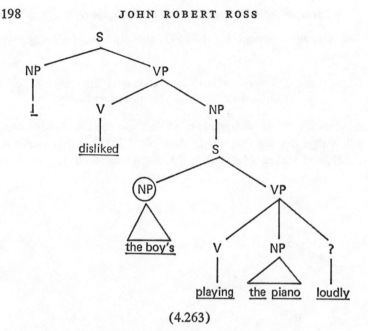

(4.263)

I have assumed that the word *playing* in (4.262) has the derived status of a noun, to account for the appearance of the preposition *of* before the object of *playing,* parallel to the *of* which occurs after such substantivized verbs as *construction, refusal, fulfillment,* etc. (cf. *his construction of an escape hatch, our refusal of help, her fulfillment of her contract*).

That the latter structure has a clausal object, while the former does not, can be seen from the difference in relativizability of the circled NP's in (4.262) and (4.263). This NP can be relativized in the former structure (cf. (4.264a)), but not in the latter (cf. the ungrammaticality of (4.264b)).

(4.264)   a.   The boy whose loud playing of the piano I disliked
              was a student.
          b.   *The boy whose playing the piano loudly I disliked
              was a student.

Although the circled NP of (4.262) is on a left branch of an NP when the Relative Clause Formation Rule applies, pied piping can be invoked to effect the adjunction of the boxed NP to the node S which dominates the clause, so a well-formed relative clause will result.

But in (4.263), if the circled NP is moved, the boxed NP cannot pied pipe, because there is a node S which intervenes between the two NP nodes, and under these conditions, pied piping cannot take place, as was pointed out in § 4.3.1 above.

Note that the object NP of *playing, the piano,* is relativizable in both (4.262) and (4.263).

(4.265)　a. ?The piano which I disliked the boy's loud playing of was badly out of tune.

　　　　　b. The piano which I disliked the boy's playing loudly was badly out of tune.

But if the action nominal or the factive gerund nominal appears in subject position, as in (4.266), the NP *the piano* can only be relativized out of the action nominal as (4.267) shows.

(4.266)　a. The boy's loud playing of the piano drove everyone crazy.

　　　　　b. The boy's playing the piano loudly drove everyone crazy.

(4.267)　a.　That piano,　$\left\{ \begin{array}{l} \text{?which the boy's loud playing of} \\ \text{the boy's loud playing of which} \end{array} \right\}$

drove everyone crazy, was badly out of tune.

　　　　　b.　*That piano,　$\left\{ \begin{array}{l} \text{which the boy's playing loudly} \\ \text{the boy's playing which loudly} \end{array} \right\}$

drove everyone crazy, was badly out of tune.

How can (4.267b) be excluded? The bottom line of (4.267b) can be blocked on the same grounds as (4.264b): since the subject NP of (4.266b) dominates the node S, pied piping cannot take place. But unless (4.454), the Sentential Subject Constraint, is added to the grammar, the top line of (4.267b) will not be excluded. Note that even condition (3.27) cannot be invoked here, because this condition must be reformulated as shown in (4.268).

(4.268)　Grammatical sentences containing an internal NP which exhaustively dominates an S are unacceptable, unless the main verb of that S is a gerund.

This reformulation is necessary in any case, in order to account for the difference in acceptability between (4.269a)–(4.269c) and (4.269d).

(4.269)   a. *Did that he played the piano surprise you?
          b. *Would for him to have played the piano have surprised you?
          c. *Is whether he played the piano known?
          d. Did his having played the piano surprise you?

Thus it appears that there are two reasons for insisting that both (4.268), the revised version of (3.27), and the Sentential Subject Constraint be included in the grammar of English. In the first place, condition (4.268) is not adequate to distinguish between (4.260a) and (4.260b), and in the second, between (4.267a) and (4.267b). These two facts indicate the necessity of adding to the conditions box of English something at least as strong as (4.254).

4.5.   To summarize briefly, in this chapter I have proposed two universal constraints, the Complex NP Constraint and the Coordinate Structure Constraint; also, a universal convention of pied piping; and a variety of language particular constraints, which are to be stated in particular grammars in a conditions box, which the theory of language must be revised to provide. I make no claim to exhaustiveness, and I am sure that the few conditions I have discussed are not only wrong in detail, but in many major ways. Not only must further work be done to find other conditions, but to find broader generalities, so that the structure of whatever interlocking system of conditions eventually proves to be right can be used with maximum effectiveness as a tool for discovering the structure of the brain, where these conditions must somehow be represented.

Review of *Language and Mind**

GILBERT HARMAN

Language and mind. By NOAM CHOMSKY. Enlarged edition. New York: Harcourt Brace Jovanovich, 1972. Pp. xii, 194.

This publication is twice the size of the original edition (Chomsky 1968), which is reprinted with three additional essays and a new preface. One of the new essays is a short, previously unpublished, lecture of 1969, 'Form and meaning in natural language', which is largely concerned with the relevance of surface structure to semantic interpretation. The other two essays have appeared before, 'The formal nature of language' as an appendix to Lenneberg 1967, and 'Linguistics and philosophy' in Hook 1969. There are therefore six chapters, the three essays making up the original *Language and mind* followed by the others in the order mentioned.

I have divided this review into three sections. The first is concerned with an historical question, whether the 'Cartesian revolution' is relevant to the history of linguistics in the way in which Chomsky supposes. Taking note of recent work that challenges C's argument, in particular Lakoff 1969 and Aarsleff 1970, 1971, I suggest that the main lines of C's argument survive these challenges. In § 2 I discuss the form of grammar that C envisions; I sketch an argument against the cyclic application of transformations, and raise a question about semantic interpretation rules. In § 3 I take up C's main thesis, that linguistics should be regarded as part of psychology. I endorse his suggestion that the full grammatical analysis of a sentence can be treated as a description of a hearer's percept; I also discuss the rationale behind his idea that principles of universal grammar constitute part of an innate schematism that plays a role in language learning. Here I attempt to make up for the unsympathetic and uncomprehending analysis in Harman 1967.

1. C begins by recalling the 'illusions of the early postwar years', when it was widely supposed that the basic problems of psychology and linguistics had been solved and that an understanding of all remaining issues could now be achieved with the aid of computers,

* Reprinted by permission of the Linguistic Society of America from *Language* 49 (1973): 453–64.

sound spectroscopes, and similar products of recent technological advances. We can now see, C says, that we are far from understanding basic issues; new insights and new concepts are still required. 'What is involved', he says in an obscure but suggestive remark, 'is not a matter of degree of complexity but rather a QUALITY OF COMPLEXITY' (p. 4, my emphasis). Nevertheless, he continues, 'there have been significant advances . . . in our understanding of linguistic competence and the ways it is put to use' (5), and these advances reflect assumptions that he traces back to Descartes.

C takes the relevant Cartesian view to be premised on what he calls 'the creative aspect of language use', namely that the normal use of language is 'innovative, free from stimulus control, and also appropriate and coherent' (13).[1] The Cartesians, he says, saw the creative aspect of language use as reflecting what is essential in human intelligence, distinguishing people from animals, but not susceptible of any sort of physical explanation. The problem, then, was to say what sort of explanation could be given. C does not suppose that the Cartesians contributed to the solution of this problem when they postulated a mental substance. He takes the significant Cartesian contribution to be the setting of a problem rather than the provision of an answer. Indeed, C says, 'we are as far today as Descartes was three centuries ago from understanding' the creative aspect of language use (12). However, the Cartesians were on the right track when they rejected physicalistic accounts: 'It seems to me', says C, 'that the most hopeful approach today is to describe the phenomena of language and of mental activity as accurately as possible, to try to develop an abstract theoretical apparatus that will as far as possible account for these phenomena and reveal the principles of their organization and functioning, without attempting, for the present, to relate the postulated mental structures and processes to any physiological mechanisms or to interpret mental function in terms of "physical causes"' (14).

C goes on to say that just this sort of approach lies behind 'the general point of view that came to be known as "philosophical" or "universal" grammar' (14), as initiated by the Port-Royal Grammar in the latter part of the 17th century. E.g., the Port-Royal theory dis-

[1] In the 'Preface to the enlarged edition,' Chomsky complains that 'a number of professional linguists have repeatedly confused what I refer to here as "the creative aspect of language use" with the recursive property of generative grammars, a very different matter' (p. viii). Professional linguists, take note!

tinguishes the surface structure of a sentence, which corresponds to its sound, from what C calls its deep structure. The deep structure of *Invisible God created the visible world* 'consists of a system of three propositions, "that God is invisible", "that he created the world", and "that the world is visible" ' (17). C suggests that what distinguishes this Port-Royal theory from the theory of ellipsis developed by the Renaissance grammarian Sanctius is that 'they are separated by the Cartesian revolution' (19). The Port-Royal theory is intended as a psychological theory according to which 'the transformations relating deep and surface structures are actual mental operations', whereas, according to C's interpretation, the theory of ellipsis developed by Sanctius 'is one of many techniques [of textual interpretation], to be applied as conditions warrant and having no necessary mental representation as an aspect of normal intelligence' (18–19).

Now C puts forward this interpretation of Sanctius only tentatively, 'with some diffidence' (19); and Lakoff has demonstrated that it is mistaken, showing that Sanctius' theory was intended to be part of a general theory of mind. More significantly, she also shows that the psychological aspect of the Port-Royal theory, as well as its distinction between deep and surface structures, derives directly from Sanctius.[2] This obviously raises a significant question about the importance and significance that C assigns to Descartes, since Sanctius preceded Descartes by half a century. However, C may be able to save most of what he wants to say, allowing for this correction concerning Sanctius.

For one thing, Lakoff's analysis actually confirms C's general thesis that there is a connection between the theory of mind and a linguistics that involves the distinction between deep and surface structures related by grammatical transformations; she shows that what might have seemed to be counter-evidence against this idea actually confirms the connection between psychology and transformational grammar. Furthermore, C could defend his claim about the relevance of

---

[2] Lakoff's account of the psychological aspect of the Port-Royal theory is more complex than this indicates; indeed, her account borders on inconsistency. On the one hand, she traces the Port-Royal distinction between deep and surface structure to a belief in 'the logical nature of mind' (348); and she says that these ideas derive from Sanctius' view that language 'is a product of the human mind. Since the mind is a rational thing, so is language' (359). It is this aspect of her discussion that I refer to in the main body of this review.

On the other hand, she says that the Port-Royal theory is 'not psychologically motivated' (352)! That is an odd thing to say, given her other remarks. Her reason for saying it is that the Port-Royal theory does not involve 'a perfectly formed psychological theory' (351). Of course, by that criterion no current linguistic theory is 'psychologically motivated'.

Descartes if he could establish the following fairly plausible points:

(a) Although attempts had been made to explain aspects of language within psychological theories before Descartes, the 17th century witnessed successes in mechanics, physiology, and the other physical sciences that posed a threat to psychology. As C observes, 'There are many far from superficial respects in which the intellectual climate of today resembles that of 17th century Western Europe. One, particularly crucial in the present context, is the very great interest in the potentialities and capacities of automata, a problem that intrigued the 17th century mind as fully as it does our own' (5).

(b) Descartes' innovation was his explicit assertion that there were aspects of mind not susceptible of mechanical or physiological explanation, including in particular the normal use of language. Actually, this led Descartes to suppose that no explanation at all could be given for these aspects of mind, which shows the power of the prevailing paradigm. Descartes did not envision an independent science of mind that would be irreducible to physical science; and when he did try to explain 'the passions of the soul', he offered an epiphenomenal physiological account.[3]

(c) But philosophers influenced by Descartes, particularly Locke and Leibniz, did try to develop an independent psychology. They accepted the Cartesian argument that certain aspects of mind could not be explained physiologically; but they rejected his view, and the prevailing view, that the only legitimate explanation was physical explanation. It was this aspect of the 'Cartesian revolution' that allowed philosophical grammar to flourish as part of an independent science of mind that was not reducible to the physical science of the time. In other words, C's claim (as I understand it) is that Sanctius is separated from Port-Royal not only by the Cartesian revolution, but also by a revolution in the physical sciences that made the Cartesian revolution necessary if there was to be any serious theory of mind.

An argument along these lines, if successful, would also meet some of the objections raised by Aarsleff, who says (1970:583–84) that he does 'not see that anything useful can be salvaged from Chomsky's version of the history of linguistics. That version is fundamentally false from beginning to end . . . Unless we reject his account, we will for a long while have no genuine history, but only a succession of enthusiastic and ignorant variations on false themes.' Much of Aarsleff's case rests on attacking C's view that rationalism involves a theory of innate ideas. He points out that many later philosophical grammarians saw themselves as followers of Locke, even though

[3] Here I am indebted to Margaret Wilson.

he had attacked the theory of innate ideas. But putting the issue of innate ideas aside,[4] Aarsleff's discussion tends to support the line of argument which I have suggested that C can appeal to, since Locke is clearly a Cartesian in all relevant respects. He accepted the Cartesian thesis that aspects of mind involving the normal use of language cannot be given a physical explanation, but unlike Descartes, he went on to develop a theory of mind that was independent of physical theory. Locke's important role in the history of linguistics, which Aarsleff has documented, illustrates the relevance to linguistics of the Cartesian revolution.

C says that philosophical grammar eventually 'reached the limits of what could be achieved within the framework of the ideas and techniques that were available' (21). A reaction set in against what seemed to be mere speculation when compared with successes in physical science. Linguists came to restrict their interest to surface forms which could be studied by objective techniques of segmentation and classification. These new techniques led to 'the remarkable successes of comparative Indo-European studies', which, says C, 'surely rank among the outstanding achievements of 19th century science' (20). These successes led to modern structural linguistics, which dominated the subject in the first half of this century. However, C says, the development of generative grammar now permits a reconstruction of the tradition of philosophical grammar.

2. C takes generative grammar to be a way of describing language as an abstract formal system, which is presumed relevant to psychological theories of language use and language learning, but which can and must be studied before specific proposals are made in that area. Although he does not put it this way, there is a kind of double Cartesian revolution involved, since we are first to conceive of a psychology that is independent of speculation concerning possible neurophysiological realizations of the psychological 'mechanisms' which we posit, and we are then to envision a formal theory of language as

[4] The issue concerning innate ideas is irrelevant as far as Locke is concerned, since Chomsky and Aarsleff agree that the theory Locke attacks as a 'theory of innate ideas' is not the theory of innate ideas held by Descartes or Chomsky or, for that matter, Locke himself! On the other hand, Aarsleff also argues that later philosophical grammarians tended to be concerned not so much with psychological issues as with questions concerning the origin of language, the implication being (I take it) that they did not try to account for linguistic universals with a theory of innate ideas in the way that C does. I discuss C's theory in § 3 below. Whether Aarsleff is right about the later philosophical grammarians I cannot say.

an abstract system which is to be studied quite apart from any consideration of possible psychological realizations of that system or the rules that describe and determine its character.

C says that nominalizations with the internal structure of noun phrases can be used as evidence that 'deep structures of the sort postulated in transformational generative grammars are real mental structures', since these nominalizations 'reflect the properties of deep structure' (107). We can speak of *John's certainty that Bill will leave,* because the surface structure of *John is certain that Bill will leave* is similar to its deep structure; but we do not speak of **John's certainty to leave,* because the deep structure of *John is certain to leave* is quite different from its surface structure, and is instead like the deep and surface structures of *That John will leave is certain.* C thus argues that deep structures are often more 'abstract' (though no less real) than surface structures, in the sense that they are not always as directly recoverable from the sound of sentences as surface structures are.

Chomsky suggests that there is a syntactic cycle determined by deep structure: a cycle of transformations is to apply first to the most deeply embedded cyclic categories (sentences, noun phrases, and adjective phrases), then to the next larger cyclic categories, etc. But the argument for this is quite weak. C cites Ross's argument (1967) that pronominalization is cyclic; but that is inconclusive, as are all other arguments for the syntactic cycle of which I am aware. An obvious objection to Ross's theory (and indeed most current theories) is that two rules of pronominalization are needed: one rule for forward pronominalization, another more complicated rule for 'backward' pronominalization. In fact, it seems to me that a unified treatment of forward and so-called backward pronominalization will be incompatible with the syntactic cycle. Such a treatment will account for apparent backward pronominalization by supposing that a clause has been moved forward after pronominalization. I will now sketch such a treatment and explain why it conflicts with the syntactic cycle.

Observe that *he* can cross-reference *John* in 1, 3, and 4, but not 2:

(1) John left, after he won.
(2) He left, after John won.
(3) After John won, he left.
(4) After he won, John left.

We can account for this if, following Harris (1968:18), we assume

that the subordinate clause follows the main clause in deep structure, and that pronominalization and optional forward clause movement can occur in either order. Pronominalization alone yields 1;
pronominalization followed by clause movement yields 4; clause
movement and then pronominalization yields 3. But no combination
of pronominalization and clause movement yields 2.

Again, observe that in most dialects *he* can cross-reference *John*
in both 5 and 6:

(5) That John won the race surprised him.

(6) That he won the race surprised John.

However, in some dialects *he* can cross-reference *John* only in 6. We
can account for these facts by supposing that the embedded sentence follows the surface object of *surprised* in deep structure. One
possibility, suggested by Postal 1970, is that 5 and 6 are derived by
a transformation of 'psych-movement' from the structure underlying
John was surprised that he won the race. If pronominalization precedes psych-movement, 6 results; if psych-movement comes first, 5
results. We can account for dialects in which 5 is ruled out by supposing that pronominalization cannot follow psych-movement in
them.

Next consider the fact that *he* can cross-reference *John* in 7, 9, and
10, but not in 8:

(7) John hit the man next to him.

(8) He hit the man next to John.

(9) The man next to John hit him.

(10) The man next to him hit John.

We can account for 10 if we suppose that *the man next to him* follows the surface object of *hit* in deep structure. E.g., we might accept
something like McCawley's account (1970) of the source of underlying NPs. Then we would have the deep structure for 9 and 10
shown in Figure 1, representing only the pertinent details.

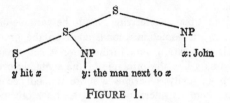

FIGURE 1.

Furthermore, we can now accept the following simple principle of
pronominalization, based on this idea that underlying NPs are
variable-binding operators:

(11) Insert a noun phrase into the leftmost variable it binds, and
pronominalize all other occurrences of that variable.

We can apply 11 to x or y in either order. Applying it first to y, then
to x, yields 9. Reversing this order yields 10. Note, however, that the
latter order of application conflicts with the principle of the syntactic
cycle.

Finally, consider the following contrast, which is exploited in the
argument by Ross to which C alludes:

(12) Learning that he had won the race surprised John.

(13) Learning that John had won the race surprised him.

In all dialects, *he* can cross-reference *John* in (12) but not in (13).
Now we have the deep structure of Figure 2.

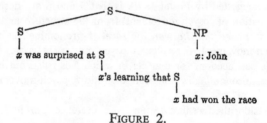

FIGURE 2.

Following C and Ross, we can suppose that the deletion of the subject of *learning* occurs as part of pronominalization. If pronominalization occurs before psych-movement, 12 results. But if the order is
reversed, 11 yields not 13 but 14:

(14) John's learning that he had won the race surprised him.

No combination of psych-movement and pronominalization gives 13.
So we can account for the fact that *he* cannot cross-reference *John*
in 13 without assuming the syntactic cycle, indeed by adopting instead a unified account of pronominalization that is not compatible
with the cycle.

An analysis that takes underlying NPs to be variable-binding operators in this way is sometimes condemned on the grounds that it
lacks syntactic motivation, and furthermore violates natural conditions on grammars like the principle of the syntactic cycle. But the
fact that such an analysis permits a more unified account of pronominalization than its alternatives is syntactic motivation for that
analysis, and furthermore, is evidence against the conditions in
question.[5]

[5] The account of pronominalization suggested here derives from Harris (81),
and a suggestion of Richard Grandy's.

In *Language and mind,* C is very concerned to emphasize the role of conditions on rules. In addition to various cyclic principles, he mentions an 'A-over-A' condition, which says, 'if a transformation applies to a structure of the form $[_S \ldots [_A \ldots]_A \ldots]_S$, for any category A, then it must be so interpreted to apply to the MAXIMAL phrase of type A' (51); and an 'erasure principle' due to Rosenbaum 1967, 'that prescribes roughly that the subject of an embedded proposition is deleted by the nearest noun phrase outside of this proposition' (58). In both cases he mentions problems that arise concerning these principles.

Among the examples that C gives as relevant to the A-over-A principle are these. We have *What is it difficult for him to understand?* from *It is difficult for him to understand what?,* but not **What is for him to understand difficult?* from *For him to understand what is difficult?* We have *What did John think that Bill had read?* but not **What did John wonder why Bill had read?* We have *Who did he see a picture of?* but not *Who did he see John's picture of?* We have *What do you believe that John saw?* but not **What do you believe the claim that John saw?* C argues that a theory of conditions on rules should account for these and other examples.[6]

Conditions on rules, the principle of the cycle, the A-over-A principle, and the like, play an important role in C's version of the theory of innate ideas. C offers his theory to account for the fact that a grammar of a language takes the form it does, including rules that form deep structures, transformational rules, phonological rules etc., with rather particular and surprising conditions that must be placed on the application of these rules. I will come back to this below.

Turning to principles of semantic interpretation and possible conditions on such principles, C observes: 'When we try to pursue such questions, we soon become lost in a tangle of confused issues and murky problems and it is difficult to propose answers that carry any conviction' (60). In my opinion this pessimistic evaluation arises from the thought that a reasonable semantic theory might, as C says,

[6] A later, more complete, and somewhat different discussion occurs in Chomsky 1974, which, by the way, advocates a cyclic syntactic principle that one might adopt instead of a principle of the cyclic application of transformational rules. The new condition prevents interaction between a phrase of a given cyclic category (sentence, noun phrase, adjective phrase) and any other except the next higher or lower such phrase. However, C says that this condition does not apply to certain rules, in particular to the rule of 'Coreference Assignment (no matter how that is formulated)' (1972, fn. 16), so it does not rule out the analysis of pronominalization that I have suggested.

'establish a universal system of semantic features and laws regarding their interrelations and permitted variety' (123) and that the semantic component of a grammar is to assign 'readings' or semantic representations to a sentence in terms of these universal semantic features. I am skeptical about the need for a theory of that sort.

Not all aspects of meaning will be expressed by the analysis a grammar assigns a particular sentence. E.g., although it is no doubt part of the meaning of a sentence that it logically implies various other sentences, we will try to capture this aspect of meaning, not by including in the analysis assigned to the given sentence a list of its (indeed infinite) logical consequences, but by stating general principles of logic and by analysing the form of sentences in such a way that the forms assigned to sentences, together with the logical principles, serve to account for the implications that hold between sentences by virtue of logical form. It is not obvious that special semantic interpretation rules are needed to assign forms to sentences on the basis of their syntactic derivations, since we might hope to frame the principles of logic so as to apply directly to the deep and surface structures of sentences.

Of course, interpretation rules of this sort may be needed. If NPs are not treated as variable-binding operators in deep structure, the ambiguity in logical form of a sentence like *Someone loves everyone* may not show up in either deep or surface structure (which might in fact be quite similar); and interpretation rules would be needed to associate the sentence with its two possible forms, as in Figure 3. But if NPs were to be treated as variable-binding operators in deep structure, the relevant differences in logical form in the two interpretations of *Someone loves everyone* would be exhibited directly in deep structure, and semantic interpretation rules would not be needed here.

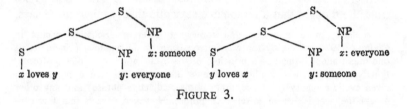

FIGURE 3.

In addition to logical principles, we will occasionally want to appeal to 'meaning postulates' and definitions, expressing equivalences and implications that do not hold simply by virtue of logical form. But there is no obvious reason to suppose that these non-logical principles must assign readings or semantic interpretations to sentences as part of their grammatical analyses. Indeed, it is a moot question whether there is a principled distinction between, on the one hand, meaning postulates and definitions, and, on the other, principles known to be generally accepted by speakers of the language.

Other aspects of meaning might be captured by appeal to conversational maxims of the sort described by Grice (ms). Consider the sentence *John is tall for a pigmy*. As C observes, 'This sentence presupposes that John is a pigmy, and that pigmies tend to be short.' In my opinion, these presuppositions are not logical implications of the sentence, but conversational implicatures that might be accounted for, on Grice's theory, by supposing that the hearer is intended to reason as follows. 'The speaker says *John is tall for a pigmy* rather than the shorter *John is tall,* so there must be some reason for saying the one rather than the other, presumably that he is not warranted in saying the shorter sentence. Therefore the speaker implies that John is tall in relation to pigmies but not in relation to people in general; and that means he is supposing that we both agree that pigmies tend to be short. He implies that there is some special reason to pick out pigmies as the reference class, presumably that John is a member of that class. Furthermore, he must assume I already know that John is a pigmy, since his remark would not by itself be an orderly way to present me with that information if I did not already possess it.'

The implicatures in question do not seem to be logical implications, since they can be easily cancelled. The fact that John is tall for a pigmy may indicate that he is not a pigmy. Similarly, C points out that we say *John is tall even for a Watusi,* this use of *even* cancelling the implication that Watusis are not tall. The opposite implication holds in this case, because we assume that the speaker has some reason for saying what he says rather than the shorter *John is tall for a Watusi.* The fact that the word *even* does not play a logical role is seen from its optional omission in contexts like the following: *If John is tall for a Watusi, he must be very tall indeed.*

To sum up, I can see how an account of meaning might appeal to deep and surface syntactic structure, rules of logical implication, non-logical meaning postulates and definitions that are not to be distinguished from other basic principles of common knowledge, rules of conversational and conventional implicature, etc. But I see no role for principles that assign semantic representation involving universal semantic features to syntactic analyses of sentences, except perhaps for principles that would assign aspects of logical form not fully indicated in the syntactic analysis. (And in fact I do not see any need for the latter principles either.)

C gives few examples of the sorts of non-syntactic information that might be part of a semantic representation. I have already referred to his discussion of *John is tall for a pigmy*. His discussion of another example begins like this: 'It is a fact of English that *a good knife* means *a knife which cuts well*. Consequently the concept *knife* must be specified in part in terms of features having to do with characteristic functions (not just physical properties)' (123, following Katz 1964). But clearly, *a good knife* does not MEAN a knife which cuts well. Knives have other functions; some are used to spread butter, some are thrown at targets, and so on. Furthermore, our knowledge of the functions that knives have is not purely linguistic knowledge, but is part of our general knowledge about the world. Moreover, in evaluating a knife as a good knife, we take into account not only function but other characteristics—appearance, weight, size etc. Finally, the way in which function and other characteristics of the knife are relevant to whether we will consider it to be a good knife is determined not by linguistic theory and the meaning of the word *good*, but by our views about what makes a good knife. Whatever general principles are involved can be stated as general principles which we accept, rather than as rules for assigning universal semantic features to sentences containing the word *good*.

C gives a number of examples of ways in which certain aspects of meaning are not determined by deep structure alone, so that surface structure is also relevant. Some of these examples involve matters of emphasis, presupposition, and focus that seem to be connected to Gricean principles of conventional implicature, e.g. the role of *even* in *John is tall even for a Watusi* or the relevance of emphasis in the contrast between *The Yankees played the* RED SOX *in Boston* and *The Yankees played the Red Sox in* BOSTON. C says that the placement of *even* or of contrastive stress is not determined in deep structure. If true, that should not be surprising: one expects the surface form of what is said to contribute to its Gricean implicatures. Other examples which C gives are meant to suggest that even logical form is not entirely a matter of deep structure. E.g., he argues that 15 and 16 have the same deep structure, but that *his* can cross-reference *the men* only in 15:

    (15) Each of the men hates his brothers.

    (16) The men each hate his brothers.

However, if the analysis of NPs and pronominalization referred to above is accepted, 15 (in the relevant interpretation) and 16 will have different deep structures, as in Figure 4.

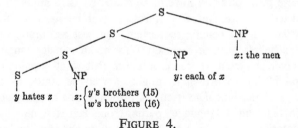

FIGURE 4.

Of course some sort of constraint on this analysis is needed to prevent the movement of *each* when *each of x* is substituted for the first occurrence of *y*, provided a later occurrence of the same variable *y* is bound by *each of x*. But that is not just an ad-hoc 'notational variant' of the way in which C might handle this, since there are independent reasons to accept this analysis of NPs and pronominalization. I believe that all examples that C and others have given to suggest that deep structure does not fully determine logical form are to be analysed in a similar fashion, although the point is controversial. If I am right, the principles of logic need refer only to deep structure and can disregard surface structure.

3. C mentions two ways in which the study of language as a formal system has a direct bearing on psychological issues. First, he says that we can take the grammatical analysis given to a sentence as a description of a possible 'percept' that a hearer might construct as an interpretation of some physical stimulus. Thus there is a connection between grammar and the theory of perception. Second, and more central to C's concerns, he argues that there is a direct connection between universal grammar and learning theory, and that universal conditions on grammars are not learned but are part of the 'schematism' with which the language learner approaches his task.

Although C does not discuss the point, it is worth observing that the first of these ideas is relevant to the issue, mentioned above, whether the semantic component of the grammar should assign readings to sentences that express their meanings in terms of universal semantic features. My doubts about this derive from doubts about the usefulness of that sort of information. How would it help a speaker or hearer to have a reading of the sentence in universal terms? Presumably he or she will make use of logical and other principles that relate various readings to other readings, perception, action etc. These principles will have to be stated so as to apply to readings constructed from universal features. It will be hard to distinguish them from general beliefs; so perhaps the best assumption is that a speaker's beliefs are not themselves formulated in his language, but in a universal system of representation. But what is gained by that assumption? These principles might as well be stated in the deep structures of the language itself, as principles the speaker accepts as true. In learning a language, perhaps one learns a new system of representation for beliefs etc. Of course there are empirical questions here, and the issues are more complex than these brief remarks can indicate.

Turning to the more central issue, let me begin by remarking that there is a trivial sense in which, in learning a language, one forms a representation of the rules of the grammar of the language. We can trivially let the principle of representation be this: a person p at time t represents grammar g if and only if, at t, p knows the language for which g is the grammar. C suggests that it is reasonable to take this idea somewhat more seriously in thinking of a model of a language learner; i.e., we might suppose that the model is designed to develop a representation in a more serious sense of an appropriate grammar when exposed to the relevant environment. This representation would be utilized by other aspects of the device in order to speak and understand the language.

Now C's idea is that such a model will make use of a schematism concerning the form of grammar. One particular proposal might be this. There are several boxes in the model, one for phrase-structure base rules, another for transformation rules, a third for phonological rules, a fourth for the lexicon, a fifth for beliefs constructed in accordance with the rules and lexicon in the other boxes, and so on. The way the model goes about learning a language is this. First, it makes one or two entries in each box, and then sees how well it manages in the relevant environment. The device is designed to respond as a typical speaker of the language described by its provisional grammar might respond. The device adds to and modifies the contents of the various boxes in order to improve its dealings with the environment as time goes on.

C's idea is that we are not to suppose that the device in question must determine that it is going to use phrase-structure rules, syntactic transformational rules, phonological rules, a lexicon etc. That schematism for grammar is built in ahead of time. Similarly, the device does not need to form representations of constraints on rules, such as principles of cyclic application or the A-over-A principle; these too are built in.

Why suppose that all this is built in? C's answer is that it is difficult to see how the device could be made to work without such a supposition. What could lead it to formulate rules for a transformational grammar rather than some other sort? How could it ever hit on anything like the right constraints on rules? The point is that we can in some sense envision how the device would work if it were to make use of such a schematism. It would try a few rules and lexical entries of a narrowly specified sort, and then modify these to improve its dealings with the environment. That is imaginable. But if some such schematism is not built in, how does the device even get started? How does it ever come to represent anything like the grammar of the language?

As Putnam 1967 remarks, this is a 'What else?' argument: 'What else could account for language learning if there were not this sort of innate schematism?' But it is a powerful argument, once it is fully understood; and C is quite convincing in his rejection of putative alternative accounts.

C points out that his way of looking at things suggests that conditions on rules will hold universally, since it will in general be difficult to see how they might be learned. That is why he says that one can learn about universal grammar by studying one language in detail. He goes on to speculate that similar innate schematisms might be involved in non-linguistic perception and even in the development of scientific theories.

> C also criticizes published reactions to his views by four philosophers; Putnam 1967, Goodman 1967, Hiz 1967, and Harman 1967. Much of this concerns his arguments about innate schematisms. Philosophers tend to worry about the possibility of alternative theories of grammar that would account for all the facts equally well. E.g., I have argued above against the principle of the syntactic cycle. But it is quite possible that one could keep the cycle if one were willing to use a more complex theory of pronominalization, since one might foresee simplifications elsewhere in the grammar. It is a familiar aspect of the current scene that different linguists make quite different assumptions about constraints and rules; and it is not at all obvious

that any of a number of rather different sets of assumptions might not be viable. But this suggests to philosophers that it may not be the language learner who uses a schematism, but the linguist. ('SCHEMA-TISM . . . A schematic arrangement; a set form for classification or exposition. Also, the schematic method of presentation, or excessive addiction to this.' *O.E.D.*) Goodman seems to be worried about this possibility; in another form it lies behind Quine's 1960 thesis of the indeterminacy of radical translation.

If theories A and B account equally well for the facts, does it make any real sense to suppose that the language learner internalizes the rules of grammar A rather than those of grammar B? What sense can be made of the supposition that he uses schematism A rather than schematism B? Even if we open up the brain and discover a representation there of the rules of grammar, we cannot expect the representation to be in English; it will require interpretation, and will receive different interpretations from proponents of different theories. Philosophers who feel that this sort of multiplicity of theories is inevitable are naturally skeptical about talk of 'the' rules which the learner allegedly internalizes, 'the' innate schematism which he allegedly has.

I suspect that C's attitude to this is that it is a good research strategy to ignore the possibility of alternative equally good theories and to assume that it is possible to decide among competing theories that are actually put forward by linguists (until they are shown to be 'notational variants'). I would add that one might attempt to avoid the philosophical worry by supposing that claims about 'the' internalized grammar and 'the' innate schematism contain an implicit parameter: 'the' internalized rules or schematism as interpreted by this sort of general approach. Then the claim is not that a given over-all hypothesis is the only one that works, but rather that it is one of those that work.

This also has a bearing on the question whether, as C says, the innateness hypothesis is a strong empirical claim needed to account for the otherwise very surprising fact that people learn language in the way that they do, as quickly as they do. A natural philosophical response to this sort of claim is 'What is so surprising about that?' The point is that C can make this seem surprising with reference to his language-learning model. What would be surprising would be to have a device that not only came to represent phrase-structure rules, transformations etc., but also somehow figured out that rules of that sort were what is needed, and also represented various sorts of rather strange-looking constraints on rules.

Pressing the philosophical point, let us ask this: 'Under what conditions would language learning not be surprising?' If we cannot answer that, then it remains obscure what it means to say that language learning is surprising. What if it had turned out that the theory of context-free phrase-structure grammar could account for all the facts? Then would it be so surprising? Presumably yes; for how would the device have 'known' to start work on the development of a context-free phrase-structure grammar? But then would any possibility have been unsurprising?

Suppose that we agree that a phrase-structure grammar would be less surprising, so that C's argument rests on the surprising character of the actual conditions on rules which we apparently need to postulate (and the conditions proposed in Chomsky 1974 are surprising indeed, and seemingly unmotivated by any sort of a-priori consideration). In that case we might wonder whether the conditions on rules in an equally good alternative theory of language wouldn't seem more natural and less surprising. Inasmuch as conditions are strange or unexpected, we will want an explanation. Having an explanation of them may well suggest a reformulation of grammar that would make them look more natural.

To this sort of philosophical worry, C offers in effect the following answer, which seems to me quite adequate. He has produced a theory of language and some speculations about language learning which make certain aspects of language learning seem quite surprising unless there is an innate schematism of the sort that he suggests. If someone wishes to argue that language learning is not so surprising, it is not enough that they point out that there MAY be alternatives to C's view. What they need to do is to develop an alternative account that makes language learning look less surprising. Until that is done, there is no reason for C to moderate his claims.

Another issue between C and the philosophers concerns his use of the word COMPETENCE for 'tacit knowledge of the language' which is 'not a skill, a set of habits, or anything of the sort'. Given the ordinary meaning of the word *competence,* this is perhaps not the best terminology (*'com·pe·tence* . . . the state or quality of being capable or competent; skill; ability', Morris 1969). Finally, there is the question whether C's theory of innateness is incompatible with contemporary philosophical empiricism, as represented e.g. by Quine. Despite what Chomsky says in this connection, I see no conflict whatever, once misunderstanding on all sides is cleared away.[7]

[7] NSF support is gratefully acknowledged.

REFERENCES

AARSLEFF, HANS. 1970. The history of linguistics and Professor Chomsky. Lg. 46.570–85.
——. 1971. Cartesian linguistics: history or fantasy? Language Sciences 17.1–12.
CHOMSKY, NOAM. 1968. Language and mind. New York: Harcourt, Brace & World.
——. 1974. Conditions on rules. In Stephen R. Anderson and Paul Kiparsky (eds.), A Festschrift for Morris Halle. New York: Holt, Rinehart & Winston.
GOODMAN, NELSON. 1967. The epistemological argument. Synthese 17.24–28.
GRICE, H. P. MS. Logic and conversation. Mimeo, n.d.
HARMAN, GILBERT. 1967. Psychological aspects of the theory of syntax. Journal of Philosophy 64.75–87.
HARRIS, ZELLIG. 1968. Mathematical structures of language. New York: Interscience.
HIZ, HENRY. 1967. Methodological aspects of the theory of syntax. Journal of Philosophy 64.67–74.
HOOK, SIDNEY (ed.). 1969. Language and philosophy. New York: New York University Press.
KATZ, JERROLD J. 1964. Semantic theory and the meaning of 'good'. Journal of Philosophy 61.739–66.
LAKOFF, ROBIN. 1969. Review of Grammaire générale et raisonnée. Lg. 45.343–64.
LENNEBERG, E. H. 1967. Biological foundations of language. New York: Wiley.
MCCAWLEY, JAMES D. 1970. Where do noun phrases come from? In Readings in English transformational grammar, ed. by R. Jacobs and P. Rosenbaum, 166–83. Waltham, Mass.: Ginn.
MORRIS, WILLIAM (ed.). 1969. American Heritage dictionary. Boston: Houghton Mifflin.
POSTAL, PAUL. 1970. Cross-over phenomena. New York: Holt.
PUTNAM, HILARY. 1967. The 'innateness hypothesis' and explanatory models in linguistics. Synthese 17.12–23.
QUINE, W. V. 1960. Word and object. Cambridge, Mass.: MIT Press.
ROSENBAUM, PETER S. 1967. The grammar of English predicate complement constructions. (MIT Research Monograph, 47.) Cambridge, Mass.: MIT Press.
ROSS, JOHN R. 1967. On the cyclic nature of English pronominalization. In To honor Roman Jakobson, 1669–82. The Hague: Mouton.

Linguistics and Epistemology*

THOMAS NAGEL

There is some reason to believe that Chomsky's views about the innate contribution to language-acquisition have a bearing on epistemological issues: on disputes over the existence of a priori knowledge, for example. Certainly if he is right, grammar provides a striking example of strong innate constraints on the form of human thought, and a natural object of philosophical fascination.

I do not propose to discuss the correctness of Chomsky's view concerning the importance and size of that innate contribution, or the adequacy of the support offered for it. The object of this paper is to investigate what epistemological consequences Chomsky's empirical hypotheses about language-learning have, it they are *correct*. The discussion will divide into two parts. First, I shall consider how Chomsky's hypotheses are most appropriately formulated, and specifically how the concept of knowledge can enter into their formulation. Second, I shall consider the bearing of these hypotheses on the epistemological status of our knowledge of natural languages, and also what they suggest about other kinds of knowledge, particularly those sometimes thought to be a priori.

I

The following, from page 58 of *Aspects of the Theory of Syntax*, gives a clear, brief statement of Chomsky's position:

> It seems plain that language acquisition is based on the child's discovery of what from a formal point of view is a deep and abstract theory—a generative grammar of his language—many of the concepts and principles of which are only remotely related to experience by long and intricate chains of unconscious quasi-inferential steps. A consideration of the character of the grammar that is acquired, the degenerate quality and narrowly limited extent of the available data,

* Reprinted by permission of the author and the New York University Press from *Language and Philosophy,* ed. Sidney Hook. Copyright © 1969 by New York University.

the striking uniformity of the resulting grammars, and their independence of intelligence, motivation, and emotional state, over wide ranges of variation, leave little hope that much of the structure of the language can be learned by an organism initially uninformed as to its general character.

I believe Chomsky means to assert that we have here a genuine case of innate knowledge. His references to the Rationalists suggest that he does. Moreover, the alternative to an organism initially *un*informed as to the general character of the structure of natural languages would seem to be an organism initially *informed* as to that general character. And elsewhere (p. 27) he speaks of ascribing tacit knowledge of linguistic universals to the child. However, for the purpose of this discussion, it is not necessary to settle the exegetical point. The fact is that Chomsky's contentions about language-acquisition will suggest to most students of epistemology, as they suggest to me, that we are presented here with an example of innate knowledge. It is this natural philosophical interpretation that I propose to examine, and I shall not in the remainder of this paper concern myself explicitly with Chomsky's philosophical views, but only with the philosophical implications of his linguistic views.

The first question, then, is whether the initial contribution of the organism to language-learning, alleged by Chomsky, is properly described as knowledge at all. Let us begin by considering what I take to be a natural but bad argument for a negative answer to the question. The argument has the form of a reductio.

It occurs to most philosophers to ask, at some point in their consideration of Chomsky's views, whether the decision to apply the concept of knowledge in this case would not also commit us to ascribing innate knowledge, perhaps even a priori knowledge, to the human digestive system (or perhaps rather to human beings in virtue of the behavior of their digestive systems). For without having to be trained, instructed, or conditioned, the individual is able to adjust the chemical environment in his stomach to break down the digestible food that is introduced, while rejecting, sometimes forcibly, what is indigestible. This formidable task of classification and variable response is carried out even by infants, so it cannot be learned entirely from experience.

Admittedly the infant is not consciously aware of the principles that govern his gastric secretions, nor is the adult, unless he has studied physiology. But this does not distinguish the case from that of language-acquisition, for neither a child, nor an adult who has not studied linguistics, is consciously aware either of the grammatical rules of his language or of the principles by which he arrives at the ability to speak the language governed by those rules, on the basis of his exposure to a subset of the sentences of that language. In light of these parallels, it might be thought that the same reasons which can be offered in support of the view that there is innate knowledge of the general character of linguistic structure would count equally well in favor of the view that there is innate knowledge of the proper chemical means of digesting various kinds of food. The consequence of this would be that either both are examples of innate knowledge, or neither is. And it would then appear that the latter possibility is the more plausible. This would allow us to say that in both cases there is an extremely important innate *capacity*—to discriminate among and digest foods, or to acquire command of natural languages having a certain type of structure—but it would not be called innate *knowledge* in either case.

The trouble with this argument is that it ignores the difference between the operations that we have in the two cases the capacity to perform. In the case of digestion, the operation is not an action at all (this is obvious even though we do not possess an analysis of action). Nor do the data on which the operation is based, i.e., the various foods introduced into the stomach, have to be brought to the awareness of the organism. In the case of language-learning, on the other hand, conscious apprehension of the data (limited as they may be) is essential; and what the individual can do as a result of his linguistic capacity is to speak and understand sentences.

Moreover, the exercise of the capacity involves *beliefs:* e.g., that a certain combination of words is, or is not, a sentence of the language. Someone who regurgitates a bad oyster, on the other hand, is not thereby said to believe that it is indigestible. Though we may not possess an adequate analysis of the distinction, it is clear that certain methods of response and discrimination warrant the attribution of beliefs and attitudes, while others do not. Only of the former category is it appropriate to consider whether they give evidence of knowledge. The phenomena of language use belong to that former category, whereas the phenomena of digestion do not.

It is clear then that such cognitive concepts are entirely appropriate to the description of linguistic capacity and performance on particular occasions. What must be settled, however, is whether the concepts of knowledge and belief can be applied at higher levels of generality and abstraction in the description of the individual's linguistic capacity, and ultimately in the description of his capacity to acquire that capacity.

We may distinguish the following two theses: (1) that the general capacity to produce a set of performances each of which provides an instance of knowledge is itself an instance of more general knowledge; (2) that the general capacity to acquire other capacities each of which is an instance of knowledge is itself an instance of still more general knowledge. The former thesis is more plausible than the latter, but both are needed to warrant the inferential ascent from cases of linguistic knowledge revealed in particular utterances to the ascription of a knowledge of linguistic universals on which language-learning is alleged to depend.

It will be useful if we try to ascend step by step from the most specific and immediate case to more general capacities. It seems obvious that we can speak of linguistic knowledge whose object is not merely the grammaticality or meaning of a particular utterance, but something more general. (In fact it is doubtful that we could speak of knowledge in the particular case unless we could also speak of it on a more general level.) To take a very simple example, we can ascribe to the ordinary speaker of English, on the basis of countless particular performances and responses, the knowledge that the plural form of a noun is usually formed by adding 's,' and that among the exceptions to this is the word 'man,' whose plural is 'men.' Now we *might* verify this ascription by finding that the individual can actually state the rule; but it is important that this is not necessary. Someone can possess general knowledge of a rule of the language without being able to state it. He may never have heard the words 'plural,' and 'noun,' for example, and may be unable to formulate the principle in any other way. When we come to the more complicated principles to which grammatical English speech conforms, that will be the usual situation. Only professional grammarians will be able to state those rules, and sometimes even that may not be true.

Under what conditions can knowledge of a language governed by certain rules be described as knowledge of those rules? It will be instructive in this connection to consider another type of knowledge that cannot be explicitly formulated by its possessor, namely unconscious knowledge in the ordinary psychoanalytic sense. This is of course a very different phenomenon from knowledge of the rules of grammar, but it has an important feature that, as Saul Kripke has pointed out to me, may bear on the linguistic case. The psychoanalytic ascription of unconscious knowledge, or unconscious motives for that matter, does not depend simply on the possibility of organizing the subject's responses and actions in conformity with the alleged unconscious material. In addition, although he does not formulate his unconscious knowledge or attitude of his own accord, and may deny it upon being asked, it is usually possible to bring him by analytical techniques to *see* that the statement in question expresses something that he knows or feels. That is, he is able eventually to acknowledge the statement as an expression of his own belief, if it is presented to him clearly enough and in the right circumstances. Thus what was unconscious can be brought, at least partly, to consciousness. It is essential that his acknowledgment *not* be based merely on the observation of his own responses and behavior, and that he come to recognize the rightness of the attribution from the inside.

It seems to me that where recognition of this sort is possible in principle, there is good reason to speak of knowledge and belief, even in cases where the relevant principles or statements have not yet been consciously acknowledged, or even in cases where they will never be explicitly formulated. Without suggesting that knowledge of the rules of a language is in other ways like the unconscious knowledge revealed by psychoanalysis, we may observe that accurate formulations of grammatical rules often evoke the same sense of recognition from speakers who have been conforming to them for years that is evoked by the explicit formulation of repressed material that has been influencing one's behavior for years. The experience is less alarming in the former case, but nevertheless recognizably similar. It can happen even if the grammatical principles are formulated in a technical vocabulary that may require a certain amount of effort to master.

So long as it would be possible with effort to bring the speaker to a genuine recognition of a grammatical rule as an expression of his understanding of the language, rather than to a mere belief, based on the observation of cases, that the rule in fact describes his competence, it is not improper I think to ascribe knowledge of that rule to the speaker. It is not improper, even though he may never be presented with a formulation of the rule and consequently may never come to recognize it consciously.

If the condition of recognizability cannot be met, however, the ascription of knowledge and belief seems to me more dubious. And this casts doubt on the possibility of carrying the ascription of knowledge to any level of generality or abstraction higher than that involved in the specification of grammatical rules for a particular natural language. Even some of those rules are highly abstract. But when we consider the alleged innate contribution to language-learning, we pass to quite another level, and there is reason to doubt that the principles of such a linguistic acquisition device, when they have been formulated, could evoke internal recognition from individuals who have operated in accordance with them.

The rules of a particular grammar deal in part with recognizable expressions, and retain some connection, in their formulation, with the speaker's conscious experience of his language. The connection in the case of linguistic universals, of the kind that Chomsky suggests are innately present, is more remote. One example that he offers is the proposal that the syntactic component of a grammar must contain transformational rules. This highly abstract condition is supposed to apply to *all* languages, and to determine the way in which a child acquires knowledge of the grammar of his native language by being exposed to samples of speech. But is it supposed that he could in principle be brought some day to recognize such a principle as the proper expression of an assumption he was making at the time (once the proper principle has been formulated and its meaning conveyed to him)? This may be a possibility, but the conditions of explanatory adequacy that Chomsky accepts seem not to demand it. Explanatory adequacy is in itself of course a very strong requirement. But a hypothesis could be shown to satisfy it on the basis of observation of the language-learning feat itself. The additional test of asking the language-learner whether he can recognize the principle as one that was activating him all along seems irrelevant. It seems not to be required even that such internal recognition should *ever* be available or possible, no matter how much effort is expended on it.

I may have misconstrued Chomsky on this point; but in light of it, I am uneasy about extending the concept of knowledge, and the related concepts of belief and assumption, to the description of those innate capacities that enable a child to acquire knowledge of a language—any natural language—on the basis of rather minimal data. If this is correct, then not every innate capacity to acquire knowledge need itself be an instance of knowledge—even though its structural description may be quite complex.

II

The difficulties raised so far about the ascription of innate knowledge on the basis of language-learning ability are really broader difficulties about the ascription of innate *beliefs* or *assumptions* on the basis of language-learning ability. I wish now to turn to the epistemologically more interesting question, whether there is any possibility that the other main type of condition for knowledge could be met in such cases. I refer to the justification condition. There has been considerable controversy over the exact nature of this condition, but I hope it will be possible to discuss the present issue without entering that maze.

The problem is this. We can imagine almost any belief to be innately present, or that there is an innate tendency to develop that belief as the result of certain minimal experiences. That is not a sufficient basis for ascribing knowledge, however. Not just any belief that one cannot help arriving at is ipso facto justified, even if it should be true.

Suppose that someone discovered that he was able on request to specify the square root of any integer to four decimal places, without reflection or calculation. The fact that his ability was innate would not of itself guarantee the validity of his answers. The grounding of his knowledge of square roots would be rather more complex: he and other persons could verify by calculation in case after individual case that the number which he unreflectively believed to be the square root of a given integer in fact was the square root. In virtue of this further evidence, his unreflective belief in any given case could be taken as strong evidence of its own truth. In that sense it would be self-justifying—not merely because of the innateness of the capacity, but because of its independently verifiable accuracy.

With knowledge of a language we face a very different subject matter, but certain features of the case are the same. Let us consider first an imaginary example analogous to the one just discussed—a case in which someone has an innate capacity that is not generally shared. Suppose someone discovers that he is able to extend his vocabulary merely by observing new species of plants and animals, because he finds himself able to say what they are called without being told. Again, the mere fact that he is innately disposed to call this bird a magpie does not guarantee that that is its name. But if it is discovered in case after case that his unreflective belief conforms to general usage, the belief itself will provide evidence for its own truth.

Now, the actual phenomenon of language-learning that Chomsky describes is different from this, because it reveals an innate capacity that we all share. All speakers of English, for example, reach agreement in an obedience to certain grammatical rules, and attain this naturally and without calculation after a certain amount of exposure to the language. Now, no one individual's innate propensity to arrive at these rules of itself guarantees that they are the rules of the language he is speaking. That depends on a more general conformity to those same rules by all speakers of the language, and this is guaranteed by the universality of those same innate propensities. Thus if any given individual knows that his own linguistic intuitions about sentences that he has not encountered before, and his own original linguistic productions, are in conformity with the linguistic intuitions of other speakers of his language, then he can regard his innate tendencies as providing strong evidence for their own accuracy. But that is simply because as a matter of natural fact they are in conformity with the linguistic propensities of speakers of the language in general, as determined presumably by a uniform innate contribution. I am not suggesting for a moment that we actually *do* step back from our linguistic intuitions in order to validate them in this way. I am suggesting only that it is because such a justification is *available* that we can plausibly describe what our innately governed linguistic propensities provide as *knowledge* of the language.

The point of all the examples is this: in each case, the fact that the tendency to arrive at a certain belief was innate, did not by itself make it a case of knowledge. In the special case of language, where the actual rules are simply those by which competent speakers generally are governed, a universal innate tendency to arrive at certain rules is enough to guarantee their accuracy; but any one individual must still know that he is in conformity with the universal tendency, in order to know that his linguistic intuitions are correct. And this is a matter that is open to empirical investigation. The crucial fact is that in any individual case the alleged innate contribution to language-learning can itself be assessed for its accuracy as a source of knowledge of the language. It may be that no one ever engages in this sort of assessment, and that the innate tendency to construct the grammar of one's language in a certain way also includes an innate tendency to assume that other speakers will construct it in the same way; in fact this seems likely. But that assumption too is open to epistemological assessment by other means.

The importance of all this is that the innate factor, which Chomsky argues must underlie our language-learning capacity, bears no resemblance to the sort of unquestionable, epistemologically unassailable foundation on which some philosophers have sought to base human knowledge, and which is generally referred to as a priori or innate knowledge. What has been sought under this heading is something that is not itself open to the usual varieties of epistemological assessment and doubt, something whose opposite is unimaginable.

But what Chomsky offers us is a system of innate propensities that we are conveniently stuck with. It is perfectly imaginable that we should be differently constituted, but we are not. A mere innate tendency to believe certain things or perform in certain ways, no matter how universal, is not a priori knowledge. Even Hume thought that we all share a natural propensity to believe that the sun will rise again tomorrow. To point out the natural phenomenon of human agreement, innately determined, is simply to turn aside the epistemological demand that motivates the search for a priori knowledge.

In fact, such a move is closely related to Wittgenstein's position[1]—the main difference being that Wittgenstein applies it much more generally, and not just to language-learning. He argues that if one follows any chain of epistemological justification far enough, one comes in the end to a phenomenon of human agreement—not conventional agreement, but natural, innately determined agreement—on which the acceptance of that justification depends. He supposes this to happen whether the justification is empirical or deductive. If he is right, the procedures by which we subject one innate contribution to epistemological assessment will themselves simply depend on another innate contribution. And if at every stage what we have reached is only a contingent feature of our constitution, then there is no unquestionable a priori foundation on which our knowledge rests. It depends on a network of innate responses and propensities; and they are simply there.

If this is so, then epistemology may be essentially impossible. Insofar as Chomsky's contentions about language suggest that similar

[1] I am aware that Chomsky does not share this view of Wittgenstein. He has been kind enough to show me a forthcoming paper that defends another interpretation.

innate contributions underlie other cognitive phenomena as well, they suggest that all knowledge is in similar straits: it lacks an unassailable foundation. Sometimes, as in the case of language, one can take further steps to justify one's confidence in the yield of one's innate mechanism. Evidence of this kind is available to any speaker who successfully uses the language to communicate with others. But the admission of such evidence may in turn depend on innate principles that, without guaranteeing their own justification, form part of one's basic constitution;[2] so the task of justification may be incompletable.

Though this is epistemologically unsettling, it has practical compensations. If we had to learn by trial and error, or by training, how to digest food, we should have a much harder time surviving. But fortunately we don't need to *know* how to digest food, for we do it in the right way automatically. Language-learning may be similar. We do not need to *know* how to construct the grammar of a natural language on the basis of our early childhood exposure to samples of it. We simply *arrive* at a command of the language after a certain period of exposure, and find ourselves convinced that other speakers are following the same rules.

It may be true in many areas of human activity and experience that if we had to rely on what we could come to know, by either empirical or rational means, we should be unable to survive. But if in these areas we are fortunate enough to possess an innate endowment that suits us to deal with the world awaiting us, we do not require the knowledge that it would be so difficult, or perhaps impossible, to obtain. We can be guided by our innate ideas instead.

[2] I believe that this is connected with Quine's thesis of the indeterminacy of translation.

The Relevance of Linguistics to Philosophy*

JERROLD J. KATZ

1. *Introduction.* In this paper I shall defend the relevance of linguistics to philosophy on the grounds that linguistic theory incorporates solutions to significant philosophical problems. My defense will be to show that a number of philosophical problems can be represented as questions about the nature of language, and that, so represented, they can be solved by conceptual constructions found in linguistic theory. The justification of these solutions, then, is provided by the same evidence that warrants the introduction of such conceptual constructions into linguistic theory.

My thesis is not that the linguist's description of locutions from natural languages reveals philosophical insights that somehow escape philosophers. It is rather that conceptual constructions, initially devised to enable linguistic theory to state uniformities in natural languages systematically, also fulfill the conditions on solutions to certain philosophical problems. If this defense proves successful, then linguistics is not incidentally pertinent to philosophy in the way that philosophy of science bears upon the clarification of methodology and theory construction in linguistics, but is directly relevant in the same way that philosophical theories themselves are.

2. *Linguistic Theory.* Synchronic linguistics involves two distinct but interrelated studies: a study of the diversity in forms of linguistic communication and a study of the limits of such diversity. In the former, linguists investigate what is unique about individual natural languages and formulate such facts in *linguistic descriptions*. In the latter, linguists investigate what is common to all natural languages and formulate these more general facts about language in *linguistic*

* Reprinted by permission from the *Journal of Philosophy* 62 (1965): 590–602. Presented in a symposium on "Philosophy and Linguistics" at the sixty-second annual meeting of the APA, Eastern Division, December 29, 1965.

This work was supported in part by the Joint Services Electronics Program (Contract DA36-039-AMC-02300(E)), the National Science Foundation (Grant GP-2495), the National Institutes of Health (Grant MH-)4737-05), the National Aeronautics and Space Administration, and the U. S. Air Force (ESD Contract AF19(628)-2487); also by a grant from the National Institute of Health (MH-05120-04) to Harvard University, Center for Cognitive Studies.

230JERROLD J. KATZ

theory. Linguistic theory specifies the universals of language—those principles of organization and interpretation which are invariant from one natural language to another.

Linguistic theory expresses such invariants in the form of a model of a linguistic description, of which each empirically successful linguistic description is an instance, exemplifying every aspect of the model. Particular linguistic descriptions describe the diverse ways in which different natural languages realize the abstract structure exhibited in the model; the model itself describes the form of a system of empirical generalizations capable of organizing and expressing the facts about a natural language.

Linguistic theory consists of three subtheories, each corresponding to one of the three components of a linguistic description. The terms 'phonological theory', 'syntactic theory', and 'semantic theory' refer to the subtheories, and 'phonological component', 'syntactic component', and 'semantic component' refer to the corresponding parts of a linguistic description. The phonological component states the rules defining the speaker's tacit knowledge of the phonetic structure of speech sounds; the syntactic component states the rules defining his tacit knowledge of how speech sounds are organized into sentential structures; the semantic component states the rules defining his tacit knowledge of how sentential structures are interpreted as meaningful messages. Jointly, phonological, syntactic, and semantic theory characterize the form of the rules in a linguistic description, specify the theoretical constructs utilized in writing actual rules in appropriate forms, and determine both the internal relations among rules within each component and the relations among the components that weld them into an integrated linguistic description.

The construction of linguistic theory and linguistic descriptions are strongly interdependent. Linguists can abstract out the common features from a set of linguistic descriptions and so generalize from them to a hypothesis about the linguistic universals. Alternatively, linguists can facilitate their task of describing a language by using the model provided by linguistic theory as a pattern on which to systematize the facts uncovered in field work. Accordingly, justification both of linguistic theory and of individual linguistic descriptions depend on a common basis. Putative linguistic universals are inductively extrapolated generalizations, projected from known regularities cutting across a set of already constructed linguistic descriptions. Since their adequacy is thus a matter of whether further facts, upon which newly constructed linguistic descriptions will be based, continue to support them, the same facts that confirm or disconfirm particular descriptions also confirm or disconfirm a linguistic theory. Also, if the general form of a particular linguistic description can be deduced from linguistic theory, so that the linguistic description is supported by a wealth of evidence from many natural languages, then it will be better confirmed than if its support derives solely from the facts about a single natural language.

3. *The Organization of a Linguistic Description.* Linguistic communication presupposes that different speakers possess a common system of internalized rules by which they are able to correlate the same speech signal with the same message. On the current model of a linguistic description,[1] a conception of how such correlations are established is embodied in the organization of a linguistic description.

The syntactic component is the generative source of a linguistic description. It generates abstract formal objects which are the input to the phonological and semantic components. Their outputs are, respectively, phonetic representations and semantic interpretations. Both these components are, therefore, purely interpretive systems. The syntactic description of a sentence consists of a set of *underlying phrase markers,* which give an account of that aspect of the syntax of a sentence which determines its meaning, and a single *superficial phrase marker,* which describes that aspect which determines its phonetic shape. The number of underlying phrase markers indicates the degree of the sentence's syntactic ambiguity. The rules of the phonological component operate on the superficial phrase marker to provide the phonetic representation of the sentence, and the rules of the semantic component operate on the underlying phrase markers to provide its semantic interpretation. The underlying phrase markers are related to the superficial phrase marker by virtue of the fact that this same superficial phrase marker is transformationally derived from each of them. Thus, the linguistic description will correlate the phonetic representation of a sentence with its semantic interpretation as desired, the correlation being effected by the transformational rules in the syntactic component and the manner in which the phonological and semantic components are organized to operate.

[1] Cf. J. J. Katz and P. Postal, *An Integrated Theory of Linguistic Descriptions* (Cambridge, Mass.: MIT Press, 1964), and N. Chomsky, *Aspects of the Theory of Syntax* (Cambridge, Mass.: MIT Press, 1965).

4. *The Psychological and the Epistemological.* Given that linguistic theory is a formal reconstruction of how speakers relate speech signals to messages, it is an explication of a human ability. This makes it a psychological theory. A philosophical problem, on the other hand, concerns the structure of concepts and the grounds for the validity of cognitive or evaluative principles, which makes it epistemological in the broad sense, not psychological. How, then, can linguistic theory offer solutions to philosophical problems when the "solutions" are apparently not even addressed to the right problems?

This criticism rests on a failure to distinguish two senses of the term 'psychological'. The distinction depends on the difference between a speaker's *linguistic competence,* what he tacitly knows about the structure of his language, and his *linguistic performance,* what he does with this knowledge. A theory in linguistics explicates linguistic competence, not linguistic performance. It seeks to reconstruct the logical structure of the principles that speakers have mastered in attaining fluency. On the other hand, a theory of performance seeks to discover the contribution of each of the factors that interplay to produce natural speech with its various and sundry deviations from ideal linguistic forms. Thus, it must consider such linguistically extraneous factors as memory span, perceptual and motor limitations, lapses of attention, pauses, level of motivation, interest, idiosyncratic and random errors, etc. The linguist whose aim is to provide a statement of ideal linguistic form unadulterated by the influence of such extraneous factors can be compared to the logician whose aim is to provide a statement of ideal implicational form unadulterated by extraneous factors that influence the actual inference men draw.

Hence, there are two senses of 'psychological': on one, the subject of a psychological theory is a competence, and, on the other, a performance. The criticism cited above applies to a proposed solution for a philosophical problem extracted from a theory that is psychological in the latter sense. But it does not apply to one extracted from a theory in linguistics that is psychological in the former sense. A theory of performance cannot solve a philosophical problem such as that of formulating an inductive logic that is a valid codification of the principles of nondemonstrative inference in science and daily life. People can be quite consistent in drawing nondemonstrative inferences according to invalid principles, and be inconsistent in their practice of using valid ones. Because a theory of performance must accept such behavior at face value, it has no means of correcting for the acceptance of invalid principles and the rejection of valid ones. In contrast, however, a theory of competence does. Since it regards performance only as evidence for the construction of an idealization, it sifts the facts about behavior, factoring out the distorting influences of variables that are extraneous to the logical structure of the competence. Such a theory has built in a means for correcting itself in cases where invalid principles were accepted or valid ones rejected. Therefore, linguistic theory cannot be criticized as prima facie irrelevant to the solution of philosophical problems.

5. *Grammatical Form and Logical Form.* But to establish the relevance of linguistic theory, it must be shown to offer solutions to significant philosophical problems. One of the pervasive problems of modern philosophy is that of distinguishing between the grammatical and logical forms of sentences. It has long been recognized that the phonetic or orthographic realization of many sentences is such that no analysis of them in terms of traditional taxonomic grammar can reveal the true conceptual structure of the proposition(s) they express. Almost invariably, however, this recognition has led twentieth-century philosophers—Russell, early Wittgenstein, Carnap, and Ryle, to mention some notable examples—to seek a philosophical theory about the logical form of propositions. They assumed that grammar had done what it could, but that its best was not good enough, so that a philosophical theory of one sort or another would be needed to exhibit the conceptual relations unmarked in grammatical analysis.

This assumption is open to a serious challenge, even aside from the fact that such philosophical theories have not achieved much success. From the same cases where grammatical form and logical form do not coincide, one can conclude instead that the traditional taxonomic theory of grammar, on which these philosophers' conception of grammatical form is based, is too limited to reveal the underlying conceptual structure of a sentence. Suitably extended, grammar might well reveal the facts about logical form, too. Philosophers who accepted this assumption simply overlooked the possibility that traditional taxonomic grammar might not be the last word on grammar.

An alternative to a philosophical theory about logical form is, thus, a linguistic theory about logical form. Support for this alternative has come, recently, from Chomsky's work on syntactic theory, which shows that traditional taxonomic grammar is too limited and revises it accordingly.[2] The feasibility of this alternative rests on whether Chomsky's criticism is directed at just the features that make traditional taxonomic grammar incapable of handling logical form and whether the revision provides the theoretical machinery to handle it.

The traditional taxonomic description of an utterance type is a single labeled bracketing that segments it into continuous phonetic stretches and classifies them as constituents of one or another sort. Chomsky's basic criticism is that such description cannot mark a variety of syntactic features because it fails to go below the surface structure of sentences. Consider the sentences: (i) 'John is easy to leave' and (ii) 'John is eager to leave'. On a traditional taxonomic description, both receive the same syntactic analysis, viz.,

$$((\text{John})_{NP}((\text{is})([\begin{smallmatrix} \text{easy} \\ \text{eager} \end{smallmatrix}])_A(\text{to leave})_V)_{VP})_S$$

This analysis, which, on the terminology introduced in section 3, is the superficial phrase marker for (i) and (ii), does not mark the logical difference that in (i) 'John' is the object of the verb 'leave' whereas in (ii) 'John' is its subject. Consider, further, a sentence like: (iii) 'John knows a kinder person than Bill'. The syntactic ambiguity of (iii) cannot be represented in its taxonomic description because a single (superficial) phrase marker cannot explicate the different propositional structures underlying the terms of its ambiguity. Finally, consider a normal imperative such as: (iv) 'Help him!' Ellipsis, which in such cases absents the subject and future-tense auxiliary constituent, cannot be handled by a traditional taxonomic description because it deals only with the phonetically or orthographically realized constituents of a sentence.[3]

These difficulties cannot be remedied by enriching the complexity of superficial phrase markers. More elaborate segmentation and subclassification cannot overcome the inherent inability of this form of description to represent relational information. Rather, the superficial phrase marker, as it stands, has a proper role to play in syntactic

---

[2] Cf. N. Chomsky, *Syntactic Structures* (The Hague: Mouton, 1957), and P. Postal, *Constituent Structure*, publication 30 of the Indiana University Research Center in Anthropology, Folklore, and Linguistics, Bloomington, 1964.

[3] For the syntactic motivation behind the claim that there are such phonetically unrealized constituents in normal imperatives, cf. P. Postal, "Underlying and Superficial Linguistic Structures," *The Harvard Educational Review*, 34, 2 (1964).

description, viz., that of providing the most compact representation of the syntactic information required to determine the phonetic shape of a sentence. What is wrong is that the superficial phrase marker, because it is the only type of description sanctioned by the traditional taxonomic theory of grammar, is made to do work that, in principle, it cannot do so long as it must still play its proper role. To right this wrong, Chomsky introduced the conception of a grammar as a generative, transformational system, to supersede the conception of a grammar as a set of segmentation and classification procedures. Within this new conception, Chomsky and others developed the concept of an underlying phrase marker,[4] a form of syntactic description in which semantically significant grammatical relations can be adequately represented and shown to underlie the phonetic form of sentences on the basis of transformational rules that derive superficial phrase markers from appropriate underlying phrase markers by formally specified operations.

The logical difference between (i) and (ii) noted above can be indicated with the underlying phrase markers:[5]

(I) $(((it)((one)_{NP}((leaves)_V(John)_{NP})_{VP})_S)_{NP}((is)(easy)_A)_{VP})_S$

(II) $((John)_{NP}((is)((eager)_A((John)_{NP}(leaves)_{VP})_S)_A)_{VP})_S$

The grammatical relations *subject of* and *object of* are defined in syntactic theory in terms of subconfigurations of symbols in underlying phrase markers as follows:

Given a configuration of the form

$$((X)_{NP}(Y)_{VP})_S \quad \text{or} \quad ((X)_{NP}((Y)_V(Z)_{NP})_{VP})_S$$

X is the subject of the verb Y and Z is the object of the verb Y.[6]

---

[4] Katz and Postal, *op. cit.*, and Chomsky, *Aspects of the Theory of Syntax*. The notion of an underlying phrase marker used here is the same as Chomsky's notion of a deep structure.

[5] For further discussion, cf. G. A. Miller and N. Chomsky, "Finitary Models of Language Users," *Handbook of Mathematical Psychology*, Vol. II, edited by D. R. Luce, R. R. Bush, and E. Galanter (New York: Wiley, 1963), pp. 476–80, and P. S. Rosenbaum, "The Grammar of English Predicate Complement Constructions," doctoral dissertation, MIT, 1965.

[6] Note that this definition reconstructs the intuitive notion that the subject is the noun phrase preceding the verb in a simple sentence and that the object is the noun phrase following it. Restricting the definition to underlying phrase markers makes it possible to have a single definition, because, then, compound sentences are handled in terms of the simple sentences out of which they are constructed.

By this definition, 'John' in (i) is marked as the object of the verb 'leaves' because it occupies the Z-position and 'leaves' occupies the Y-position in the appropriate subconfiguration of (I), and 'John' in (ii) is marked as the subject of 'leaves' because it occupies the X-position and 'leaves' occupies the Y-position in the appropriate sub-configuration of (II).

Further, since a sentence can have more than one underlying phrase marker in a generative, transformational syntactic component, syntactic ambiguities, such as the ambiguity in (iii), can be repre-sented in terms of appropriately different underlying phrase markers transformationally associated with the same superficial phrase marker. Thus, the superficial phrase marker for (iii), viz.,

$$((\text{John})_{\text{NP}}((\text{knows})_{\text{V}}((\text{a})(\text{kinder})(\text{person})(\text{than})(\text{Bill}))_{\text{NP}})_{\text{VP}})_{\text{S}}$$

is associated with two underlying phrase markers both of which have the general form[7]

$$((\text{John})_{\text{NP}}((\text{knows})_{\text{V}}((\text{a})(.\ .\ .)_{\text{S}}(\text{person}))_{\text{NP}})_{\text{VP}})_{\text{S}}$$

but in one of which

$$.\ .\ . = (\text{the person})_{\text{NP}}((\text{is})(\text{more})(\text{than})((\text{Bill})_{\text{NP}} \\ ((\text{is})(\text{kind})_{\text{A}})_{\text{VP}})_{\text{S}}(\text{kind})_{\text{A}})_{\text{VP}}$$

where, in the other,

$$.\ .\ . = (\text{the person})_{\text{NP}}((\text{is})(\text{more})(\text{than})((\text{the})(\text{Bill})_{\text{NP}}(\text{knows})_{\text{V}} \\ (\text{the person})_{\text{NP}})_{\text{VP}})_{\text{S}}(\text{person}))_{\text{NP}}((\text{is})(\text{kind})_{\text{A}})_{\text{VP}})_{\text{S}}(\text{kind})_{\text{A}})_{\text{VP}}$$

The former case underlies the term of the ambiguity on which the person that John knows is kinder than Bill is, and the latter case underlies the term on which the person that John knows is kinder than the person Bill knows.

Finally, in ellipsis, phonetically unrealized constituents can be specified in underlying phrase markers and deleted in the transforma-tional derivation of the superficial phrase marker. This enables us to account for their syntactic relations and their semantic contribution without falsely characterizing the phonetic shape of the sentence, as would be required if we modified the superficial phrase marker to account for them.

But, although it is clear from these examples that the distinction

---

[7] For further discussion, cf. C. S. Smith, "A Class of Complex Modifiers in English," *Language* 37 (1961): 342–65.

between underlying and superficial syntactic structure is a significant step toward the philosopher's distinction between logical form and grammatical form, even a fully developed transformational syntactic component would not provide all the theoretical machinery necessary to deal adequately with logical form. Philosophers have rightly held that an analysis of the logical form of a sentence should tell us not only about the formal relations among its constituents but also about the semantic properties and relations of the proposition(s) expressed by it. In particular, an account of the logical form of a sentence should specify whether it is (1) *semantically anomalous* (i.e., whether it expresses any proposition at all), (2) *semantically ambiguous* (i.e., whether it expresses more than one proposition, and if so, how many), (3) *a paraphrase of a given sentence* (i.e., whether the two sentences express the same proposition), (4) *analytic,* (5) *contradictory,* (6) *synthetic,* (7) *inconsistent with a given sentence,* (8) *entails* or *is entailed by a given sentence,* (9) *a presupposition of a given sentence,* and so on.

The fact that a transformational syntactic component does not suffice, by itself, to determine such semantic properties and relations has brought about the formulation of a conception of a semantic component designed to determine them.[8] This conception is based on the idea that a speaker's ability to produce and understand sentences he has never before spoken or heard depends on his mastery of principles according to which the meanings of new and unfamiliar sentences can be obtained by a process in which the meanings of syntactically compound constituents are composed out of the meanings of their parts. The semantic component formally reconstructs these compositional principles. It has a *dictionary* that contains an account of the meaning of each syntactically atomic constituent in the language, i.e., representations of the senses of *lexical items,* and a set of *projection rules* that provide the combinatorial machinery for representing the senses of compound constituents on the basis of representations of the senses of the lexical items that make them up. The dictionary is a list of *entries,* each of which consists of a lexical item written in phonological form, a set of syntactic features, and a set of *lexical readings.* A lexical reading, which represents one sense

[8] Katz and Fodor, "The Structure of a Semantic Theory," *Language* 39 (1963): 170–210; reprinted in *The Structure of Language: Readings in the Philosophy of Language,* Fodor and Katz, eds. (Englewood Cliffs, N.J.: Prentice-Hall, Inc., 1964), pp. 479–518.

of a lexical item, consists of a set of *semantic markers* and a *selection restriction*.

A semantic marker is a theoretical term representing a class of equivalent concepts. For example, the semantic marker (Physical Object) represents the class of concepts of a spatially and temporally contiguous material entity each of us has in mind when we distinguish the meanings of words like 'chair', 'stone', 'man', 'building', etc. from the meanings of words like 'virtue', 'togetherness', 'shadow', 'emrose', etc. Semantic markers enable us to state empirical generalizations about the senses of words (expressions, and sentences), for, by including the semantic marker (Physical Object) in a lexical reading for each of the words in the former group and excluding it from the lexical readings for words in the latter, we thereby express the generalization that the former words are similar in meaning in this respect but that the latter are not. A selection restriction states a condition—framed in terms of a requirement about the presence or absence of certain semantic markers—under which a reading of a constituent can combine with readings of other constituents to form *derived readings* representing conceptually congruous senses of syntactically compound constituents.

The semantic component operates on underlying phrase markers, converting them into *semantically interpreted underlying phrase markers,* which formally represent all the information about the meaning of the sentences to which they are assigned. Initially, each of the lexical items in an underlying phrase marker receives a subset of the lexical readings that it has in its dictionary entry. Then, the projection rules combine lexical readings from sets assigned to different lexical items to form derived readings, and these are combined to form further derived readings, and so on. Each derived reading is assigned to the compound constituent whose parts are the constituents whose readings were combined to form the derived reading. In this way each constituent in the underlying phrase marker, including the whole sentence, is assigned a set of readings that represents its senses. Thus, a semantically interpreted underlying phrase marker is an underlying phrase marker each of whose brackets is assigned a maximal set of readings (where by 'maximal' is meant that the set contains every reading that can be formed by the projection rules without violating a selection restriction).

We are now in a position to define the notions 'logical form' and 'grammatical form': *The logical form of a sentence is the set of its semantically interpreted underlying phrase markers; the grammatical form of a sentence is its superficial phrase marker with its phonetic representation.* Accordingly, the syntactic and semantic components for a language comprise a theory of logical form for that language, whereas the syntactic and phonological components for the language comprise a theory of grammatical form for it. Similarly, syntactic theory and semantic theory comprise a theory of logical form in general, whereas syntactic theory and phonological theory comprise a theory of grammatical form in general.

6. *Semantic Properties and Relations.* However, semantic theory does much more than complete the account of the distinction between logical form and grammatical form. It also provides solutions to the philosophical problems of explicating concepts such as (1) through (9) above. Definitions of these concepts thus constitute further support for the relevance thesis that I am defending.

Restricting our attention to syntactically unambiguous sentences, we can provide a general idea of such definitions. First, a sentence is semantically anomalous just in case the set of readings assigned to it is empty. This explicates the notion that what prevents a sentence from having a meaningful interpretation are conceptual incongruities between senses of its parts that keep these senses from compositionally forming a sense for the whole sentence. Second, a sentence is semantically unique, i.e., expresses exactly one proposition, just in case the set of readings assigned to it contains one member. Third, a sentence is semantically ambiguous just in case the set of readings assigned to it contains n members, for $n > 1$. Fourth, a sentence is a paraphrase of another sentence just in case the sets of readings assigned to the two sentences have a member in common. Fifth, two sentences are full paraphrases just in case both are assigned the same set of readings. Sixth, a sentence is analytic if there is a reading assigned to it that is derived from a reading for its subject and a reading for its verb phrase such that the latter contains no semantic markers not already in the former.[9] Finally, a sentence entails another sen-

[9] This is a simplified version of the definition of analyticity given in Katz, "Analyticity and Contradiction in Natural Language," and in Katz, *The Philosophy of Language* (New York: Harper & Row, 1965). This concept of analyticity can be regarded as a linguistically systematized version of Kant's concept of analyticity, with two refinements: (1) that Kant's somewhat vague and restricted notions of subject and predicate are replaced by the formally defined grammatical relations *subject of S* and *verb phrase of S,* and (2) that Kant's metaphorical notions of concept and of containment are replaced by

tence if each semantic marker in the reading for the latter's subject is already contained in the reading for the former's subject and if each semantic marker in the reading for the latter's verb phrase is already contained in the reading for the former's verb phrase.[10]

The adequacy of these definitions as solutions to the philosophical problems to which they are addressed is entirely a matter of their empirical justification. Since such definitions are part of semantic theory, which, in turn, is part of linguistic theory, they must be justified on the same evidential basis as any other linguistic universal. Thus, their empirical evaluation consists in verifying the predictions to which they lead about the semantic properties and relations of sentences from natural languages. Given the semantically interpreted underlying phrase marker for a sentence S in a language L and the definition of a semantic property P or relation R, we can deduce a prediction about whether S has P or bears R to some other sentence. This deduction is merely a matter of determining whether or not S's (their) semantically interpreted underlying phrase marker(s) possess the formal features required by the definition of P or R. Such predictions can be checked against the ways that fluent speakers of L sort sentences in terms of their naive linguistic intuitions. Hence, the justification of these definitions depends on whether such predictions accord with the judgments of fluent speakers about the clear cases from L.

To remove from these definitions the stigma that automatically attaches to definitions of semantic properties and relations since Quine, I will show how the above definition of analyticity avoids the criticism that Quine leveled against Carnap's explication of this concept.[11] One of Quine's major criticisms was that Carnap's explications of analyticity, contradiction, and related concepts merely defined one of these concepts in terms of another, whose own definition quickly brought us back to the first without offering a genuine analysis of any of them. The above definition of analyticity cannot be criticized

---

the formal analogues of a reading and the inclusion of a set of semantic markers in another set. The semantic properties of contradiction and syntheticity can also be defined, and so can inconsistency and other related cases, but their definitions involve too many technicalities for them to be given here.

[10] A conditional sentence is analytic just in case its antecedent entails its consequent.

[11] W. V. O. Quine, "Two Dogmas of Empiricism," in *From a Logical Point of View* (Cambridge, Mass.: Harvard, 1953).

on grounds of such circularity, because it is not the case that any of these related terms were used to define others. The unique feature of the above definitions is that the defining condition in each is stated exclusively in terms of a different set of formal features in semantically interpreted underlying phrase markers. Moreover, Quine criticizes Carnap for merely labeling sentences as analytic without ever indicating just what is attributed to sentences so labeled. On Carnap's account, the term 'analytic' is just an unexplained label. But, on my account, labeling a sentence as analytic attributes to it that linguistic structure formalized in the definition that introduces 'analytic' in linguistic theory. Lastly, the definitions in semantic theory cannot be criticized for being too particularistic, because, as Quine requires, they are formulated for variable 'S' and 'L'. This is guaranteed by the fact that they are given in linguistic theory and that their defining conditions are formulated in terms of semantically interpreted underlying phrase markers, which are associated with each sentence in any linguistic description.

7. *Conclusion*. My defense of the relevance of linguistics to philosophy is admittedly incomplete. Not only is more in the way of clarification and justification of linguistic theory needed, but the treatment of the philosophical problems discussed needs to be considerably expanded. In addition, to indicate adequately the scope of the defense, the range of problems considered should be extended to include others that have already been dealt with in linguistic theory, e.g., categories, innate ideas, presupposition, etc. But these omissions are not sins, since there is a substantial literature available in which these subjects are treated.

Semantics for Natural Languages*

DONALD DAVIDSON

A theory of the semantics of a natural language aims to give the meaning of every meaningful expression, but it is a question what form a theory should take if it is to accomplish this. Since there seems to be no clear limit to the number of meaningful expressions, a workable theory must account for the meaning of each expression on the basis of the patterned exhibition of a finite number of features. But even if there were a practical constraint on the length of the sentences a person can send and receive with understanding, a satisfactory semantics would need to explain the contribution of repeatable features to the meaning of sentences in which they occur.

I suggest that a theory of truth for a language does, in a minimal but important respect, do what we want, that is, give the meanings of all independently meaningful expressions on the basis of an analysis of their structure. And on the other hand, a semantic theory of a natural language cannot be considered adequate unless it provides an account of the concept of truth for that language along the general lines proposed by Tarski for formalized languages. I think both linguists and philosophers interested in natural languages have missed the key importance of the theory of truth partly because they have not realized that a theory of truth gives a precise, profound and testable answer to the question how finite resources suffice to explain the infinite semantic capacities of language, and partly because they have exaggerated the difficulties in the way of giving a formal theory of truth for a natural language. In any event the attempt is instructive, for insofar as we succeed in giving such a theory for a natural language, we see the natural language as a formal system; and insofar as we make the construction of such a theory our aim, we can think of linguists and analytic philosophers as co-workers[1].

* Reprinted by permission from *Linguaggi Nella Società e Nella Tecnica*, Edizioni di Comunità, Milan 1970, pp. 177–88.

[1] I have been promoting this view in lectures and papers since 1953. Recent papers of mine that touch on the subject include "Truth and Meaning", *Synthese*, 17 (1967), pp. 304–23, "Theories of Meaning and Learnable Languages," in *Logic, Methodology and Philosophy of Science, Proceedings of the*

By a theory of truth I mean a set of axioms that entail, for every sentence in the language, a statement of the conditions under which it is true. Obviously if we have a definition of a truth-predicate satisfying Tarski's Convention T we have a theory of truth[2], but in general the characterization of a theory of truth demands much less. If no further restrictions are imposed, some theories of truth will be of little intrinsic interest. For example, we could simply take as axioms all sentences of the form "*s* is true if and only if *p*" where "*s*" is to be replaced by a standardized description of a sentence and "*p*" by that sentence (assuming that the metalanguage contains the object language). Such a theory would yield no insight into the structure of the language and would thus provide no hint of an answer to the question how the meaning of a sentence depends on its composition. We could block this particular aberration by stipulating that the non-logical axioms be finite in number; in what follows I shall assume that this restriction is in force, though it may be that other ways exist of ensuring that a theory of truth has the properties we want.

What properties do we want? An acceptable theory should, as we have said, account for the meaning (or conditions of truth) of every sentence by analyzing it as composed, in truth-relevant ways, of elements drawn from a finite stock. A second natural demand is that the theory provide a method for deciding, given an arbitrary sentence, what its meaning is. (By satisfying these two conditions a theory may be said to show that the language it describes is *learnable* and *scrutable*). A third condition is that the statements of truth conditions for individual sentences entailed by the theory should, in some way yet to be made precise, draw upon the same concepts as the sentences whose truth conditions they state.

Theories of the sort Tarski showed how to devise clearly enough have these desirable characteristics. The last condition, for example, is satisfied in an elementary way by a theory couched in a metalanguage that contains the object language, for in the required statements of the form "*s* is true if and only if *p*" the truth conditions of *s* are given by the sentence that replaces "*p*", namely *s* itself, and so make no use of any concepts not directly called upon in understanding *s*.

1964 International Congress (Yehoshua Bar-Hillel, ed.), Amsterdam 1965, pp. 383–94, and "On Saying That", *Synthese*, 19 (1968–69), pp. 130–46.

[2] A. Tarski, "The Concept of Truth in Formalized Languages", in *Logic, Semantics, Metamathematics*, Oxford 1956, pp. 152–278.

If the metalanguage does not contain the object language, it is less obvious when this criterion is satisfied: and natural languages raise further problems that will be touched upon presently.

It seems natural to interpret the third condition as prohibiting the appearance of a semantic term in the statement of the truth conditions of a sentence unless that sentence already contains the semantic term (or a translation of it). It is not clear whether or not this would rule out explicit resort to semantic concepts in the statement of truth conditions for modal sentences (since it is uncertain whether or not these should be construed from the start as semantic in nature). But this constraint does appear to threaten theories that appeal to an un-analyzed concept of denoting or naming, as well as those that make truth in a model the fundamental semantical notion[3].

To put this interpretation on the third condition is, it seems, to judge much recent work in semantics irrelevant to present purposes; so I intend here to leave the question open, along with many further questions concerning the detailed formulation of the standards we should require of a theory of truth. My present interest is not in ar-guing disputed points but to urge the general relevance and produc-tiveness of requiring of any theory of meaning (semantics) for a natural language that it give a recursive account of truth. It seems to me no inconsiderable merit of this suggestion that it provides a framework within which a multitude of issues and problems can be sharply stated.

To give a recursive theory of truth for a language is to show that the syntax of the language is formalizable in at least the sense that every true expression may be analyzed as formed from elements (the "vocabulary"), a finite supply of which suffice for the language by the application of rules, a finite number of which suffice for the lan-guage. But even if we go on to assume that falsehood may be defined in terms of truth, or independently and similarly characterized, it does not follow that sentencehood or grammaticalness can be recursively defined. So arguments designed to establish that a formal recursive account of syntax (sentencehood or grammaticalness) cannot be given for a natural language do not necessarily discredit the attempt to give a theory of truth. It should also be mentioned that the sug-gested conditions of adequacy for a theory of truth do not (obviously, anyway) entail that even the true sentences of the object language

[3] Here and elsewhere in this paper I am much in debt to John Wallace.

have the form of some standard logical system. Thus supposing it were clear (which it is not) that the deep structure of English (or another natural language) cannot be represented by a formal language with the usual quantificational structure, it still would not follow that there was no way of giving a theory of truth.

A theory of truth for a natural language must take account of the fact that many sentences vary in truth value depending on the time they are spoken, the speaker, and even, perhaps, the audience. We can accommodate this phenomenon either by declaring that it is particular utterances or speech acts, and not sentences, that have truth values, or by making truth a relation that holds between a sentence, a speaker, and a time.

To thus accommodate the indexical, or demonstrative, elements in a natural language is to accept a radical conceptual change in the way truth can be defined, as will be appreciated by reflection on how Convention T must be revised to make truth sensitive to context. But the change need not mean a departure from formality[4].

The fear is often expressed by philosophers that a formal theory of truth cannot be made to cope with the problems of ambiguity in natural language that absorb so much of the energy of linguists. In thinking about this question it may help to distinguish two claims. One is that formal theories of truth have not traditionally been designed to deal with ambiguity, and it would change their character to equip them to do so. This claim is justified, and harmless. Theories of truth in Tarski's style do not in general treat questions of definition for the primitive vocabulary (as opposed to questions of translation and logical form); on the other hand there is nothing in a theory of truth inimical to the satisfactory treatment of the problems a lexicon is designed to solve. The second claim is that some sorts of ambiguity necessarily prevent our giving a theory of truth. Before this thesis can be evaluated it will be necessary to be far clearer than we are now about the criteria of success in giving a theory of truth for a natural language. Without attempting a deep discussion here, let me indicate why I think the issue cannot be settled by quoting a few puzzling cases.

[4] Whether we want to consider theories of this sort part of semantics is a matter for choice: if theory of truth is semantics, we are still within the domain of semantics; while if any reference to speakers or speech acts is a move to pragmatics, then theory of truth for a natural language belongs to pragmatics.

Bar-Hillel gives an example like this: "They came by slow train and plane"[5]. We can take "slow" as modifying the conjunction that follows, or only "train". Of course an adequate theory would uncover the ambiguity; a theory of truth would in particular need to show how an utterance of the sentence could be true under one interpretation and false under another. So far there is no difficulty for a theory of truth. But Bar-Hillel makes the further observation that the context of utterance might easily resolve the ambiguity for any normal speaker of English, and yet the resolution could depend on general knowledge in a way that could not (practically, at least) be captured by a formal theory. By granting this, as I think we must, we accept a limitation on what a theory of truth can be expected to do. Within the limitation it may still be possible to give a theory that captures an important concept of meaning.

In a related, and ingenious, case, Bar-Hillel points out that in most contexts someone who knows English will have no trouble resolving the ambiguity in an utterance of "The box was in the pen"; the hearer will know that the pen is a playpen and not a writing pen[6]. Bar-Hillel maintains that machine translation can never be perfected to handle such cases (assuming that the language into which we are translating does not have a word that reflects the ambiguity of "pen"). Bar-Hillel may well be right about this and hence about the "nonfeasibility of fully automatic machine translation"; but it would be a mistake (which he does not make) to argue from this to the impossibility of a theory of truth. For example, a theory might handle the troublesome sentence along these lines:

(T1) "The box was in the pen" is true for an English-speaker x at time t if and only if either the box was in the playpen before t and the circumstances surrounding v at t meet condition $c,$ or the box was in the writing pen before t and the circumstances surrounding x at t meet condition c'.

Whether such a theory was acceptable would depend on what we were prepared to allow in the description of the relevant conditions. In any case, it is worth remarking that T1 could be translated into a (meta) language containing no single word with the ambiguity of "pen", thus illustrating the fact that it might be possible to give a

[5] Yehoshua Bar-Hillel, *Language and Information,* Jerusalem, 1964, p. 182.
[6] *Ibid.,* pp. 174–79.

theory of truth for a language L in another language M without being able (automatically) to translate from L into M.

We have touched lightly on a few of the considerations that have led linguists and philosophers to doubt whether it is possible to give a formal theory of truth for a natural language. I have suggested that the pessimism is premature, particularly in the absence of a discussion of criteria of adequacy. On the other hand, it would be foolish not to recognize a difference in the interests and methods of those who study contrived languages and those who study natural languages.

When logicians and philosophers of language express reservations concerning the treatment of natural languages as formal systems, it may be because they are interested mainly in metatheoretical matters like consistency, completeness and decidability. Such studies assume exact knowledge of the language being studied, a kind of precision that can be justified only by viewing the relevant features of the object language as fixed by legislation. This attitude is clearly not appropriate to the empirical study of language.

It would be misleading, however, to conclude that there are two kinds of language, natural and artificial. The contrast is better drawn in terms of guiding interests. We can ask for a description of the structure of a natural language: the answer must be an empirical theory, open to test and subject to error, and doomed to be to some extent incomplete and schematic. Or we can ask about the formal properties of the structures we thus abstract. The difference is like that between applied and pure geometry.

I have been urging that no definite obstacle stands in the way of giving a formal theory of truth for a natural language; it remains to say why it would be desirable. The reasons are of necessity general and programmatic, for what is being recommended is not a particular theory, but a criterion of theories. The claim is that if this criterion is accepted, the empirical study of language will gain in clarity and significance. The question whether a theory is correct can be made reasonably sharp and testable; the theories that are called for are powerful in explanatory and predictive power, and make use of sophisticated conceptual resources that are already well understood. Among the problems which a satisfactory theory of truth would solve, or help solve, are many which interest both linguists and philosophers; so as a fringe benefit we may anticipate a degree of convergence in the methods and interests of philosophy and linguistics. Let me try, briefly, to give color to these remarks.

One relatively sharp demand on a theory for a language is that it give a recursive characterization of sentencehood. This part of theory is testable to the extent that we have, or can contrive, reliable ways of telling whether an expression is a sentence. Let us imagine for now that we can do this well enough to get ahead. In defining sentencehood what we capture, roughly, is the idea of an independently meaningful expression. But meaningfulness is only the shadow of meaning; a full-fledged theory should not merely ticket the meaningful expressions, but give their meanings. The point is acknowledged by many linguists today, but for the most part they admit they do not know how to meet this additional demand on theory, nor even how to formulate the demand[7]. So now I should like to say a bit more in support of the claim that a theory of truth does "give the meaning" of sentences.

A theory of truth entails, for each sentence *s,* a statement of the form "*s* is true if and only if *p*" where in the simplest case "*p*" is replaced by *s*. Since the words "is true if and only if" are invariant, we may interpret them if we please as meaning "means that". So construed, a sample might then read " 'Socrates is wise' means that Socrates is wise".

This way of bringing out the relevance of a theory of truth to questions of meaning is illuminating, but we must beware lest it encourage certain errors. One such error is to think that all we can learn from a theory of truth about the meaning of a particular sentence is contained in the biconditional demanded by convention T. What we can learn is brought out rather in the *proof* of such a biconditional, for the proof must demonstrate, step by step, how the truth-value of the sentence depends upon a recursively given structure. Once we have a theory, producing the required proof is easy enough; the process could be mechanized.

To see the structure of a sentence through the eyes of a theory of truth is to see it as built by devices a finite number of which suffice for every sentence; the structure of the sentence thus determines its relations to other sentences. And indeed there is no giving the truth conditions of all sentences without showing that some sentences are logical consequences of others; if we regard the structure

---

[7] See, for example, Chomsky's remarks on semantics in "Topics in the Theory of Generative Grammar", in *Current Trends in Linguistics* (ed. by Thomas A. Sebeok), vol. III, The Hague, 1966.

revealed by a theory of truth as deep grammar, then grammar and logic must go hand in hand.

There is a sense, then, in which a theory of truth accounts for the role each sentence plays in the language insofar as that role depends on the sentence's being a potential bearer of truth or falsity; and the account is given in terms of structure. This remark is doubtless far less clear than the facts that inspire it, but my purpose in putting the matter this way is to justify the claim that a theory of truth shows how "the meaning of each sentence depends on the meaning of the words". Or perhaps it is enough to say that we have given a sense to a suggestive but vague claim; there is no reason not to welcome alternative readings if they are equally clear. In any case, to accept my proposal is to give up the attempt to find entities to serve as meanings of sentences and words. A theory of truth does without; but this should be counted in its favor, at least until someone gives a coherent and satisfactory theory of meaning that employs meanings.

Convention T, suitably modified to apply to a natural language, provides a formal criterion of success in giving an account of meaning. But how can we test such an account empirically? Here is the second case in which we might be misled by the remark that the biconditionals required by Convention T could be read as giving meanings, for what this wrongly suggests is that testing a theory of truth calls for direct insight into what each sentence means. But in fact, all that is needed is the ability to recognize when the required biconditionals are true. This means that in principle it is no harder to test the empirical adequacy of a theory of truth than it is for a competent speaker of English to decide whether sentences like " 'Snow is white' is true if and only if snow is white" are true. So semantics, or the theory of truth at least, seems on as firm a footing empirically as syntax. It may in fact be easier in many cases for a speaker to say what the truth conditions of a sentence are than to say whether the sentence is grammatical. It may not be clear whether "The child seems sleeping" is grammatical, much less meaningful; but surely "The child seems sleeping" is true if and only if the child seems sleeping.

I have been imagining the situation where the metalanguage contains the object-language, so that we may ask a native speaker to react to the familiar biconditionals that connect a sentence and its description. A more radical case arises if we want to test a theory stated in our own language about the language of a foreign speaker. Here again a theory of truth can be tested, though not as easily or directly as before. The process will have to be something like that described by Quine in Chapter 2 of *Word and Object*[8]. We will try to notice under what conditions the alien speaker assents to or dissents from, a variety of his sentences. The relevant conditions will, of course, be what we take to be the truth-conditions of his sentences. We will have to assume that most of his assents are to true, and his dissents from false, sentences—an inevitable assumption since the alternative is unintelligible. Yet Quine is right, I think, in holding that an important degree of indeterminacy will remain after all the evidence is in; a number of significantly different theories of truth will fit the evidence equally well[9].

Making a systematic account of truth central in empirical semantics is in a way merely a matter of stating old goals more sharply. Still, the line between clarification and innovation in science is blurred, and it seems likely that the change will shift priorities in linguistic research. Some problems that have dominated recent work on semantics will fade in importance: the attempt to give "the meaning" of sentences, and to account for synonymy, analyticity and ambiguity. For the first of these, the theory of truth provides a kind of substitute; the second and third become unnecessary appendages; the fourth reappears in a special form. What will emerge as the deep problems are the difficulties of reference, of giving a satisfactory semantics for modal sentences, sentences about propositional attitudes, mass terms, adverbial modification, attributive adjectives, imperatives and interrogatives; and so on through a long list familiar, for the most part, to philosophers.

It is a question how much of a realignment we are talking about for linguistics. This depends largely on the extent to which the structure revealed by a theory of truth can be identified with the "deep structure" transformational grammarians seek. In one respect, logical structure (as we may call the structure developed by a theory of truth) and deep structure could be the same, for both are intended to be the foundation of semantics. Deep structure must also serve, however, as the basis for the transformations that produce surface structures, and it is an open question whether logical structure can

---

[8] W. V. Quine, *Word and Object,* New York, 1960.
[9] For further discussion of this point see "Truth and Meaning", *cit.*

do this job, or do it well. No arguments to show logical structure won't serve seem conclusive; and it would be strange if the structure essential to an account of truth were not effectively tied to the patterns of sound we use to convey truth.

Finally, deep structure is asked by some linguists to reflect the "internalized grammar" of speakers of the language. Chomsky in particular has argued that the superiority of transformational grammars over others that might be equally good at accounting for the totality of grammatical sentences lies in the fact that transformational grammars can be made to "correspond to the linguistic intuition of the native speaker"[10]. The problem is to find a relatively clear test of when a theory corresponds to a speaker's linguistic intuition. I would like to suggest that we can give empirical bite to this idea if we take deep structure to be logical form. I will illustrate by commenting on a passage in Chomsky[11].

Chomsky says that the following two sentences, though they have the same surface structure, differ in deep structure:

(1) I persuaded John to leave
(2) I expected John to leave

The demonstration rests chiefly on the observation that when an embedded sentence in a sentence somewhat like (2) is transformed to the passive, the result is "cognitively synonymous" with the active form; but a similar transformation does not yield a synonymous result for the analogue of (1). The observation is clearly correct, but how does it show that (1) and (2) have radically different deep structures? At most the evidence suggests that a theory that assigns different structures to (1) and (2) may be simpler than one that does not. But how our linguistic intuitions have been tapped to prove a difference here is certainly obscure.

But of course Chomsky is right; there is a contrast between (1) and (2), and it emerges dramatically the moment we start thinking in terms of constructing a theory of truth. Indeed we need go no further than to ask about the semantic role of the word "John" in both sentences. In (1), "John" can be replaced by any coreferring term without altering the truth-value of (1); this is not true of (2). The contribution of the word "John" to the truth-conditions of (1) must therefore be radically different from its contribution to the truth-

[10] N. Chomsky, *Aspects of the Theory of Syntax*, Cambridge (Mass.), 1965, p. 24.

[11] *Ibid.*, p. 22 ff.

conditions of (2). This way of showing there is a difference in the semantic structure of (1) and (2) requires no appeal to "the speaker's tacit knowledge" of the grammar or the "intrinsic competence of the idealized native speaker". It rests on the explicit knowledge any speaker of English has of the way in which (1) and (2) may vary in truth under substitutions for the word "John".

Yet these last remarks do not begin to do justice to the method of truth. They show that by bearing the requirements of a theory of truth in mind we can throw in relief far more plainly than Chomsky succeeds in doing our feeling of a difference in structure between (1) and (2). So far, though, the evidence to which we are appealing is of much the same sort as Chomsky uses: mainly questions of the loss or preservation of truth value under transformations. Such considerations will no doubt continue to guide the constructive and analytic labors of linguists as they long have those of philosophers. The beauty of a theory of the sort we have been discussing is that these intimations of structure, however useful or essential they may be to the discovery of a suitable theory, need play no direct role in testing the final product.

Languages, Language, and Grammar*

DAVID LEWIS

THESIS

What is a language? Something which assigns meanings to certain
strings of types of sounds or of marks. It could therefore be a function, a set of ordered pairs of strings and meanings. The entities in
the domain of the function are certain finite sequences of types of
vocal sounds, or of types of inscribable marks; if σ is in the domain
of a language L, let us call σ a *sentence of L*. The entities in the
range of the function are meanings: if σ is a sentence of L, let us
call $L(\sigma)$ the *meaning of σ in L*. What could a meaning of a sentence be? Something which, when combined with factual information
about the world—or factual information about *any* possible world—
yields a truth-value. It could therefore be a function from worlds to
truth-values—or more simply, a set of worlds. We can say that a sentence σ is *true in* a language L *at* a world w if and only if w belongs
to the set of worlds $L(\sigma)$. We can say that σ is *true in L* (without
mentioning a world) if and only if our actual world belongs to $L(\sigma)$.
We can say that σ is *analytic in L* if and only if every possible world
belongs to $L(\sigma)$. And so on, in the obvious way.

ANTITHESIS

What is language? A social phenomenon which is part of the natural
history of human beings; a sphere of human action, wherein people
utter strings of vocal sounds, or inscribe strings of marks, and wherein

* Reprinted with permission of the author and the publishers from David
Lewis, "Languages and Language," from *Minnesota Studies in Philosophy of
Science,* Volume VI, edited by Keith Gunderson, University of Minnesota
Press, Minneapolis, © University of Minnesota; and from David K. Lewis,
Convention: A Philosophical Study, Cambridge, Mass.: Harvard University
Press. Copyright 1969 by the President and Fellows of Harvard College. It
should be noted that the treatment of convention in "Languages and Language"
is not in full agreement with the treatment in the earlier book, *Convention.*

people respond by thought or action to the sounds or marks which they observe to have been so produced.

This verbal activity is, for the most part, rational. He who produces certain sounds or marks does so for a reason. He knows that someone else, upon hearing his sounds or seeing his marks, is apt to form a certain belief, or act in a certain way. He wants, for some reason, to bring about that belief or action. Thus his beliefs and desires give him a reason to produce the sounds or marks, and he does. He who responds to the sounds or marks in a certain way also does so for a reason. He knows how the production of sounds or marks depends upon the producer's state of mind. When he observes the sounds or marks, he is therefore in a position to infer something about the producer's state of mind. He can probably also infer something about the conditions which caused that state of mind. He may merely come to believe these conclusions, or he may act upon them in accordance with his other beliefs and his desires.

Not only do both have reasons for thinking and acting as they do; they know something about each other, so each is in a position to replicate the other's reasons. Each one's replication of the other's reasons forms part of his own reason for thinking and acting as he does; and each is in a position to replicate the other's replication of his own reasons. Therefore the Gricean mechanism[1] operates: X intends to bring about a response on the part of Y by getting Y to recognize that X intends to bring about that response; Y does recognize X's intention, and is thereby given some sort of reason to respond just as X intended him to.

Within any suitable population, various regularities can be found in this rational verbal activity. There are regularities whereby the production of sounds or marks depends upon various aspects of the state of mind of the producer. There are regularities whereby various aspects of responses to sounds or marks depend upon the sounds or marks to which one is responding. Some of these regularities are accidental. Others can be explained, and different ones can be explained in very different ways.

Some of them can be explained as conventions of the population in which they prevail. Conventions are regularities in action, or in action and belief, which are arbitrary but perpetuate themselves because they serve some sort of common interest. Past conformity

[1] H. P. Grice, "Meaning," *Philosophical Review* 66 (1957): 377–88.

breeds future conformity because it gives one a reason to go on conforming; but there is some alternative regularity which could have served instead, and would have perpetuated itself in the same way if only it had got started.

More precisely: a regularity R, in action or in action and belief, is a *convention* in a population P if and only if, within P, the following six conditions hold. (Or at least they almost hold. A few exceptions to the "everyone"'s can be tolerated.)

(1) Everyone conforms to R.

(2) Everyone believes that the others conform to R.

(3) This belief that the others conform to R gives everyone a good and decisive reason to conform to R himself. His reason may be that, in particular, those of the others he is now dealing with conform to R; or his reason may be that there is general or widespread conformity, or that there has been, or that there will be. His reason may be a practical reason, if conforming to R is a matter of acting in a certain way; or it may be an epistemic reason, if conforming to R is a matter of believing in a certain way. First case: according to his beliefs, some desired end may be reached by means of some sort of action in conformity to R, provided that the others (all or some of them) also conform to R; therefore he wants to conform to R if they do. Second case: his beliefs, together with the premise that others conform to R, deductively imply or inductively support some conclusion; and in believing this conclusion, he would thereby conform to R. Thus reasons for conforming to a convention by believing something—like reasons for belief in general—are believed premises tending to confirm the truth of the belief in question. Note that I am *not* speaking here of practical reasons for acting so as to somehow produce in oneself a certain desired belief.

(4) There is a general preference for general conformity to R rather than slightly-less-than-general conformity—in particular, rather than conformity by all but any one. (This is not to deny that some state of *widespread* non-conformity to R might be even more preferred.) Thus everyone who believes that at least almost everyone conforms to R will want the others, as well as himself, to conform. This condition serves to distinguish cases of convention, in which there is a predominant coincidence of interest, from cases of deadlocked conflict. In the latter cases, it may be that each is doing the best he can by conforming to R, given that the others do so; but

each wishes the others did not conform to R, since he could then gain at their expense.

(5) R is not the only possible regularity meeting the last two conditions. There is at least one alternative R' such that the belief that the others conformed to R' would give everyone a good and decisive practical or epistemic reason to conform to R' likewise; such that there is a general preference for general conformity to R' rather than slightly-less-than-general conformity to R'; and such that there is normally no way of conforming to R and R' both. Thus the alternative R' could have perpetuated itself as a convention instead of R; this condition provides for the characteristic arbitrariness of conventions.

(6) Finally, the various facts listed in conditions (1)–(5) are matters of *common* (or *mutual*) *knowledge:* they are known to everyone, it is known to everyone that they are known to everyone, and so on. The knowledge mentioned here may be merely potential: knowledge that would be available if one bothered to think hard enough. Everyone must potentially know that (1)–(5) hold; potentially know that the others potentially know it; and so on. This condition ensures stability. If anyone tries to replicate another's reasoning, perhaps including the other's replication of his own reasoning . . . , the result will reinforce rather than subvert his expectation of conformity to R. Perhaps a negative version of (6) would do the job: no one *dis*believes that (1)–(5) hold, no one believes that others disbelieve this, and so on.

This definition can be tried out on all manner of regularities which we would be inclined to call conventions. It is a convention to drive on the right. It is a convention to mark poisons with skull and crossbones. It is a convention to dress as we do. It is a convention to train beasts to turn right on "gee" and left on "haw." It is a convention to give goods and services in return for certain pieces of paper or metal. And so on.

The common interests which sustain conventions are as varied as the conventions themselves. Our convention to drive on the right is sustained by our interest in not colliding. Our convention for marking poisons is sustained by our interest in making it easy for everyone to recognize poisons. Our conventions of dress might be sustained by a common aesthetic preference for somewhat uniform dress, or by the low cost of mass-produced clothes, or by a fear on everyone's part that peculiar dress might be thought to manifest a peculiar character, or by a desire on everyone's part not to be too conspicuous, or—most likely—by a mixture of these and many other interests.

It is a platitude—something only a philosopher would dream of denying—that there are conventions of language, although we do not find it easy to say what those conventions are. If we look for the fundamental difference in verbal behavior between members of two linguistic communities, we can be sure of finding something which is arbitrary but perpetuates itself because of a common interest in coordination. In the case of conventions of language, that common interest derives from our common interest in taking advantage of, and in preserving, our ability to control others' beliefs and actions to some extent by means of sounds and marks. That interest in turn derives from many miscellaneous desires we have: to list them, list the ways you would be worse off in Babel.

Synthesis

What have languages to do with language? What is the connection between what I have called *languages,* functions from strings of sounds or of marks to sets of possible worlds, semantic systems discussed in complete abstraction from human affairs, and what I have called *language,* a form of rational, convention-governed human social activity? We know what to *call* this connection we are after: we can say that a given language L is *used by,* or is a (or the) language *of,* a given population P. We know also that this connection holds by virtue of the conventions of language prevailing in P. Under suitably different conventions, a different language would be used by P. There is some sort of convention whereby P uses L—but what is it? It is worthless to call it a convention to use L, even if it can correctly be so described, for we want to know what it is to use L.

My proposal[2] is that the convention whereby a population P uses a language L is a convention of *truthfulness* and *trust* in L. To be truthful in L is to act in a certain way: to try never to utter any sentences of L that are not true in L. Thus it is to avoid uttering any sentence of L unless one believes it to be true in L. To be *trusting* in L is to form beliefs in a certain way: to impute truthfulness in L to others, and thus to tend to respond to another's utterance of

[2] This proposal is adapted from the theory given in Erik Stenius, "Mood and Language-Game," *Synthese* 17 (1967): 254–74.

any sentence of L by coming to believe that the uttered sentence is true in L.

Suppose that a certain language L is used by a certain population P. Let this be a perfect case of normal language use. Imagine what would go on; and review the definition of a convention to verify that there does prevail in P a convention of truthfulness and trust in L.

(1) There prevails in P at least a regularity of truthfulness and trust in L. The members of P frequently speak (or write) sentences of L to one another. When they do, ordinarily the speaker (or writer) utters one of the sentences he believes to be true in L; and the hearer (or reader) responds by coming to share that belief of the speaker's (unless he already had it), and adjusting his other beliefs accordingly.

(2) The members of P believe that this regularity of truthfulness and trust in L prevails among them. Each believes this because of his experience of others' past truthfulness and trust in L.

(3) The expectation of conformity ordinarily gives everyone a good reason why he himself should conform. If he is a speaker, he expects his hearer to be trusting in L; wherefore he has reason to expect that by uttering certain sentences that are true in L according to his beliefs—by being truthful in L in a certain way—he can impart certain beliefs that he takes to be correct. Commonly, a speaker has some reason or other for wanting to impart some or other correct beliefs. Therefore his beliefs and desires constitute a practical reason for acting in the way he does: for uttering some sentence truthfully in L.

As for the hearer: he expects the speaker to be truthful in L, wherefore he has good reason to infer that the speaker's sentence is true in L according to the speaker's beliefs. Commonly, a hearer also has some or other reason to believe that the speaker's beliefs are correct (by and large, and perhaps with exceptions for certain topics); so it is reasonable for him to infer that the sentence he has heard is probably true in L. Thus his beliefs about the speaker give him an epistemic reason to respond trustingly in L.

We have coordination between truthful speaker and trusting hearer. Each conforms as he does to the prevailing regularity of truthfulness and trust in L because he expects complementary conformity on the part of the other.

But there is also a more diffuse and indirect sort of coordination. In coordinating with his present partner, a speaker or hearer also is coordinating with all those whose past truthfulness and trust in

L have contributed to his partner's present expectations. This indirect coordination is a four-way affair: between present speakers and past speakers, present speakers and past hearers, present hearers and past speakers, and present hearers and past hearers. And whereas the direct coordination between a speaker and his hearer is a coordination of truthfulness with trust for a single sentence of *L,* the indirect coordination with one's partner's previous partners (and with *their* previous partners, etc.) may involve various sentences of *L*. It may happen that a hearer, say, has never before encountered the sentence now addressed to him; but he forms the appropriate belief on hearing it—one such that he has responded trustingly in *L*—because his past experience with truthfulness in *L* has involved many sentences grammatically related to this one.

(4) There is in *P* a general preference for general conformity to the regularity of truthfulness and trust in *L*. Given that most conform, the members of *P* want all to conform. They desire truthfulness and trust in *L* from each other, as well as from themselves. This general preference is sustained by a common interest in communication. Everyone wants occasionally to impart correct beliefs and bring about appropriate actions in others by means of sounds and marks. Everyone wants to preserve his ability to do so at will. Everyone wants to be able to learn about the parts of the world that he cannot observe for himself by observing instead the sounds and marks of his fellows who have been there.

(5) The regularity of truthfulness and trust in *L* has alternatives. Let *L'* be any language that does not overlap *L* in such a way that it is possible to be truthful and trusting simultaneously in *L* and in *L',* and that is rich and convenient enough to meet the needs of *P* for communication. Then the regularity of truthfulness and trust in *L'* is an alternative to the prevailing regularity of truthfulness and trust in *L*. For the alternative regularity, as for the actual one, general conformity by the others would give one a reason to conform; and general conformity would be generally preferred over slightly-less-than-general conformity.

(6) Finally, all these facts are common knowledge in *P*. Everyone knows them, everyone knows that everyone knows them, and so on. Or at any rate none believes that another doubts them, none believes that another believes that another doubts them, and so on.

In any case in which a language *L* clearly is used by a population *P,* then, it seems that there prevails in *P* a convention of truthfulness and trust in L, sustained by an interest in communication. The converse is supported by an unsuccessful search for counterexamples: I have not been able to think of any case in which there is such a convention and yet the language L is clearly not used in the population P. Therefore I adopt this definition, claiming that it agrees with ordinary usage in the cases in which ordinary usage is fully determinate:

> a language L is *used by* a population P if and only if there prevails in P a convention of truthfulness and trust in L, sustained by an interest in communication.

Such conventions, I claim, provide the desired connection between languages and language-using populations.

Once we understand how languages are connected to populations, whether by conventions of truthfulness and trust for the sake of communication or in some other way, we can proceed to re-define relative to a population all those semantic concepts that we previously defined relative to a language. A string of sounds or of marks is a *sentence of P* if and only if it is a sentence of some language L which is used in P. It has a certain *meaning in P* if and only if it has that meaning in some language L which is used in P. It is *true in P at* a world w if and only if it is true at w in some language L which is used in P. It is *true in P* if and only if it is true in some language L which is used in P.

GRAMMARS

Not just any arbitrary infinite set of verbal expressions will do as the set of sentences of an interesting language. No language adequate to the purposes of its users can be finite; but any language usable by finite human beings must be the next best thing: finitely specifiable. It must have a finite grammar, so that all its sentences, with their interpretations, can be specified by reference to finitely many elementary constituents and finitely many operations for building larger constituents from smaller ones.

A good deal of recent effort in linguistic theory has been devoted to finding a suitable normal form for grammars.[3] The plan is to cut

[3] See, for instance, Noam Chomsky, *Aspects of the Theory of Syntax* (Cambridge, Mass.: MIT Press, 1965), Chap. 1.

down the class of possible languages by cutting down the class of possible grammars, until the only possible languages left are the ones that are serious candidates for human use. In practice, this is done by restricting the normal form of grammars as far as can be done without leaving any actual language grammarless.

It will do us no harm to have many extra entities counting as possible languages, as well as the ones we really want. So we will not stipulate that our possible languages must have grammars of any specified form. In fact, we need not include possession of *any* grammar as a defining condition for possible languages. We can save ourselves the trouble of trying to say, with adequate precision and generality, what it is to have a grammar. But we must bear in mind that languages without grammars—or without grammars of whatever turns out to be the appropriate normal form—are called possible languages only because we have been too lazy to rule them out.

Let me nevertheless try to say how one sort of grammar for a possible language *L* might work. I distinguish three parts of the grammar, called the lexicon, the generative component, and the representing component.

The *lexicon* is a large finite set of elementary constituents, marked to indicate their grammatical categories. Most of these will be words, or morphemes smaller than words.

The *generative component* is a finite set of *combining operations*. Each of these operates on a given number of constituents of given categories, concatenating them to build a new, larger constituent of a given category. It also provides this new constituent with a marker showing its category and the constituents of which it is built. Starting with the lexical elements, the generative component builds up larger and larger constituents. More precisely: a constituent is any member of the smallest set containing the lexical elements and closed under the combining operations. Thus constituents are strings of lexical elements, carrying a hierarchy of category markers, as shown in Figure 1.

The *representing component* operates on some of the constituents built by the generative component—those of the category *sentence*—to produce verbal expressions. The verbal expressions thus representing sentential constituents are the sentences of *L*. In the special case of a *phrase-structure grammar,* the representing component has little work to do. It merely strips off the category markers and replaces

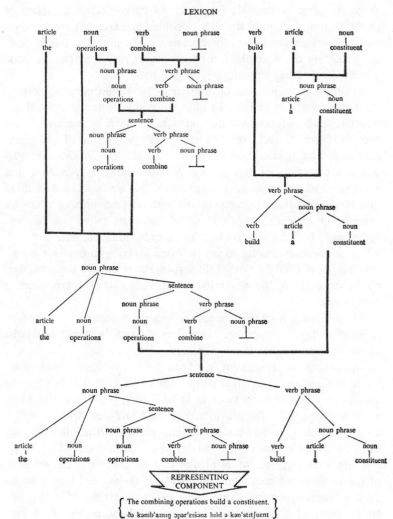

LEXICON

REPRESENTING COMPONENT

The combining operations build a constituent.
ðə kəmb'aɪnɪŋ ɔpər'eɪʃənz bɪld ə kən'stɪtʃuənt

FIGURE 1.

the lexical items, in order, by suitable strings of sounds or marks. Grammars for formalized languages—at least, those with simple systems of punctuation—are phrase-structure grammars. In the more general case of a *transformational grammar,* the representing component does much more. Using information contained in the category markers, it may permute parts of the sentential constituent, delete parts, and add new parts, before it produces a verbal expression.

I do not stipulate that there must be a one-to-one correspondence between sentential constituents and the verbal expressions representing them. One sentence might represent several different sentential constituents: syntactic ambiguity. Or one sentential constituent might be represented by several different sentences: one kind of stylistic variation. Or a sentential constituent might fail to be represented; by permitting the representing component to be selective, we can simplify the generative component.

The grammar should give not just the sentences of L but also their interpretations on their occasions of utterance. It can do this by (1) assigning interpretations—we shall soon consider what sort of things these are—to the lexical elements, (2) providing, for each combining operation used to build a new constituent ξ out of old ones $\xi_1 \ldots \xi_k$, an accompanying *projection operation* to derive an interpretation for ξ, given an interpretation for each of $\xi_1 \ldots \xi_k$, and (3) passing on the interpretations of sentential constituents to the sentences representing them. As the combining operations build up infinitely many larger and larger constituents, starting with the lexical elements, the corresponding projection operations work in parallel to derive interpretations for those constituents, starting with interpretations of the lexical elements.

A sentence may have more than one interpretation passed on to it; this can happen in either or both of two ways. The sentence may be syntactically ambiguous, representing—and receiving interpretations from—more than one sentential constituent. An example is Chomsky's "John was frightened by the new methods," which is ambiguous although it contains no ambiguous word. Or the sentence may be ambiguous because it represents one sentential constituent that already has several interpretations. For a lexical element may be ambiguous. When it is built into a larger constituent, the different interpretations of the lexical element will in general yield different interpretations of the larger constituent. And so on, up to an ambiguous sentential constituent, represented by an ambiguous sentence. An example is "Owen is going to the bank."

We need not assume that when a new constituent ξ is built out of old ones $\xi_1 \ldots \xi_k$, *every* possible combination of interpretations of $\xi_1 \ldots \xi_k$ yields an interpretation for ξ. If that were so, ambiguity would run wild. The projection operations may be selective, working only on input combinations of interpretations which satisfy certain restrictions. But in that case, it could happen that ξ received no interpretation at all, although it was properly built up from $\xi_1 \ldots \xi_k$, all of which did have interpretations. For no combination of interpretations of $\xi_1 \ldots \xi_k$ might be an acceptable input for the projection operation. If ξ is built in turn into another constituent, that too will normally have no interpretation; for the projection operation will not be given even one complete combination of interpretations to work on. And so on, up to sentential constituents without interpretations. If such an anomalous sentential constituent is represented by a sentence, it will have no interpretation to pass on to the sentence. That is why it is possible for sentences themselves to have no interpretations. (I do not say that any good grammar for any familiar language would yield sentences without interpretations; but, as I said earlier, it seems advisable to leave the possibility open.)

A lexical element may be indexical, receiving different interpretations on different possible occasions of its utterance. (Let us say that an occasion of utterance of a constituent is any occasion of utterance of a sentence representing a sentential constituent containing it.) This dependence on occasion is passed along through projection operations to larger and larger constituents, and finally to sentences.

My sketch of the nature of a grammar for L has been designed to have enough generality to cover two special cases: (1) the sets of formation and valuation rules used by logicians to specify the formalized languages they study, and (2) transformational grammars for natural languages, of the form recently proposed by Chomsky, Jerrold Katz, and others.[4] There are earlier proposals by Chomsky and his associates which would have allowed grammars not fitting my description; but no convincing case has been made that this original generality is needed. In any case, it does not matter whether I have given an adequate definition of a grammar, provided I have shown roughly what one would look like.

I have subscribed to Katz's account of the way in which a grammar derives interpretations for a sentence by starting with interpretations for lexical elements, using projection operations to derive interpretations for larger and larger constituents, and finally handing over

---

[4] Chomsky, *Aspects of the Theory of Syntax;* Jerrold Katz, *Philosophy of Language* (New York: Harper & Row, 1966), chap. 4. My constituents, since they carry hierarchies of category markers, are the same as Chomsky's underlying phrase markers, or subtrees thereof.

interpretations from sentential constituents to the sentences representing them. But I have not endorsed Katz's account of the nature of these interpretations; that is a separate question. Katz takes them to be expressions built out of symbols called "semantic markers" which represent "conceptual elements in the structure of a sense."[5] I find this account unsatisfactory, since it leads to a semantic theory that leaves out such central semantic notions as truth and reference.

Then what is an interpretation for a constituent? We have already decided one case. An interpretation for a sentence, and hence for a sentential constituent, is a pair of a mood and a truth condition: a code number and a set of possible worlds. The mood is something peculiar to sentences; but the truth condition suggests a general strategy for providing constituents with appropriate interpretations.

Referential semantics in the tradition of Tarski and Carnap provides constituents with extensions appropriate to their categories: truth values for sentences, denotations for names, sets for one-place predicates, sets of *n*-tuples for *n*-place predicates, and so on. Given extensions for lexical elements, appropriate extensions for larger and larger constituents are derivable by projection operations (valuation rules). Interpretations had better not be mere extensions, of course, since the extension depends both on the interpretation and on accidental facts about the actual world; for instance, constituents that ought to have different interpretations turn out to be accidentally coextensive. Nevertheless, referential semantics looks like a near miss.

A truth condition specifies truth values for a sentence; but in all possible worlds, not just in whichever world happens to be actual. We can interpret a constituent of any category on the same principle, by giving it an extension (appropriate to its category) in every possible world. The idea is Carnap's; it has recently been applied to the semantics of formalized languages with intensional operators, in work by several philosophers in the tradition of Tarski and Carnap.[6]

[5] Katz, *Philosophy of Language*, pp. 155–56.

[6] See Rudolf Carnap, *Meaning and Necessity*, 2nd ed. (Chicago: University of Chicago Press, 1956), pp. 181–82; Jaakko Hintikka, "Modality as Referential Multiplicity," *Eripainos Ajatus*, 20 (1957), pp. 49–64; Saul Kripke, "Semantical Considerations on Modal Logic," *Acta Philosophica Fennica* 16 (1963), pp. 83–94; David Kaplan, *Foundations of Intensional Logic* (Ann Arbor: University Microfilms, 1964); Richard Montague, "Pragmatics," *Contemporary Philosophy—La Philosophie Contemporaine,* ed. Raymond Klibansky (Florence: La Nuova Italie Editrice, 1968); Montague, "On the Nature of Certain Philosophical Entities," *The Monist,* 53 (1969); Dana Scott, "Advice

For instance, an interpretation for a name should give the thing named (if any) in every possible world. It can be taken as a function from possible worlds to things therein. An interpretation for a one-place predicate should give the things of which that predicate is true in any given world; it can be taken as a function from worlds to sets of things therein (or, if nothing inhabits more than one world, perhaps just as a single set containing things from various worlds). An interpretation for an n-place predicate can be taken as a function from worlds to sets of n-tuples of things therein. It is possible to provide interpretations even for constituents that resist treatment within referential semantics confined to the actual world. An interpretation for a modal operator, for instance, might be taken as a function from possible worlds to sets of truth conditions—that is, sets of sets of possible worlds.

It is this sort of interpretation—an assignment of extension in every possible world—which, I suggest, should be attached to constituents by the grammar, in order to build up to sentence interpretations of the kind we want. (Some sort of special provision would have to be made in the grammar for attaching moods.) Obviously such interpretations—like extensions in a single world—are capable of being given relative to features of occasions of utterance; for that reason, a meaning for a constituent is not any one interpretation, but rather the function whereby its interpretation (or its set of alternative interpretations) depends on its occasions of utterance.

---

on Modal Logic," presented at the Free Logic Colloquium held at the University of California at Irvine, May 1968. Montague and Scott propose a unified treatment of intension and indexicality in which extensions are assigned relative to *points of reference:* combinations of a possible world and several relevant features of context—a time, place, speaker, audience, etc. Montague classifies his work as pragmatics because of this relativity to context; it does not deal with the sort of pragmatic considerations that determine which possible language is used by a given population.

Toward a Grammar of Meaning*

DENNIS W. STAMPE

The concept of meaning is as dismayingly complex as any concept which suffers the attentions of philosophy. So diverse and apparently miscellaneous are the senses, uses, and meanings of the words *mean* and *meaning* that the very integrity of "the concept of meaning" is subject to doubt. Yet we will surely not understand the concept of meaning, or any concept, until we understand how its parts hang together, as it were, to the extent that they do; until we have an analysis of the concept which reflects such univocity as the concept possesses. The provision of such an account would seem to depend in part on our discovering and describing relationships between the various uses and senses and grammatically diverse occurrences of the words which, as one says, "express" the concept in question. The statement of whatever syntactical, including transformational, relations may exist between sentences involving these words, and the placing of this description within the context of analyses of kindred expressions and ultimately within the broader context of a theory of the entire language, seems likely to prove essential to this undertaking.

I

The verb *mean,* like any other word, is subject to a number of classifications in terms of which its syntactic behavior may be described and explained. I am particularly concerned with the place of this verb in two of the word classes to which it belongs. I suggest first that, contrary to first appearances, *mean* is in the senses in question an *intransitive verb,* and consider the ramifications of its intransitivity with respect to the character of the complements of the verb and thus to such nominals as *meaning.*

Secondly, *mean* will be examined together with a number of verbs which so far as I know have not before been considered as a distinct class. A verb belongs to this class, which I shall call the class of

* Reprinted by permission of the author and the *Philosophical Review* from the *Philosophical Review* 77 (1968): 137–74.

factive-agentive (*FA*) verbs, if and only if it can take subject expressions of both of two kinds: (*a*) expressions referring to persons or agents and (*b*) expressions referring to occurrences or facts. That is, *FA* verbs will occur in both these environments: (*a*) Agent-Verb-Noun phrase; (*b*) That *p*-Verb-Noun phrase. I will be mainly concerned with a subset of *FA* verbs, which I shall call *FA-t* verbs: namely, those which can take a *that*-clause as object or complement in both (*a*) agentive environments ('John meant [proved, indicated] that *p*'), and (*b*) factive environments ('That he was late meant [proved, indicated] that he had failed'). Thus *frighten* and *astonish* are *FA* verbs, but not *FA-t* verbs. We have 'John astonished Sally,' but not *'John astonished that *p*.' (An asterisk marks a construction as grammatically deviant.) *FA-t* verbs will include *mean, indicate, imply, prove, suggest, show, reveal, demonstrate, warn, tell, inform,* and *remind:* words which, as it turns out, belong to one and the same semantic family, pertaining broadly speaking to the giving and gaining of information.

It should be remarked at the outset that there is no *one* sense of the word *mean* which meets the condition for inclusion among the class of *FA* verbs. Rather the verb in one of its senses satisfies condition (*a*) and in another of its senses condition (*b*). I am referring to the familiar distinction between that sense the word has in '*Fumée* means smoke' or 'John means that *p*,' called by Grice[1] the "nonnatural" sense (*mean$_{nn}$*), and that so-called "natural" sense in which it occurs in 'Smoke means fire' and 'That he was late meant that he had failed.' In its nonnatural sense *mean* satisfies condition (*a*), in its natural sense condition (*b*). My excuse for ignoring this distinction in sense for purposes of classification will emerge in Section VIII.

---

[1] H. P. Grice, "Meaning," *The Philosophical Review*, LXVI (1957), 377–88. I employ these terms as being the most nearly established for the purpose. Better, perhaps, would be "factive" (= natural) and "agentive" (= nonnatural). But in the context of the present argument their use might seem tendentious, since it is part of my purpose to argue that such sentences as '*Covert* means veiled' are derived by grammatical transformation from such agentive contexts as 'By *covert* one means veiled' (sec. VIII ff.). I shall occasionally allude to "natural" and "nonnatural" interpretations of sentences involving *FA* verbs other than *mean*, corresponding to the factive and agentive interpretation or construction of their subjects. (Of the criteria Grice employs on p. 377 to distinguish natural from nonnatural meaning, only the third and the fifth are of general applicability to *FA* verbs.)

II

Dictionaries generally mark the distinction between these two senses of the verb by labeling *mean* transitive in its nonnatural sense and intransitive in its natural sense.[2] The grammatical grounds for this classification might be that, while in both senses the verb requires completion by a noun or noun phrase (that is, requires a "complement," as I shall use the term), only in the nonnatural sense does it permit the passive transformation. We say 'Smoke is what is $meant_{nn}$ by *fumée*,' but not *'Fire is what is $meant_n$ by smoke.' And capacity for passive conversion is a mark of verb transitivity.

But this rationale is defective, considering that 'y is what is meant by x' is *not* the passive of 'x means y.' The complement of the verb in the active form does not reappear as the subject of the verb *mean* in the transformed sentence, as it would under the passive transformation. (Compare: x hit $y \rightarrow y$ was hit by x; x means $y \rightarrow *y$ is meant by x.) Sentences of the form 'y is what is meant by x' are produced not from simple active sentences but rather from such so-called "cleft sentences" as 'what x means is y.'[2a] Accordingly, I will distinguish (true) passive from such "cleft-passive" sentences. Sentences of the form 'x means y' are deviant (not to say unheard of) in the true passive: *'y is meant by x.'

The distinction between $mean_n$ and $mean_{nn}$ is not, on this evidence, a simple distinction between a transitive and an intransitive sense of a verb. But the intransitivity of $mean_{nn}$ does differ curiously from that of $mean_n$ in that only in the former sense do cleft-passives occur. For *'Fire is what is meant by smoke' is as unacceptable as *'Fire is meant by smoke.' (This difference needs explaining: I make an attempt in Section XI.)

There is a rather heterogeneous class of English verbs, sometimes called "middle" verbs,[3] which are distinguished by the following fea-

[2] *Transitive* and *intransitive* are used throughout as adjectives of *verbs,* thus in their grammatical sense, not in the sense they have in the logic of relations. According to the traditional definition, a transitive verb "may be followed by a substantive denoting that which receives the action or is produced by it."

[2a] These are more usually called "pseudo-cleft."

[3] I am not clear why they *ought* to be called "middle" verbs. Presumably they are so called because they bear some analogy to "middle verbs" in languages such as Greek, which have a middle as well as an active and passive

tures: although the verbs in question require a complement (and are thus far atypical intransitive verbs) they do not permit the passive transformation, and, secondly, neither do they admit qualification by adverbs of manner. (Manner adverbs are those answering to questions of the form 'How did so and so [verb]?,' such as *quickly, haphazardly, slyly*.) Middle verbs include *resemble, have, cost, lack, weigh* ('He weighed 200 pounds'). *Mean* is in both its natural and its nonnatural senses a middle verb. In neither sense does it permit passivization, and in neither sense does it admit qualification by manner adverbs. The adverbs that ostensibly modify *mean*, and other middle verbs, are in fact mainly sentence adverbs. Thus: '*x* clearly (obviously, probably) means *y*' means 'It is clear (obvious, probable) that *x* means *y*.' '*X* normally (perhaps, often) means *y*' means 'It is normally (perhaps, often) the case that *x* means *y*.'

In this important respect *mean* is unlike other *FA* verbs, which do take manner adverbials and do have true passive forms. Thus we may say 'John (or: the fact that *p*) proved decisively (indicated plainly, suggested forcefully) that *q*,' and these adverbs are not, in this context, taken to modify the entire sentence. Any of these sentences will go naturally into the passive: 'That *q* was proved etc. by John (or: by the fact that *p*).' *Mean* is the lone exception, permitting neither passivization nor qualification by manner adverbials.

The fact that the passive transformation is restricted by and large to just those verbs which freely take manner adverbs is taken prominently into account, and perhaps accounted for, by a treatment of passives (originated, I believe, by Katz and Postal[4]) which enjoys current favor. On this view, in the phrase structure component of a generative grammar of English, "the Manner Adverbial should have as one of its realizations a 'dummy element' signifying that the passive transformation must obligatorily apply."[5]

Before proceeding to the consideration of the semantic facts which

voice. But as I understand it the Greek middle is *reflexive*, "referring the action back to the subject," as in the direct middle intransitive *loúomai* ("I wash [myself]"). But I see no such reflexivity in the case of *lack, cost, have, resemble,* etc. Cf. Parti and Sweet, *New English Grammar* (Oxford, 1891), pt. i, pars. 254 and 316.

[4] J. J. Katz and P. M. Postal, *An Integrated Theory of Linguistic Descriptions* (Cambridge, Mass., 1964), pp. 72–73. Exceptions to this generalization would apparently include *know* and (perhaps) *believe*.

[5] N. Chomsky, *Aspects of the Theory of Syntax* (Cambridge, Mass., 1965), p. 103. See pp. 103–6 and 218–19.

perhaps help to explain these syntactical peculiarities of *mean* (*vis à vis* other *FA-t* verbs), a related symptom of the intransitivity of *mean* may be mentioned. *Mean* is the only *FA-t* verb (with the possible exception of *imply*) which does not freely take so-called indirect or second objects. We have '*x* indicated (proved, suggested) *to so-and-so* that *p*,' but ***'*x* meant *to so-and-so* that *p*' is deviant. Neither do other middle verbs have indirect objects. In saying this I am distinguishing a nonaccusative occurrence of a *to*-phrase, as in (1) 'Those spots meant measles to the doctor,' from such a phrase occurring accusatively, as in (2*a*) 'Those spots indicated to the doctor that he had measles' or (2*b*) 'His argument proved to me that *p*.' In nonaccusative occurrences the *to*-phrase often functions as a sentence adverbial. We construe (1) as 'In the judgment of the doctor (or: the doctor knew that), those spots meant measles.' But no analagous construction can fully paraphrase (2*a*) and (2*b*). There are furthermore these syntactic grounds for classifying the *to*-phrase in (1) as a sentence adverb, and not as an indirect object: generally, those verbs which take an indirect object may be followed immediately by that expression (or *to* plus that expression). Thus: '*x* suggested (proved, indicated) to John that *p*,' '*x* showed John that *p*.' If the *to*-phrase declines to follow the verb immediately, its behavior is in this respect unlike that of indirect objects and like that of sentence adverbials, for neither do the latter occur (nonparenthetically) immediately following the verb. Thus, in 'John clearly showed (proved, indicated) that *p*,' the adverb, preceding the verb, is interpreted as modifying the entire sentence: 'Clearly, John showed . . . .' (Such adverbs as *obviously, surprisingly, strangely,* and *unfortunately* seem never to follow nonparenthetically immediately after the verb; they are invariably sentence adverbs.) On the other hand, in 'John proved to Jim that *p*,' the phrase *to Jim,* following the verb immediately, is interpreted as an indirect object. Where the phrase occurs initially—'To Jim, John proved that *p*'—the sentence is ambiguous; it may mean (adverbial interpretation) 'In Jim's estimation, John proved that *p*' or (accusative interpretation) 'It was proved to Jim by John that *p*.' But 'To Jim, John meant that *p*,' which permits no accusative interpretation of *to Jim,* is not thus ambiguous.

III

I have so far considered three facets of the intransitivity of *mean,* and have displayed the contrasting transitivity of other *FA* verbs. What accounts for this syntactic difference between *mean* and its fellow *FA* verbs? In the case of *mean$_{nn}$* where it takes agent as subject, the crucial semantic difference appears to be this: to say that someone meant something by such and such is not to say what he *did,* is not to answer the question, What did so-and-so do? But to say that someone proved, indicated, suggested, demonstrated, or showed something is or may be to say what that person did. That sentences of the form Agent-means-that-*p* do not tell what someone *did* is further indicated by the fact that action nominalizations of such sentences are deviant: 'His suggesting that *p* was rude' is all right, but *'His meaning that *p* was rude' is not. Neither are there imperatives: *'Mean that *p*.' If a sentence of the form Agent-Verb-that-*p* does not say that some person did something, it is not to be expected that its verb will admit qualification by adverbs which have the function of indicating how something is done.

But while this semantic account of the inapplicability of manner adverbs works well enough in the case of Agent-mean$_{nn}$-NP, it is of little worth in the case of *mean$_n$,* or in the case of constructions such as '*Feu* means$_{nn}$ fire,' where an expression-denoting term serves as the subject of *mean$_{nn}$.* For it seems unlikely that the key difference between, say, 'The red spots indicated$_n$ measles,' on the one hand, and 'The red spots mean$_n$ measles' and '*Feu* means$_{nn}$ fire,' on the other, is that the former sentence says what its subject "did," whereas the latter do not.

An account along these same lines of the difference between *mean* and *indicate* (suggest, etc.) as they follow agent-denoting subjects is more successful. Here it is possible to say why 'Smith meant that *p*,' unlike 'Smith indicated that *p*,' does not report what Smith did. For the former sentence would be used to *explicate* something Smith said or did—to say, on one view, with what intention it was said or done. Thus it implies, but does not say, that Smith did something. 'So-and-so meant *y* by *x*' is in this respect like 'So-and-so *intended to do* such and such': neither says that so-and-so *did* something that could have been done in one manner rather than another. This explains why *mean* is not modified by manner adverbs, which in turn explains, on the Katz-Postal-Chomsky view of passives, why the passive transformation does not apply. But this kind of explanation is only as compelling as the initial observation—that '*x* means *y*' does not say that *x* "did" something. We still require, then, some account of why we accept 'The spots indicated clearly (= in a clear manner) that he had measles,' but not *'The spots meant clearly (= in a clear manner) that he had measles,' and accordingly accept 'That he had measles was indicated by the spots,' but not *'That he had measles was meant by the spots.' The difference is especially puzzling since such sentences as 'Smoke means$_n$ fire' and 'Smoke indicates$_n$ fire' would seem to mean very nearly the same thing. Why should *mean* be intransitive in this context? To answer this question one must examine the grammatical character of the complement of the verb.

IV

The passive transformation moves the object of the verb in the active construction to the subject position of the resulting sentence. If, as we commonly suppose, the subject expression of a sentence characteristically fulfills a referring function, or is a "referring expression," it would seem that a sentence will have a passive version only if the expression which serves as the complement of the verb is of a kind suitable to fulfill this referring function. But in the case of 'Smoke means$_n$ fire,' this condition is not satisfied—and neither, for that matter, is it satisfied in the case of '*Feu* (or: Pierre) means$_{nn}$ fire.' The complement expressions in these sentences are syntactically incapable of being used to make reference, and it is in my submission this fact which explains the inapplicability of the passive transformation, and thus the intransitivity of *mean*.

That the complement of *mean* in such sentences as '*Masticate* means chew' is syntactically unfit to make reference is obvious, for here the complement is not a nominal expression. It is also, I think, intuitively clear even when the complement is nominal, as in '*Feu* means fire,' that that expression does not refer to anything. I do not mean that the noun *fire* can never be used to refer—obviously it can—but that its occurrence as the complement of *mean* blocks the possibility of its having a referring use, in that sentence or in any transformation thereof.[6] But should this not be obvious, it is in any case a hypothesis which accounts for certain syntactic peculiarities of *mean, vis à vis* other *FA* verbs.

It seems reasonable to suppose that if an expression genuinely refers to something, it is in principle possible to say, in terms either more general or more specific, what *kind* of thing it is to which that expression refers—that in any case a statement purporting to do so may be made within the bounds of grammar and without contradicting the statement in which the original reference is made. Thus, generally, if the complement of a verb in a given sentential context is a referring expression, it will be possible to substitute for that expression some more general or more specific expression "categorizing" what is referred to, producing a sentence (in which the verb retains its original sense) which is grammatical, and which does not necessarily say anything inconsistent with what the original sentence said. But this (very weak) condition is not satisfied in the case of *mean,* in the sense of the verb here in question.

For while '*Feu* refers to fire' can be altered in the way described, '*Feu* means fire' cannot be, where *means* does not have the sense 'refers to.' Thus, if fire can be categorized as a form of oxidation, we may say, nondeviantly and even truly, '*Feu* refers to a form of oxidation.' But '*Feu* means a form of oxidation' is deviant (unless *means* is heard as 'refers to') or else it must be construed in such a way that it is false, *if* it is true that '*Feu* means fire': for the ex-

[6] We may distinguish at least two possible uses of this difficult term "referring expression." The first would make any expression a referring expression if it can, in some syntactic context or other, be used to refer to something. The second use would be confined to expressions which in a given sentential context might be used to refer to something. This latter notion would make "referring expression" a functional term, rather as the term "subject" is.

Alston, in his admirable paper, "The Quest for Meanings" (*Mind,* LXXII [1963], 81), allows that sometimes, at least, "what follows 'is' [in a 'meaning-statement' of the form 'The meaning of *x* is *y*'] is a referring expression." He gives as an example "The meaning of *courage* is—steadfastness in the face of danger," about which he says " 'steadfastness in the face of danger' certainly does refer to something, to a certain trait of character." The concession rather blunts the point of Alston's argument. But he need not have made the concession. What counts is not whether "what follows 'is' " is a referring expression in the first of the two senses I distinguish, but whether it is, *in the sentential context in question,* a referring expression—i.e. a referring expression in the second sense. That it is not is shown by the considerations under discussion.

pressions *fire* and *a form of oxidation* plainly do not have the same meaning.[7] The operative point here is that if an expression *B* says to what more general or more specific category the thing referred to by another expression *A* belongs, then *B* cannot have the same meaning as does *A* (but must instead have some "broader" or "narrower" meaning). Consequently, 'NP means *A*' and 'NP means *B*' will be inconsistent.

It is often permissible to incorporate into a sentence information concerning the kind of thing being referred to, by the device of placing the referring term in apposition to some categorizing expression. Thus, we may say 'The *word feu* means fire,' placing the referring expression *feu* in apposition to an expression saying what sort of thing *feu* refers to. But by contrast we cannot say *'The word *feu* means the word *fire*,' without automatically altering either the sense of *mean* or contradicting the original assertion: for the only constructions which can properly be put on this latter sentence are the (unlikely) one according to which *means* means 'refers to,' and one according to which the sentence says, what is false, that *feu* means 'the word fire'—that being instead what the phrase *le mot «feu»* means.

One finds the same incapacity to stand in apposition to a "categorizing" preface displayed by *that*-clause complements of *mean*.[8] We have, on the other hand,

> NP reveals the fact that *p*
> NP suggests the possibility that *p*
> NP proves the contention that *p*

(where NP may be either factive or agentive) as we may say that what is proved is a contention, what is suggested is a possibility or

[7] The word *feu* means fire if and only if the word *feu* has the same meaning (means the same thing) as does the word *fire*. But this is not to say, nor is it true, that the sentence 'The word *feu* means fire' says the same thing as does the sentence 'The word *feu* means the same thing as does (the word) *fire*." A French teacher might tell a pupil, as a hint, that *feu* means the same as (the German word) *feuer*, without saying what *feu* means. Cf. G. E. Moore, *Commonplace Book 1919–1953* (London, 1962), p. 304.

[8] Concerning such constructions as *the fact that p*, it is a suggestion of Austin's that "It is a usage grammatically *like* (not of course in all ways the same as) the *apposition* usage with proper names, as when we say 'The person Caesar'" ("Unfair to Facts," *Philosophical Papers* [Oxford, 1961], p. 113).

an alternative, and so forth. But there are no nondeviant sentences of the form

   *NP means the (Noun) that p,[8a]

unless *mean* means 'refer to' (as in 'John means the fact that p' or '*The Bard* means the poet Shakespeare'), or the sentence implies that NP has the same meaning as *the (Noun) that p*. This peculiarity of *mean* is accounted for by the fact that its complements refer to nothing of any general or particular kind or "category" (in however broad a sense), a circumstance best accommodated by allowing that they refer to nothing at all: and this supposition also accounts for the inability of such sentences to undergo conversion into the passive.

The hypothesis that the passive transformation applies only to verbs the complements of which may be made to stand in apposition to some categorizing phrase is confirmed by the case of other verbs pertaining to communication, including the *FA-t* verbs *warn, inform, tell,* and *remind,* as well as *remark* and (perhaps) *say.* All these verbs are like *mean* in that (in at least one of their senses) their *that*-clause complements cannot be prefaced by a categorizing noun phrase. (We have 'NP warned [informed, told] me *of* the fact that p,' but not *'NP warned [informed, etc.] me the fact that p.' And in 'remarked the fact that p,' *remarked* must mean 'noticed,' not 'said.') The verbs cited differ from *mean* in taking an indirect object, and (unless that object requires introduction by *to,* as do the objects of *remark* and *say*) the passive transformation may produce, for example, 'I was warned (informed, etc.) that p by Jane.' But there is no passive in which the *that*-clause occupies the subject position. Thus, *'That p was warned (informed, told, reminded, said) by Jane' is, depending on the particular verb, more or less badly deviant.

These considerations are related to the fact that *mean,* unlike most transitive verbs, and unlike most *FA* verbs, has no past participle—that being an adjectival form of the verb which tends to modify the expression which serves as the verb's object. Thus: 'The bull broke the china' $\rightarrow$ 'The china was broken by the bull' $\rightarrow$ 'the china (which was) broken by the bull' $\rightarrow$ 'the broken china.' A verb which has no passive form will have no past participle. An intransitive verb such as *mean,* having no direct object, will have no past participle—there

[8a] That is to say, the constructions that serve as complements of *mean,* in the relevant sense, do not have nouns as their "head" constituents.

being nothing such an adjectival expression might serve to modify. In the case of *FA-t* verbs generally, the past participle does not directly modify the *that*-clause object of the verb (*'the proven that *p*'), but rather the expression to which that clause stands in implicit apposition: 'the proven contention (that *p*),' 'the suggested possibility,' and so forth. Accordingly, an *FA-t* verb such as *mean, remind,* or *warn,* the complement of which cannot be prefixed by some such categorizing phrase, will not have a past participle form: *'the meant such and such.'

It has often been maintained (notably by A. J. Ayer, G. Ryle, and W. S. Sellars) that such a sentence as *'Feu* means fire' is not to be understood as expressing a proposition of relational form, as if to say what a word means is to say that it stands in a certain relation to some concept, idea, or intensional whatnot indicated by 'fire.' Now to show that *mean* is not a transitive verb is not yet to show that it is not a relational term. *Resemble* is not a transitive verb, and yet it is evidently a relational term. What shows that *mean* is not relational, that "meaning" is not a relation, is that the complements of that verb are not referring expressions; and if not on that supposition, how do we account for the intransitivity of the verb and related syntactic peculiarities? It is not just that it is *open* to us, should it suit our philosophical predilections, to construe *'Feu* means fire' in a nonrelational way. What the foregoing grammatical considerations show is that the sentence *is* so construed. The relational analysis of propositions expressed by such sentences is simply mistaken.

V

All this has a connection with Austin's animadversions upon the phrase "the-meaning-of-a-word" and upon the pseudo-question, What is the-meaning-of-a-word?[9] (In the idiom of the present discussion, we may understand Austin's hyphens as intended to mark the misguided fusing of the phrase into a referring expression.) The meaning of a word is, of course, what a word means. Asking what the-meaning-of-a-word is, or what what-a-word-means is, is asking for what the foregoing considerations show to be impossible to give—

[9] J. L. Austin, "The Meaning of a Word," *Philosophical Papers,* pp. 23–43.

namely, a categorization of what a word means. Compare: John's suggestion, which is the same as what John suggested. But the analogous question, What is what-John-suggested?, does admit grammatically unexceptionable answers: what-John-suggested is an alternative, or a possibility. Compare: What is what he proved? A theorem. A contention. What is what he danced? A waltz. A dance. These answers may or may not be so general as to be entirely uninformative; but they are, however that may be, grammatical. The question, What is what-he-meant?, on the other hand, cannot grammatically be answered even in some perfectly uninformative way. He did not, certainly, mean a meaning: *meaning* is not the internal accusative of *mean*. Nor is concept, idea, proposition, or anything else. What a dancer dances, however, is inevitably a dance, however pointless it may be to say so.

It is wrong to suppose (as Austin was perhaps inclined to suppose) that the fundamental trouble with the question, What is what a word means? is that it is illicitly general. For the question is *illicitly* general only because it is a general version of particularized questions which are themselves equally illicit, when the misinterpretation in question (in which *what-x-means* is taken to refer) is imposed upon them. Compare Austin's own "specimen of nonsense" (1.211): What is the-meaning-of-(the-word)-'rat'? The question, What is what a proof proves? is perhaps a perfectly aimless generality, and one who ventures such a question might well get "stared at as at an idiot." But the idiocy manifested in asking, What is what a word means? is of another order.

VI (MEANING)

The intransitivity of the verb *mean* ramifies into the grammar of the noun *meaning*. The expression *meaning* is of course related to the expression *what x means:* generally, the meaning of *x* is what *x* means, and conversely. (Only 'generally,' because, for example, *what Smith means* does not go over into *the meaning of Smith,* although the other genitive form *Smith's meaning* is sometimes heard.) Both these expressions—both the genitive nominal forms *the meaning of x* and *x's meaning,* and also *what x means*—are nominalizations of a sentential expression *x means y.* I have pointed out, in trying to explain why '*x* means *y*' has no passive, that the object of such a sentence is syntactically unfit for duty as a referring expression: thus, it cannot be moved to the subject position as the passive transformation requires. The nominals *what x means* and *the meaning of x,* by contrast, do occur in the subject position. But while *what x means* and *the meaning of x* may serve as grammatical subjects, neither is a nominal expression of a kind which has anything to do with referring.

We may distinguish between relative clause nominalizations and interrogative nominalizations. Relative clause nominalizations are elliptical forms of some Noun Phrase-Relative Clause construction—*the x which such and such*—the relative clause serving to specify to which thing the noun phrase refers. By contrast interrogative nominals are used in allusion to some question or piece of information. For example, compare:

(1) What was in the tub was hard.
(2) What was in the tub was hard to determine.

'What was in the tub' is a relative clause nominal in sentence (1), which is transformationally related to 'The stuff (which was) in the tub was hard.' In the second sentence *what was in the tub* is an interrogative nominal. Sentence (2) may be converted into 'It was hard to determine what was in the tub'; but (1) is not convertible into *'It was hard what was in the tub' nor (2) into *'The stuff (which was) in the tub was hard to determine.' Other sentences—for example, 'What was in the tub was discovered by Smith'—are ambiguous, often owing in part to some ambiguity in the verb phrase. (Here, *discovered* may mean either 'found out' or 'found.')

The ambiguity of such nominal expressions is occasionally a considerable source of mischief. Philonous exploits it when he says: "though I hear a variety of sounds, I cannot be said to hear the causes of those sounds."[10] If the expression *the causes of those sounds* (*what causes those sounds*) is construed as being an interrogative nominal, Philonous' claim is at least arguable: I find out the causes of, or what causes, those sounds—for example, by making an inference—but I do not *hear* what causes them. But if *what causes those sounds* is a relative clause nominalization (further transformable into *the causes of those sounds*), then the assertion that we cannot be said to hear what causes sounds is plainly false. It may be a locomo-

[10] Berkeley, "Three Dialogues between Hylas and Philonous," *The Works of Berkeley,* ed. by Luce and Jessop (London), II, 174.

tive that is the cause of those sounds, and it is false that we cannot hear locomotives. Similarly, the confusions engendered by the dictum "who wills the end wills the means" result from an ambiguity of this sort. It is in one sense analytic that one who intends to do *x* intends to do "what is necessary" (interrogative nominal) in order to do *x*. But *what is necessary* may mean *the y which is necessary*. Then, since one may intend to, say, get rich, but not realize that he will in fact have to kill his rich aunt if he is ever to get rich, it may happen that he does *not* intend to do "what is necessary" (relative nominal) if he is to get what he intends to get.

To turn then to such nominal expressions occurring as subjects of *FA* verbs. Compare:

(3*a*) His proof (of the claim) was conclusive.
(3*b*) What he suggested was obscene.

with

(4*a*) The meaning (of the passage) was clear.
(4*b*) What he meant was obscure.

The first pair of sentences is introduced by nominals related transformationally to relative clauses ('The proof that he offered was conclusive,' 'The suggestion that he made was obscene'—but not: *'It was conclusive his proof [of the claim]' or *'It was obscene what he suggested'). Thus these nominal phrases may serve a referring function. But the subject expressions of the second pair of sentences, (4*a*) and (4*b*), are interrogative nominals, as those sentences would normally be construed—that is, as meaning 'It was clear what the meaning of the passage was' and 'It was obscure what he meant.' Such noun phrases are not referring expressions.

VII

It would be going too far to suggest that such a phrase as *the meaning of the passage* cannot possibly be paraphrased by a Noun Phrase-Relative Clause construction. 'The meaning (that) the passage has is clear' is not an intolerable paraphrase of 'The meaning of the passage is clear.' But such constructions, where they do occur, are grammatical sports. For ordinarily what is predicated of a relative clause nominal may sensibly (if not correctly) be predicated of a specification of that thing to which the nominal purports to refer. Thus: what is in the tub is rancid; what is in the tub is butter; the butter is rancid. Similarly: what he suggested is attractive; what he suggested is (the possibility) that *p;* the possibility (that *p*) is attractive. But compare: what *x* means is clear; what *x* means is that *p;* but not: *'the . . . that *p* is clear.' There is no way to predicate *clear* of *that p* since there is no noun permitted to fill in the blank. 'That *p* is clear' is a perfectly good sentence, but of course it means 'It is clear that *p*'—that is, 'That *p* is clearly true'—which is not what *clear* presumably means in 'What he means is clear.' When the verb involved is *mean,* these transformations will appear to be acceptable only if the sense of either the verb or the predicate in question is allowed to shift in certain ways.

It becomes apparent that there are certain predicate expressions (for example, *fat, obscene*) which may be attached to relative clause nominals but not to interrogative. There are certain other predicate expressions (*obscure, clear, apparent, well-known*) which are ambiguous in such a way that in one of their senses (as, for example, *obscure* in the sense of 'difficult to understand,' in one "sense" of *understand*) they form predicates of interrogative but not of relative clause nominals, while in another (as *obscure* = visually or auditorily indistinct) they form predicates of relative clause but not of interrogative nominals. Such predicates, and the sometimes similarly ambiguous verbs of cognition and perception in terms of which they are often defined, afford rich and multifarious opportunities for confusion and Platonizing.

Suppose a philosopher is for some reason intent on construing *x's meaning,* or *the meaning of x,* or *what x means* as a referring expression. To speak of what *x* means or *x*'s meaning is, on such a view, to speak of the *y* which *x* means or the *y* which is the meaning *x* has. Presumably, then, this philosopher would consider the sentence 'The meaning of *x* is obscure' to be equivalent to 'The *y* which is the meaning of *x* is obscure.' For something to be obscure is for it to be either difficult to understand or difficult to perceive distinctly. A dilemma arises. Our Platonist may, on the one hand, electing to understand *obscure* (*clear, apparent*) as relating to ease of perception, take the hoary view that understanding is a kind of mental perception, involving not the bodily but the mental eye. In this he exploits or is gulled by the ambiguity of *obscure* and perhaps *see*. Thus he may construe being obscure in every context as being difficult to see. Compare Church:

> The extreme demand for a simple prohibition of abstract entities under all circumstances perhaps arises from a desire to maintain the connection between theory and observation. But the preference of (say) *seeing* over *understanding* as a method of observation seems to me capricious. For just as an opaque body may be seen, so a concept may be understood or grasped. In both cases the observation is not direct but through intermediaries—light, lens of eye or optical instrument, and retina in the case of the visible body, linguistic expressions in the case of the concept.[11]

Our Platonist is in a sense forced into mental ophthalmology; if he declines to take this route, a regress awaits him. For if 'The y which is the meaning of x is obscure' does not mean '. . . is perceptually indistinct,' it must mean, again, '. . . is difficult to understand.' But if 'The y which is the meaning of x is obscure' means the y which is the meaning of x is difficult to understand, then the meaning of y which is the meaning of x is obscure—that is, the z which is the meaning of y which is the meaning of x is obscure. And so on. It would follow that to understand the word x is to understand infinitely many things. For to understand the word x will be to understand the y which is the meaning of x, and to understand y will be to understand its meaning z, and so on. But this is surely an absurd result. The regress can be evaded only by equivocating at some point on *know, understand,* or *see,* and on associated predicates like *obscure* and *clear*. For instance, instead of allowing the regressive paraphrase of 'The y which is the meaning of x is difficult to understand' as above, he might, equivocating on *understand,* take 'y is difficult to understand' to mean not 'It is difficult to understand the meaning of y,' but something like 'It is difficult to understand the nature of y, the meaning of x.' (Compare the ambiguous 'Women are hard to understand.')

This is familiar stuff, but it is perhaps worth insisting on even today, when the search for the nature of meanings seems to be cropping up anew, and in respected quarters. Chomsky, for example, refers with apparent approval to a view which has "abstract ideas constitut-

[11] Alonzo Church, "The Need for Abstract Entities in Semantic Analysis," reprinted in Katz and Fodor, *The Structure of Language* (Englewood Cliffs, N.J., 1964), p. 442.

ing the meanings of sentences,"[12] and Katz says such things as "the meanings of words are not indivisible entities but, rather, are composed of concepts in certain relations to one another,"[13] implying, it would seem, that the meanings of words are (composite) entities.

VIII

Skepticism concerning the integrity of the concept of meaning may be inspired by the polysemy of the verb *mean,* or again by the grammatical promiscuity of a verb which takes as its subject and object so great a variety of expressions or constructions. But it is in fact just the diversity of syntactic contexts in which *mean* appears which enables us to cope with the ambiguity of the word. For the syntax of the sentence in which the verb occurs largely determines which of its interpretations the verb is given.

If, for example, *mean* is followed by an adverbial occurrence of an infinitive, as in 'She means to leave him,' *means* generally means 'intends.'[14] If it is followed by an adverbial of quantity, as in 'She means a lot to him,' the sentence may say how much or how little such and such *matters.* If *means* is followed by a phrase introduced by a "determiner" (*the such and such* . . .) it will mean 'is referring to.' If the subject of the verb denotes an agent, and its complement is a pronominal expression referring to what that agent said, wrote, or the like—as in 'He means it' or 'He means what he says'—*means* means 'is serious and sincere in saying.'

Similarly, the distinction between the natural and nonnatural senses of *mean* is correlated with and marked by the occurrence of syntactically distinct kinds of subject expressions. This is true not only of the verb *mean,* but of all those (*FA-t*) verbs, which (curiously, without, in their cases, a corresponding diversity of senses) analogously take *that*-clause objects and subject expressions denoting

[12] N. Chomsky, *Cartesian Linguistics* (New York, 1966), p. 38.

[13] J. J. Katz, *The Philosophy of Language* (New York, 1966), p. 154.

[14] From which derives, perhaps, the somewhat degenerate use in the indignant query, 'What did you mean by doing that? (by saying such a thing?),' meaning simply, 'What's the idea?' One responds with an explanation or excuse, not literally, with an answer of the form 'What I meant by saying what I said (treating him as I did) was that *p*'—a peculiar sentence. Thus, 'What did you mean by saying what you said?,' in which the preposition is followed by an *action* nominal, is distinguished from 'What did you mean by what you said?'

agents as well as subject expressions (such as factive nominals) denoting states of affairs.

While certain subject expressions, wearing their syntax on their sleeves, make clear the sense to be given to *mean,* certain "deformations" of these subject expressions may obscure their syntax and leave the resulting sentence ambiguous. For example, the sentence 'That there is a lantern placed in the tower means that they are coming by sea' has a clear ("natural") sense. (Suppose the tower is used as a beacon for incoming ships.) But if those elements of the subject expression which mark it as being a factive nominal are deleted, an ambiguous sentence results: 'A lantern placed in the tower means they are coming by sea.' Here, both the signaling or nonnatural *and* the natural interpretation are available. 'His argument proved (demonstrated) his incompetence' is a syntactical homonym of the same sort: it may be a comment on the inferiority of his argument, or it may mean that he argued successfully that he is incompetent. Even 'Smoke means fire' has the same potential for ambiguity. (Of course, the written version of the sentence 'Smoke means fire' would not be taken as meaning 'The *word smoke* means fire' unless *smoke* occurred in italics or within inverted commas. But this is an orthographical convention which does not necessarily reflect any phonetic feature of the utterance.)

It is proper, I think, to regard such sentences as 'Smoke means fire' and 'A lantern placed in the tower means that *p'* as *syntactic* homonyms, even though one could alternatively say that their ambiguity is lexical—that is, attributable to the ambiguity of a *word.* The verb *mean* does have two senses, properly so called, and what is not clear in the ambiguous sentences is in which sense the word *mean* is being used, the natural or the nonnatural. But lexical ambiguities generally have a syntactic dimension: the ambiguities of words are concealed or revealed by the syntax of their occurrence. In any case—and this is the argument for treating these homonyms as syntactic—ambiguities between natural and nonnatural interpretations are not peculiar to sentences involving the ambiguous verb *mean.* Homonyms of the same sort can be found involving any *FA-t* verb whatever—*prove, indicate, show, imply,* and so forth. But these *FA-t* verbs, unlike *mean,* do *not* have two senses, properly so called, corresponding to a natural and a nonnatural interpretation. Thus the ambiguity which can be perceived in 'Smoke indicates fire' or 'His argument proved his incompetence' cannot be characterized as lexical, for these verbs are univocal with respect to the two interpretations of the sentences. Thus there are good grounds for treating 'Smoke means fire' as a syntactic homonym. A grammar which failed to account for this ambiguity in a way analogous to that in which the plainly analogous ambiguity of 'Smoke indicates fire' is to be accounted for, would contain a needless anomaly.

It is not the superficial phrase structure of these sentences which is ambiguous. Both 'Smoke means$_n$ fire' and *'Covert* means veiled' could be represented on the level of phrase structure simply as Noun-(Verb-Noun). There being no reason to diagram the two sentences differently, the differences between the normal interpretation of the two sentences cannot be represented on this level as being a function of syntactic structure. 'Smoke means fire' and 'His argument proved his incompetence' are instances of a now familiar kind of structurally ambiguous sentence, the ambiguity of which cannot be explicated by attributing to the sentence alternative characterizations of the internal relations of its elements (alternative ways of construing its phrase structure). In such a case it is by now generally accepted that we may look for the explanation of the ambiguity to the external relations of the sentence—that is, to the relations the ambiguous sentence bears to other sentences. If we can associate the ambiguity of a sentence with the existence of two sets of structurally diverse sentences, such that the sentence is on one interpretation syntactically related in certain ways to one of these sets and on another to the other set, then we will have a hypothesis that accounts for the (two-way) ambiguity of the sentence. The diverse structures of these related sentences may be said to constitute the deep structures of the ambiguous sentence, and the ambiguity of the sentence attributed to its having more than one deep structure. In a generative grammar the relations of which I am speaking are called transformational relations.[15] The ambiguity of the sentences in question is said to be owing to the sentences' having diverse transformational histories.

[15] Sentences are related by transformation only if they are syntactically related. Sentences are "syntactically related" if, for example, there are grammatical constraints on the selection of an element of one sentence which may be stated with reference to constraints on the selection of certain elements of another sentence. (This situation is called a co-occurrence relation.) Thus, for example, active and passive are syntactically related because the set of expressions which may serve as the object of the verb in the active is restricted to just those expressions which may serve as the subject of the verb in the passive (i.e. in the context '. . .-be-Verb-past-by NP').

I submit, then, that the aforementioned syntactic homonyms involving *mean* have two distinct transformational histories, one corresponding to each of the possible interpretations in question. On the one hand, under their "natural" interpretation, they are produced by a deletion transformation operating on strings the subject of which is factive nominalization. On the other hand, under its "nonnatural" interpretation, the sentence is derived from another transformation or chain of transformations which operates on strings having an agent-denoting expression as subject and an adverbial prepositional phrase, deleting both Agent and Preposition, on the model of:

> with a turn of the key he started the engine
> . . . a turn of the key . . . started the engine.

The effect of such a transformation or chain of transformations would be to promote expressions occurring in an adverbial context, indicating the means or "instrument" which is used, to the role of subject of the verb. Such a transformation might accordingly be called an "instrument promotion" transformation. My suggestion, then, is that the following display of relationships accurately represents the kind of ambiguity under discussion, the arrows indicating transformational relationships, and the direction of derivation in a generative grammar:

> (*nn*) By a lantern placed in the tower the sentry means that the invasion is by sea.
>
> (*nn*/*n*) A lantern placed in the tower means that the invasion is by sea.
>
> (*n*) The fact that there is a lantern placed in the tower means that the invasion is by sea.

The postulation of the instrument promotion transformation accounts for one term of the ambiguities in question. There is furthermore independent syntactic motivation for postulating its existence. The proposed rule will state a regularity or co-occurrence phenomenon which ought to be represented by the grammar as something more than coincidence: namely, that set of expressions, other than agent-denoting expressions, which are permitted as the subject of *FA* verbs is precisely that set of expressions which are permitted as the object of certain prepositions (for example, *by, with, in*) in prepositional phrases modifying sentences of the form, Agent-Verb$_{fa}$-NP.

That is, those expressions which occur in the environment Prep$_i$-. . .-Agent-Verb$_{fa}$-NP (where "Prep$_i$" stands for a certain set of prepositions, and the prepositional phrase has a certain history, discussed below) are the only expressions other than Agent which occur in the environment . . .-Verb$_{fa}$-NP.

There are verbs other than *FA* verbs which seem to exhibit this same principle of subject selection. These include certain other verbs relating to speech acts. Compare, for example, 'In his letter he said (stated, promised, mentioned, announced, etc.) that he would arrive today' and 'His letter said (etc.) that he would arrive today.'

I am inclined to think that a transformation of this sort also operates on strings containing *frighten, help, encourage, shock, surprise*—that is, *FA* verbs which do not take *that*-clause complements. In *Syntactic Structures* Chomsky considered and offered an analysis of a homonym involving *frighten*—namely, 'John was frightened by the new methods.' He was there dealing with a homonym of much the same sort as those I have mentioned, although Chomsky's example is in the passive. It is comparable then to 'The election of a new Pope was indicated by the white smoke.' (They might possibly have been executing the old Pope at the stake.) Or 'The election of a new Pope was indicated by the new methods.' (The new methods being employed, or the new methods of indicating elections?) Chomsky's treatment of such cases is not what I have suggested:

> Consider such pairs as
> (113) (*i*)   the picture was painted by a new technique
>   (*ii*) the picture was painted by a real artist.
> These sentences are understood quite differently, though identically represented as NP-was-Verb-en-by-NP on the level of phrase structure. But their transformational history is quite different. (113*ii*) is the passive of "a real artist painted the picture." (113*i*) is formed from, e.g., "John painted the picture by a new technique" by a double transformation; first the passive, then the elliptical transformation (mentioned in fn. 7 on p. 81) that drops the 'agent' in the passive. An absolute homonym on the model of (113) is not hard to find. For example,
> (114) John was frightened by the new methods.
> may mean either that John is a conservative—new methods frighten him; or that new methods of frightening people were used to frighten John (an interpretation that would be the more normal one if "being" were inserted after "was"). On the transformational level,

(114) has both the analysis of (113*i*) and (113*ii*), which accounts for its ambiguity.[16]

On Chomsky's treatment, the ambiguity of (114) is resolved in one direction, since the source 'Someone frightened John by the new methods' is unambiguous. But the ambiguity is *not* resolved in the other direction, since 'The new methods frighten John' is ambiguous in precisely the same way as is 'John was frightened by the new methods.' 'The new methods frighten John' can mean either what Chomsky implies it always means—that John is a conservative, as he puts it—or it can mean, again, that a person can frighten John by means of the new methods. It would receive the latter interpretation in the context 'Jim can be frightened only by the old methods, but the new methods frighten John.'

This defect in Chomsky's analysis suggests the need for a better account. In particular, an adequate account must account for the ambiguity of *both* the active and the passive forms. Apparently, then, the active form itself must be further derived. Chomsky's treatment fails, in so far as it does, because he fails to relate the ambiguous active form 'The new methods frighten John' to any unambiguous source. (It is of course not surprising that ambiguities present in the passive of a sentence, especially one involving no quantifiers, are present in the active form as well.) Certainly the account I suggest, of deriving the sentence under its 'John is a conservative' interpretation by a deletion transformation operating on a factive nominal subject of *frighten,* will not be open to this complaint. For the source will on this account be something like 'The fact that they are employing the new methods frightens John,' and this sentence is not ambiguous. On the other side, 'The new methods frighten John' is derived by an instrument-promotion transformation from 'Agent frightens John by the new methods' or 'One may frighten John by the new methods.'

IX

If there is an extensive range of verbs which permit the application of the proposed instrument promotion transformation, there are obviously other verbs upon which such a transformation must not be

---

[16] N. Chomsky, *Syntactic Structures* (The Hague, 1957), pp. 89–90.

allowed to operate. From 'By eavesdropping, he discovered their plan,' we do not get *'Eavesdropping discovered their plan.' Nor does 'He ate the pie with his fingers' have a transform, *'His fingers ate the pie.'

But neither, for that matter, may the proposed transformation be allowed to operate upon every sentence involving an *FA* verb, simply because that sentence contains the sequence, By-NP-Agent-Verb-NP. For instance, it cannot be allowed to apply to 'By five o'clock he proved the theorem,' giving us *'Five o'clock proved the theorem.' Of course in this sentence the prepositional phrase does not indicate the "means, method, or instrument" by which the theorem was proved. But there are still other sentences, in which the prepositional phrase does have that *sort* of semantic function, which are nevertheless not subject to the transformation, such as 'He indicated his position by telephone,' from which we do not want *'Telephone indicated his position.'

The stipulation that the grammar be "mechanical" requires that we be able ultimately to provide a suitably formal specification of the strings upon which the suggested transformation is to operate. This requires that we discover some formal distinction between such prepositional phrases as *by five o'clock* and *by that remark*. A generative grammar of English will for reasons quite independent of the present proposal have to incorporate such a classification of prepositional phrases. For example, constraints on the conjoinability of prepositional phrases will have to be imposed to prevent the generation of certain kinds of zeugma. Such a sentence as 'He filled the hole with water and sand' would derive (in a grammar employing "binary" transformations) from a binary transformation on some such pair of sentences as 'He filled the hole with water' and 'He filled the hole with sand.' But such a transformation cannot be allowed to conflate 'He filled the hole with sand' and 'He filled the hole with a steamshovel' into the zeugma, *'He filled the hole with sand and a steamshovel.' Similarly, we ought to be able to say why the two sentences, 'He proved the theorem by mathematical induction' and 'He proved the theorem by five o'clock,' are not to be conflated into *'He proved the theorem by mathematical induction and five o'clock.' So the operation of acceptable conjunction transformations of this sort would presumably presuppose a set of classifications adequate for restricting the domain of a deletion transformation of the kind proposed.

It is perhaps possible to indicate in rough outline how the required specification may be obtained. We may, in the case of 'He proved it by midnight,' appeal to the existence of certain related sentences—for example, 'He proved it after midnight'—in order to isolate such prepositional phrases as being spatial or temporal sentence modifiers, not subject to the proposed transformation. In the case of 'He proved it with ease,' from which we must not derive *'Ease proved it,' we may appeal to the existence of related sentences containing manner adverbs, such as 'He proved it easily.' And so forth. More generally, it seems that the strings on which the instrument promotion transformation ought to operate are strings (of the form Prepositional phrase-Sentence) which might be derived by binary transformation of certain pairs of strings—namely, pairs subject to certain related binary transformations. Thus the pair 'He said x'-'He meant y' may be taken by related transformations into 'He said x and (or: by which) he meant y,' 'When he said x he meant y,' as well as 'By x, he meant y.'

This accords with Chomsky's note "that many of the Manner Adverbials, like many other Adverbials, are Sentence transforms with deleted Subjects."[17] The *by*-phrases we want here to isolate are manner adverbials when they modify transitive verbs; they say how something was done. The *by*-phrase in 'By x so-and-so means y' cannot be construed as saying how something is done because meaning something is not doing anything. Thus its semantic function differs from that of manner adverbials proper because of the character of the verb it modifies: but its underlying grammar is the same—that of a sentence transform with deleted subject and verb.

We can see from this why 'John meant that p' entails that John did or said something, whereas 'John meant (intended) to do such and such' does not entail that he actually did anything. The former, but not the latter, contains an implicit *by-x*, which is a transform of a sentence which says John did or said x—that is, which says that John (actually) did something. We may expect to find that a sentence of the form 'x means y' which cannot be traced to these roots—to something said or done—will not exhibit normal semantic liaisons with 'by x Agent means y.' Such a case is discussed in Section XII.

17 *Aspects,* pp. 218–19.

X (Meaning and Use)

There is a little-understood connection between the way an expression is used and what the expression means. Perhaps some light may be shed from the present angle. Sentences within the domain of the instrument promotion transformation can be identified with considerable success by reference to another transformational relationship in which those sentences stand. Thus, 'He persuaded her by (with) subtle argument' has a relation to 'He used subtle argument to persuade her,' and is accordingly subject to instrument promotion: 'His subtle argument persuaded her.' On the other hand, 'He persuaded her by midnight' is not analogously related to *'He used midnight to persuade her,' and predictably there is no *'Midnight persuaded her.' Similarly, 'By *idea* Hume means such and such' is related to 'Hume uses *idea* to mean such and such,' and thus by instrument promotion to '*Idea,* as used by Hume, means such and such.'

The construction we put on 'uses the expression to mean' this or that is not entirely analogous to the construction we put on, say, 'uses his teeth to crack nuts.' The latter phrase is related to 'cracking nuts with his teeth' (but compare *'meaning *y* with *x*'), and 'using one's teeth is one way to crack nuts' (compare *'using *x* is one way to mean *y*'). These differences are explicable on the assumption that meaning something is a matter of having certain intentions; it is relatively clear why there is no such thing as a *way* of intending something. ('In what way do you mean that?' or 'How do you mean that?' —compare 'How do you crack nuts?'—does not mean *'By what means do you mean that?')

Chomsky has pointed out that the preposition *with* is quite generally a transform of *have*. Thus, "underlying the sentence 'John gave the lecture with great enthusiasm,' with the Adverbial 'with great enthusiasm,' is the base string 'John has great enthusiasm.'"[18] In other occurrences, *with* (and *by*) may for the same reason be regarded as transforms of *use*. Compare 'He used sand to fill it' → 'He filled it with sand'; 'He used an ax to do it' → 'He did it with an ax'; 'He used *x* to mean *y*' → 'He meant *y* by *x*.' (It would seem that a verb of such meager semantic content that it can be absorbed into

[18] *Ibid.*

a preposition offers small purchase to philosophical analysis.) To investigate the use of an expression is to investigate what is done *with* it, *by* or *in* uttering it, and so forth. But of course not a few of the uses of an expression are irrelevant to its meaning. To investigate those that are relevant is presumably to investigate what it is used to *mean*—that is, what is meant by it.

XI

We are now in a position to attempt to deal with a difficult problem postponed from Section II. I remarked there that while *mean* is subject to true passivization in neither its natural nor its nonnatural senses, a passive construction which I called the cleft-passive could be formed[19] in the case of $mean_{nn}$ which could not be formed in the case of $mean_n$. Thus, it requires explanation why 'Fire is what is $meant_{nn}$ by *feu*' is acceptable English, while *'Fire is what is $meant_n$ by smoke' is not. Presumably this requires us to find some structural difference between 'Fire is what *feu* means' and 'Fire is what smoke means,' for while both these cleft sentences are grammatical, only the former is subject to this sort of passive transformation.

It is a mistake to suppose that the passive transformation applies to such sentences only if they have Agent as subject, or are derived from such a string (as is 'Fire is what *feu* means' on the present hypothesis). This is a rather natural thought, since one might think that the active-passive relation implies an agent and a patient. But the cleft-passive 'Fire is what is indicated by (the presence of) smoke' is perfectly acceptable, and (*the presence of*) *smoke* is not an agentive but a factive construction. It is also wrong to suppose that what is lacking in *'Fire is what is $meant_n$ by smoke' is a "patient." Another natural thought, considering 'Fire is what is indicated by

---

[19] I am supposing that such sentences as 'Fire is what smoke means' are derived by an operation which might be called "object extraction": that is, they are derived from sentences like 'Smoke means fire' by extracting the object, placing it together with an appropriate copula either initially ('Fire is what . . .') or terminally ('What smoke means is fire'), and inserting a Wh pronoun before the subject of the verb. This operation is a kind of interrogative nominalization. The derived sentence corresponds to the question 'What does smoke mean?,' and corresponding to the question 'What means fire?' there is the sentence 'What means fire is smoke,' derived by "subject extraction."

smoke': here it sounds rather as if the presence of fire is indicated *to* an implicit *someone*—the patient. This might suggest that since $mean_n$ does not take such indirect objects, the trouble is that there is no patient to "receive the action" in the case of *'Fire is what is meant$_n$ by smoke.' The trouble with this line is that neither does the grammatical 'Fire is what is meant$_{nn}$ by *feu'* have an implicit indirect object, if the argument of Section II was correct. So the possession of such an implicit indirect object cannot be a necessary condition of the application of this transformation. That is, a rule which sought simply to restrict cleft sentence passivization either to sentences with Agent as implicit or explicit subject, or to sentences having an implicit or explicit indirect object (Patient), would not fit the data.

To solve this puzzle we must first segregate the conditions for passivization of transitive verbs (*indicate, prove,* and so forth) from the conditions for the application of this transformation to intransitive or middle verbs such as *mean*. I suggest the following rule: (1) the passive transformation is permitted to operate on cleft sentences involving any transitive verb whatever—that is, by any verb which permits the genuine passive. (Thus there are cleft-passives involving all *FA-t* verbs other than *mean,* whether with factive or agentive subject constructions.) (2) The cleft-passive transformation is permitted in the case of middle or intransitive verbs (that is, is permitted to operate on strings, produced by object extraction, of the form NP_2-be-Wh-NP_1-V_{intr}) if and only if the strings in which they figure are derived from a string containing a *by*-phrase of the appropriate sort —that is, a string of the form Agent-V_{intr}-NP_1-by-NP_2.

This rule says, in effect, that the subject of a middle or intransitive verb can be transformed (by cleft sentence passivization) into a *by*-phrase if and only if it has originated from a *by*-phrase (by something like our instrument promotion transformation). *Smoke,* the subject of $mean_n$ in 'Fire is what smoke means$_n$,' has *not* come from this source; it has not come from By-smoke-Agent-means-fire. Accordingly, it cannot be returned to that occurrence in an acceptable sentence, *'By smoke what is meant$_n$ is fire' or *'Fire is what is meant$_n$ by smoke.' On the other hand, *fumée,* the subject of $mean_{nn}$ in 'Smoke is what *fumée* means' is on my hypothesis derived from 'By *fumée* Agent means smoke.' Consequently, it *can* be returned to the context *by*-. . . , in an acceptable sentence 'Smoke is what is meant by *fumée.'* The suggested rule, then, accurately expresses a certain co-occurrence phenomenon: namely, there is a nondeviant cleft-passive context NP-be-Wh-be-Verb$_{intr}$-Past-. . . , in which a by-phrase may occur, if and only if a by-phrase may occur in the context NP-Verb$_{intr}$-NP-. . . .

Thus we may predict correctly that since there are sentences of the form 'Jim means$_{nn}$ y by x,' there will be sentences of the form 'y is what is meant$_{nn}$ by x' and 'y is what is meant$_{nn}$.' And we predict, again correctly, that since there are no sentences of the form *'NP means$_n$ y by the fact that p,' we will find sentences of the form *'y is what is meant$_n$ by the fact that p' unacceptable.

The permissibility of the cleft-passive transformation of sentences like 'Feu means$_{nn}$ fire' is explained by these considerations. The existence of cleft-passive sentences can be predicted from the hypothetical deep structure assigned to them; and the predictability of such sentences is, on the hypothesis that they have *such* a deep structure, relatively intelligible. For the rule in question relates in a suitably nonarbitrary way the occurrence of cleft-passive constructions involving *mean$_{nn}$* to a stage in the derivation of such constructions in which an identical syntactic structure occurs—namely, the by-phrase. Conversely, it relates the absence of cleft-passives involving *mean$_n$* to the absence of such a stage in the derivation of sentences of the form 'y is what x means$_n$.' Thus, supposing this rule provides the correct explanation of the phenomena in question, it lends additional support to the hypothesis it crucially invokes—namely, that such a sentence as 'Feu means$_{nn}$ fire' is derived from a construction of the form 'By *feu* Agent means$_{nn}$ fire.'

XII

I have argued that sentences which say what some expression (utterance, remark, etc.) means are transformationally related to, and in fact derived from, sentences which say what a person means by that expression. I want now to consider what philosophical importance it would have were this grammatical contention in fact correct.

Taking an Olympian view of philosophical goings-on, one might argue that this grammatical analysis serves to explain, at least along one dimension, the peculiar tendency of philosophers, at least English-speaking philosophers, to say that it is basically persons that mean things, and not expressions. Hospers, for instance, says,

"Strictly speaking, it is not *sentences* that mean at all; we speak as if this were so, but this way of speaking is an ellipsis; actually it is *we* who mean various things by our sentences."[20] But the murky question remains: supposing this philosophical view is in part an expression of grammatical intuition, is the grammar—is English—in this regard philosophically perspicuous or philosophically misleading? Of course, the view in question is not *merely* an expression of grammatical insight into English. For one thing the view is very much older than the English language; I quote from the Kneales' discussion of Stoic logic:

> Now the word 'mean' has two uses which it is important to distinguish in this connexion. We can ask what a person means and we can ask what a sentence means. The Stoics, on the other hand, had two different words where we have only one; for Greek uses λέγειν of persons, σημαίνειν of sentences. But they deliberately identified *semainomena* with *lekta*. . . . What a sentence means, then, in their view is what a person means when he utters it.[21]

The grammatical analysis of a word is of philosophical interest to the extent that it contributes to or is congruent with a philosophical analysis of the "concept" expressed by the word. Of course, whether the Stoic view can constitute a successful philosophical analysis is inseparable from the question whether the analysans, the notion of "a person's meaning something by an utterance," is itself independently analyzable. Grice has indicated, I think, that it is: that the concept of a person's meaning something by an utterance can be analyzed in terms of the peculiar configuration of intentions with which such an utterance is made. His published formulation of that (by now extensively revised) analysis was this:

> "*A* meant$_{nn}$ something by *x*" is (roughly) equivalent to "*A* intended the utterance of *x* to produce some effect in an audience by means of the recognition of this intention"; [and he further adds that] . . . the intended effect must be something which in some sense is within the control of the audience, or [such that] in some sense of "reason" the recognition of the intention behind *x* is for the audience a reason and not merely a cause.[22]

[20] John Hospers, *An Introduction to Philosophical Analysis* (Englewood Cliffs, N.J., 1953), p. 75.

[21] W. and M. Kneale, *The Development of Logic* (Oxford, 1962), p. 157.

[22] Grice, *op. cit.,* p. 385.

(There are, of course, recognized difficulties in extending such an analysis as this to cope with "utterance parts," such as words and phrases.) The great gain of such an analysis as Grice's is that, whatever its difficulties, the concept of intention, unlike the concepts of an idea, a concept, semantic marker, semantic regularity, and so forth, at least does not swim the same orbit of conceptual space as does "meaning" itself.

I wish to advance the cause of this analysis only within the limited terms of the grammatical analysis presented here. Thus I will say nothing here about the adequacy of Grice's analysis of "meaning something by an utterance," itself a seemingly inexhaustible topic. Instead I will consider only the claim that what an expression means may be identified (with certain qualifications) with what a person means by that expression. Thus I will consider whether the proposed instrument promotion transformation "preserves meaning" between the source and the transform.[23] To the extent to which it does so, the philosophical credentials of the transformational analysis will be confirmed.

The transformation under discussion is a deletion transformation. Unfortunately, deletion transformations are not the best exemplars of the meaning preservative properties of transformations. We are not here dealing with a case in which a redundant element is deleted, as in, for example, 'Jim ordered peas and John ordered beans' → 'Jim ordered peas and John beans.' In such an instance the deleted element carries no information, as it were, which is not available from the transform. Thus such a transformation would meet a condition generally imposed on transformations, which stipulates that the source must be recoverable from the transform.[24] The principle operating here is an extension of the Saussurean one that an element of a sentence which is predictable from its sentential environment bears no meaning: as *to,* in the environment 'I want . . . go,' being predictable, has no meaning. By an extension of this principle, those elements of a transformational source which are predictable from the

[23] According to some current formulations of transformational theory, this question cannot receive a negative answer, for, in these formulations, *all* transformations preserve meaning. (This threatens to become a matter of definition.) See Katz and Postal, *op. cit.* I think it is neither necessary here to take issue with this view nor, given the highly fluid state of the subject, to be hidebound by it.

[24] Chomsky, *Aspects,* pp. 138, 144–45.

transform are deletable without alteration of meaning, either because they have no meaning or because they, and hence their contributions to the sense of the sentence, are implicit in the transformed sentence.

If this deletion transformation were supposed to take 'By x *John* means y' into 'x means y,' it would plainly not preserve meaning; in no sense would the source and transform mean the same thing. (One cannot tell from the fact that x means y that it is John who means y by x.) I have accordingly written the source form as 'By x *Agent* means y,' employing the "abstract" or indefinite element "Agent" to indicate the underlying subject of the verb. This element "Agent" has of course *some* semantic content; its "values," so to speak, must be expressions referring, in one way or another, to agents—to those higher animals, and so forth, or aggregates thereof, to which action and intention may be ascribed. But although "Agent" is neither devoid of meaning nor redundant, its deletion results in no loss of meaning, for the deleted element is recoverable or predictable from the transform. That is, only some expression referring (in some sense) to an agent or agents can occur as the subject of *mean* in an acceptable sentence of the form 'By x . . . means y.' Thus, the transform is properly diaphanous with respect to its source.

Whether and in what sense this transformation "preserves meaning" depends in part upon whether and in what sense such an abstract element as "Agent" *has* meaning to be either lost or preserved. This question partakes of a general difficulty concerning the sense in which any transformation may be said to preserve meaning. The input and the output of a transformation are not generally conceived (except, I understand, by Zellig Harris) as being actual sentences. Rather they are "abstract formal structures underlying actual sentences," or the like. If so, there is a (not insurmountable) general difficulty about the sense in which such structures have meaning to be either lost or preserved. Whether a certain transformation preserves meaning may perhaps be discussed in disregard of this technical point, without endorsing any particular view about the semantic properties of the abstract structures on which transformations operate. To do so is to discuss the semantic relation of certain actual sentences variously associated with such structures by the grammar.

Consider, then, the claim that the Agent deletion-Instrument promotion transformation preserves meaning in just this sense: For every sentence of the form (*i*) by-x-Agent-Aux-mean-y-(adverbial phrase), there is some sentence of the form (*ii*) x-Aux-mean-y-(adverbial phrase), which means the same thing, and conversely. (This would perhaps serve as a fair statement of Grice's proposal.[25]) There is, I think, little doubt that this claim is at least generally true; and I am inclined to think that the philosophical importance of this semantic generalization would not greatly be diminished by the existence of a few exceptions to the rule.

It would, I suppose, be conceded that we do quite often use the two forms of words, (*i*) and (*ii*), interchangeably. We also distinguish between what (the word, or expression) *x* means and what a certain person means by *x* on a certain occasion. This distinction, however, is not tied to the difference between the two forms of words. For we may equally well state the distinction as that between what *x* means ordinarily (or what *x* means properly speaking) and what *x* means as used by (or in the mouth of) a particular person on a particular occasion.

The point to be emphasized is this. There is often a restriction on the scope of a meaning statement implicit in the reference made in a form (*i*) sentence to a particular person: but in general such a restriction may be preserved in and by an adverbial phrase, modifying a sentence of form (*ii*). For instance, we may say 'By *idea* Hume means such and such,' restricting our remark to Hume's use of the word; but we can as well say '*Idea,* as used by Hume, means such and such.' It is a mistake to suppose that sentences of form (*i*) are *bound* to refer to idiosyncratic or nonce or misuses, and that sentences of form (*ii*) are bound to assert general and comparatively unrestricted synonymy claims. The resources for preserving synonymy made available by adverbial modifiers are often underestimated in discussions of the thesis in question; it is in fact as if the meaning of a statement of the form '*x* means$_{nn}$ *y*' is left indeterminate or ambiguous by the omission of an adverbial restrictor.

Consider, next, whether it is possible to find some sentence of form (*i*) to express what is expressed by, for example,

(1) *Aggravate* means make some condition more serious.

It has been objected that

(2) By *aggravate* people mean make some condition more serious.

[25] *Op. cit.,* p. 385.

(the formula suggested by Grice) is not equivalent to (1), because as a matter of fact what people mean by *aggravate* is exasperate or irritate. People (let us suppose) generally misuse the word, so (1) is true and (2) is false. But such form (*i*) sentences as

(3) By *aggravate* people, when speaking correctly, mean make some condition more serious.

(4) By *aggravate* one means make some condition more serious.

would seem to accommodate this observation; for what they say is true, and is true if and only if (1) is true.[26]

The complaint has been made that Grice's proposal is objectionably "empiricist." Thus it has been said that it does not accommodate the projective character of language. A sentence may have meaning even if it has never before been uttered, in which case it is not true that "people mean" (or that "one means") anything by it. But it *is* true that *were* one to utter it one *would* (generally) mean such and such by it. Again, ambiguities pose no great problem. If a word means either *y* or *z,* a person, by that word, *might* mean *y* or he *might* mean *z*. The "charge" of empiricism is a misunderstanding. Sentences of form (*i*) do not *necessarily* refer to actual historical use, and are not necessarily generalizations from or quasi-statistical reports of the (to some extent) irrelevant facts of usage. Thus there are sentences of the form 'By *x* one (or: a person) means *y*' available for paraphrasing such sentences as (1), and this is no more a statistical report on actual behavior than is 'One (or: a man) rises when a lady enters the room.' In other words, the proposal in question is not independent of that essential commonplace of linguistic theory, the ideal speaker, who is not, certainly, to be met with in experience.

It is, I think, entirely true and important to realize that the present account does nothing whatever to *elucidate* (though it does accommodate) the central phenomenon of language, its projective character, its capacity, so to speak, to enable its speakers to know what a person would mean were he to say something that has never before

[26] It is true, but in no way incompatible with the present view, that such a cleft-passive sentence as "What is meant by *aggravate* is exasperate" has a greater tendency than does the active form to be interpreted as a comment on usage. This comes out in such a sentence as *"Aggravate* means make some condition more serious, but by *aggravate* what is meant is exasperate," which is not necessarily construed as inconsistent.

been said. Ziff has complained that Grice's "alloy lacks the basic ingredient of meaning: a set of projective devices."[27] So it does lack this ingredient, but neither is that the basic ingredient of *meaning*, though it is, certainly, basic to *language*. It would seem that meaning comprehends more, and less, than language: that, for example, a code containing only three messages and no means for going beyond that finite vocabulary would still, while certainly not a language, be such that its signals had meaning, in precisely the same sense of the word *meaning* in which words and sentences of a language have meaning.

Another complaint is that the proposal involves the objectionably empiricist idea that one determines what a word or sentence means by means of investigating or determining in some way what people mean or generally mean by it. But this is a misunderstanding. The proposal is that the two forms of words are *equivalent* in the sense explicated earlier. That is, to determine what a word or sentence means *is, eo ipso,* to determine what one means or would mean by it, and conversely. The form of the proposal implicitly precludes the idea that the two matters are related as evidence to conclusion: it has virtually nothing to do with such matters as *how* one finds out what words or sentences mean.

I pointed out that in adverbial modifiers, verbal auxiliaries (*would, should, might*), and indefinite pronouns, the language provides rich resources for paraphrasing form (*i*) sentences by form (*ii*) sentences and vice versa. But these resources do have their limits. There is, for example, the case mentioned by Grice: we may say that a red traffic light means$_{nn}$ Stop, but as Grice observes, "it would be very unnatural to say 'Somebody (for example the Corporation) meant$_{nn}$ by the red light that the traffic was to stop,'" or 'by a red light someone or one means Stop.'[28] But this exception is not particularly unsettling, for on our paradigm one can see why the case should be exceptional. A sentence of the form 'By x Agent means y' is, on the present analysis, derived from a double source, 'Agent-Verb-x' and 'Agent-mean-y.' (A typical case would derive from 'Agent said x' and 'Agent meant y.') The anomaly in the stoplight

[27] P. Ziff, "On H. P. Grice's Account of Meaning," *Analysis,* XXVIII (1967), 1–8. For further discussion of this and other of Ziff's criticisms, see T. Patton and Stampe, "The Rudiments of Meaning: on Ziff on Grice," *Foundations of Language* 5 (1969), p. 2–19.

[28] *Op. cit.,* p. 385.

case is that the first of these deep sources is unrealized. No one, certainly not the Corporation, did (or 'uttered') anything when the light turned red, no one turned the light to red, hence no one intended or meant anything when the light turned red. (One cannot mean anything unless one utters or does something.) The peculiarity is in a sense owing simply to the designed peculiarity of automated stop signs, which are devices designed to eliminate the need for human gesticulation and utterance at the crossroads.

There are also apparent exceptions to the semantic generalization going the other way, which adverbial modifiers cannot easily bring into line. Suppose that what a person says is not merely idiosyncratic but perfectly mad. Crazy George, for instance, sitting in the dark, makes the sounds *Gelug glugid,* and we discover that in his madness what he meant when he made these noises was Let there be light. Here it will be unnatural to say that *Gelug glugid* meant Let there be light. It will not be enough to add the adverbial restrictor, 'as George used it.' That would imply that others use it, as they do not, in other ways. Such adverbial modifiers function normally to contrast one accepted or tolerated use with another. Against this, however, it might be argued that the unacceptability of *'Gelug glugid* means Let there be light' arises from the fact that as the case is described we are invited to conceive the utterance as a specimen of nonsense (that is, to think of it as having no meaning). The suggestion is that while a person may mean something by a nonsensical utterance, such an utterance will not, by virtue of that fact, mean anything. But if we suspend our preoccupation with the nonsensicality of George's utterances—if, say, we should become interested in cataloguing and studying the vocal behavior of such patients—it seems that we might well record that *Gelug glugid* meant Let there be light, *Blugot negub* meant Leave me alone, and so forth. It is not obvious that we would have to use the other form of words. If it is replied that this would just be shorthand for 'By *Gelug glugid* George meant . . . ,' then perhaps we have reached agreement.

But even supposing that it is determined that we have here or elsewhere a genuine counterinstance, it is not clear that it would matter greatly. The importance of any such counterinstances must be weighed against the explanatory success of the paradigm here presented, against its capacity to elucidate the syntactic and semantic subsystem of *FA* verbs. It would surely be defective judgment which would allow a handful of exceptions (if they be such) involving automata, madmen, and brains stuck with electrodes to hold sway over a paradigm which successfully aspires to that unified account of meaning we desire. Whether these aspirations are to some extent realized is another question.

Linguistic Metatheory*

BARBARA HALL PARTEE

A picture of linguistic theory in 1971 is a picture of a field very much in flux. It was much easier to teach a course in syntax in 1965 or 1966 than it is now. In 1965 we had Chomsky's *Aspects* model, and if one didn't pay too much attention to disquieting things like Lakoff's thesis and Postal's underground *Linguistic anarchy notes,* one could present a pretty clear picture of syntax, with a well-understood phonological component tacked on one end and a not-yet-worked-out but imaginable semantic component tacked on the other end. There were plenty of unsolved problems to work on, but the *paradigm* (in Kuhn's sense) seemed clear. But now we're in a situation where there is no theory which is both worked out in a substantial and presentable form and compatible with all the data considered important. So what I find myself doing in syntax classes is first showing some of the many elegant solutions to exciting syntactic problems that have been worked out in the *Aspects* framework, and then showing them the additional data which doesn't seem to be amenable to treatment in that framework at all.

What I want to do here is threefold: first, I'll give a brief historical sketch of the theory of syntax and its relation to semantics since 1957; the focus of this will be the rise and fall of the Katz-Postal hypothesis. (See also Partee 1971.) Second, I'll outline the main features of three current approaches: the interpretive semantics and generative semantics variants of transformational grammar, and, very briefly, Richard Montague's quite different approach. I won't attempt to choose sides, because I think it's way too early to judge and because all three seem worth exploring as far as possible if only for negative results. What I will do as my third task is describe what I consider to be some of the key problem areas, areas where I expect the choice among alternative theories may eventually lie.

* Reprinted with permission from William Orr Dingwall (ed.), *A Survey of Linguistic Science* (University of Maryland: 1971). Copyright © September 1971 by William Orr Dingwall.

I. HISTORY

I don't want to go into detail here on the evolution of the *Katz-Postal hypothesis* that deep structure is the only level of syntactic structure which is needed as input to semantic interpretation rules. I've discussed it in Partee (1971), and it's pretty familiar by now anyway. There are really only two points which seem at all surprising in retrospect, one a rather significant point in Chomsky's *Syntactic structures* and one apparently just a historical accident in the evolution of the Katz-Postal hypothesis.

The first point concerns Chomsky's view of syntax in 1957. In *Syntactic structures,* Chomsky expressed doubts about the possibility of *any* systematic connection between syntax and semantics. Furthermore, he believed it not only necessary, but even possible, to describe syntax in completely autonomous terms. This may seem surprising in retrospect, particularly from one who was so articulate in rejecting the idea of trying to do autonomous phonetics. I think his outlook was probably very much affected by his concurrent work on formal languages, where classes of languages could be very rigorously described in syntactic terms, and very interesting formal properties of the languages could be deduced from the form of their grammars. And these approaches *did* bear fruit in the investigation of natural languages. In particular, it was possible, using only the most universally agreed-on judgments of *grammatical* and *ungrammatical,* to demonstrate very elegantly that natural languages were neither finite-state languages nor context-free languages. Since those were not straw men in the fifties, that was a great theoretical advance. And since that advance was made within an *autonomous syntax* approach, that approach gained at least *prima facie* plausibility.

The rise of the Katz-Postal hypothesis that deep structure as described in the *Aspects* model provided a sufficient basis for semantic interpretation was also marked by interesting results which similarly provided a *prima facie* justification for their approach. In case after case it was shown that a more careful syntactic analysis led to derivations in which transformations were meaning-preserving. The surprising historical accident that I alluded to earlier is that the behavior of quantifiers was not really noticed until the Katz-Postal hypothesis had for most linguists reached the status of a necessary condition on writing rules. I think this historical accident is one of the major causes of the state of turmoil in the theory today. Let me give a few examples of derivations that would have been given in the standard theory, and leave you to reflect on whether the Katz-Postal hypothesis would have even been suggested if these had been noticed beforehand.

(1) a. Every man voted for himself. *From:*
    b. Every man voted for every man.
(2) a. Every candidate wanted to win. *From:*
    b. Every candidate wanted every candidate to win.
(3) a. All pacifists who fight are inconsistent. *From:*
    b. $\begin{cases} \text{All pacifists fight.} \\ \text{All pacifists are inconsistent.} \end{cases}$
(4) a. No number is both even and odd. *From:*
    b. No number is even and no number is odd.

This is the kind of data that has led to the downfall of the Katz-Postal hypothesis in conjunction with the classical *Aspects* kind of *independently motivated* syntax. There are clearly two ways to react to such data: either keep the Katz-Postal hypothesis and revise the deep structure; or abandon the Katz-Postal hypothesis and keep the deep structure. The first of these is the *generative semantics approach,* the second the *interpretive semantics approach.* Of course there is another alternative, which is to try a completely different model, and I'll get to an example of that, too.

II. THREE CURRENT APPROACHES

Although what I just said about generative and interpretive semantics is a gross oversimplification, I think it fairly represents their historical beginnings. What there seemed to be in 1965 was a maximally elegant theory, elegant in two directions: first, there was a level of deep structure which could be established on purely syntactic grounds and which had a remarkable convergence of properties: it was the level at which all the key grammatical relations could be defined, all the lexical items could be inserted, and all of their contextual restrictions defined, and it also served as input to the transformations. The other elegant feature of the theory, the contribution of Katz and Postal, was that at this same level of structure there appeared to be a one-for-one correlation between syntactic and semantic rules (not that these were ever worked out, but it certainly appeared possible in principle).

Given this two-sided elegance, it's not hard to see why it was difficult to give the theory up, and why, when it had to be given up, linguists should be divided about which part was more worth fighting for. Let me try to make this vivid by arguing for each side.

A. Interpretive semantics: PRO

Think back to the examples where certain transformations changed meaning when quantifiers were involved, e.g., *every candidate wanted every candidate to win = every candidate wanted to win*. There's nothing ungrammatical about either sentence, so there's no purely syntactic reason to rule out such a derivation. Most of the time the rule preserves meaning: e.g., *John expected John to win = John expected to win*. Furthermore, there's no very plausible "better" source for *every candidate wanted to win*. Furthermore, the semantic change wrought by the transformation can be described perfectly well in terms of the surface structure—two independent quantifiers in one sentence, only one in the other, which is just what the difference in logical form is. Similar remarks can be made about the other examples. I'll get back to counterarguments in a minute. But the main thrust of the arguments *for* this approach seem to be as I've just sketched: the derivations which change meaning do not change grammaticality, so we have no syntactic basis for rejecting them; and furthermore the semantics can be done at the surface.

B. Generative semantics: PRO

Now let me bring in a different sort of quantifier example: *a hundred soldiers shot two students*. Here we have a sentence which apparently has had no transformations, so there's no problem of meaning-changing transformations. But the sentence is ambiguous; it has either two or three readings depending on one's dialect: either (1) there were a hundred soldiers each of whom shot two students or (2) there were two students each of whom was shot by a hundred soldiers or (3) there was a group of a hundred soldiers who altogether shot a pair of students. It doesn't have any ambiguous *words* in it (a *hundred* isn't ambiguous and *two* isn't ambiguous), so the ambiguity must be structural. And structural means syntactic. But the standard theory only assigns one deep structure, and therefore it predicts that the sentence is unambiguous: that was a principle enunciated by Chomsky as far back as *Syntactic structures.* The ambiguity is one of relative scope of the two quantifiers, so the obvious emendation to the syntax is to indicate quantifier scope in a structural way. So just as adverbs have typically been attached higher or lower in a tree to show whether they modify the *VP* or the whole *S,* so could quantifiers be given an appropriate hierarchical structure. Classical quantifier logic in fact works just this way—not with a tree representation but with a kind of a bracketing which is equivalent to it. Once we have done this, it becomes clear how the derivations which appeared to change meaning can be revised in a simple way so they no longer do: a sentence like *every candidate wants to win* can be handled by also bringing in from logic the notion of a variable, and we have as a deep structure something like: (*for every x:candidate*) (*x wants x to win*). Here there is just one occurrence of the quantifier: *every* and a variable which is somehow attached to the noun: *candidate;* the same variable occurs twice in the representation of the sentence: *every candidate wanted to win,* while in the representation of the sentence: *every candidate wanted every candidate to win* there would be two different quantifiers and two different variables.

This somewhat artificial sketch might be called a *hypothetical Stage One*—each side laying out how neatly it can preserve one of the two elegant sides of the doomed Katz-Postal-*Aspects* model, and not talking too much about the other side. The interpretivists don't say much about *how* their semantics works, and the generativists don't say much about the syntactic rules that will turn their elegant deep structures into English. Now without trying to maintain this fiction of clear historical "stages," let me describe some of the subsequent arguments. (It will be noted that I am focussing on just a small part of the data that is fought over. There are also negation, conjunction, pronominalization, causatives, derived nominals, and many other phenomena talked about by one side or the other or both.)

[1] Against the interpretivist view that grammaticality is never affected by the meaning-changing transformations, there has been offered a considerable amount of counterevidence. For instance, the *EACH*-HOPPING RULE which converts (5a) to (5b):

(5) a. Each of the men won a prize.
   b. The men each won a prize.

sometimes changes meaning, as in (6):

(6) a. Each of the men hates his brothers.
    b. The men each hate his brothers.

(where the *his* in (6b) cannot be interpreted as *his own*). Dougherty and Chomsky argued for surface interpretation, on the basis of the rule itself being too clear and simple to give up. But the same rule converts the grammatical (7a) into the ungrammatical (7b):

(7) a. Each of the men shaved himself.
    b. *The men each shaved himself.

and in order to derive (8b) one has to posit the ungrammatical source sentence (8a):

(8) a. *Each of the men shaved themselves.
       [acceptable in some dialects]
    b. The men each shaved themselves.

Similarly, the interpretivist theory of pronominalization, which generates all pronouns freely in the base, and interprets pronoun-antecedent relations semantically, generates such ungrammatical sentences as (9) and (10):

(9) *Mary asked John to help herself.
(10) *The boy shot her own father.

The counterargument to this line of criticism has been interesting, and is one I find both unsettling and hard to attack. It has been to retract one of the premises of *Syntactic structures* which many people had been dubious about anyway, namely that native speakers have clear intuitions about *grammaticality*. It is claimed instead that while certain sentences will be judged in some way deviant or unacceptable by native speakers, the classification of deviance into *syntactic* and *semantic* is not part of the raw data of speaker intuitions, but will simply be a product of whatever theory attains the greatest overall simplicity. Therefore if the simplest overall theory deems the sentence *I saw himself* to be syntactically well-formed but semantically ill-formed, so be it; we have no pre-theoretic notions of syntax vs. semantics to falsify such a claim. What a linguist might take as intuitions to the contrary are just prejudices born of habit. Notice how easily *colorless green ideas sleep furiously* slid over the fence and back again—grammatical in *Syntactic structures*, ungrammatical in

Aspects, grammatical again once McCawley showed what should have been obvious—that selection restrictions must be semantic and not syntactic.

I once asked Chomsky if the distribution of the word *please* didn't show the influence of semantic factors on grammatical well-formedness, since it is request interpretation and not interrogative or imperative form that governs its possibility of occurrence. I take his reply as typical of the new view of grammaticality: he answered in effect that the only thing that needed to be included in the syntax about *please* was that it occurred sentence-initially, in the auxiliary, or sentence-finally (at least as a rough approximation); there was no *a priori* reason to call the deviance of *will I please help you tomorrow?* syntactic.

[2] A second argument against the interpretive semantics position is that the semantics part of it is just a claim and not a theory. I believe that Jackendoff is doing some interesting and promising work to try to rectify that inadequacy, but that it has to a large extent been a fair criticism. (Certainly it was a fair criticism of the interpretivist claims that I made in Partee (1969).) I still find the interpretivist approach to semantics a plausible one, but at this point that's a matter of temperament and "gut feelings"; not a subject for polemics but simply for further work.

[3] In an earlier paper of mine (Partee 1969) I pointed out one serious defect in Lakoff's treatment of quantifiers. Lakoff had posited two different deep structures to account for the different meanings of (11) and (12).

(11) Few men read many books.
(12) Many books are read by few men.

But because of the way he was accounting for the ambiguity of *a hundred soldiers shot two students,* his transformations would permit either deep structures to turn into either surface form, thereby *not* accounting for the fact that (in the dialect he was describing) each sentence has only one interpretation. In response there arose the *theory of derivational constraints.* In general, the generative semantics approach started out with a rather unspecified syntax (deep structures but very few transformations) just as the interpretive approach started with an unspecified semantics. I think generative semanticists have done more work to fill in their syntax than interpretivists have for their semantics, though it is a matter of opinion whether the syntactic innovations Lakoff and others have made have strengthened or weakened their claims for their theory. I think they have weakened them, but I accept their reply that they foresee corresponding weaknesses in interpretive semantics if and when its semantics is specified in detail.

[4] Another point at which the generative semantics view is quite specific is in its claim that semantic representations are basically of the same form as syntactic representations, namely labelled trees. I find this aspect of the theory rather mystifying. At one time, around 1969, McCawley at least was saying that that abstract tree structure *was* the semantic interpretation. But I think it has been generally conceded since then that there must be more to semantics than drawing trees. For instance, in addition to the notion of synonymy, which *might* be capturable as *same tree,* a semantic theory must indicate when one sentence entails another—e.g., it is part of our linguistic competence to know that *John barely caught the train* entails *John caught the train;* whereas *John nearly caught the train* entails *John didn't catch the train.* Furthermore, there are sentences like *the glass is half empty* and *the glass is half full* whose "synonymy" is probably best captured as mutual entailment without sameness of deep structure.

Since I see the task of semantics as consisting in large part of explicating relations *among* sentences such as synonymy and entailment, I can only see a role for a notion like a *semantic representation* as something like *a structural representation on which semantics can be based.* Hence I feel that so far there is in fact a serious incompleteness in even the *semantic* part of generative semantics.

One potential rebuttal to this criticism is that the semantic representations give the logical form of the sentences, so the rules of logic, presumably universal, will do the rest. The counterargument to that is that logicians are only just beginning to formulate logics that will go beyond the treatment of *all, some, and, not, or, if-then, necessarily,* and *possibly,* and that even what has been done in logic so far is extremely syntax-sensitive. That is, a logic and a syntax can never be specified independently of one another, and to give abstract syntax-like structures without simultaneously specifying a logic to operate on them is almost empty. Not quite, because to give different syntactic forms to sentences with different entailment-potentials is one step in the process. I think the near-vacuousness of the theory in this respect is being recognized and worked on; but it is as far from being worked *out,* I believe, as any other linguistic approach to semantics.

In many respects, I believe that generative and interpretive semantics are in essential agreement, and jointly in opposition to the Katz-Postal-*Aspects* theory, which was more elegant than either but unfortunately wrong. The major point of agreement now is that there are many points of connection between syntax and semantics, not just one (the classical *deep structure*). Derivational constraints and interpretive rules can both be designed to capture the fact that the relative scope of logical elements depends on at least the following factors:

Surface Structure Word Order
   (13) a. Many men read few books.
        b. Few books are read by many men.

Stress
   (14) a. John and Mary can't come to the party.
        b. John *AND* Mary can't come to the party.

Subordination in Surface Structure
   (15) a. To please everyone is hard.
        b. Everyone is hard to please.

Idiosyncratic Lexical Differences among Quantifiers
   (16) a. Every soldier shot several students. [unambiguous scope]
        b. Several soldiers shot three students. [ambiguous scope]

Part of the problem involved here is that of describing the weighting of these different factors relative to each other, and this certainly does not seem to be extremely simple.

There is also, I think, still essential agreement among generative and interpretive semanticists about the form of the syntax, though this is not entirely clear. The interpretivists have essentially retained the standard theory's PS-rules and T-rules although the PS-rules may generate more *dummy nodes* or *empty nodes* than the standard theory did (cf. especially Emonds 1970; Dougherty 1968, 1970). The generative semanticists seem less clear on this point; Lakoff (In press) talks about the grammar specifying whole derivations as well- or ill-formed, but he only mentions transformations and *global constraints* and does not specify how either the set of inputs or outputs is specified. Presumably *deep structure constraints* plus *surface structure constraints* would have to add up to something at least as restrictive as phrase-structure rules.

Montague's theory of grammar is different from any version of transformational grammar in at least this last respect. The theory is in some ways reminiscent of the early *Katz-Fodor theory* where both PS-rules and transformations had corresponding projection rules, but his view of syntax is one in which rules much like PS-rules and rules much like transformations may apply in mixed and variable orders, with the order of operations often of crucial semantic significance. There is also a notion of noun phrases substituting for variables that is unique, though it has points of similarity with several transformational theories. Thus for an ambiguous sentence like (17):

(17) John is looking for a little girl with red hair.

in a Montague-grammar, there will be one derivation in which the noun phrase *a little girl with red hair* is substituted for *x* in *looking for x before* the phrase-structure rules (operating "bottom-up") attach the verb phrase to the subject to make a sentence. On that interpretation, *John* is simply described as having the property of *looking for a little girl with red hair,* i.e., what linguists have called the nonspecific reading. The other interpretation will be associated with a derivation which builds up a sentence *John is looking for x* and *then* substitutes the noun phrase for *x*. Although Montague, before his recent tragic death, had formalized only a relatively small fragment of English, his formalization was complete, i.e., the semantics, including the associated logic, was completely specified.

It remains for linguists and logicians to see whether the treatment can be extended to larger fragments of natural language.

Incidentally, Montague himself was not particularly interested in narrowing down the class of grammars to a subset just large enough for natural languages, but there is no reason to suppose it will be any harder (or easier) to do so in his framework than in any of the presently far-too-rich transformational approaches even though they avow such a purpose.

III. KEY PROBLEMS

I want to close with a brief mention of what seem to me key problems to focus on in searching for an adequate theory.

[1] The first is one I have been illustrating in my examples—the *logical form* problem, particularly the treatment of quantifiers, negation, and conjunction. This area has been receiving plenty of attention, and there have been many new insights gained about how

natural language expresses logical form, but we are still waiting for an adequate and fully specified theory.

[2] The second (and none of these are really independent) is the problem of PRONOMINALIZATION, EQUI-NP DELETION, and ELLIPSES. I lump these together because they are all parts of the problem of how best to represent the native speaker's competence in understanding as part of the interpretation of a sentence things that are missing in the surface structure. The standard theory and generative semantics both postulate fully-specified deep structures with processes of pronominalization and deletion. *SLOPPY-IDENTITY* DELETION (as in *if you can stand on your head, I'm sure I can*) is a recent addition to this repertoire. At this point discourse may become relevant in a way that it hasn't usually been taken to be for syntax. If you say to me *you're staring at me* and I reply *no, I'm not,* are we to say that the deep structure of my sentence *includes* a transformed version of your sentence? It certainly wouldn't include *you're staring at me;* if it included any thing, it would be *I'm staring at you,* but even that hardly seems plausible. And if the deep structure of my sentence does not include as a sub-part some transformed version of your sentence, then what is my deletion based on? It might be worth working on that question as a source for new ideas about deletions in general.

[3] The third big problem area is *lexical unity vs. lexical decomposition.* It is by now abundantly clear that *dissuade* has systematic relations to *persuade . . . not, kill* to *cause-to-die,* etc.; but the unity of lexical items also needs to be captured. *Either* as a quantifier and *either* as part of *either-or* are not unrelated. The different subsenses of *remind* are clearly closely related, and only one of them is equivalent to *strike as similar.* Charles Bird and Tim Shopen have been arguing this kind of point; it remains to find a way to reconcile the two kinds of generalizations.

There are many aspects of the current scene I haven't even touched on. Things are very exciting these days. I don't think a little polemics hurts—I might never have gotten started writing papers if I hadn't gotten worked up about some of the things George Lakoff was doing with quantifiers and I hereby thank him for that. I'm not at the moment very optimistic about any of the presently available theories; I'm by now sure that the Katz-Postal-*Aspects* model can't work, and I consider that a great pity. But I think that a lot of new insights are being gained that will stand, whatever theoretical framework they are eventually made a part of. And the linguists' belated discovery of logical form and formal semantics has opened up contacts between linguists and philosophers which promises to pay off richly in both fields. For the faint at heart the absence of a working paradigm may be distressing; I know that for the student, the field worker, the language teachers who would like to "apply" linguistics, it is certainly aggravating. But if one bears in mind how much was discovered and explained with the *Syntactic structures* model, and how much more with the *Aspects* model, and that those are being rejected only because we see a lot *more* things we'd like to explain, it can only be a very encouraging and exciting scene.

REFERENCES*

BIRD, CHARLES S. 1970. Associational phrases in English and Bambara. Presented at the 45th Annual Meeting of the Linguistic Society of America.

CHOMSKY, NOAM. 1957. Syntactic structures. The Hague: Mouton.

———. 1965. Aspects of the theory of syntax. Cambridge: The M.I.T. Press.

———. 1970. Deep structure, surface structure and semantic interpretation. Studies in general and oriental linguistics presented to Shirō Hattori, ed. by R. Jakobson and S. Kawamoto, 52–91. Tokyo: TEC Company, Ltd.

DOUGHERTY, RAY C. 1968. A transformational grammar of coordinate conjoined structures. Unpublished Ph.D. dissertation. Cambridge: M.I.T.

———. 1970. A grammar of coördinate conjoined structures: I. Lg. 46.850–98.

EMONDS, JOSEPH. 1970. Root and structure-preserving transformations. Unpublished Ph.D. dissertation. Cambridge: M.I.T.

KATZ, J. and J. FODOR. 1963. The structure of a semantic theory. Lg. 39.170–210.

[* For additional bibliography and sources relating to current issues in syntax and semantics see Ruwet, N. 1969. Bibliographie. Languages 14.134–44; Krenn, H. and K. Müllner. 1970. Generative Semantik. Linguistische Berichte 5.85–106; Dingwall, W. O. 1971. A bibliography of linguistic esoterica: 1970. Edmonton/Champaign; Linguistic Research, Inc.; Studies in linguistic semantics, ed. by C. J. Fillmore and D. T. Langendoen, 291–96. N.Y.: Holt, Rinehart and Winston, 1971; Kisseberth, C. (ed.). To appear. Studies in the linguistic sciences. Vol. 2, No. 1 [Special issue devoted to generative semantics]. Urbana: Dept. of Linguistics, U. of Illinois.]

KATZ, J. and PAUL M. POSTAL. 1964. An integrated theory of linguistic descriptions. Cambridge: The M.I.T. Press.

KUHN, THOMAS S. 1962. The structure of scientific revolutions. Chicago: The University of Chicago Press.

LAKOFF, GEORGE. 1966. On the nature of syntactic irregularity. Ph.D. dissertation. Bloomington: Indiana University. [=Lakoff, George. 1970. Irregularity in syntax. N.Y.: Holt, Rinehart and Winston.]

———. In press. On generative semantics. Semantics: An interdisciplinary reader in philosophy, linguistics, anthropology and psychology, ed. by D. Steinberg and L. Jakobovits. N.Y.: Cambridge U. Press.

MONTAGUE, RICHARD. 1970. English as a formal language. Linguaggi nella società e nella tecnica, 189–224. Milan: Edizioni di Comunità.

———. To appear. Universal grammar. Theoria.

———. To appear. The proper treatment of quantification in ordinary English. Approaches to natural language: Proceedings of the 1970 Stanford workshop on grammar and semantics, ed. by J. Moravcsik and P. Suppes. Dordrecht-Holland: D. Reidel Pub. Co.

PARTEE, BARBARA HALL. 1970. Negation, conjunction and quantifiers: Syntax vs. semantics. Foundations of Language 6.153–65.

———. 1971. On the requirement that transformations preserve meaning. Studies in linguistic semantics, ed. by C. J. Fillmore and D. T. Langendoen, 1–21. N.Y.: Holt, Rinehart and Winston.

———. To appear. Comments on Richard Montague's *The proper treatment of quantification in ordinary English*. Approaches to natural language: Proceedings of the 1970 Stanford workshop on grammar and semantics, ed. by J. Moravcsik and P. Suppes. Dordrecht-Holland: D. Reidel Pub. Co.

POSTAL, PAUL M. 1967. Linguistic anarchy notes: Series A: Horrors of identity: No. 2, Coreferentiality and physical objects. Unpublished MS. Yorktown Heights: I.B.M.

Review of *Noam Chomsky**

DELL HYMES

Noam Chomsky. By JOHN LYONS. (Modern masters, ed. by Frank Kermode.) New York: Viking Press, 1970. Pp. xii, 143. Cloth $5.75, paperback $1.85.

1. In this book Chomsky, and in a sense linguistics, join the company of Albert Camus, Frantz Fanon, Herbert Marcuse, Che Guevara, Claude Lévi-Strauss, Ludwig Wittgenstein, George Lukács, and James Joyce—the other 'modern masters' already treated in books published in the series edited by the distinguished English literary critic, Frank Kermode. Lyons has chosen to introduce his readers as much to transformational grammar as to Chomsky, on the premise that it is not possible to understand the impact of Chomsky's ideas in a number of different disciplines without going into some of the details of the formal system for the description of language that he has constructed (vii–viii). His main purpose, he writes, has been to provide enough historical and technical background so that a reader can go on afterward to Chomsky's own works. The readers of this journal presumably already have such a background and are already familiar with Chomsky's own works. Yet in pursuit of his purpose Lyons has provided a very readable short introduction to the character of transformational grammar, one that many linguists may wish to recommend. And the fact of such a book merits some comment. I shall discuss Lyons' account of the context and development of Chomsky's work, then say something about the book's assessment of Chomsky as intellectual figure.

2. Lyons devotes Chapter 2 to a short sketch of relevant ways in which modern linguistics departs from traditional grammar, assuming that his readers are familiar with the latter and that many may not be at all acquainted with the former. (The introduction, Chapter 1, belongs with later discussion of Chomsky's significance.) The sketch is intended to comprise principles common to all of modern linguistics, certainly to all 20th-century schools concerned with the description of languages. (Historical linguistics has no part in the

* Reprinted by permission of the author and the Linguistic Society of America from *Language* 48 (1972): 416–27.

sketch or book.) The principles are very much those of the 'equality, diversity, relativity' of forms of speech. Modern linguistics focuses upon the spoken language; eschews the stigma of 'incorrectness', regarding all dialects of English as worthy of equal consideration; has as a chief aim a theory of grammar appropriate for all human languages, not biased in favor of a few; rejects the category of 'primitive' languages; and recognizes two particularly striking properties of human language, duality of structure (syntactic, phonological) and creativity (or 'open-endedness'). While traditional grammar is noted as having recognized duality, the notion is used to bring out the distinction between syntax and semantics, and to characterize a grammar as containing at least three interrelated parts; syntax, semantics, and phonology.

I think Lyons is mistaken in his discussion of the vocabularies of languages. Swadesh found a ratio of about 2:1 (2000:1000 in order of magnitude) between the minimal morphemic elements of world languages, such as English and Spanish, and regional or local languages such as Nahuatl. To say (18–19) that every language has a sufficiently rich vocabulary for the expression of all the distinctions that are important in the society using it is to beg a host of questions; it is a form of 'functionalist optimism', or Panglossia, that would not pass muster for a moment in the political circles in which Chomsky figures, if seriously considered: cf. 'every society has sufficiently rich resources for the satisfaction of all the needs that are important to it', the general form of the proposition. Or consider the following recent note (Berman 1970:85): 'The corruption of language that dulls men's critical faculties, and blurs the disparity between things as they are and things as they should be (and could be) is a leitmotif in contemporary radical thought . . . Orwell . . . Gellner . . . Mills . . . Marcuse . . . All these writers err, it seems to me, in portraying this sleight-of-mind as a peculiarly contemporary problem. As Auerbach's material (in his essay, "La Cour et la Ville") suggests, it is rather an old story. Indeed, it is only in modern times, through Rousseau and his contemporaries, that a psychological vocabulary has emerged in which the potentialities of the self and the conditions for its fulfillment (or "actualization") could be talked about.'

If it is assumed that previous societies had no important interest in such a vocabulary, it still does not follow that the addition of such a vocabulary is not a difference. A parallel argument with regard to other instruments of human activity, such as material technology, would be spotted instantly as ridiculous. It is simply the case that one aspect of science is to have a name for everything in the universe, and that this ticketing of reality is an aspect of certain languages, not of most. One does not have to approve of the fact—one can deplore it—but only ideological blinders of the sort pervasive in linguistics and philosophy would enable one to ignore it. The plain truth of the matter is that most linguists have accepted unquestioningly a liberal humanist ideology formed earlier in the century to justify the study of all languages and to combat racist, imperialist, and other ethnocentric notions about 'primitive' languages. This ideology is right in what it denies: that there are any languages 'primitive' in the sense of being of a fundamentally different plan, lacking definite grammar or phonological systems, having to eke out words with gestures, etc. It is wrong in what it affirms: that 'all human societies of which we have knowledge speak languages of roughly equal complexity' (18)—no one has ever measured the 'roughly equal complexity' of languages, and it is ideological confidence rather than empirical knowledge that leads linguists to say such things. There is every reason to think that languages are differentially elaborated along different lines, and possibly over-all, as part of the adaptation of their communities and speakers; certainly with respect to vocabulary, at least, a criterion of evolutionary advancement can be established. Phenomena of this sort are a matter of regular experience, and a problem of some significance for language policy and planning in Third World countries. If linguists were to cease treating vocabularies as functionally perfect by definition, returning to the study of lexical creation and change and the more general question of a theory of vocabularies, a great deal of good might result.

Again, it is not at all certain that differences of grammatical structure among languages cannot be correlated with the cultural development of peoples, although the differences that have been observed do not of course contradict the existence of formal and perhaps substantive universals. The evolutionary theory of human language that Lyons has in mind, or considers his audience to have in mind, may well be something of the 19th century sort—isolating, agglutinating, inflecting and the like—and his point is no doubt well taken in such a case. It might have been possible to be more specific, however, so as to allow for the renewed study of languages from an evolutionary, developmental, adaptive standpoint on a different basis (cf. Hymes 1961, Berlin & Kay 1969, Swadesh 1971). Many linguists would probably agree with Lyons that it is best not even to suggest something that would give aid and comfort to a prejudiced enemy still entrenched. But there is a general issue to which we must return (§ 4.1 and fn. 3, below).

3. Chapter 3, 'The "Bloomfieldians"', sketches the American

background of Chomsky's work, taking up Boas, Sapir, and Bloomfield. The chapter is perceptive and sensible, bringing out the importance of the American Indian work for the earlier period, the congruence of many of Sapir's views with those of Chomsky, some of the complexities of assessing Bloomfield's views, and the initial dependence of Chomsky's advances on the work of scholars such as Harris. It is worth noting, however, how much there is still to discover and explain about this very recent history.

For one thing, Boas' central role is still inadequately understood. American anthropologists had been concerned with American Indian languages long before Boas, but without Boas' impact. The very fact that he concentrated on the writing of grammars caused comment at the time. The truth of the matter appears to be that writing grammars was not an inescapable activity, elicited simply by encounter with the languages, but was motivated for Boas by a theoretical concern, a 'mentalism' derived partly from the German tradition of Herder, Humboldt, Steinthal, and Wundt, and partly from his personal transition from a psycho-physical to a 'social psychological' perspective, through discovery of the complementary misperceptions of sounds by speakers of different languages. Salient ethnocentric concepts of unwritten languages at the time were that they changed more rapidly and lacked definite systems of sounds.[1] In Boas' contribution on the latter subject (1889) may be seen, as Stocking has remarked, the gist of his entire later intellectual development. In sum, the direction taken by notions of linguistic description at the time, while clearly reflecting (as Lyons notes) the particular task of recording unwritten languages and certain notions of objectivity, reflected also quite general theoretical purposes, stemming from a mentalist tradition more recent than the 'Cartesian', and forming part of an approach to the 'mental (human) sciences' as a whole.

The point is worth making here, because it is so recurrently tempting to explain American linguistics earlier in this century by the encounter with American Indian languages (cf. Bolinger 1968). Yet the linguist most articulate and influential in defining phonological discovery procedures in the 'neo-Bloomfieldian' period of the 1940's and 1950's was a man of European philological training, whose linguistic field work was in connection with American English dia-

[1] On the former, cf. § 1.1 of Hymes (MS a); on the latter, Wells (MS) and Stocking (MS). The role of Horatio Hale in both these respects deserves closer study; he was early in the field on the first point, and anticipated Boas on the second.

lectology (Bernard Bloch); while the man who most thoroughly defined grammatical discovery procedures for the period (33–34) was connected with the anthropological tradition more by fraternity than by research involvement (Zellig Harris). The two linguists who might be regarded as the field workers par excellence of the period, Pike and Swadesh, were both quite critical of the neo-Bloomfieldian direction, both as to its discard of meaning and its algorithmic approach to field work (Pike 1947, 1952; Swadesh 1948). Recall also Swadesh's controversy in the 1930's with Twaddell, an early exponent of an 'operationalism' that rejected a physical reality (and a fortiori, a mental reality) as object of investigation. Twaddell, like Bloch and Joos, had an academic background in a European language-and-literature field. It would appear that the appeal of various forms of operationalism, positivism, and behaviorism, at least as a style and ideology, had a great deal to do with the emergence of a new professional identification on the part of a small group of young men, coming out of and reacting against traditional humanistic fields, against which they wished to define their difference. The appeal also no doubt had a great deal to do with the climate of opinion in the period after World War I, marked by skepticism and even cynicism as to traditional concepts and rationalism in all fields. Cognitive interests had been strong in anthropology and linguistics before the debacle of the 'Great War'; witness not only Boas but also Bloomfield's first book (cited by Lyons, p. 30, fn. 2). Lyons notes a suggestion from the psychologist John Marshall that 'Bloomfield's behaviorism was more radical than that of many of the psychologists who influenced him because he was himself a "convert" from mentalism' (30, fn. 1). I am suggesting that a great deal of the explanation of the climate of opinion dominant immediately before Chomsky lies in factors of this kind (cf. Hymes 1964:8)—as well as of the dominant climate of opinion following Chomsky, as Lyons hints (12).

Another factor needing to be taken into account more fully is the role of Sapir. Lyons sketches Sapir's merit appreciatively, but limits attention to his *Language* of 1921, as contrasting with Bloomfield's *Language* of 1933. He is without doubt correct in singling out the two men and the two books; but a closer reading of the period would direct attention to Sapir's articles on phonology and semantics, the first of which were rediscovered early by transformationalists, and from one of which ('Sound patterns in language', Sapir 1925) stems not only the form of such titles as *Sound pattern of Russian* and *Sound pattern of English,* but also a methodological perspective of continuing relevance (cf. Pike 1967). On this subject I cannot agree with Lyons that 'there never has been a "Sapirian" school in the sense in which there has been, and still is, a "Bloomfieldian" school of linguistics in America' (29). I submit that in the 1930's there was at the very least a Sapir tradition, and a group of younger scholars whose work was thoroughly informed by it (Haas, Newman, Swadesh, Whorf and others; cf. Hymes 1971b). Before World War II, to be sure, there was not the sense of opposition between a Sapir and a Bloomfield tradition that was to be fostered in the 1940's, after Sapir's death in 1939, in terms of Sapir as 'vague' and 'intuitive' vs. Bloomfield as 'hard-headed' and precise (a view that conveniently neglected to note that Sapir's grammars represented the high point of precision in actual description at that time). The elements of a distinct outlook, retaining close connection with anthropology, can be discerned in the memorial volume to Sapir (Spier et al. 1941); and what the climate of American linguistics might have been, had Sapir lived, is worth conjecture. As it was, Whorf also died before World War II (in (1941), and the continuity of the perspective became raveled and peripheral. The methodological climate came to be dominated by men who took a certain conception of Bloomfield as its symbol (cf. Hymes 1970). This was not inevitable and needs investigation.

It is worth recalling that it was in the self-conscious development of methodology in this period that the connection of linguistics with anthropology became strained; if anthropological field work shaped theory, it was more in its image than in its practice. Pike's appeals to the experience of practice (1952), like those of Swadesh to mentalism (1948), got short shrift.

Another thread of the story needs to be brought out here as well, for it has much to do with the impact of Chomsky's work. The succession is not only of theoretical attitudes, but also of research foci. In this connection it is somewhat misleading to dub Boas a 'structuralist', however tentatively, for his view that every language has its own unique grammatical structure and that the task of the linguist is to discover for each language the categories of description appropriate to it (27). On the one hand, Boas—like Sapir, Jakobson, and many a true structuralist—had a concept of linguistic universals as well as of unique structures. On the other hand, the dominant note of Boas' work was to AVOID imposing alien categories of description. His own descriptions teased out elements and noted processes, but were remarkably reluctant to discover, infer, impute, or, as he might well have felt, IMPOSE implicit and underlying relations. In my opinion, structuralism proper may be said to begin with descriptions that not only recognize that each language has a definite, distinct set of elements of its own (as did Boas), but that also proceed to account for each language by a methodology that permits one to go beyond identification of elements to inference and statement of patterns, and sometimes of abstract elements—at least at a very low level of abstraction. This Boas did not do, Sapir and Bloomfield did. For Boas the 'phoneme' lost information. If he was right in his criticism of some uses of a more abstract representation, he was a 'pre-structuralist' in having cleared the way for, but refusing to take up, the possibility of such representation and analysis.

Structuralism proper in linguistics began with phonology, wherein lies a story in itself. But surely an essential factor in Chomsky's impact is that he proposed a new orientation and role for syntax at a time when structural linguistics had REACHED syntax, so to speak, having elaborated methods and controversy successively in the sectors of phonology and morphology. (Note in passing that it may seem only natural that an American, anthropology-linked linguistics would begin with phonology, because of its field-work orientation toward unwritten languages; but it remains to be explained both why Boas had earlier concentrated on grammatical categories, and why a phonology-focused structuralism dominated the linguistic scene in all countries in the 1930's. One factor was presumably the exhilaration of capturing and exploring a sector of speech that had previously seemed to lie outside the human sciences in the domain of natural science, of discovering in a sector of physical behavior mental patterns of great regularity and rigor. Such certainly is the thrust of Sapir 1925. Such a novel sector was well calculated to encourage a new discipline, a linguistics distinct from the study of language in departments of languages.)

There is no monograph or handbook or even set of studies from which one could expect to learn the story of linguistics in the first half of the 20th century, and the above discussion is directed, not at Lyons, but at our need for closer, non-ideological study of the period. Chomsky's status as a master of modern thought depends on the two stages on which he has had the opportunity to perform, first in the profession of linguistics, then in the world intellectual community. If as linguists we take responsibility for our own history, we have much to do to explain adequately the first of those stages.

4. Chapters 4–7 describe the development of Chomsky's transformational grammar, taking up first 'The goals of linguistic theory', then

'Generative grammar: a simple model', 'Phrase structure grammar', and 'Transformational grammar'. Ch. 4 is based very much on Chomsky's chapter, 'On the goals of linguistic theory', in his *Syntactic structures* (1957). The principal stress is on the rejection of 'discovery procedures' in favor of an evaluation procedure, and on the creativity (or 'open-endedness') of human language as setting a goal for grammatical theory that requires going beyond a corpus. In this connection Lyons notes the 'Bloomfieldian' fear of prescriptive (or normative) grammar as a cause of its unwillingness to venture judgments as to the grammaticality of sentences, apart from attestation in actual usage and texts (cf. Harris & Voegelin 1953).

It should be noted that texts were also valued as an opportunity to discover forms which the linguist might not think to elicit, or be able to, and as an independent test of the adequacy of his analysis. In Chomsky's successful introduction of the goal of generating all and only the grammatical sentences of a language, we can see the completion, or carrying through to syntax, of structuralist principle. It was just such a criterion of relevance and goal that had made phonology a new field, as against either physical phonetics or Boasian delineation of sound types, and it was inconsistent and incomplete for linguists not to establish the corresponding principle in the rest of grammar. No doubt the reason was, as Lyons says, a fear of normative considerations, a fear perhaps not ungrounded in practice, apart from the general principle (39). If linguistics eschews the sampling approach of many sciences, it has its own 'simpling' approach that tends to reproduce the difficulties of prescriptive grammar, even if the intentions are professional rather than social. If we let the clear cases, or the grammar, decide (47), we sever the result from any claim to account for the tacit knowledge of actual speakers; we put the entire significance claimed for grammar, as an explication of speakers' competence, into question. If Chomsky established grammaticality as an effective criterion, as against occurrence in a corpus, the next step in linguistics would appear to be to establish appropriateness and acceptability. That is not part of the present story, for it leads not only to the human mind but also to human life. Yet the significance of Chomsky's work for disciplines other than linguistics is said to derive primarily from the acknowledged importance of language in all areas of human activity, as well as from the peculiarly intimate relation that is said to hold between the structure of language and the innate properties or operations of the mind (5). It should probably have been noted that Chomsky's conception of the scope of linguistics so far has permitted significance of the second type, but not of the first. The study of language as human activity calls for ethnography as well as logic, and for a reconsideration of the foundational notions of linguistics, as to what is to be accounted for and how it is organized (cf. Hymes 1964, 1971a; and fn. 3 below).

5. Again in ch. 4, Lyons states (43): 'Chomsky's most original, and probably his most enduring, contribution to linguistics is the mathematical rigor and precision with which he formalized the properties of alternative systems of grammatical description.' This theme runs through the following three chapters on forms of grammar. The chapters are clear, straightforward accounts, well worth recommending to any interested person.

> One or two unfortunate errors in the first printing should be pointed out. In the account of an illustrative underlying string and associated phrase marker, the statement of domination inexplicably has '*V* by *V* (this is an instance of "self domination")' (75), whereas throughout the rest of this example elements of the underlying string itself are cited (*the* + *man* is wholly dominated by *NP*' etc.); so '*open* by *V*' surely is required. Again, the explanation of a rule for word-boundary symbol works neatly if 'first' and 'second' are interchanged in lines 1 and 2 of p. 81!

> Also, it is remarked that the derivation of a phrase marker in a purely abstract example begs an important theoretical question (75), and merely follows conventions (77), but there is no indication that any alternatives for the form of the result are possible, and none are likely to occur to the reader. The 'convention' appears inescapable and natural.

Beyond this, I have only the testimony of a participant-observer to make with regard to these three chapters. Lyons' book has the advantage of having been read and commented upon by its subject, and in ch. 6, fn. 2 (p. 67) Lyons reports: 'Chomsky tells me that he is not himself aware of any change in his attitude over the years with respect to the role of simplicity measures and intuition. He thinks that some confusion may have been caused by the fact that *Syntactic structures* was "a rather watered-down version of earlier work (at that time unpublished)" and that, for this reason, it "emphasized weak rather than strong generative capacity". I am sure [comments Lyons] that most linguists who read *Syntactic structures* when it was first published in 1957 interpreted Chomsky's general views on linguistic theory in the way that I have represented them in Chapter IV (39–40). One can only wonder whether Chomsky's work would have had the effect that it did within linguistics if *Syntactic structures* had not been "watered down".'

Lyons' account in ch. 4 is that the 1957 work treated 'intuitions' as independent evidence, whose explanation is secondary to the principal task of generating the sentences of the language, and that it is in later work that the intuitions of the speakers of a language are included as part of the data to be accounted for by the grammar. Correspondingly, less weight is given to 'simplicity' and more weight to reflecting the 'intuitions' and being semantically more 'revealing', in arguing for the superiority of transformational grammar (67). For what it is worth, my recollection of the impact of *Syntactic structures* is that it showed the existence of phenomena which existing grammar (esp. immediate-constituent phrase-structure grammar) could not account for at all—or if it could, could not do so in other than a cumbersome way. By God, native speakers DID associate active and passive counterparts, did know how to formulate a passive from an active; yet the two were different and even unrelated in a phrase structure analysis. Lyons may be right that intuitions were initially taken as independent evidence, and then later as part, the essential part, of what was to be explained. I can only report that they appeared salient, dramatically salient, from the outset; and that I recall a conference in 1961 in which Robert Lees stressed, as his goal, accounting for his intuitions as a native speaker. Chomsky's 1959 review of Skinner, and his remarks in various contexts (e.g., an exploratory meeting that led to a SSRC Committee on Intellective Processes) were to the same effect. The notions of simplicity and intuition, and the possibility of validating grammatical analysis (40) by various tests, have had a history within the school more complex than can be accounted for by a distinction of an earlier and a later period. Recall, for instance, that Halle's simplicity metric, and debates with Lamb as to what counted as simpler, were issues of the 1960's. I would guess that each of the three notions has seemed attractive and important in different degree at different times; Chomsky has perhaps never been committed to any one way of warranting transformational deep structure and its significance for the human mind, but has from the beginning been committed to the reality of that structure and that relationship.

6. In chapters 8 and 9 ('The psychological implications of generative grammar', 'The philosophy of language and mind') Lyons

turns to the broader significance of Chomsky's work. Throughout the book Lyons stresses a development of Chomsky's views from the largely 'Bloomfieldian' matrix in which they had been formed in his studies with Harris (34–36, 91). One who lived through the period of the impact of Chomsky's earlier views may be puzzled, not at the indications of continuity with earlier work, but at the soft-pedaling, to the point of inaudibility, of any note of the dramatic impact of Chomsky's 'largely "Bloomfieldian"' views at the time. Lyons, I think, is judging the matter in retrospect, and a bit in prospect. From the standpoint of ultimate significance, not local impact, it is Chomsky's research on the formalization of linguistic theory that is seen as the irreversible, decisive contribution to linguistics; and it is the views on psychological and philosophical issues of mind that now constitute much of his larger intellectual significance. The formalization was not itself directly a challenge on these later grounds. Thus many a linguist, viewing the history internal to his discipline, might regard 1957 as the decisive moment, and the attack on then-current linguistic practice as the decisive thrust, with what follows being part of an increasingly complex, but continuous, story; but Lyons sees the less widely known, highly technical formal investigations into the properties of grammars—investigations quite independent of linguistic practice—as the essential thing. To Lyons, the point at which Chomsky begins to refer to linguistics as a branch of cognitive psychology is seen as decisive, at least from the standpoint of general intellectual history.

Lyons' manner of 'periodizing' Chomsky's intellectual history has its justification, but a somewhat different distribution of emphasis might be fairer to the histories of both linguistics and rationalism. Lyons writes (35) that 'Chomsky's general views on linguistic theory as presented in *Syntactic structures* are in most respects the same as those held by other members of the "Bloomfieldian" school, notably by Zellig Harris'; and he introduces Chomsky's views on creativity and discovery procedures with these words (36): 'However, there are one or two points that sharply distinguish even Chomsky's earlier work from that of Harris and the other "Bloomfieldians".' From this, the general reader is unlikely to form an accurate picture of the revolutionary impact within linguistics that has provided the base for Chomsky's later impact on other fields. The wording hardly suggests that *Syntactic structures* was published by Mouton after being turned down by several American publishers, presumably on 'Bloomfieldian' advice. And though the mathematical and logical foundations may ultimately be the essential thing, most linguists in 1957 were not prepared to follow the mathematics and logic, which indeed were not widely available, being either unpublished or published outside common linguistic channels. It was the evidence of new empirical possibilities, and the showing of the inadequacy to them of other approaches, that captured the field and a new generation. As Lyons himself observes in a note previously quoted, a formal work might not have had the same reception as *Syntactic structures*. At the same time, most linguists would agree with Lyons that Chomsky's work has become the central reference point for all of them, quite apart from Chomsky's own motives for doing linguistics, or what he may consider linguistics to be capable of showing with regard to mind and human freedom.

A formulation that may do better justice to Chomsky's periodization and impact would be that, in his earlier period, he applied philosophy to linguistics, and in the later period he has applied linguistics to philosophy. In the first period he brought philosophy of science to bear in a critical way, and mathematical logic in a constructive way, together liberating linguistic practice and setting new goals for it. In the second period (stage might be the better term, for the two emphases overlap in time) he has brought linguistics to bear on dominant assumptions in the study of mind in a way that has been both critical of one dominant line of work, and stimulating to the development of another. (Regarding the effect of Chomsky's impact on philosophy, apart from the stimulation of the study of formal grammars within mathematics, I am not able to speak, but cf. Hook 1969.)

In the course of his discussion, Lyons several times refers to the autonomy and the independence of modern linguistics as synonymous terms (12–13, 91, 95, 107, 119). He has in mind the rejection, especially among Bloomfieldians, of dependence on other fields, especially psychology and philosophy, and, I suppose, the general thrust of structural linguistics within the century for recognition as a distinct discipline. (Recall the end of Saussure's *Cours*, Sapir's recurrent reference to the formal completeness of language, and Bloomfield's remark that the study of language had been many times begun but never fully entered upon.) I would like to enter a mild protest and to suggest that the two terms can be usefully distinguished. AUTONOMY may be used to refer to linguistics as master in its own house (as the etymology suggests), INDEPENDENCE to refer to a claim that it is or should be without dependence or connection with other fields. Chomsky himself does not recommend that lin-

guistics cease to be autonomous (95–96), but rather that it understand its role in relation to the study of mind, and conceive of itself
as a branch of cognitive psychology in the sense of contributing to
that study. Therein lies a certain dependence: i.e., some directions
of work are more relevant than others; some considerations are
crucial, others are not. But there is no loss of autonomy, no psychologists defining linguistic concepts or dictating base structures. This
distinction between autonomy and independence is very much like
that which Jakobson has repeatedly stressed between integrative
and isolationist views of linguistics, and is, I think, one worth a lexical quibble (cf. Hymes 1964:8, 1968).

Lyons' presentation of Chomsky's views on psychology and philosophy is careful and sensitive. He is especially clear about the
fallacy of categorizing Chomsky's views by one horn of any anti-
quated dilemma. However, in the psychology chapter I miss any mention of the recent critical investigations of Fodor, Bever, and others.
In the philosophy chapter I miss any suggestion of a connection between Chomsky's views on mind and his views on the humanities,
social sciences, and politics, though there is some mention of these
connections in the introduction. Now Chomsky's views go beyond received philosophical categories, such as 'rationalism' vs. 'empiricism',
and this is a point that Lyons brings out splendidly. Chomsky's views
also go beyond received categories as to the boundaries between academic and non-academic activity, and as to the separation of roles.
It would be a natural step to show how Chomsky's conception of
mind and human nature seems to inform parts of *American power
and the new Mandarins,* for example, as in the critique of existing
accounts of the Spanish Civil War for their failure to give anarchist
uprisings their due—a fault attributable to a pervasive failure to allow for successful spontaneous political activity. Or, ethics being a
branch of philosophy, and one coming to be cultivated again, it would
be desirable to treat Chomsky's essay, 'The responsibility of intellectuals' (1967), as a contribution to current ethical debate (cf. Hymes
1969). (Chomsky's Bertrand Russell lectures at Cambridge in 1971
were of course given after the writing of this book.) His role in the
organization of Resist and in related activities of civil disobedience
merits consideration also; it receives warm and honorable mention
(6), but needs assessment, as an attribute of the book's subject.

    7. Here, I am sorry to say, appears the great limitation of the

book.[2] It ends (Ch. 10, 'Conclusion') with mild demurral on Chomsky's rationalist claims, as not proved, and concise indications that there are criticisms of his views within linguistics—that he is not an unquestioned hero there. The final note is, again, that even if Chomsky's particular formulations should fail, the attempt (and the direction) constitute a 'Chomskyan revolution' that 'cannot help being successful' (131). But there is another 'Chomskyan revolution', that of a style of being a linguist and academic—not wholly due to him, to be sure, but one of which he is an exemplar. Can this 'help being successful'? Lyons describes Chomsky's role at one point in terms of the defense of traditional values, too often left to scholars unfitted for the kind of argument needed, but finding in Chomsky a redoubtable champion who can match opponents at their own game (7–8). There is indeed a sense in which Chomsky stands for the defense of traditional values, but there is another sense in which he stands for the realization of an alternative form of social order, as necessary to the realization of human values. What is the significance of the joint role of linguistic and political figure?

Chomsky's political role is advertised on the book jacket, sympathetically sketched in Lyons' introduction (5–6), and noted as not unconnected with his theory of language. It is not much analysed, and the consideration is prefatory. The book ends on Chomsky's significance in linguistics alone. Now, having been in England at the time, I should like to enter an informed doubt that the more than a thousand who attended his lectures on language and mind at Oxford in the spring of 1969, or who filled the streets in London waiting for a lecture there, were moved by visions of a better base structure. Many of them came moved by the figure of a dramatically successful scholar who would put his mind and to some extent his body on the line for causes that matter—a man who publicly and committedly broke with the age-old tradition of trahison des clercs, in which so many of us, recovered from our fright of the young in the 60's, are beginning to wallow again, rationalizing our toleration of the intolerable as defense of the academy of civility. Chomsky

[2] Lyons has informed me that he undertook the book with two understandings: that Chomsky did not object, and that he need not assess Chomsky's political role, a subject which he did not feel prepared to treat. The publisher at one point suggested an appendix on the latter topic, to be provided by someone else, but later dropped the idea. I am sorry to criticize the book for not being what its author did not intend it to be; I offer as apology that Chomsky's public role no doubt looms especially large on the American scene, where, I believe, it has significantly influenced the character of the profession.

was a man who said simply that intellectuals should not lie, and more than that, a man who exposed some of the lies and liars.

There is more here than a man playing well a dual role. There may not be a perfect integration of Chomsky's linguistic and political activities (cf. Hymes 1972), but the connection needs to be explored. It is more than a matter of defense of traditional values. Chomsky himself has given one lead in his long footnote on Rousseau in *Cartesian linguistics* (1966:91–93, fn. 51). Another is to be found in his mention (1967:254) of reading Dwight Macdonald's essay, 'The root is man', in the mid-1940's. Lyons records that Chomsky has been interested in politics since childhood; that his views were formed in the radical Jewish community in New York, and have always tended toward socialism or anarchism; that Chomsky himself has explained that it was really his sympathy with Harris' political views that led him to work as a graduate student in linguistics (xii). In one sense, personal history of this sort may seem irrelevant—experience and disappointment in a kibbutz, a turn from politics to linguistics, then from political pessimism to activity. In another sense, all this is essential to the story, for if a link can be found among most of the 'modern masters' in the series, it is that the work of each speaks in some way to the question of the responsibility of the intellectual—of the relation between thought and action in the century of Guernica, Lidice, Buchenwald, Hiroshima, and Vietnam. In Chomsky's career there is some reflection, one would guess, of the defensive retreat from political action in the years of Joseph McCarthy and institutionalized McCarthyism, and then of the eventual breaking of the political hegemony of coldwar liberalism with the increasing agony of Vietnam. There is some connection between Chomsky's views, based on a conception of human nature close to that of natural law in function, and their impact at a time when official intellectuals claimed a monopoly of fact and thereby a monopoly of decision. True, the framework within which official information was obtained and evaluated might have been analysed in such a way as to discredit the presumed monopoly;[3] events and independent analysis eventually DID discredit it. At

[3] Needless to say, as an anthropologist as well as linguist, I do not accept Chomsky's conception of social scientists as universally whoring after the surface features of other sciences, neglecting all fundamental problems, and taking refuge in spurious precision and trivialities (Lyons, p. 7). There is much of this, one knows, but there is much else besides. Chomsky's notion of the social sciences may have been shaped (and warped) by close proximity to representatives of the type he describes in his own institution. Lyons appears to follow Chomsky in this, referring to 'academic advisers to the American government who, posing as "experts" in a field where there is no such thing as scientific expertise

the time when Chomsky came to prominence in resistance to the war policy, a moral critique—informed by knowledge of the true history, colonial heritage, and character of the war—was the one rallying point (and it is a fair question how many would have come to oppose the war, despite knowledge of its character, if they thought it could still be won). It is fair to say that the intelligence, principles and will to launch a moral attack against an apparent hegemony of information and influence was the crucial step, and that Chomsky played a vital role.

One cannot portray Chomsky as an unquestioned hero of the left (for recent attacks, cf. Thompson 1969; Newmeyer & Emonds 1971). There are never unquestioned heroes on the left. But one can recognize that he deserves a book in this series, because he has understood the difference between intellectuals and intellect-workers (in the phrase of the late Paul Baran); has understood that true intellectuals have a responsibility for the ends of their work, as well as the means; has understood that the ultimate justification of freedom for the intellectual and the academy is not that, being harmless, they should be left alone, but rather that only with such freedom can they serve society by independent criticism. In his time and with his means, Chomsky has acted on such understanding.

This book will well serve the reader who wishes an introduction to the linguistic work which is central to Chomsky's intellectual

---

and where consideration of common morality should have prevailed' (6). I agree that the advisers frequently offered spurious expertise, and that common morality should have prevailed; but there *is* such a thing as scientific expertise. Chomsky has gone a fair way to acquiring it, one essential reason for the effectiveness of his arguments (as I argue just below). The true danger of such experts is that they can sometimes be right as to the means to secure the ends they advocate or accept. A page later Lyons applauds Chomsky as being able to manipulate the conceptual and mathematical apparatus of the social sciences. Passing by the contextual implication that social scientists are on the side of the enemy and eschewing here any critique of Chomsky as, say, an anthropologist, Lyons would here seem to agree that there is such a thing as a serious content to the social sciences that requires mastery, moral protest alone being unavailing. Just so. Elsewhere I have argued that the serious content of the social sciences is essential also to the solution of problems in linguistics; that the trajectory from phonology through syntax to semantics is essentially unified and structuralist, Chomsky's conception of linguistics serving in many ways as its ultimate ideological justification; and that the political and social relevance which many linguists seek should come in part through a recasting of linguistics to enable it to deal with the ways in which language is part of social life (Hymes 1972, MS b). Such an approach will have ultimately an evolutionary, adaptive perspective, seeking to explain the origin, maintenance, decline, and replacement of ways of speaking.

332 DELL HYMES

stature. There are indeed many such readers: the reviewer in the New York *Times* was one such, surprised to find that Chomsky was a famous linguist and that his linguistics had some connection with his public role. Where the book falls short is in its picture of the man and figure as a whole. The impact of Chomsky, as of other men, has been jointly a product of the man, the work, and the times. We have here essentially the work. I doubt very much that the work alone would have led to a publisher and an audience for such a book. To say this is in no sense to belittle Chomsky. For one thing, it is to say that credit goes to the man as well as to the work. For another, it is to say that the career of such a man can also reveal to us something of our times. I have tried to suggest some of the additional factors of the times, in the discipline of linguistics and in the political climate of the United States, but do not claim adequacy for the suggestion. Perhaps one must always wait a generation, for memoirs, retrospection and the like, before the owl of Minerva can take her flight.

REFERENCES

BERLIN, BRENT, and PAUL KAY. 1969. Basic color terms. Berkeley & Los Angeles: University of California Press.

BERMAN, MARSHALL. 1970. The politics of authenticity: radical individualism and the emergence of modern society. New York: Atheneum.

BOAS, FRANZ. 1889. On alternating sounds. American Anthropologist (o.s.) 2.47–53.

BOLINGER, DWIGHT. 1968. Aspects of language. New York: Harcourt, Brace & World.

CHOMSKY, NOAM. 1957. Syntactic structures. The Hague: Mouton.

——. 1959. Review of Verbal behavior, by B. F. Skinner. Lg. 35.26–58.

——. 1966. Cartesian linguistics. New York: Harper & Row.

——. 1967. The responsibility of intellectuals. The dissenting academy, ed. by Theodore Roszak, 254–98. New York: Pantheon Books.

HARRIS, Z. S., and C. F. VOEGELIN. 1953. Eliciting in linguistics. Southwestern Journal of Anthropology 9.59–75.

HOOK, SIDNEY (ed.) 1969. Language and philosophy. New York: New York University Press.

HYMES, DELL. 1961. Functions of speech: an evolutionary approach. Anthropology and education, ed. by F. Gruber, 55–83. Philadelphia: University of Pennsylvania Press.

——. 1964. Directions in (ethno-)linguistic theory. Transcultural studies in cognition, ed. by A. K. Romney and R. G. D'Andrade, 6–56. American Anthropologist 66:3, part 2 (special publication).

————. 1968. Linguistics–the field. International Encyclopedia of Social Sciences 9.351–71. New York: Macmillan.

————. 1969. Review of The dissenting academy, ed. by Theodore Roszak. Bulletin of the Atomic Scientists, vol. 24, November, 29–34.

————. 1970. Linguistic method of ethnography: its development in the United States. Method and theory in linguistics, ed. by Paul L. Garvin, 249–325. The Hague: Mouton.

————. 1971a. Sociolinguistics and the ethnography of speaking. Social anthropology and linguistics, ed. by Edwin Ardener, 47–93. (ASA monographs, 10.) London: Tavistock.

————. 1971b. Morris Swadesh and the first 'Yale School'. In Swadesh 1971:228–70.

————. 1972. Models of the interaction of language and social life. Directions in sociolinguistics, ed. by John J. Gumperz and Dell Hymes, 35–71. New York: Holt, Rinehart & Winston.

————. MSa. Lexicostatistics and glottochronology in Paris (1834, 1862). To appear in a volume ed. by Isidore Dyen. The Hague: Mouton.

————. MSb. Toward communicative competence. To be published by the University of Pennsylvania Press.

NEWMEYER, FREDERICK J., and JOSEPH EMONDS. 1971. The linguist in American society. Papers from the 7th regional meeting, Chicago Linguistic Society, 285–303.

PIKE, KENNETH L. 1947. Grammatical prerequisites to phonemic analysis. Word 3.155–72.

————. 1952. More on grammatical prerequisites. Word 8.106–21.

————. 1967. Language in relation to a unified theory of the structure of human behavior. 2nd ed. The Hague: Mouton.

SAPIR, E. 1925. Sound patterns in language. Lg. 1.37–51.

SPIER, LESLIE; A. I. HALLOWELL; and S. S. NEWMAN (eds.) 1941. Language, culture, and personality: essays in memory of Edward Sapir. Menasha, Wisc.: Banta.

STOCKING, G. W., JR. MS. The Boas model for American Indian linguistics. Studies in the history of linguistics, ed. by Dell Hymes, to appear. Bloomington: Indiana University Press.

SWADESH, MORRIS. 1948. On linguistic mechanism. Science and Society 12.254–59.

————. 1971. Origin and evolution of languages. Ed. by Joel Sherzer. Chicago: Aldine-Atherton.

THOMPSON, J. S. 1969. The reactionary idealist foundations of Noam Chomsky's linguistics. Literature and Ideology 4.1–20.

WELLS, RULON S. MS. Phonemics in the nineteenth century, 1876–1900. Studies in the history of linguistics, ed. by Dell Hymes, to appear. Bloomington: Indiana University Press.

Index

Notes on Contributors

JOHN HOLLANDER, the poet and critic, is Professor of English at Hunter College. His books include *A Crackling of Thorns, Visions from the Ramble,* and *The Night Mirror.*

GILBERT HARMAN, Professor of Philosophy at Princeton University, is the author of *Thought* and editor (with Donald Davidson) of two anthologies, *Semantics of Natural Language* and *The Logic of Grammar.*

JOHN SEARLE, Professor of Philosophy at the University of California at Berkeley, has written widely about language and about the nature of the university. His books include *The Campus War, Speech Acts,* and *Philosophy of Language.*

ROBERT B. LEES, chemical engineer, meteorologist, and linguist, is Professor of Linguistics at Tel-Aviv University. He has written *The Grammar of English Nominalizations, The Phonology of Modern Standard Turkish,* and *Konuşulan Ingilizce.*

HILARY PUTNAM, Professor of Philosophy at Harvard University, has written papers in philosophy and logic. He is the author of *Philosophy of Logic* and edited (with Paul Benacerraf) an anthology, *Philosophy of Mathematics.*

W. V. QUINE, the logician, geographer, philosopher, and linguist, has written many books, including *Word and Object, Set Theory and Its Logic,* and *The Roots of Reference.* Quine is Edgar Pierce Professor of Philosophy at Harvard University.

THOMAS G. BEVER, Professor of Psychology at Columbia University, is the editor of the journal *Cognition.* He has written *The Psychological Basis for Linguistic Universals* and (with J. A. Fodor and M. Garrett) *The Psychology of Language.*

JAMES R. LACKNER teaches in the Department of Psychology at Brandeis University.

ROBERT KIRK is a psychologist-philosopher-logician who teaches in the Department of Philosophy at the University of Washington.

JOHN R. ROSS has written widely in linguistics. His dissertation, *Constraints on Variables in Syntax,* is an underground classic. Ross is Professor of Linguistics at the Massachusetts Institute of Technology.

THOMAS NAGEL, Professor of Philosophy at Princeton University, is the author of *The Possibility of Altruism* and numerous essays about the nature of mind and about moral issues. He is an associate editor of *Philosophy & Public Affairs.*

JERROLD J. KATZ, the linguist and philosopher, is the author of *Semantic Theory, The Underlying Reality of Language and Its Philosophical Import, Philosophy of Language,* and *The Problem of Induction and Its Solutions.* With J. A. Fodor, Katz edited *The Structure of Language.*

He is Professor of Philosophy at the Massachusetts Institute of Technology.

DONALD DAVIDSON, Professor of Philosophy at The Rockefeller University, is the author (with P. Suppes and S. Siegel) of *Decision-Making: An Experimental Approach*. He is (with G. Harman) editor of *Semantics of Natural Language* and *The Logic of Grammar*.

DENNIS STAMPE is Professor of Philosophy at the University of Wisconsin. He has written a number of articles about meaning and the philosophy of language.

BARBARA HALL PARTEE is Professor of Linguistics at the University of Massachusetts. With R. P. Stockwell and P. Schachter she wrote *The Major Syntactic Structures of English*.

DAVID LEWIS, Professor of Philosophy at Princeton University, has written a great deal about language and related topics. He is the author of *Convention* and of *Counterfactuals*.

DELL HYMES, Professor of Anthropology at the University of Pennsylvania, has written about language and culture. His books include *Language in Culture in Society* and *Pidginization and Creolization of Languages*. He is editor of the journal *Language in Society*.

John Lyons on Chomsky

Fromkin + Rodman, An Introduction to Language, (N.Y. : Holt, Rinehart, & Winston, Inc., 1974).

Lenneberg on Lang.